Riberalta
BOLIVIA
La Paz
Sucre
PARAGUAY
HILE
ARGENTINA

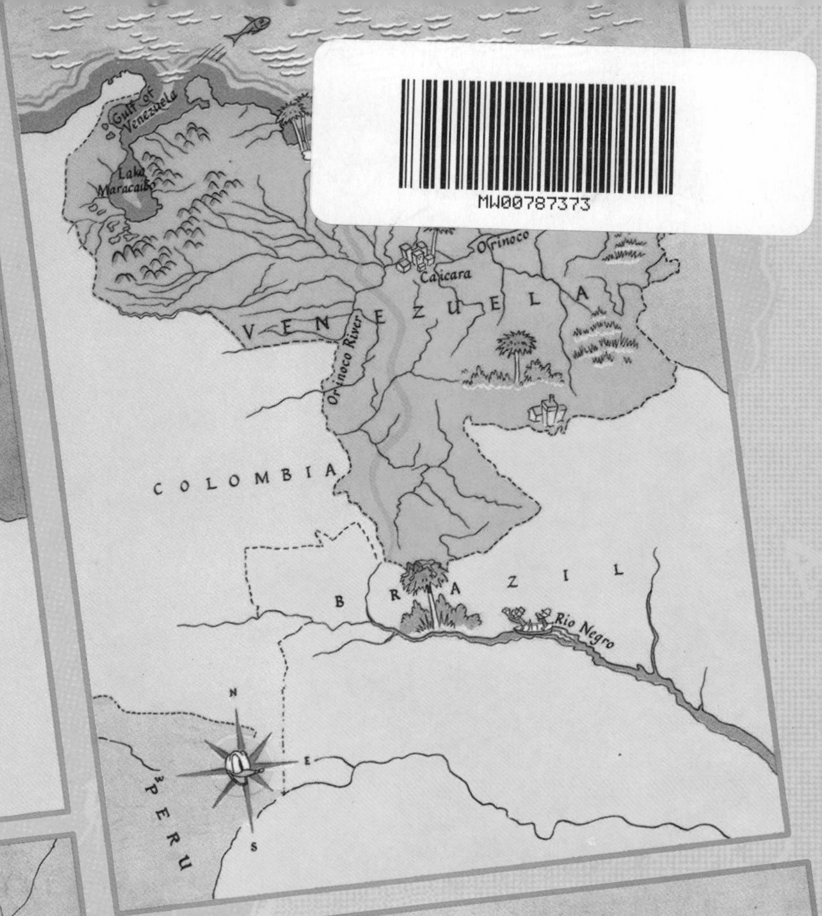

Gulf of Venezuela
Lake Maracaibo
Orinoco
Caicara
VENEZUELA
Orinoco River
COLOMBIA
BRAZIL
Rio Negro
N
E
S
PERU

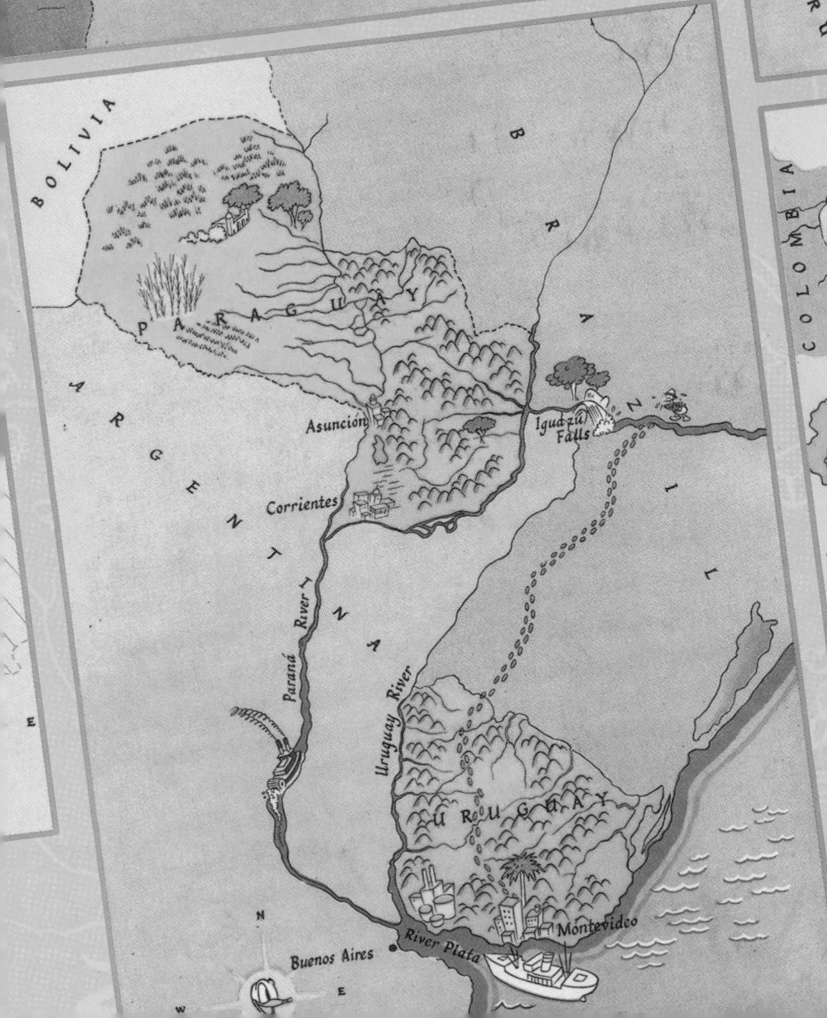

BOLIVIA
BRAZIL
PARAGUAY
Asunción
Iguazú Falls
Corrientes
ARGENTINA
Paraná River
Uruguay River
URUGUAY
Montevideo
River Plata
Buenos Aires
N
W
E

COLOMBIA
VENEZUELA
BRITISH GUIANA
DUTCH GUIANA
FRENCH GUIANA
Belém
Natal
Recife
Rio Negro
Manáos
Amazon River
BRAZIL
PERU
BOLIVIA
PARAGUAY
São Paulo
Santos
Rio de Janeiro
URUGUAY
ARGENTINA
CHILE
ATLANTIC OCEAN
N
W

SEA
Gatun Lake
Canal
Panama
Balboa
PANAMA
Gulf of Panama
COLOMBIA
PACIFIC OCEAN

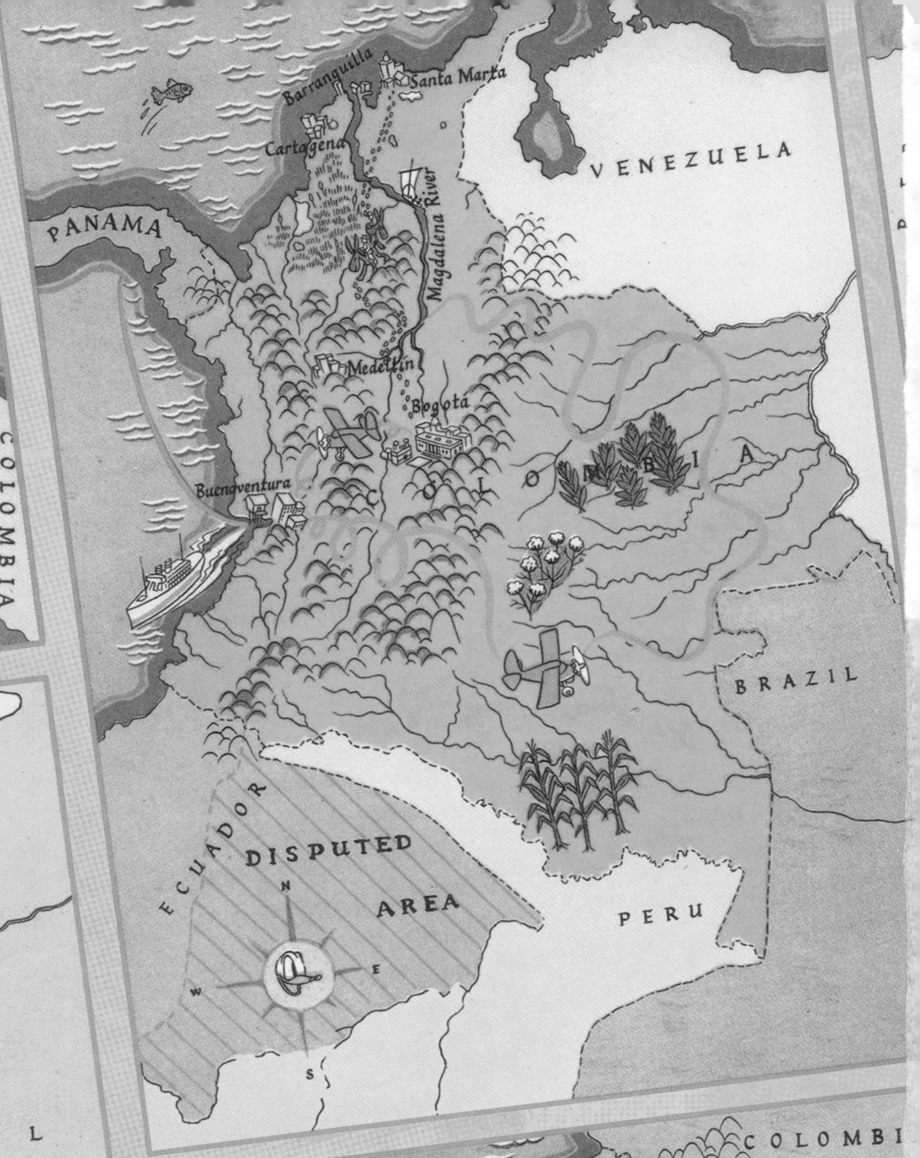
Barranquilla
Santa Marta
Cartagena
VENEZUELA
PANAMA
Magdalena River
Medellin
Bogota
Buenaventura
COLOMBIA
BRAZIL
ECUADOR
DISPUTED AREA
PERU
N
E
W
S

COLOMBIA
ECUADOR
DISPUTED AREA
BRAZIL
PERU
Ucayali River
Lima
BOLIVIA
Lake Titicaca
SOUTH PACIFIC OCEAN
CHILE
N
E
W

COLOMBI
Quito
Cotopaxi
Mt
Mt Chimborazo
Riobamba
Guayaquil
Gulf of Guayaquil
ECUADOR
DISP
AREA
SOUTH PACIFIC OCEAN

South of the Border with Disney

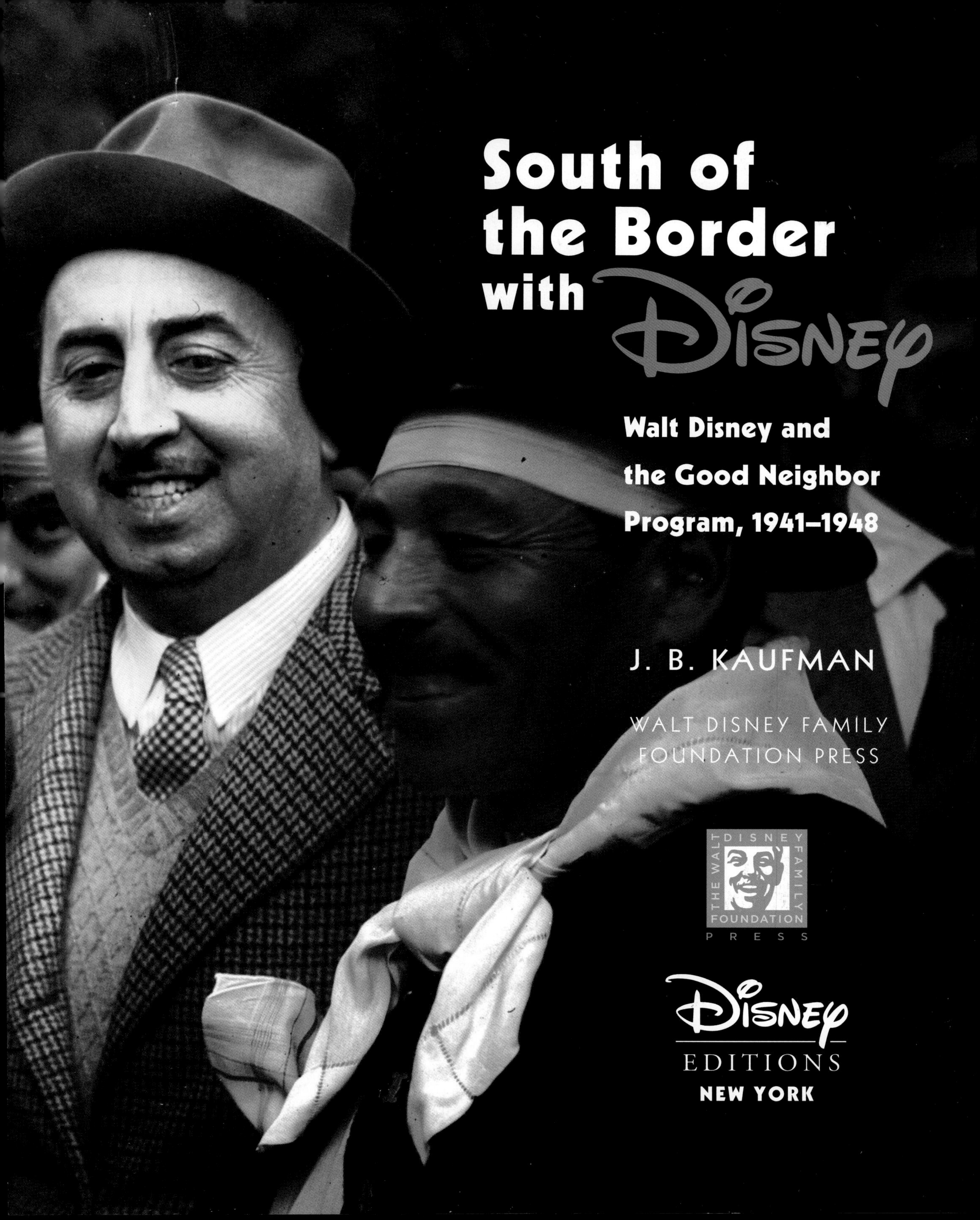

South of the Border with Disney

Walt Disney and the Good Neighbor Program, 1941–1948

J. B. KAUFMAN

WALT DISNEY FAMILY FOUNDATION PRESS

THE WALT DISNEY FAMILY FOUNDATION PRESS

Disney EDITIONS
NEW YORK

Published by Disney Editions, an imprint of Disney Book Group. No part of this book may be reproduced or transmitted in any form or by any means, electronic or mechanical, including photocopying, recording, or by any information storage and retrieval system, without written permission from the publisher.

For information address
Disney Editions, 114 Fifth Avenue,
New York, New York 10011-5690.

Editorial Director: Wendy Lefkon
Assistant Editor: Jessica Ward

Designed by Jon Glick, mouse+tiger
Edited by Christopher Caines

Library of Congress Cataloging-in-Publication Data on file

ISBN 978-1-4231-1193-1

First Edition
10 9 8 7 6 5 4 3 2 1

Printed in Singapore

PAGE 1: Donald Duck sets out to visit South America in this illustration from H. Marion Palmer's *Donald Duck Sees South America* (1945), one of a series of books published by D. C. Heath and Company for the Disney Studio in the 1940s. Donald's adventures closely follow the routes Walt Disney and his team followed during their research trips south of the border. All the maps charting Donald's travels are reproduced in the endpapers to this book.

PAGES 2–3: Walt Disney with Ramón Columba at an *asado* (festive outdoor barbecue), Argentina, September 1941.

RIGHT: Lee and Mary Blair sketch the sights of Rio de Janeiro, Brazil, August 1941.

CONTENTS

FOREWORD

The year 1941 was one of worldwide turmoil and instability. Europe was at war, and at the end of the year the United States would be fully engaged in that war too. The loss of the European markets represented nearly half the income of Walt Disney Productions. My father, who had led his organization to a level of artistic achievement that exceeded all expectations for the cartoon medium, was forced to severely modify his ambitions. *Pinocchio* had been released in February 1940, and *Fantasia* in November of that year. Both were artistic triumphs for the studio but did not do well at the box office. *Bambi* was in the works but moving slowly. My uncle Roy advised that in order to raise enough capital to keep things going the company would have to issue preferred stock, something that the brothers had never wanted to do. This was also a time of labor unrest everywhere in the nation and burgeoning union activity, which found fertile ground in the film industry. It was a time of great stress for Dad and Roy and of doubt and insecurity for their employees.

Early in 1941 Dad addressed the entire studio, detailing the situation that the studio found itself in—"the real crisis that we are facing." It was an honest, gut-wrenching speech. Things were happening that threatened the existence of the studio, and he was puzzled and distressed by the situation. The crisis culminated on May 29, when the strike began. Dad arrived that morning to find a picket line in place. The strike was a nasty one, very personally directed against Dad. Picket signs were cruel and vicious. My sister and I were aware of all of this. "Pickets is bad peoples," Sharon solemnly pronounced, and I shouted it from the car window as we drove by. Our dear, precious daddy was being attacked unjustly.

The South American project intervened at this time, and it was a wonderful, bright, creative, intensely productive interlude that took Dad out of the arena of conflict and thrust him into the colorful, musical world of Latin America. Of course, those countries had their own serious problems at that time too, with the Axis making inroads into several of the South American nations. But they weren't Dad's problems. He went there with a handpicked team, they set up shop, and they worked. The trip was well planned at a time when travel was primitive by today's standards. Air travel wasn't easy, and communication slow. Everyone on the trip was anxious about what was going on at home, but the creative stimulation and demands of travel didn't give them too much time to ponder it.

I was seven years old, my sister was four, and our parents were to be gone for about three months. We could have been miserably lonely, but Mother arranged to have our cousin Marjorie, daughter of her sister Hazel, stay with us. We adored Marjorie and her husband. He was in medical school at the time, but he found time to play with us, to arrange treasure hunts for us. Mother's older sister, Grace, was also nearby. (She might even have even been living with us at that time. I forget. . . .) We were well and lovingly cared for, but we did miss our parents terribly.

J.B. suggested the idea of this book to me several years ago, and I was delighted with the idea of it. J.B.'s sphere of interest is really silent films in general, with a special focus on the early silent films of Walt Disney. His book *Walt in Wonderland*, coauthored with Russell Merritt, deals with that period, and I had found it fascinating and well done. I was pleased that J.B. wanted to take this new project on, and knew he'd do a good job with it. I think that it is a wonderful story, and an interesting and important piece of history. Ted Thomas's film *Walt & El Grupo* was begun at just about the same time. Both capture, each in their medium, the energy and excitement of the South American adventure and assess its value.

Our parents returned sometime in November, after attending the *Dumbo* premiere in New York. Less than a month later, on Sunday, December 7, the Japanese attacked Pearl Harbor, and the U.S. Army moved into the Walt Disney Studio and more or less took them over. But that's another story.

Diane Disney Miller

INTRODUCTION

In 1942, moviegoers who had long been familiar with Donald Duck and Goofy—two of the beloved characters in the animated cartoons of Walt Disney—suddenly saw their old cartoon friends in an unaccustomed setting. Abandoning the generic (but recognizably North American) barnyards, houses, and cities where they were usually seen, "the Duck" and "the Goof" traveled to South America and embraced exotic, fascinating cultures very different from their own. This unexpected film was *Saludos Amigos*, and it was produced by the Disney studio in support of the United States' Good Neighbor program. In time it would be followed by another feature-length film, *The Three Caballeros*, along with a wide assortment of short subjects, produced both for entertainment and for education, which were likewise built along Latin American lines.

This book is the story of those years, and those films. Millions of viewers have enjoyed *Saludos Amigos* and *The Three Caballeros*, during the 1940s and ever since, often without realizing that the films were produced for a specific diplomatic purpose. But these and Disney's other Good Neighbor films become much more fascinating and entertaining when we see them in context, and understand the circumstances that created them. Certainly they marked a significant change in direction for Walt Disney. During the 1930s he had established his studio as unquestionably the world's premier animation company, producing both short and feature-length films that powerfully defined, and continue to define, the scope of animated film art. Now, at the onset of World War II, that immense power was to be harnessed in the service of the United States—both to participate explicitly in the war effort, with training and overt propaganda films; and, more subtly, to help cement sincere bonds of friendship and goodwill between the American republics.

What was the Good Neighbor program, and how did Walt Disney get involved in it?

The roots of the Good Neighbor program go back at least as far as the nineteenth century and the rise of the Pan-American movement. A growing recognition of the need for a balance of political and economic power among the Americas had led to the establishment of a series of Pan-American Conferences, beginning in 1889. These were intended to promote both peaceful relations and commercial trade among the American nations. The application of the term "Good Neighbor" to this effort seems to have originated with Franklin D. Roosevelt, apparently coined by the man who was his foreign policy adviser at the time, Sumner Welles. In his first inaugural speech in March 1933 Roosevelt declared: "In the field of world policy I would dedicate this nation to the policy of the Good Neighbor—the neighbor who resolutely respects himself and, because he does so, respects the rights of others—the neighbor who respects his obligations and respects the sanctity of his agreements in and with a world of neighbors." A month later, addressing the 1933 Pan-American Conference in Montevideo, he repeated those sentiments, adding, "The essential qualities of a true

Walt Disney poses with indigenous dancers and musicians in Lima, Peru, during his visit there on 8 October 1941. The singer to Walt's immediate right is the young Yma Sumac, who had just turned nineteen and had not yet achieved international fame.

Pan-Americanism must be the same as those which constitute a good neighbor, namely, mutual understanding, and, through such understanding, a sympathetic appreciation of the other's point of view."

These warm sentiments were repeatedly expressed during the 1930s, but they suddenly took on a dramatic new importance at the end of the decade. The key figure in this development was Nelson Rockefeller, who was at this time still firmly entrenched in the private sector. Because of his family's extensive financial holdings in South America, Rockefeller visited that continent several times in the late 1930s and realized a disturbing fact: the Axis powers, then waging an armed struggle for supremacy in Europe, were also establishing a growing presence in South America. Argentina, in particular, was becoming a hotbed of Nazi propaganda activity. The United States was still not officially involved in the war, but the country's neutrality was becoming increasingly shaky, and the establishment of a strong Nazi power base in Argentina would have made *all* the American republics extremely vulnerable. Strong and friendly relations between the U.S. and the Latin American countries were no longer just a desirable goal; suddenly they were a chilling necessity.

Rockefeller took his concerns to Washington, urging immediate action that might cut through the red tape of existing bureaucratic procedure. The result was the creation in 1940 of a new government post, the Coordinator of Commercial and Cultural Relations Between the American Republics, and Rockefeller received his initiation into Washington politics by taking this post himself. Subsequently the name of his office was simplified to Coordinator of Inter-American Affairs, known as the CIAA for short. It has sometimes been claimed that Rockefeller's agency was a part of the State Department. In fact the CIAA existed independently of, and sometimes in competition with, the State Department, and Rockefeller and Secretary of State Cordell Hull were frequently at odds with each other in various political skirmishes. Undeterred by such opposition, Rockefeller plunged into an ambitious program with two main functions: "economic warfare"—initiatives designed to meet Latin America's immediate financial, agricultural, educational, and health needs—and "psychological warfare," designed to foster a strong spirit of friendly hemispheric unity, so that all the Americas might stand together against the Axis powers.

The psychological warfare, or propaganda, division inevitably enlisted the help of the United States' most powerful mass medium: the movies. Rockefeller himself, busily engrossed in running his agency, had little to do with its motion-picture activities—although his family connection with the Museum of Modern Art was of prime importance: the museum became a center of the CIAA's film program, producing a series of 16 mm nontheatrical films and dubbing existing short subjects into Spanish and Portuguese for Latin American distribution. But for the day-to-day running of these activities, and for his agency's contact with Hollywood, Rockefeller delegated responsibility to Francis Alstock and to John Hay "Jock" Whitney. Whitney's Hollywood credentials were impeccable: during the previous decade he had involved himself in the filmmaking community and had invested in Technicolor and in the formation of David O. Selznick's independent production company. Together, Alstock and Whitney approached all the major Hollywood producers and asked them to produce films that would reflect the spirit of the Good Neighbor campaign.

Rockefeller could hardly have asked for a better spokesman than Walt Disney. In order to understand the significance of the Disney studio's contribution to the Good Neighbor effort, it's important to understand that Walt Disney was, in the late 1930s and early 1940s, at the zenith of his powers as an artist. In the preceding decade his studio had completely redefined the medium of the animated cartoon, exploding all its perceived limitations and carrying it to undreamed-of heights. The Disney technological breakthroughs in the use of sound and color were great accomplishments, but even greater was the studio's development of the *artistic* side of its craft: dramatic and storytelling principles and, perhaps most important of all, *personality animation*—the ability to convey a compelling characterization through the design and movement of a drawn figure.

Nor were these advances lost on viewers; Walt's development as an artist had brought with it overwhelming worldwide acclaim.[1] Mickey Mouse, stepping accidentally into the role of a mascot for Depression-era America in the early 1930s, had enjoyed an unprecedented level of popularity for a cartoon character. The Silly Symphonies had expanded the studio's prestige still further, exploring new horizons of musical brilliance and subtle wit and satire. Building on this foundation, Walt had made a bold move into feature production with *Snow White and the Seven Dwarfs*, *Pinocchio*, and *Fantasia*, establishing a standard of artistic and technical excellence that still remains unequaled by any animation studio. Each of these advances was greeted by popular and critical acclaim. In these golden years, not only were the Disney films overwhelmingly successful with audiences, but Walt himself became the darling of critics and intellectuals. In later years, as the studio made its decisive move into "family entertainment," critics would become more divided; but on the threshold of the 1940s, the appeal of the Disney films was truly universal.

[1] In this book Walt Disney, the man, will generally be referred to as "Walt"—not to imply that I had any personal relationship with him, but to distinguish between Walt and Roy Disney; and also between Walt and Roy, on one hand, and Disney, the production company, on the other.

In this outpouring of public adulation, Central and South America had been as vocal as any other part of the world. As early as 1933, Argentina's Escuela de Artes Decorativas de la Nación had sent Walt an elaborate leather-bound certificate expressing admiration for the Mickey Mouse and Silly Symphony pictures. More recognition and awards had followed from Ecuador, Brazil, and the other South American republics. As plans for the 1941 Disney goodwill tour began to take shape, one researcher asked to assess the situation in Brazil reported that "Walt Disney is not considered a movie producer, in the category of a Goldwyn, but is accepted as an artist on a level with Toscanini, etc." The subsequent experience of the tour group would bear out the truth of this statement, not only in Brazil but throughout South and Central America.

Too, Latin American atmosphere and music had occasionally cropped up in the Disney shorts of the previous decade, as if to lay the groundwork for the Good Neighbor films of the 1940s. The second Mickey Mouse short, *The Gallopin' Gaucho* (1928),

is explicitly set in Argentina and even features an ostrich, which could be seen as a forerunner of the later *avestruz* character in *Saludos Amigos*. A subsequent Mouse short, *The Cactus Kid* (1930), takes place in a vague, undefined "Southwestern" setting, but its musical score includes such public-domain tunes as "La paloma" and Emile Waldteufel's "Estudiantina," the latter performed by Minnie Mouse as a fiery, Spanish-speaking cantina singer. Donald Duck, who made his first appearance in the mid-1930s and who would become the leading member of the Disney "gang" to appear in the Good Neighbor films, indulged in these side trips too. When he suddenly launches into an impromptu medley of "La cucaracha" and "Cielito lindo" in *Orphans' Picnic* (1936)—or, even more, when he appears wearing a huge sombrero in a recognizably Mexican setting in *Don Donald* (1937)—the effect, in hindsight, is almost eerie.

Thus, when Walt Disney and his cartoon creations set out to help strengthen the United States' bonds of friendship with Latin America, they were building on a preexisting basis of mutual admiration and affection. In retrospect, their participation in the Good Neighbor project seems almost inevitable. They were only waiting for someone to ask.

ABOVE: **In 1936, Disney fans in Argentina sent this autograph album to "Donald Duck, King of the Irritable Ones."**

OPPOSITE: **Mickey Mouse rides the pampas in his second film, *The Gallopin' Gaucho* (1928).**

1 AMBASSADORS OF GOODWILL

On Thursday, 31 October 1940, Roy Disney, the business and financial head of Walt Disney Productions, sat down to write a memo to his younger brother Walt. The previous day, Roy wrote, he and company lawyer Gunther Lessing had had lunch with John Hay "Jock" Whitney and Francis Alstock, and the luncheon conversation had centered on a diplomatic mission undertaken by Nelson Rockefeller, in which Whitney and Alstock were participating. At issue was the relationship between the United States and the various republics of South America. Rockefeller, Roy explained, had "been appointed by President Roosevelt to follow through on the general subject of working up closer cooperation between the United States business and social life, and that of the South American countries. In other words, as a national policy the government [was] trying to foster better understanding and relationship and better business between our country and the South American countries." Whitney and Alstock had encouraged Roy to maintain a friendly relationship between the Disney studio and the South American movie market. Roy had replied that the studio's two features, *Snow White and the Seven Dwarfs* and *Pinocchio*, had already been released in Latin America with specially dubbed Spanish and Portuguese sound tracks, and that many of the studio's shorts had been similarly dubbed for Latin American markets until the cost became prohibitive.

Almost as an afterthought, Roy added, "Whitney also wanted to know if it would be possible for you to consider putting some South American atmosphere in some of the short subjects in order to help the general cause along—some such thing as el Gaucho. I told him that I thought possibly that could be worked out and I would suggest it to you. Maybe two or three pictures of such a nature could be put in work, just as well as not, if good story material could be thought up."

Neither Roy nor anyone else could have imagined the vast scope of the events that would spring from that modest suggestion. The Disney studio could easily have satisfied Whitney's and Alstock's request during the ensuing war years with only a minimal effort. To see just how minimal, we need only look at the wartime output of the other cartoon studios, whose Latin American content rarely ventured beyond an occasional good-natured caricature of Carmen Miranda. One example will suffice: Rudolf Ising's cartoon *The Boy and the Wolf*, released in 1943 by MGM. Ising's cartoon is essentially a retelling of "the boy who cried wolf," transplanted to a Mexican setting for no particular reason except as a friendly gesture. The boy and the landscape are clearly Mexican, but with a pointed avoidance of the demeaning stereotypes that had marked such earlier cartoons as Warner Bros.' *Little Pancho Vanilla* (1938) or MGM's own *The Lonesome Stranger* (1940). It's a nice thought, but it's not a particularly bold move.

OPPOSITE: Walt Disney enjoys a private audience with Roberto M. Ortiz, the president of Argentina, on 15 September 1941.

Walt Disney's response would be considerably more ambitious. No written record has survived to document his immediate reaction to Roy's memo, but we can infer his instinctive response from the flurry of studio activity that began almost immediately. The Coordinator of Inter-American Affairs (CIAA) was seeking nothing more than a smattering of "South American atmosphere" in a few of the Disney short subjects. By contrast, Disney artists were soon laying the groundwork for something far more profound and exciting: an entire special series of Latin American pictures, produced in cooperation with Rockefeller's agency. Not for Walt a halfhearted modification of something that had already been done; he envisioned something entirely new, a combination of Disney style with authentic Latin American characters, themes, culture, and music. The CIAA, which could not have been expecting this good fortune, happily agreed. In one way this was a purely pragmatic undertaking: both the Disney studio and the CIAA had something to gain from the arrangement. The fledgling CIAA, eager to prove itself, was anxious for the prestige that a Disney connection would bring to its program; while the Disney studio, heading into troubled financial waters in late 1940 and early 1941, welcomed the security of a government guarantee against losses on this new venture. Negotiations were conducted during the spring of 1941, and by June a tentative agreement had been reached: the studio would produce a special series of twelve Latin American–themed short subjects, all in Technicolor, over a period of two years.

Anticipating this new endeavor, the Disney story department began to assemble a body of Latin American research during the early months of 1941. Gradually a still more ambitious plan began to emerge: Walt and some of his artists would supplement this research by actually traveling *to* South America to record their own firsthand impressions of the land and its cultures. It's not clear exactly when this idea was proposed; Disney interoffice correspondence is, again, noticeably quiet about it in early 1941, and the sketchy evidence suggests that the notion originated within the CIAA. Such a trip would certainly be in line with the agency's interests: it would double as both a research venture and a goodwill mission. By mid-June the CIAA had issued its tentative approval of a Disney goodwill tour of South America. Walt and a group of his artists would visit Buenos Aires and other locations around the continent, sketching and studying the sights and cultures of the South American republics for use in their planned series of films. At the same time they would serve as ambassadors of goodwill, forging professional contacts with other prominent cartoonists, painters, musicians, and filmmakers in those republics.

The problem was that, by the summer of 1941, the Good Neighbor program had already started to sour with the very Latin American neighbors Rockefeller was trying to reach. The CIAA and its affiliates, charging into their mission with far more enthusiasm than expertise, had bungled many of their initial attempts, their well-intentioned gestures frequently coming across as merely condescending or even insulting. Press and radio propaganda, intended to cement friendly relations, often backfired when the writers made embarrassing mistakes, revealing their complete ignorance of Latin American political and cultural realities. Universal Pictures, in answer to Jock Whitney's call for Latin American themes in motion pictures, responded in 1940 with the hastily assembled *Argentine Nights*. When the film was shown in Buenos Aires the following spring, with its wildly inaccurate portrayal of Argentina and its jumble of Spanish dialects, audiences were so infuriated that riot police were called to quell the disturbance, and the feature was pulled after two days.

North American celebrities making "goodwill tours" of South America similarly did more harm than good. "Those charged with their entertainment have gained the impression that these 'goodwill missionaries' felt they were on sort of a 'slumming' party," reported a syndicated article in the *San Diego Union*. "Often they expect to be entertained royally from budgets already strained to the breaking point. Few speak Spanish or Portuguese and insist on giving their message of goodwill in English over the radio." By the spring of 1941 these unwanted ambassadors had become an active irritant in South American culture. "The next good-will mission that arrives in Rio," said Oswaldo Aranha, Brazil's foreign minister, "Brazil will declare war on the United States."

Small wonder that some knowledgeable observers advised Walt to drop the idea of a Latin American film program altogether. "If I were Disney I would save this for some future time when political conditions are not so tense," wrote Julien Bryan, a documentary filmmaker already working with the CIAA. J. R. Josephs, of the CIAA's Motion Picture Subcommittee in Buenos Aires, agreed: "STOP SUCH PICTURES. OR AT LEAST CHECK THEM VERY VERY CAREFULLY, BEFORE IT IS TOO LATE." Josephs pointed out that diplomacy toward South American countries was a far more delicate matter than some North Americans realized: "Miami may be happy if Hollywood makes a picture called 'Moon Over Miami' but Argentina won't be overly pleased even with a picture which represents her perfectly. They want U.S. pictures from the U.S." Similar concerns applied, of course, to the idea of a Disney goodwill tour.

Another factor weighing heavily on the tour was the strike currently in progress at the Disney studio. This bitter, divisive dispute between the studio and a newly formed cartoonists' union had erupted early in 1941 and would become the pivotal crisis in Disney history, tearing at the very fabric of the studio. Some latter-day accounts have suggested that the South American trip was undertaken largely as an excuse to get Walt out of the way during the studio's heated confrontations with the union. The facts are nearly the opposite: the ongoing labor struggle *jeopardized* the South American venture, and CIAA correspondence indicates that delays in launching the tour were caused primarily by the strike. "The Walt Disney project has been approved by the State Department," Whitney reported at the end of June. "Contracts are now being drawn and will be executed immediately upon solution of the Disney labor problem." The CIAA offered its help in resolving the labor dispute, and at one point Whitney personally offered to guarantee a settlement of the strike, simply to expedite the tour. Other observers objected to such support, and in fact objected to the tour, on the grounds that Walt's labor troubles might compromise his role as a goodwill ambassador. Kenneth Thomson, a former actor who had become deeply involved with the Screen Actors Guild, wrote to Whitney: "LABOR IS OF COURSE INTERNATIONAL AND THE COMMITTEE WOULD BE IN THE POSITION OF SENDING AS A GOOD WILL EMISSARY TO THE OTHER

AMERICAN REPUBLICS A MAN WHO WILL NOT DEAL WITH LABOR." He concluded that sending Walt to South America to represent the U.S. "WOULD BE A SERIOUS MISTAKE FROM THE STANDPOINT OF THE ROCKEFELLER COMMITTEE."[2]

By this time, of course, both Walt and the CIAA were seriously committed to the idea of the tour, but there was general agreement that Walt should take all possible steps to avoid the diplomatic mistakes made by other public figures. For starters, he should avoid public identification with the CIAA or any other government agency. John Rose, after a meeting in Washington on the eve of the trip, sent a wire to the studio that confirmed this explicitly: "COMMITTEE DESIROUS OF REMAINING ENTIRELY IN BACKGROUND PROJECT IS ALL DISNEY AND IN NO WAY TO BE IDENTIFIED WITH GOVERNMENT." Instead Walt would represent himself simply as a working artist, gathering research material for his films—which, of course, as far as it went, was the truth.

[2] Thomson's assessment, offered in response to Whitney's request, was clearly colored by his heavy union involvement. He had nothing to say against Walt personally except for his connection with Willie Bioff, who represented the studio in strike negotiations; most of his ire was reserved for Bioff.

In order to distance itself further from the government, the studio encouraged public identification with Pan American Airways instead. The enormously complicated logistics of moving a large group of artists around an unfamiliar continent required expert assistance, and the studio originally planned to contract a travel bureau to help with the arrangements. American Express, in fact, campaigned energetically for the job, courting Roy in June 1941 with sample itineraries and enthusiastic descriptions of its tour management service. In the end, however, the studio decided to eliminate the middleman and deal directly with Pan Am. This was due largely to a lavish demonstration of personal attention from the airline's George Strehlke, who went so far as to bring two of Pan Am's Latin American representatives—Paulo Einhorn, of Rio de Janeiro, and George Smith Jr. of Buenos Aires—to the United States to meet with Walt at the studio. "Believe me," Strehlke commented, "when those two gentlemen left Los Angeles they were ready to fight dragons, and I don't mean reluctant ones, for dear old Walt." Einhorn's and Smith's commitment to the success of the tour, combined with their intimate knowledge of South American cultures, would play a tremendous part in accomplishing the goals of the tour. So grateful was the studio for Strehlke's help that both John Rose, the tour group's business manager, and Roy Disney wrote to Pan Am in an effort to have Strehlke accompany the party on the trip. This could not be arranged, but the benefit of Einhorn's and Smith's input during preparation for the tour, and their personal assistance at two of the key stops, meant that ultimately Pan Am contributed far more than transportation.

Thanks to this assistance—and despite some minor friction between the studio and the airline in August 1941, on the very eve of the trip, when a promised 30 percent discount in the party's airfares failed to materialize—the studio determined to acknowledge Pan Am on the screen in some way. Earlier in 1941, Disney writers Joe Grant and Dick Huemer had written a story about a baby airplane called Petey O'Toole, after the identification number on his wings: P-T O-2-L. Petey's father was a mail plane, and Grant and Huemer's story concerned Petey's coming of age and

Rough sketches by Joe Grant for the original version of "P-T O-2-L."

P-T

learning to fly the mail route himself. Their original story was completely unrelated to the Latin American enterprise, and in fact two surviving drafts from the spring of 1941 are written as if for publication as a children's book. By mid-July, however, Petey had been pressed into service in support of the Good Neighbor program. On 18 July, Rose wrote to Pan Am's H. W. Peterson, enclosing "rough sketches of a new character whom we are hoping to develop as the hero of a story based upon a courageous flight across the Andes. Strehlke will tell you of our recent discussion regarding the possibility of identifying this little airplane character with Pan Air[3] in some way." In the end, Petey's story did in fact evolve into one of the Disney Latin American subjects.

Along with Pan American, the Disney studio also agreed to a public show of solidarity with its distributor. It was one of the serendipitous factors surrounding the Disney Good Neighbor venture that the studio's films were distributed in this period by RKO Radio Pictures; thanks to the Rockefeller family's heavy investment in RKO, that studio was predisposed toward any subject that interested Nelson Rockefeller—such as South America.[4] Moreover, from RKO's point of view, the prospect of a goodwill tour by Walt Disney represented a golden public relations opportunity. For one thing, RKO's South American sales convention was conveniently scheduled for late August in Rio de Janeiro, and if Walt happened to be in Rio at the time he could make several well-publicized appearances at the convention. A tentative schedule featuring several such appearances arrived at the studio late in July. Secondly, *Fantasia*, which had opened in North America in November 1940, had not yet been seen in the South American countries and was due for its openings there. Personal appearances by Walt Disney and his artists would create invaluable publicity for the premiere showings.

Part of the idea behind the Disney tour was to encourage an international creative exchange between artists. The CIAA's project authorization for the tour included this ambitious announcement: "Mr. Disney plans to ask well-known South American caricaturists, cartoonists, artists, musicians and technicians to join the United States group and work with them professionally in the project." This idea led to an even more daring concept: the establishment of a branch Disney studio in South America. Jack Cutting suggested such an idea to Walt in June 1941, pointing out that a skeleton crew from the main studio could work with regional artists to combine the distinctive Disney technique with equally distinctive South American styles, themes, and characters: "After all, General Motors, Eastman Kodak, General Electric, etc. all have plants in South America for the purpose of being better able to compete with the markets there, so why not Disney[?]" This intriguing possibility was absorbed into the early plans for the tour and even suggested in one of the studio's press releases. However, by the time Walt arrived in Uruguay in September, he was already denying that any such plans were in the works.

[3] In some areas of South America, Pan American Airways was also known as Pan Air for short. On the West Coast the airline was affiliated with the W. R. Grace shipping line; the resulting combine was known as Panagra.

[4] In the early 1930s, when RKO had gone into receivership and been unable to pay the rent on its New York office space in Rockefeller Center, the Rockefellers had received a large block of RKO stock in compensation. This asset eventually became a controlling interest in the studio, and when RKO was reorganized later in the decade, Nelson Rockefeller took an active role in the proceedings.

The plan for the finished film, retitled *Pedro,* called for the little plane to skywrite the main title card himself (*see* page 99).

In the spring and summer of 1941, of course, *any* plans involving South America were contingent on a finalized contract with the CIAA, which was in turn delayed pending the outcome of the strike. As the months dragged on, Roy Disney resolutely held out for a formal agreement before making any public announcements about either the tour or the films. In the meantime, however, plans for both went ahead on the assumption that the contract eventually would be executed. As always, the studio excelled by virtue of exhaustive preparation. In particular, between March and August of 1941, various departments within the studio assembled a voluminous amount of research.

One topic of research was the question of how to avoid the embarrassing gaffes that had marred Hollywood's earlier approaches to Latin America. Staff writer Bob Carr concluded that the problem had been one of simple carelessness. "Ignorant and arrogant Hollywood fleshfilm producers," Carr wrote, "lump together a vast continent, 19 separate and distinct Republics, two major languages and several races under the meaningless term, 'South America.' In an effort to please these mythical 'South Americans,' they dump into their pictures a mixture of junk which they call 'South American atmosphere.' There is no such thing, any more than there is a 'Southern European atmosphere.' There are, however, 44,000,000 Brazilians; 12,000,000 Argentinians; 9,000,000 Colombians; and so on down the line. Each country has its own culture, traditions, and peculiarities. Each is very touchy about his own distinct national identity. All are infuriated when Yankees brush them off as 'South Americans.' All have a fantastically sensitive pride."

Carr suggested, in place of "the wishy-washy mixture of sombreros, guitars, and rhumbas" that had characterized earlier films, that the Disney films should be built around individual countries, in particular the two biggest South American markets: Argentina and Brazil. "Despite local rivalries, the South American Republics are now acquiring a certain sense of continental solidarity," Carr wrote. "That is why, if a film producer does justice in a decent, respectful way, to one country down there, they all appreciate it more than Hollywood's futile attempts at 'general South American atmosphere.'" In other words, Walt was already on the right track with in-depth research on individual countries. In the end, as we'll see, this approach would succeed brilliantly—both in the short term, during the 1941 goodwill tour, and in the long term with subsequent film production. Let other Hollywood studios commit their careless cultural mistakes; the Disney studio would consistently strike a responsive chord with Latin American audiences by picturing their cultures in authentic detail.

The studio's South American research took a variety of forms. Much of it was compiled in a large "South American Research" booklet, distributed among the staff, which exhaustively catalogued the history, geography, flora and fauna, and culture of individual South American countries, principally Argentina, Brazil, and Chile. Sources for this information ranged from Pan Am representatives Einhorn and Smith in South America to various U.S. authorities, some of them recommended by the CIAA. One such authority, Dr. Victor von Hagen, visited the studio in April with some of his books and 16 mm footage to consult with Rose. For information about South American music, the staff relied heavily on an article by Carleton Sprague Smith, chief librarian of the New York Public Library's music division, who had recently toured South America for the Pan American Union. Based on his writings and their own research, the team started assembling a large collection of recordings of contemporary South American, Cuban, and Mexican music. Numerous books of South American folklore and literature were added to the studio library.

Because of the proposed artistic interchange between countries, the staff researched prominent artists. Among those investigated was Dante Quinterno, whose comic character Patoruzú was then a popular favorite in Argentina. John Rose, upon seeing the recent Mexican film *Ni sangre ni arena*, was enthused over the comic actor Cantinflas. Still more than a decade away from his international success in *Around the World in 80 Days*, Cantinflas was already extraordinarily popular in Mexico and had come to the attention of Hollywood producers. Describing him as "one of the funniest comics I have ever seen," Rose suggested the intriguing idea of a combination live-action–animated version of *Don Quixote* with Cantinflas as Sancho Panza, an idea that was never realized.[5]

One South American artist who loomed large in the studio's pretrip research was F. Molina Campos. Despite little formal training, Florencio Molina Campos had years earlier established himself as a popular artist in Argentina with his painted caricatures of gauchos and gaucho life. Thanks to his calendar-art contract with a company that manufactured a rope-soled canvas shoe called the *alpargata*, Molina Campos's paintings had

[5] The possibility of a Disney version of *Don Quixote* was suggested the following month in an internal CIAA document. Subsequently Walt did meet Cantinflas, inviting him to the studio in November 1941 and later visiting him on the set of the film *El circo* on one of Walt's trips to Mexico.

been distributed throughout the region since 1930. He was widely regarded, not least by himself, as the artistic spokesman of the gaucho, and his fame had become international through exhibitions in Europe and the United States. Advance research by the Disney studio clearly established two facts: that cooperation with Molina Campos would considerably boost Argentine acceptance of Disney's film venture, and that the artist's ego would make him difficult to deal with. Dr. Henry C. Niese, the honorary consul for Argentina in Los Angeles, told the staff that "Campos had told him that if he (Campos) were ever associated with the making of a cartoon, it would have to be Campos-produced, Campos-drawn, Campos-written." On the other hand, the artist had already shown an interest in Disney (he had visited the studio on one of his previous trips to the United States), and clearly understood that association with Disney would enhance his own prestige.

In the field of music, the staff focused particularly on the Brazilian classical composer Heitor Villa-Lobos. This was hardly surprising for the studio that had recently completed *Fantasia*, and given Villa-Lobos's international reputation. That reputation owed something to his colorful, flamboyant personality, which one staff member compared to that of Leopold Stokowski. Moreover, Villa-Lobos's wide-ranging musical exploration already included some film experience: in 1937 he had composed the score for director Humberto Mauro's *Descobrimento do Brasil*. It was one of his subsequent projects that struck Bob Carr's imagination. In 1940 Villa-Lobos had captured international attention by composing melodic lines based on the physical contours of mountains like Sugarloaf and Corcovado, then applying the same principle to the New York City skyline and to the profiles of human beings. "His weird method of composing music from people's profiles suggests the basis for a unique cartoon," Carr wrote to Walt. "You could commission him to do an original score for a short in which he gave 'musical profiles' of Mickey, Donald and other characters. Or he could himself play on the piano 'musical caricatures' of Hollywood stars, while you supply the cartoon caricatures." In the summer of 1941 this seemed a logical direction for Disney's Latin American venture to take. Conveniently, a concert of Villa-Lobos's music had been presented at the Museum of Modern Art in October 1940, giving him a ready-made connection to Nelson Rockefeller and the CIAA.

Another aspect of preparation for the trip involved preliminary story work. The gathering of story material would be an important part of the studio's mission in South America, but the Disney story artists knew from experience the value of thorough preparation and research. Accordingly, a variety of Latin-themed story ideas began to circulate in the story department long before the trip. The P-T O-2-L outline that John Rose had mentioned to Pan Am was only the beginning; by the time of Rose's letter many other ideas were also in the works.

Earlier in 1941, Bill Cottrell had suggested that two types of Latin American story ideas should be developed: "a musical group; or stories on the Silly Symphony style," and "a comedy group; including Mickey Mouse, Donald Duck, Pluto, etc. in South America. Also a few cartoons with an original character of a Gaucho and his horse." In other words, Cottrell was thinking along the same binary lines the studio had pursued during the 1930s, with the Mickey Mouse and Silly Symphony series. This approach was adopted by the story department at large. In mid-July Walt met with the writers, agreed to this general plan, and tentatively assigned story crews to the two budding groups of films: Ted Sears, Webb Smith, and Jack Miller on the "comedy" series; Cottrell, Lee Blair, and Jim Bodrero on the "musical" series.

As Cottrell had suggested, a leading candidate for the comedy pictures was a series built around a gaucho. The notion of a gaucho series can be considered the earliest story idea in the Disney Latin American project; Roy's original memo to Walt in October 1940 had made a vague suggestion regarding "el Gaucho," and now, in the summer of 1941, Ted Sears began actively to develop the idea. An undated document preceding the trip already incorporates the idea of styling the backgrounds for the series after Molina Campos's paintings and indicates that the idea of a series built around "a Gaucho, his horse and his dog" was suggested by Walt. By mid-June Sears had produced a four-page outline proposing a "little gaucho" character provisionally named Pio, but stressing that he "would not be a boy—sort of an ageless character like Chaplin." Sears tentatively set forth a story about the gaucho and a singing horse. A week later he submitted another outline in which the gaucho (now renamed Panchito) and his horse find a lost lamb that turns out to belong to a pretty shepherdess. Further ideas followed, and by the time of the July meeting five tentative stories were lined up for the gaucho series, leading off with "The Singing Horse." (Third on the list was an item called "The Winged Donkey.")

The "Pan-American Symphonies," on the other hand, were (like the Silly Symphonies of the 1930s) not built around continuing characters. At the mid-July meeting, Cottrell proposed three unrelated story ideas for the series, beginning with the P-T O-2-L idea, now known as "The Mail Plane." His other ideas were inspired by Brazil: a ballet "featuring the beautiful birds, butterflies and flowers of the country," and a "Carioca Carnival" short built around a "special Samba pop tune to be written by a South American composer."[6] Elements of both of these ideas would find their way into the studio's first Brazilian short. In addition to the ideas proposed for the two series, the story department generated a list of vague "Tentative Alternates" designed to be adaptable for generic use. Some of these were based on native animals of the countries in question—among them a "Parrot Story" set in Brazil—and one, "Paul, the Peculiar Penguin," concerned a penguin who strayed from his antarctic home to South America.

As always, personnel from all departments of the studio were invited to submit story ideas for consideration. Walt's response to one such submission from Lee Blair reveals something of his own priorities for the Good Neighbor films: "Thanks for sending in the story, SUME. However, I think we should find legends and stories that can be done with animals—animating humans is no cinch. . . . We should particularly lay off anything that leans toward religion."

As the story ideas continued to accumulate, it was clear that Sears, Cottrell, and the other contributing writers were likely candidates for the group that would make the trip to South America. Walt continued to assemble the group with care during the

[6] Although nothing was said about it in this memo, Cottrell had suggested on two other occasions that this short might be similar to the 1935 Silly Symphony *Water Babies*.

summer of 1941, constantly adding and subtracting names on the list. For a time he considered the idea of including experienced South American travelers from outside the studio. Roy tried repeatedly to enlist the services of Dudley "Dud" Easby of the State Department, who was friendly with some of the studio staff, but his request was denied because of the necessity of avoiding identification with the government. Similar efforts to recruit Pan Am's George Strehlke, who had already done so much to expedite the trip, were no more successful. In the end, all the creative and administrative members of the party were drawn from within the studio. The selection process was complete by 23 July, when Roy wrote a formal letter of introduction for each of the travelers. Walt had handpicked fifteen members of his staff:

Norm Ferguson had been one of the studio's top animators during the 1930s, the man who had done more than any other artist to develop the character of Pluto the pup—and, through that character, had done much to establish the craft of *personality animation*, the studio's triumphant innovation of the '30s. By 1941 Ferguson had begun to assume more administrative responsibilities, having directed a Pluto short and sequences in *Fantasia* and *Dumbo*. Walt appointed him supervisor of the South American tour group, and later Ferguson would become the supervising director of the studio's most important Latin American films. He was an inspired choice; his intimate familiarity with the creative side of animation gave him a substantial background for supervision of the other artists.

Ted Sears was one of the strongest talents in Disney's story department, a man with a seemingly inexhaustible supply of droll story ideas, always infused with a quiet, intelligent wit. His inclusion in the South American tour group was a sign that Walt was putting the best talent in his studio behind this project. Sears' prolific output of Latin American story ideas, even before the trip started, was characteristic.

Bill Cottrell was another leading light in the Disney story department. He was also Walt's brother-in-law, but this was hardly a case of nepotism; Cottrell's fertile imagination, often teamed with that of Joe Grant, had produced the stories for such delightfully clever Disney shorts as *Who Killed Cock Robin?* and *Pluto's Judgement Day* (both 1935). Whereas Sears tended to think expansively in terms of *groups* of films, Cottrell took a personal interest in individual stories, and many of the resulting films bear his personal stamp.

Webb Smith, another Disney story stalwart, was a former newspaper cartoonist who was known as one of the studio's best gag men. Where Cottrell's story ideas were long on charm, Smith's were rich in gags; among many other things he was credited with the idea for the famous "Flypaper Sequence" in *Playful Pluto* (1934). His presence in the South American group ensured that the resulting films would never lack for solid, down-to-earth humor.

Frank Thomas, one of the newer generation of animators, was well on his way to becoming one of the fabled "Nine Old Men" of the studio. He was the only member of the animation staff at the time to make the trip, and in fact was originally included in the group largely because Walt wanted to keep him from being drafted. When the Selective Service age requirements were changed so that he was no longer at risk, Thomas recalled, "Walt came around and said, 'Hey, you don't have to go to South America!' And I said, '*Have* to go? I was looking forward to it!' I had to talk him into it."

Herb Ryman, a former art director in live-action films, was one of the most distinctive painters in the group. In a studio bursting with artistic talent, Ryman's talent and artistic intuition were particularly respected by his peers. His creative instincts would lead him to forge bonds with the other artists the group would meet in South America, and the studio's later films would benefit from his eye for accurate visual details.

Lee Blair, a serious watercolor painter and former president of the California Watercolor Society, had been supervising color treatment and making inspirational paintings at the studio for several years. His impromptu painting skills would be invaluable in recording the atmosphere of the various South American locales—and, as a bonus, he could handle a 16 mm camera and became one of the three cameramen to film the group's activities on their tour.

Mary Blair, Lee's wife, was also a serious watercolorist and had made story and inspirational paintings at the studio, but had quit in June 1941 to concentrate on her own art. When she heard that Lee was going to South America with a studio tour group, she impulsively went to Walt and asked to be rehired so she could go along too. Walt agreed—but neither he, Mary, nor anyone else was prepared for the creative explosion that would take place in Mary Blair's art in South America. The trip proved a pivotal event in her career, and she in turn exercised a great influence on the studio's Latin American films.

Jim Bodrero was an obvious choice for the tour group: he was not only a tremendously talented concept artist, given to robust, evocative sketches springing from an endless fund of rich visual ideas, but also a social animal with a wide-ranging cosmopolitan background who had already formed a South American connection. In 1932, when the Olympics were held in Los Angeles, Bodrero had struck a lasting friendship with the visiting

Argentine polo team. In 1938, just before starting to work at the Disney studio, he had published the children's book *Bomba*, about a little Mexican wild donkey adopted by a U.S. family. Clearly Bodrero had an affinity for Latin American culture, and his contacts—and his ability to form new ones—would be an asset in South America.

Charles Wolcott, the musician of the group, had joined the Disney music department as an arranger in 1938 and had quickly graduated to musical direction. To him would fall the responsibility of recording, auditioning, cataloguing, and assimilating the wide array of native South American musical traditions the group would encounter in their travels—not to mention overseeing the installation and operation of the "Fantasound" stereophonic sound system at the various openings of *Fantasia*. As the Good Neighbor project progressed in succeeding years, Wolcott would become the studio's resident Latin American musical specialist, marshaling and refining the vast repertoire of Latin music for use in the films, and occasionally contributing an original song of his own.

Larry Lansburgh, a staff assistant director, had expected the worst from the labor troubles at the studio: "I went out to the parking lot to get in my car and ran into Walt, and I was a little sad about things. And he said, 'Larry, how's your Spanish?' And I said, 'Well, it's the same as ever, I'm not completely bilingual but almost.'" Walt, as it turned out, had Lansburgh in mind for the South American trip. "And God, I would have been out of work, and I jumped at it, really. I said, 'Sure,' and we were off."[7] Lansburgh would function as Norm Ferguson's assistant director on the trip, and would also serve as one of the three 16 mm cameramen, along with Lee Blair and Walt himself.

[7] Lansburgh had submitted a South American story outline (accompanied by story sketches by Jim Bodrero) to Walt on 8 May 1941. The story was not used, but Lansburgh's initiative and his familiarity with South American cultures may have been a factor in his selection for the tour.

Jack Miller, one of the contingent of story sketch artists, was currently enjoying special status at the studio as the artist behind the *Baby Weems* segment of *The Reluctant Dragon*. *Baby Weems* had represented a breakthrough in the notoriously painstaking and expensive process of Disney animation; its story had been conveyed almost entirely through Miller's static story sketches, with only a modicum of actual animation. Thanks to Miller's evocative still drawings, the sequence had been produced at minimal cost but without any sacrifice of quality. This principle, producing maximum effect from restricted means, would assume more importance as the Good Neighbor project continued.

Jack Cutting had found a unique niche at the studio: as the Disney features entered the international market, the erudite Cutting was chosen to supervise the recording of their foreign-language sound tracks. In that capacity he had already traveled to Buenos Aires the previous year to oversee the Spanish sound track for *Pinocchio*. Cutting's value to the South American tour group was self-evident; along with providing the benefit of his experience, he could also take advantage of the opportunity to record Spanish sound tracks for the new features *The Reluctant Dragon* and *Dumbo*. So well did Cutting distinguish himself that he would remain in Rio, at the request of the Brazilian film industry, to act as a consultant after the rest of the Disney group had returned to California.

John Rose, from the studio's administrative side, was designated as the business manager for the group. This was a tall order: along with accounting for all financial expenditures, Rose was expected to coordinate the schedules of all the group members in a way that would ensure maximum effective use of their time *and* unfailingly courteous diplomatic relations—all the while conforming to a schedule that was revised daily, and sometimes hourly, in response to Walt's whims and the unexpected demands of circumstance. Much of our knowledge of the 1941 trip comes from Rose's correspondence and the reports he filed with the CIAA during and after the trip.

Janet Martin, Larry Lansburgh's wife, was the unit publicist. As such she functioned as Rose's indispensable right hand, maintaining cordial public relations with the South American press even as she coordinated the written and photographic documentation of the trip for future reference. We can be thankful that Janet made the trip; along with Rose's accounts, her public and private writings give us our fullest sense of the tour group's experiences.

Along with these fifteen studio employees, three more travelers rounded out the group: Walt's wife, Lillian; Bill Cottrell's wife, Hazel; and of course Walt himself. Hazel Cottrell was the former Hazel Sewell, Lillian Disney's sister, who had supervised the studio's ink and paint department during the late 1920s and early '30s, but by 1941 she had retired from the studio and did not act in a professional capacity on the trip.

In addition to the human element, it was of course necessary to prepare the equipment and supplies that would be going on the trip. To Larry Lansburgh, as Norm Ferguson's assistant, fell the job of organizing, selecting, packing, and accounting for the supplies that would be needed. Two long itemized lists, prepared in July 1941, indicate the enormity of Lansburgh's task. To begin with, equipping a team of artists to record their impressions of South America called for great quantities of paper, sketch pads, pencils, pens, brushes, paints, ink, pastels, erasers, rubber cement, drawing boards, and other assorted paraphernalia. A full complement of office supplies, for conducting normal business and correspondence (including a supply of the studio's *Fantasia* letterhead, since *Fantasia* would be opening in South America during the trip), would also be needed. The tour's public-relations function called for a supply of publicity materials, including stills, portraits of Walt, and some of the studio's standard publicity handouts, duly translated into Spanish and Portuguese. And finally, to allow for some actual production work in the field, Lansburgh gathered a supply of production equipment—ranging from editing scissors and tape and rough animation training reels to two full-size animation boards and a complete Moviola, disassembled and shipped directly to Buenos Aires.

One of the objects of the tour was to film a 16 mm record of the group's travels, and the matter of 16 mm camera equipment, and responsibility for using it, was an issue of particular concern to Walt. Herb Ryman was regarded as an excellent cinematographer, and it was assumed by some that he would be responsible for the 16 mm shots of the trip. Walt vetoed this idea, feeling that Ryman's painting ability was more important to the success of the tour and not wanting him to be distracted by any other responsibilities. Instead the 16 mm duties were passed to another painter, Lee Blair, and to Lansburgh. A new Eastman camera with tripod and telephoto lens was purchased for their use, and in addition Walt took along his own Bell & Howell Filmo 141-A camera and shot a considerable amount of footage himself. The studio's original intent, to shoot 16 mm footage strictly for internal reference, took on an added dimension as the departure date neared. Kenneth Macgowan, an erstwhile producer for Twentieth Century–Fox who was now director of the CIAA's Motion Picture Section, issued a public "call for 16 mm. film taken of Latin American countries," especially "film taken by stars, directors, writers and others," to be edited into documentaries for nontheatrical exhibition. The Disney tour was of special interest to Macgowan, and he sent Walt a telegram in early August: "WOULD LIKE VERY MUCH TO DISTRIBUTE IN 16-MM. NON-THEATRICALLY A THREE OR FOUR-REEL PICTURE ON YOUR SOUTH AMERICAN TRIP. OUR OFFICE WILL PAY COST OF THE KODACHROME FILM EXPOSED FOR THIS PURPOSE." So the tour group's 16 mm "home movies" became yet another aspect of their work for the CIAA.

Despite these intricately detailed preparations, and a departure date now tentatively set for mid-August, the studio still had no signed formal agreement with the U.S. government authorizing the South American tour. Roy was growing increasingly concerned over this, and pressured Alstock for a decision: "MOST MEN CONTEMPLATING TRIP ARE KEY MEN AROUND WHOM CONSIDERABLE WORK REVOLVES. THE MORE TIME ELAPSES THE MORE ALL OUR PLANS ARE UPSET INCLUDING BOTH CURRENT AND FUTURE PRODUCT." Alstock tried to apply pressure of his own within the CIAA, but the wheels were turning very slowly, and until the contract was executed Roy was loath to issue any public statements about the studio's Latin American plans.

This put the studio publicists in an awkward position. Keeping the trip a secret was an impossible task; a major South American tour by a public figure of Walt Disney's stature was an event, and rumors began to circulate in June 1941, almost as soon as the trip was proposed. Janet Martin, bombarded with queries from the trade press, blankly denied that a South American trip was even contemplated. This of course did not prevent the trade papers from publishing their own speculation and rumors, and the efforts at secrecy were not helped by confusion and miscommunication within the ranks. When Ben Cammack, an RKO representative in Buenos Aires, issued an announcement that Walt would attend the local premiere of *Fantasia*, Janet asked Gunther Lessing to help defuse the story. Lessing contacted the trade press and explained that the trip was still in the "conversational" stage, then cabled Roy: "SUGGEST YOU TELEPHONE [RKO vice president Phil] REISMAN TO TELL BEN TO SOBER UP." As late as August, J. R. Josephs, representing the CIAA in Argentina, heard rumors of the impending Disney visit and dismissed them as sheer fantasy: "This sounds like pure imagination but if it is true, somebody had better inform B.A. [Buenos Aires] and Cesar Civita, Disney's local representative who knows nothing of it." As the departure date loomed, Roy warned Alstock: "NO SIGNED CONTRACT HAS YET BEEN RECEIVED. POSITIVELY I CANNOT AND WILL NOT LET THESE PEOPLE START THIS WEEKEND WITHOUT IT."

Finally, on 5 August 1941, the formal agreement was executed: Contract NDCar-110 between the United States of America and Walt Disney Productions, providing for the field survey in South America and for a subsequent series of twelve one-reel cartoons. A flurry of transcontinental telegrams confirmed the signing of the contract; both Alstock and John Lockwood, general counsel for the CIAA, hastened to reassure Roy that this crucial step had finally been taken. John Rose, who was in Washington preparing for his departure, corroborated the story: "HAVE JUST SEEN SIGNED CONTRACT WITH OWN EYES." Janet Martin, released from her enforced silence, issued an official press release announcing the trip, identifying the personnel in the group, and even hinting at the "strong possibility" of a permanent branch of the Disney studio in South America. She later noted ruefully: "The initial newsbreaks were disappointing, and can be laid to the fact that the story did not have an element of first-hand news, due to the fact that there have been rumors and stories of this trip all over town for so long."

On 6 August 1941, *one day* after finalization of the CIAA contract, Jack Cutting left Miami on a Pan Am Clipper bound for Brazil. He arrived in Rio de Janeiro on the eighth and was followed a few days later by the other advance man, John Rose. Rose had left the studio in late July for a trip across the U.S. to confer with CIAA officials in New York and Washington, intending to return to California before beginning the South American journey. Instead, when his departure date was moved up to 10 August, he was instructed to proceed from Washington directly to Miami. Amid a barrage of last-minute instructions from Roy and others at the studio, Rose left Miami for the two-day trip to Rio, joining Cutting there on the twelfth. Together they met with Pan Am and RKO representatives and secured hotel reservations, paving the way for the arrival of the rest of the party.

On 13 August, a party of nine representing the first main Disney group left Miami for South America. Last of all, on Friday the fifteenth, Walt's own party made their departure. Janet Martin had done her advance publicity work well, and at each stop on the two-day flight Walt was besieged by the press. Arriving in Belém on the sixteenth, he was met by Celestino Silveira, a prominent Brazilian radio commentator and editor-in-chief of *Cine-Rádio Jornal*. Silveira had been deputized by the Brazilian press, not to wait until Walt arrived in Rio, but to go to Belém himself to welcome Walt on his official arrival in Brazil (and, incidentally, to obtain an exclusive interview). Silveira recalled in later years that he dined with Walt at the hotel that evening, and that a small band in the dining room played, very badly, a selection of North and South American music. One melody in particular, despite its mangled performance, seemed to catch Walt's ear. The song was Ary Barroso's "Aquarela do Brasil."

The following day, Walt, Silveira, and the rest of the party continued their flight to Rio de Janeiro. Arriving at the airport at 4:30 in the afternoon, they were met by a crowd of at least a thousand people. The Disney South American tour had officially begun.

BRAZIL

After months of preparing and imagining, the Disney artists suddenly found themselves immersed in the vivid reality of Brazil. "Rio was an exciting, wonderful city," Bill Cottrell recalled. "The architecture, it's European architecture; the harbor, which I think is supposed to be the most beautiful harbor in the world; the sidewalks, with their wonderful patterns and colors; and the music, the enthusiasm of the music itself, the modern music, the songs, the rhythm." "There just seemed to be decorative stuff everywhere," said Frank Thomas, "and the big palm trees, and the people all so happy." The artists eagerly plunged into their mission: sketching, painting, filming, and photographing expeditions throughout the bustling city. "I saw all the street vendors singing out their wares," said Thomas. "There was a knife sharpener that would drive by the hotel, and he had a special little song about sharpening knives, 'I sharpen knives.' Another guy had a dry cleaning [business] in the back of the hotel where he'd clean things up at night, and he had a little song about his dry cleaning business. So that made it all pretty colorful for us."

Accommodations for the Disney party were split between two hotels. Although the entire group's reservations at the Copacabana Palace Hotel had been confirmed before the trip, Jack Cutting and John Rose discovered on arrival that they had not been honored and that, moreover, Rio was suffering from a hotel shortage. In the end Walt and Lillian Disney, Bill and Hazel Cottrell, Larry Lansburgh and Janet Martin, and Rose did stay at the Copacabana, while the rest of the party checked into the more economical Hotel Glória. This divided living arrangement made it difficult to coordinate the group's activities, so the group was split into four teams, each with a "captain" who delegated responsibilities among the rest of the team. Walt asked Jim Bodrero, Jack Miller, and Frank Thomas to concentrate on character sketches, while the Blairs and Herb Ryman were to give their attention to scenery and atmosphere paintings. Larry Lansburgh was charged with the 16 mm film detail. All were encouraged to explore Rio and its surroundings: Sugarloaf and Corcovado, the botanical and zoological gardens, libraries, and museums.

Chuck Wolcott's assignment was to survey the music of Brazil, and Brazil offered a wealth of musical treasures to choose from. Initially, in line with their advance plans, the group pursued the idea of working with serious Brazilian music. Walt did meet with Villa-Lobos and with other composers, including Francisco Mignone and Hekel Tavares, discussing the possibility of a "Brazilian *Fantasia*-type short." From the day of their arrival, however, the Disney party was captivated with Brazilian *popular* music, and in particular the infectious rhythm of the samba. The samba was everywhere: in the streets, on the radio, in concerts. At the first meeting of the entire Disney group, two days after Walt's arrival in Rio, he stressed the importance of using samba rhythms in the studio's Brazilian films. Over the next three weeks he and Wolcott, along with the rest of the party, were treated to samba concerts, samba auditions, and even a samba school. These activities brought Wolcott into contact with such notable musicians as Dorival Caymmi, Sílvio Caldas, Radamés Gnattali—and the composer of the tune that had so impressed Walt at that Belém hotel: Ary Barroso.

Wolcott soon learned it was small wonder that "Aquarela do Brasil" had found its way into a hotel band's repertoire; it was an enormously popular tune in Brazil. Ary Barroso had been all but overlooked in the studio's preliminary musical research, but he had a fanatical popular following in his own country, and his "Aquarela," introduced in 1939, had become practically an unofficial national anthem. At a series of meetings with Barroso and his publisher, Irmãos Vitale, Walt and his associates arranged to buy the film rights to "Aquarela" and another Barroso composition, "Os quindins de Yayá." "We are extremely pleased to have accomplished the clearance on 'Aquarela do Brasil,' which is unquestionably the most popular musical composition in all Brazil," Rose wrote to Francis Alstock. "Dona Alzira, the president's daughter, told us that in her opinion it is the most beautiful piece of music ever written. This opinion seems to be shared with most of the Brazilians with whom we have talked." Another tune, Zequinha de Abreu's instrumental "Tico-tico no fubá," a popular favorite in South America for more than two decades but as yet little known in the U.S., was also acquired in these conferences.

The Brazilian parrot, or *papagaio*, the party soon learned, was another popular feature of local culture. This was particularly impressed on them by an exhibition arranged in their honor, featuring the work of prominent Brazilian cartoonists. Walt and the rest of the party were particularly struck by a group of parrot drawings by the popular artist J. Carlos.[8] Before the trip, Ted Sears and Bill Cottrell had tentatively suggested ideas for parrot stories; now it became clear that those suggestions had been more apt than they realized. Soon artists were being dispatched to zoos and museums to sketch and photograph parrots. Norm Ferguson sent his family a newspaper photograph of himself and Sears with a trained parrot that, he wrote, "sings, dances, and talks Portuguese!" The group wasted no time in applying all this parrot research to their story work. "We have publicly announced our intent to develop a new character inspired by the Brazilian parrot—*papagaio*," Rose reported to Alstock at the end of the month. "This announcement has met with widespread approval."

[8] Studio records of the trip make no reference to Walt's meeting with J. Carlos. However, Daniella Thompson points out that the meeting was widely documented in the Brazilian press, which also claimed that Walt invited Carlos to the U.S. to work with the artists at the Disney studio. If Carlos had accepted, he might have influenced the studio's Brazilian subjects as F. Molina Campos influenced the Argentine ones. In any case, we know that the Disney artists were aware of J. Carlos's work; Jack Cutting had called it to Walt's attention even before the trip.

Hazel and Bill Cottrell, Ted Sears, Lilly and Walt, Norm Ferguson, and Frank Thomas disembark in Rio.

The Disney artists recorded their impressions of Rio in vivid watercolors and sketches. This one is probably the work of Lee Blair.

Ferguson and Rose did their best to keep these various sketching and photographing expeditions organized. The Hotel Glória had a salon adjacent to the dining room, where the artists held impromptu meetings to compare notes and plan upcoming activities. It was apparently at one of these meetings, during their first week in Rio, that the Disney party coined their distinctive self-nickname: "El Grupo." Throughout the rest of the trip, and on subsequent Latin American research trips for years afterward, this and other teams of Disney artists would be known affectionately as El Grupo.

"[The Glória] was a nice old hotel," Frank Thomas recalled, "very traditional, and the restaurant would only be open certain times of the day. And I would usually be shipped off to the market to make drawings of something, or to see the parrots or to see some kind of animal out there that somebody had on a little chain, and I'd get back to the hotel about one minute after two, and the restaurant always closed at two. There'd be all the food just sitting there within reach, and I'd say, 'Why can't I knock somebody down and get a sandwich for myself or something?' 'No, no, no sir, sorry, sir.' So I lost, what was it, twenty pounds in Rio, I think, because I couldn't figure out when they ate!"

If the Disney artists were much taken with Brazil, Brazilians were delighted to host Walt Disney. Those pretrip jitters over Walt's reception in South America quickly proved groundless; everywhere he went he was mobbed by fans. "Walt

Disney is far more successful as an enterprise and as a person than we could have dreamed," reported an elated Jock Whitney, who dropped in on the party in Rio, to the CIAA home office. "His public demeanor is flawless. He is unruffled by adulation and pressure—just signs every autograph and keeps smiling. . . . The cultural and scientific big names alike have accepted him and we had the right thought that he was the one representative we might send who above all others was outside the range of criticism." This sounds like press agent hype, but it comes from private interoffice correspondence, never intended for public scrutiny.

Walt and the rest of El Grupo scrupulously maintained their original plan to avoid identification with the U.S. government, but such precautions were probably unnecessary. Indeed, thanks to John Rose's advance work, Walt was welcomed to Rio as an official guest of the *Brazilian* government. The invitation was extended by Dr. Lourival Fontes, director of the Department of Press and Propaganda, or DIP. Throughout Walt's stay in Brazil the DIP kept him under its wing, arranging meetings with prominent artists and dignitaries and coordinating an endless round of parties, banquets, and receptions—and taking care to film those activities for its self-produced newsreel, the *Cine jornal Brasileiro*. Walt's first night in Rio set the tone: an intimate dinner party at Cassino da Urca[9] quickly escalated into a large-scale publicity event. "We were supposed to have a quiet and informal dinner," Jack Cutting wrote to Roy. "Well, the table prepared for us was right along the dance-floor and between two bands playing continuously, floor-show, flash-bombs and newspaper-men, plus some

[9] The Urca was one of Rio's most popular nightclubs. Its huge electric sign was a local landmark that would be featured in the studio's first Brazilian film.

Ted Sears, Herb Ryman, and Norm Ferguson observe a trained parrot.

hundreds of people sitting nearby, Walt had quite a peaceful time of it. The climax came when they turned the flash-light on him. I must say, however, that he was a good sport about the whole thing, as I am sure it was quite tiring after the long plane trip." These attentions continued throughout the Brazilian visit: Walt was formally received by Presidente Getúlio Vargas and other notables and, in a special ceremony, was presented with the Order of the Southern Cross. Oswaldo Aranha—the *ministro das relações exteriores* (foreign minister) who had threatened military retaliation against further Good Neighbor missions—hosted a luncheon for Walt and some of his party.

One highlight of the visit was the Rio opening of *Fantasia*, presented at the Cine Pathé-Palacio on Saturday, 23 August. This was a major event of the social season in Rio, sponsored by the *primeira-dama*, dona Darcy Vargas, as a benefit for her favorite charity, Cidade das Meninas. In keeping with the high-profile nature of the event, Wolcott and Cutting personally supervised the installation of the Fantasound sound system for the occasion. "The only thing people comment about is the selection of the house," Cutting noted privately. "It will be in the Pathé Theatre which, while being centrally located, is small and rather second rate. [Bruno] Cheli [the manager of RKO's Brazilian office] has assured us that the place will be dressed up for the occasion." Indeed it was. Walt and Lilly were invited by Presidente Vargas to join

Between diplomatic functions, Walt incessantly shot 16 mm footage and still pictures.

the presidential party, and the event was attended by a glittering array of prominent social and government figures. Celestino Silveira broadcast the proceedings, and Walt and some of the artists spoke a few words of Portuguese on the air. Next day, the newspaper reviews were rapturous. "Fortunately *Fantasia* was an enormous success, even with the most critically aloof," Whitney reported happily, "and after that the applause and decorations came in showers of glory."

A similar scene was enacted three days later when *Fantasia* opened at the Cine Rosário in São Paulo. This was another charity benefit, this time sponsored by dona Anita Silveira Costa, wife of the governor of São Paulo. At the urging of RKO's Brazilian office, Walt took a side trip in order to make another personal appearance at this opening. Aside from Lillian, Walt's traveling companions were RKO vice president Phil Reisman and Albert Byington, Jr., a Brazilian media mogul. The rest of El Grupo remained behind in Rio, carrying on with their survey work.

Even apart from the openings of *Fantasia*, Walt maintained a high profile with the Brazilian public. Beginning with a broadcast from Belém when his plane first landed there on 16 August, he was a popular radio subject and made numerous broadcasts. Perhaps most notable of these was a guest appearance on the *Hora do Brasil* program, in which Walt, as the voice of Mickey Mouse, spoke in Portuguese to the children of Brazil. Written by Dr. Julio Barata, director of the radio division of the DIP, this special address was recorded on acetate at the commercial station Rádio Club do Brasil on 19 August, then broadcast the following day. One can only imagine the seeds of goodwill that were planted when an audience of Brazilian children heard Mickey Mouse speaking to them in their own language.

Walt also made several appearances at the RKO convention, which conveniently was being held at his hotel, the Copacabana Palace. (Currently appearing at the hotel's Cassino Copacabana was the U.S.-born entertainer Ethel Smith, who was building a reputation in the Latin American music world and who would herself be involved in the Disney Good Neighbor project several years later.) More importantly, Walt and several of his artists made personal appearances for the benefit of several professional arts organizations. One of these, presented at the DIP auditorium on 25 August, amounted to a summit conference between Disney artists and Brazilian artists: the Disney crew displayed sketches and paintings representing their first impressions of Brazil, while the DIP presented Walt with manuscripts, charts of Brazilian flora and fauna, and other materials gathered to help with the group's survey activities. At another program later the same day, Ferguson, Thomas, and Bodrero presented an informal "chalk talk," sketching Disney characters—including preliminary designs of the new *papagaio* character—on easels onstage, while Wolcott, at the piano, played Disney music. A charity auction of original *Fantasia* paintings capped the proceedings.[10] Some of these programs provided Brazilian artists with a preview of works in progress: screenings of rough animation from the still uncompleted *Bambi*, and of the celebrated *Baby Weems* sequence from *The Reluctant Dragon*, which had not yet been released in Brazil.

[10] The evening's entertainment also included a performance by U.S. singer Grace Moore, who was herself making a goodwill tour of South America. Although her tour had no formal connection whatever with that of the Disney group, her itinerary coincided with theirs at several stops in Brazil and Argentina.

El Grupo's visit to Brazil, originally planned to last ten days, was ultimately extended to three weeks. With the notable exceptions of Walt, Lilly, and the Cottrells, most of the group came down with colds, "which we are told is quite proper in Rio this time of year," Rose noted. While the rest of the group was occupied with survey activities, Jack Cutting concentrated on his familiar specialty: dubbing Spanish and Portuguese dialogue tracks for recent and upcoming Disney features. Operating independently of the main group's timetable, Cutting shuttled between Rio and Buenos Aires, supervising the casting of voices and recording of dialogue for *Dumbo*, *The Reluctant Dragon*, and *Bambi*. In addition, taking advantage of Chuck Wolcott's presence in the group, Cutting was able to call on Wolcott's musical expertise in recording the songs for the Spanish and Portuguese editions of *Dumbo*.

This latter activity led to a Good Neighbor project that had not been part of the original plans: recording true Brazilian music, played by Brazilian musicians, in a Brazilian recording studio for possible use in future Disney films. After weeks of negotiation and technical consultation with local RCA representatives,[11] several sambas, including "Aquarela do Brasil," were recorded at Carmen Santos's studio in Rio. The sessions began on Wednesday, 3 September, with Radamés Gnattali's orchestra and special guest musicians. "I think they were like studio musicians," said Frank Thomas, "and, I don't know, at least forty players in the group, and they had nice arrangements for these. It takes a rhythm section for a samba dance, because it takes about twelve people to play all those noisemakers, and get the right rhythm in the right order. They made a great sound; you'd find yourself hopping around, with no lessons or anything!"

[11] The RCA sound system was the standard system used by the Disney studio to record all its sound tracks at this time. (Coincidentally, RCA was also one of the parent companies of RKO Radio Pictures, currently Disney's theatrical distributor.)

Unfortunately, the technical conditions for these sessions were less than ideal. It seems likely that Cutting chose the Carmen Santos studio for this project because the Sonofilm studio, where he had recorded the Portuguese dialogue tracks for *Pinocchio* the previous year, was unavailable, having burned down in the meantime.[12] Sonofilm's recording equipment, salvaged from the flames, had been moved onto the Santos stage. Carmen Santos herself was a Brazilian actress who had been popular in the silent era. Her stage, newly fitted with this second-hand recording equipment—adequate for recording dialogue and small musical ensembles—was less successful in recording a large orchestra. "Spent about five hours getting six takes," Wolcott wrote to his wife. "Many, many problems to balancing this combination. Our 'two mike' set up didn't work out because of the drain on volume, so we had to go back to a single 'mike'. Trying to separate voice from orchestra with one 'mike' is practically impossible, so we had to sacrifice orchestra. Thursday, two takes were recorded. . . ." None of these takes were satisfactory, and finally Wolcott eliminated the large orchestra.

[12] Ted Thomas, who unearthed much of this information, also points out that Sonofilm was part of the Byington media empire—which, by a suspicious coincidence, suffered several other fires at its various properties around the same time.

On Friday, 5 September, he tried again with a smaller group. This time the results were far more pleasing, and Wolcott successfully recorded a variety of selections. For a time he and Norm Ferguson held out for the possibility of using these Brazilian tracks in production, possibly with some additional dubbing. In the end, however, only one of the recordings made that day would be heard in a Disney film. The instrumental "Flauta e Pandeiro," performed by its composer, Benedicto Lacerda, was used three years later on the sound track of the second Disney Good Neighbor feature, *The Three Caballeros*. Other recordings from the Carmen Santos session would be used only for reference, and the music rerecorded for production at the Disney studio in Burbank.

Still, the recording experiment was not a wasted activity. In terms of diplomacy, it was a gesture that created incalculable goodwill. "These efforts were appreciated by the Brazilian Government and the local movie industry, who recognized the sincerity of our desire to use local talent and spend money in Brazil," the staff later noted. "From a 'good neighbor' standpoint, therefore, the results were excellent."

This incident led, in fact, to yet another unexpected development. So favorably had Jack Cutting's technical abilities impressed the Brazilian filmmakers that he found his services in further demand. Gustavo Capanema, Brazil's minister of education, formally requested the assistance of a Disney artist/technician to assist in developing Brazil's educational film industry. The request was relayed to Walt on 30 August, about a week before his departure for Argentina, and he immediately agreed to "loan" Cutting to the Brazilian government. As a result, after the rest of El Grupo finished its stay in Buenos Aires and moved on, Cutting would return to Rio and remain there, working with the Brazilian film industry, until early 1942.

Argentine artist F. Molina Campos visits Rio to discuss his paintings with Walt.

Other miscellaneous activities in Rio included a meeting with F. Molina Campos, who was on his way to New York. The group's extended stay in Brazil meant that, by the time they arrived in Argentina, they would miss seeing Molina Campos there; consequently, he stopped off to see *them* in Rio on 3 September. The Disney visit to Brazil officially concluded with the events of 7 September, Brazil's Independence Day. The morning was marked by a lengthy parade, demonstrating the massed might of Brazil's armed forces. El Grupo turned out for the occasion, Walt watching the parade from Oswaldo Aranha's palace. Later in the day, another kind of celebration took place at the Estádio Vasco da Gama: Heitor Villa-Lobos conducted a choral group composed of thirty thousand schoolchildren. All this was faithfully recorded on 16 mm film by Walt and Larry Lansburgh. It was an appropriately stupendous finish to an eventful three weeks in Brazil's capital city.

Early the next morning, the party took their leave of Brazil at the Rio airport—the Disneys and the Cottrells taking the regular 8:30 flight, the rest of the group following on a specially chartered plane an hour later. A crowd of well-wishers turned out to see them off: officials of Pan Air, representatives of the DIP, and members of the press, along with a throng of curious fans. With the thanks and farewells of their new Brazilian friends ringing in their ears, El Grupo set off for Buenos Aires.

By popular demand, Walt was frequently costumed as a gaucho during his visit to Argentina.

ARGENTINA

Argentina was in some ways the focal point of the South American tour. It was Axis influence in Argentina that had first prompted Nelson Rockefeller to pursue a "Good Neighbor" program, for here the Nazi propaganda machine in South America was at its strongest. Motion pictures were a key part of this enterprise; several important theaters in Buenos Aires fed their patrons a steady diet of pictures from UFA[13] and other German studios, sometimes adding a Mickey Mouse or Donald Duck cartoon to the bill to lure audiences. John Rose, in one of his last-minute meetings in Washington before leaving the U.S., had been specifically asked by the CIAA to concentrate on Argentine material during the trip. Axis propaganda forces in Argentina, anticipating the Disney visit, were prepared to attack; *El Pampero*, the Nazi newspaper in Buenos Aires, published a stinging five-column assault on Walt in late August, while the Disney party was still in Brazil. Of course this resistance

[13] UFA (also known as Ufa), or Universum Film AG, was the principal studio of the German film industry from 1917 to 1945.

had itself been anticipated by the CIAA and by the Disney studio. Those months of exhaustive research had been calculated to leave Walt fully prepared when he walked into the political minefield that was Argentina in 1941.

Once again, they needn't have worried. When Walt's plane, delayed for two hours by inclement weather, taxied into Morón Airport on 8 September, it was greeted by what was described as the largest crowd in the airport's history. If Disney fans in Brazil had been enthusiastic, those in Argentina were ecstatic. A special interview script had been prepared for Walt's arrival in Buenos Aires, but he never got to use it. Instead Chas de Cruz, a popular broadcasting personality for Radio Belgrano, bounded up the steps to the plane, ambushed Walt as he emerged from the door, and asked him to say a few words into the microphone.[14] This was followed by a more formal welcoming speech from the well-known artist Ramón Columba, representing the official reception committee, who greeted Walt as "a peaceful Ambassador of Humor" and "a true benefactor of Humanity" and concluded with words heavy with meaning: "Welcome, then, greatest pictorial genius of our time, to this land of peace and liberty." The stage was set: just as in Brazil, the overwhelming popularity of Walt and his films effortlessly swept away any opposition.

[14] This incident can be glimpsed briefly in the *Sucesos Argentinos* newsreel.

Nor was the entry into Buenos Aires uneventful for the rest of El Grupo. Studio lore would later relate how Jim Bodrero's old friends from the Argentine polo team, alerted to his arrival, swarmed onto the airfield to greet the second plane, crying, "Jimmy! Jimmy!" Other members of the party were pleasantly surprised at the luxury of their accommodations. Janet Martin privately noted her pleasure at discovering "the first good food since leaving Miami—Rio food is uniformly nothing to rave about, no matter where you go, and all of us lost a little weight there I think, but we'll certainly get fat here. Everybody in B.A. loves to eat. And of course the meat is the best you ever tasted."

As in Rio de Janeiro, John Rose had preceded the rest of the party by several days to confirm formal arrangements. The idea of establishing a temporary "studio" in Buenos Aires had been part of the plan from the beginning, and Larry Lansburgh had assembled and shipped a large complement of production equipment directly to Argentina when the group left Burbank. For the question of *where* to set up the studio, Rose relied largely on Pan Air. George Smith, of Pan Air's local office, tentatively suggested the Continental Hotel, which had the advantage of being centrally located in Buenos Aires (and was directly across the street from Pan Air's offices). In the end, however, Rose opted for both living and working quarters at the Alvear Palace Hotel. By the time El Grupo arrived in the city, Rose had established the "studio" in the Alvear Palace penthouse, a large, airy, high-ceilinged room used as a ballroom during the winter season. With its large windows, the penthouse made an ideal working space for artists, and it opened onto a roof garden that afforded a scenic view of the city. Rose also established an office in room 407 of the hotel and, mindful of the disorganization that had handicapped his efforts in Rio, advertised for secretarial help. Two bilingual secretaries, Sara Short and Diana Bohm, were quickly added to the ranks.

Ramón Columba, visiting the Alvear Palace studio, is caricatured by Jim Bodrero as a gaucho pursuing one of the *Fantasia* centaurettes (*see* p. 50).

Ramón Columba, the artist who had so eloquently welcomed Walt on his arrival in Argentina, proved to be an unexpectedly valuable ally. Columba was the president of the Asociación de Dibujantes Argentinos, an organization of Argentine cartoonists who eagerly welcomed Walt and his party as kindred spirits. For the Disney group, anxious to maintain their image as working artists on a field trip, this was a perfect connection. The Dibujantes enjoyed wide publicity through their own periodical and their affiliation with the *Sucesos Argentinos* (Argentine Events) newsreel, and Columba himself, besides being a high-profile public personality, was also well connected in government circles. "Don Ramón was a frequent visitor at the hotel, and accompanied Walt on a number of visits," wrote Doug Clark, Pan Air's local public relations chief. "The frequency of Don Ramón's visits became a standing joke among the group. Nevertheless, the publicity value of photographs of Walt and Don Ramón together was inestimable, especially since Don Ramón is a very popular and esteemed figure among the Argentine public, and is the confidant of many leading Argentine Statesmen."

Tuesday, 9 September, the day after the group's arrival, marked the Argentine opening of *Fantasia* at the Cine Broadway. Once again the premiere was a charity benefit, this time sponsored by a group of the social elite of Buenos Aires. The Spanish edition of the film had been personally prepared by Jack Cutting, along with his other duties, on his advance trip to the city from Rio. A press preview was held on the afternoon of the ninth, and Chuck Wolcott took the opportunity to supervise sound levels throughout the house and to consult with the manager about vibration noise behind the screen.

The rousing welcome Walt had received at the Buenos Aires airport paled in comparison to his reception at the *Fantasia* premiere. "You never saw such a mob!" wrote Janet Martin. "The mob reached clear out into the street, and packed the lobby. However, as many as there were, the crowd was very quiet and well-behaved. When Walt arrived there was really a jam. He was closed in on and had to sign hundreds of autographs. John [Rose] rescued Mrs. D. and got her inside, and after

RIGHT: The facade of the Trocadero Cine in Montevideo, spectacularly decked out for the opening of *Fantasia.*

Walt spoke on the radio, he finally worked his way inside too." Lee Blair recorded the general pandemonium on 16 mm. Once the crowd had packed into the theater, *Fantasia* scored another smashing success with both audience and critics. The evening concluded with a party at the Embassy Club, sponsored by RKO, which started after midnight and lasted until 4:00 a.m.

To avoid a repetition of the Buenos Aires mob scene, extra police protection was hired for the Uruguayan opening of *Fantasia* in Montevideo three days later. As he had done in Rio de Janeiro, Walt made a side trip to attend this out-of-town opening, but this time he took several members of El Grupo with him. Late on the evening of the eleventh, the Disneys, the Cottrells, Norm Ferguson, Chuck Wolcott, and Larry Lansburgh and Janet Martin boarded the night boat *Ciudad de Montevideo* for the trip across the Río de la Plata. Arriving the next morning in cold, drizzly Uruguay (sometimes known as "the Scotland of South America"), the group was treated to another royal reception. Walt was formally welcomed as a Guest of Honor of the city of Montevideo, and was later accorded an audience with Presidente Baldomir. He was also besieged by the press, and several members of the group noted the front page of the day's *Montevideo Ilustrado*: a banner headline, festooned with Disney characters, reading "WELCOME Walt"—directly above a story about the expulsion of the German ambassador.

WELCOME Walt

DEBE SER EXPULSADO DALDORF

MIENTRAS OCHO AGENTES NAZIS ESTAN PRESOS, DICE EL DR. BRENA, SU JEFE SIGUE EN PERSONAJE

Deben Procesarlo por su Acción Contra

SALUDA EL MAGO DE LA PANTALLA

The group's first order of business was to proceed to the Trocadero Cine, where *Fantasia* was to be shown that evening. The minister of education had declared a school holiday so that the schoolchildren of Montevideo could present a program in Walt's honor, ending by presenting him with a large bouquet. The facade of the Trocadero was decorated for the occasion with a huge portrait of a decidedly Hispanic-looking Walt. That evening, the showing of *Fantasia* scored another sensational success.

The next morning, instead of returning the way they had come, Walt's party was taken by bus to the picturesque settlement of Colonia, originally built by the Portuguese in the eighteenth century. "When we arrived," said Janet Martin, "members of the town band were scurrying around, popping in and out of doors on the main street like rabbits, and it was obvious we had surprised them by arriving a little too soon. So we took a drive around the city. Upon our return to the little dock to take the boat, the band was all nicely assembled and played for Walt. People swarmed around him getting autographs, and once again he was presented with a big bouquet all wired together. He was really mobbed here, but once again it was obvious that these people were really enjoying something they'd talk about for years." Larry Lansburgh, standing on the hood of a nearby car, filmed the crowd surrounding Walt. After the obligatory autographs and radio broadcast, Walt's party boarded the boat and sailed back across the Río de la Plata.

Meanwhile, back in Buenos Aires, the Alvear Palace penthouse studio officially opened on Thursday, 11 September. This studio fulfilled a dual function: it was both a practical working space and a public relations nerve center. It quickly became a beehive of activity. "The whole gang's there in one big room," Ted Sears wrote to his wife, "sketching—trying to write & meeting people—reporters, local artists, celebrities, cameramen, musicians, dancers, singers & people from the Argentine studios—pianos going, phones ringing, waiters rushing around with trays, all of us going out on the roof to pose—everyone trying to get an interpreter to find out what the visitors are talking about." Reporters, artists and musicians, dignitaries, writers, filmmakers, all found their way to the Alvear Palace studio for an audience with Walt or another member of El Grupo. Dante Quinterno, creator of the popular Argentine comic strip character Patoruzú, visited one day to discuss a two-reel animated cartoon he was producing. An artist who made *fotoesculturas* ("photosculptures"), life-size photographic portraits embedded on carved and painted busts, called at the Alvear Palace to immortalize Walt. On another occasion Chas de Cruz, the indefatigable radio personality, treated his listeners to a broadcast direct from the studio.[15]

At the same time, the Disney artists were actively pursuing their creative work in the same space. ("And it's obvious that the studio is really being used for work," Janet Martin observed, "because it's as messy looking as any animator's room in full swing of production.") Rose ordered some large bulletin boards that could be used as storyboards, and a local citizen, Carlos S. Lottermoser, loaned the group a grand piano for Chuck Wolcott's use. The production equipment that had been shipped from Burbank was more of a problem: it was held up in customs and extricated only with some difficulty. The raw 16 mm film stock shipped from the U.S. was especially problematic for some reason. Even with the help of the U.S. embassy, Rose was unable to secure the film until 20 September, near the end of the group's stay in Buenos Aires. In the meantime Rose prevailed on the local Eastman Kodak office, which provided the group with a substitute supply of Kodachrome. (Not having the magazine-loading film the Disney party required, Kodak also loaned a camera compatible with their stock.)

The most complex piece of equipment shipped from Burbank was a Moviola viewing machine, which had been disassembled for shipment. Frank Thomas was assigned the task of reassembling it. Customs officials took a particular interest in this item; in the tense atmosphere currently reigning in Argentina, with enemy agents establishing covert shortwave radio operations, a two-head Moviola attracted their attention. "When this big thing arrived and no one knew what it was, they assigned two Army men, big guys, that just stood there, didn't speak any English," Thomas recalled. "They wanted to see what I was going to do with this thing. So I had to unpack it, and of course I'd never seen a Moviola that wasn't assembled already, and I was trying to remember where the belts on it went and where the pedals were and what they connected to, and everything

[15] In addition to the notables who visited the Alvear Palace, El Grupo also had contact with the pioneer animator Quirino Cristiani, who had produced the feature-length political satire *El apóstol* in Argentina in 1917. John Rose's daily notes indicate that Cristiani called on Monday, 22 September, and that Jack Cutting went to meet him at his studio.

At work at the Alvear Palace studio, left to right: Frank Thomas, Norm Ferguson, Chuck Wolcott at the piano, Bill Cottrell, an unidentified man (back to camera), and Jim Bodrero.

like that. It took me an hour and a half to get it together! And I was pretty sure that it was all going to work, that was all I could do with it. So I said, 'Well, let's see now,' so I went over and plugged it in, not remembering that their electricity down there is 220, not 110. And so this thing took off like a jumping robot or something, jumped and chattered all over the floor. The guys pulled out their guns and jumped up on chairs and things: 'Live monster! Live monster!'" Thomas laughed at the memory. "I think they figured they'd seen enough for one day, and they left. We were able to get a transformer to take it down to 110, and we used it quite a bit after that."

El Grupo's sketching, painting, and photographing expeditions took a different tack from their similar missions in Rio. "The Brazilian theme, from the outset, was obvious to everyone," Herb Ryman later wrote. "The gay and colorful amusing parrot, the exotic backgrounds of the jungle near Rio and Bahia, the cariocas [a variant of the samba native to Rio], the rhythms of the samba at carnival time—each romantic and indigenous setting had its own provocative appeal. The Argentine theme, on the contrary, was not so easy, nor so obvious. Here was a temperate country, with none of the glamour of the rich jungle background of flora and fauna. The most conspicuous common denominator of understanding was the pampas and the hardy colorful gauchos. The vast seas of grass, the simple humor and hardships of those rugged horsemen of the plains seemed the source and the clue to our best efforts." Gaucho culture became the group's primary focus. Ted Sears's pretrip story suggestions for a gaucho series were now augmented with direct primary research into the customs, costumes, and lore of the real gauchos. Members of the group visited gaucho museums and gaucho libraries, attended gaucho concerts, and entertained authorities on gaucho culture at the Alvear Palace.

Larry Lansburgh took this pursuit a step further by going to the Mataderas Municipal stockyards to see working gauchos in action. After putting his command of Spanish to the test, explaining his purpose there, Lansburgh was allowed inside. "The yards are immense, covering a square mile," he noted. "Some of the gauchos were having maté before changing to fresh horses. They invited me into their small saddle room to sit for a while. There were [Molina] Campos prints all over the walls, well fly-specked. These people idolize Campos' drawings."

Thanks to Jim Bodrero's contacts, the entire group was invited to an all-day *asado*, an Argentine version of an outdoor barbecue, at Estancia el Carmen on Sunday, 14 September. This was the first sight of the Argentine countryside for the group as a whole, and the artists feasted on a banquet of mouthwatering food, sketched animal and plant life, shot copious amounts of 16 mm[16] film and still pictures, and were treated to an exhibition of gaucho riding and roping. This *asado* was followed by similar outings, later in the tour. On several of these occasions, the locals enjoyed costuming Walt as a gaucho. This was a token of their sincere affection for him and, happily, he looked the part. "He had the dark eyebrows and the dark eyes and the mustache," Herb Ryman later pointed out to Katherine and Richard Greene. "And they'd dress him up like a gaucho and put him on a

[16] Although the party would attend other *asados* during their stay in Argentina, these are the shots that appear in the documentary *South of the Border with Disney*.

A cultural exchange at the Dibujantes' *asado*: Walt poses as a gaucho, Columba as a North American cowboy. Larry Lansburgh is behind them on horseback.

horse, and he looked more like a gaucho than the gauchos did." One of Walt's prized souvenirs of the South American trip was a genuine gaucho saddle.

Wednesday, 17 September, was another special occasion. Andrés de Chazarreta, an authority on traditional Argentine music and dance, arranged with Chuck Wolcott to bring a dance troupe to the Alvear Palace to perform for the Disney party in the outdoor roof garden adjoining the studio. Here the Pepita, the Malambo, the Palapala, and other traditional dances were demonstrated while the artists busily sketched and painted. Here again Lee Blair and Larry Lansburgh shot great quantities of 16 mm, and careful notes were kept on their individual takes so that the artists could study the dances later on.

During the Chazarreta troupe's performance at the Alvear Palace roof garden, Walt joins in the dance.

While all these activities were taking place, Walt's social obligations continued—and so did his unflagging popularity. "I remember one time he called me up at the hotel," said Lansburgh, "and he said, 'Larry, come over here, there's somebody sleeping in front of my room and I can't open the door!' They were waiting for him to come out, to get an autograph or something. He was that popular." Vincent de Pascal, the Buenos Aires stringer for *Hollywood Reporter*, took a special interest in the Disney visit and reported at length on Walt's phenomenal acceptance by the Argentine press and public. "The newspapers devoted columns, some of them half pages, to Disney," wrote de Pascal. "All agreed he is one swell egg. At the reception for the press, he simply leaned against a wall, talking to the group gathered around him. Amiable and not easy to ruffle, Disney's manner convinced even the most hard-boiled that he is the best good-will builder to come down here so far. For he hasn't come to get anything out of the country, hasn't even come ostensibly to bring Argentine good-will back with him. That he has already bagged without having said he wanted it. He made it plain that he is not on any official mission, that he is here just to 'work and study.' And Argentines will be mighty proud if the creator of Mickey Mouse brings back something of themselves which will be immortalized by his studio."

In the face of this show of adulation, the negative publicity that had been threatened against Walt quickly evaporated. As Kenneth Thomson had predicted, the Screen Cartoonists Guild in Hollywood, fuming over the Disney studio strike, tried vainly to undermine Walt's mission in Argentina. A letter from the guild, translated and published in the Communist paper *La Hora*, urged a boycott of Disney films, but this was a feeble gesture that had no visible effect on attendance for *Fantasia*. "Curiously enough," wrote de Pascal at the end of the Buenos Aires visit, "the Nazi [newspaper] 'Pampero' had promised to tear into the Disney crowd upon their arrival here. Throughout their stay in this city, however, 'Pampero' kept its printed face clam-shut. Belief is that any attack against a figure as popular as Disney would have only served to kick back on them."

Ramón Columba and the Asociación de Dibujantes continued to play a vital role in Walt's public relations success. Columba figured prominently in one incident that attracted notice in the press: Walt was introduced to the president of Argentina, Roberto M. Ortiz; the vice president, Ramón S. Castillo; the president of the Chamber of Deputies (legislature), José Luis Cantillo; and the minister of foreign affairs, Enrique Ruiz Guiñazu, in a single afternoon. Before day's end, Walt also accompanied Columba to the offices of *Sucesos Argentinos*, the newsreel company affiliated with the Asociación, to view some earlier reels and to be filmed for an upcoming edition. *Sucesos Argentinos* also managed to film other highlights of Walt's visit, and months later, after the Disney party's return to California, Columba sent them a print of the finished reel. The print survives today, a precious record of the Disney visit (far more extensive than the coverage in the earlier *Cine jornal Brasileiro*) through the eyes of his Argentine hosts. Here, captured by the newsreel camera, Walt arrives at the airport, attends a banquet (with Norm Ferguson also visible in the group),[17] visits the Asociación offices, creates a "lightning sketch" of Mickey Mouse as a souvenir of his visit,[18] and faces off with Columba as they caricature each other. Here too is the Disney party's visit to Molina Campos's rancho studio on 19 September, where they are welcomed by the absent artist's wife, Elvirita, and participate in another *asado*. Walt joins in the festivities, gamely attempts to eat a meal via the one-handed gaucho method, strums a guitar, and poses with a duckling that has been volunteered to stand in for Donald (as a beaming Janet Martin looks on). As a bonus the newsreel includes a brief glimpse of the Alvear Palace studio interior, where Jim Bodrero soberly goes about his artistic duties. The sequence concludes with some fanciful drawings donated to *Sucesos Argentinos* by El Grupo, reflecting the Disney characters' immersion in Argentine culture. (In one of these Ramón Columba, caricatured as a gaucho, pursues one of the centaurettes from *Fantasia*.)

[17] This banquet was staged especially in Walt's honor by the newly formed Asociación Cinematografica Argentina, an organization of filmmakers and distributors, who presented Walt with a medal and prevailed on him to sign the minutes of their founders' meeting.

[18] This "lightning sketch," filmed by a stop-motion camera, is reminiscent of Walt's fledgling efforts in animation, the *Newman Laugh-O-grams*, created in Kansas City a full two decades earlier.

The Disney visit was also a major occasion for the children of Buenos Aires. Thanks to the cooperation of RKO and the Asociación Cinematográfica Argentina, morning programs of Disney shorts for orphan and handicapped children were presented daily at the Cine Opera and at another theater, the Gran Rex, directly across the street. On the morning of Sunday, 21 September, the same theaters presented a special event: an audience of eager children

Walt, on the stage of the Cine Opera, is observed at very close quarters by his young audience.

convened at the Opera at 11:00 a.m. to watch Walt Disney and his artists drawing Disney characters onstage. Among the general public, the exact nature of Walt's work was widely misunderstood; many assumed that he still drew the animated characters in his films. In fact, of course, his personal role had long since shifted to the story and directorial side of production, and he was out of practice as a cartoonist. Asked by the promoters to put his drawing skills on public display, Walt was nervous. Frank Thomas and Norm Ferguson, who were to appear onstage with Walt, met with him before the event to help him prepare some drawings of Goofy. "So we finally decided, well, we'll draw in light blue pencil where the head is and what this guy's doing," Thomas told Don Peri in later years. "'If you just follow those lines, you'll be in it.' So he picked up his confidence a little at that." Unfortunately for Walt's confidence, some children from the audience were allowed onstage to watch him at arm's length, where the blue lines on the paper were plainly visible. Photographs of the occasion show the children crowding around Walt, who works at his drawing of Goofy while, on adjacent easels, the other artists sketch their signature characters: Thomas puts the finishing touches on Dopey, Ferguson on the Big Bad Wolf. At the end of the thirty-minute program, the three men walked across the street and repeated their performance at the Gran Rex. Both programs were followed by special showings of *Snow White and the Seven Dwarfs* and selected Disney shorts.

During the hectic activity of the tour, Walt of course maintained constant contact with Roy and the studio. Roy kept Walt posted on the grim progress of the strike, including the final government settlement, which imposed harsh terms on the studio. More troubling news arrived on 13 September: Roy's telegram to Walt advising him of the death of their father, Elias Disney. Walt was shaken, but plunged ahead with the activities of the tour, perhaps finding solace in the pressure of his grueling schedule. "Walt took it very well," Ferguson wrote to Roy, "but we knew just about how he felt on getting the news."[19]

As the Disney visit to Buenos Aires began to wind down, a gradual development that had begun in Brazil was becoming increasingly clear to members of the group: something powerful, exciting, and unexpected was happening in the art of Mary Blair. Mary had always been recognized as a skillful painter, but she was *surrounded* by skillful painters and had originally been considered a junior member of the group, included mainly to tag along with her husband, Lee. Now, touched off by some subliminal catalyst in the South American atmosphere, a new artistic voice was emerging in her paintings. Striking, original color combinations and deceptively simple renderings expressed the Brazilian and Argentine environment in a raw, primal, and thoroughly personal way. "She'd always been following in other people's footsteps," Frank Thomas explained. "And she could draw like anybody else and paint like anybody else, but she wasn't expressing herself. And down there, looking at something very—like Paul Gauguin trying to find out in Tahiti the real honest roots of a civilization or a people or their beliefs. And I think Mary picked up some of that down there, something very simple and direct and sharply in focus. It was just great stuff." The other artists began to look at Mary and her work with increased respect. Her legendary affinity

[19] This condolence letter to Roy also served as a progress update on the tour. Ted Sears wrote a similar letter a few days later: "I was very sorry to hear about your dad passing, and I'm sure the rest of the boys shared the same sentiments. I remember having quite a pleasant chat with him on the lot a few months ago."

with the children of differing cultures was already in evidence: she devoted an entire afternoon at the Alvear Palace to interviewing young Argentine artists, ranging in age from ten to fifteen years, and taking careful notes of their names and interests.

Mary Blair, in action in South America, is caricatured by Jack Miller.

An indication of Mary's rising status in the group can be seen in John Rose's notes for the 21 September program at the Cine Opera and Gran Rex. When the Disney group had presented a "chalk talk" the previous month in Rio de Janeiro, the artists sketching Disney characters for a delighted public were Norm Ferguson, Jim Bodrero, and Frank Thomas. By mid-September, in preparing for this similar Argentine program, the artists tentatively suggested for the same function were Thomas, Ferguson, Jack Miller—and Mary Blair.

By the day of the program, however, Mary, Lee, and two other artists had already left Buenos Aires. The studio's original plans for the trip had focused on Brazil and Argentina and had only vaguely sketched in the balance of the itinerary, allowing for opportunity, inspiration, and circumstance. Once the party landed on South American soil, their plans had become even more volatile, constantly fluctuating and evolving, and numerous plans for visiting the remaining countries and for returning home were proposed and discarded. The final solution was to split the party into four smaller groups, each exploring some as yet unseen region of South America for a period of days or weeks. Then most (but not all) of the group would reconvene in Chile and, instead of returning home by air, would sail up the west coast of South America on a Grace Lines ship,[20] briefly visiting the coastal areas, traversing the Panama Canal, and then sailing on to New York.

Accordingly, the Disney group began to take steps to wrap up their stay in Buenos Aires. In gratitude for the help the Asociación de Dibujantes had provided, the Disney artists hosted a cocktail party for them. The Dibujantes presented a souvenir album of sixty original drawings to Walt, who reciprocated with a specially created scroll, depicting Disney characters "gone gaucho" and signed by all the members of El Grupo.[21] Lee Blair, a former president of the California Watercolor Society, arranged for exchange art exhibitions between the artists of California and those of Argentina and Brazil. Walt, on one of his last nights in the city, appeared on the *Tribuna de América* radio broadcast to participate in a panel discussion on "The Importance of Films as a Means to Promote Better Understanding Between the Americas." Jack Cutting left for Rio to begin his work as a consultant to the Brazilian film industry, and the rest of the party—their portfolios packed with sketches and paintings, their bags filling up with bolas, maté cups and other souvenirs—organized into smaller groups to embark on their individual assignments.

[20] This was a natural substitution because, as noted above, on the west coast of South America, W. R. Grace and Co. was affiliated with Pan American Airways under the name Panagra.

[21] Actually one signature was missing: that of Lilly Disney.

As the trip continued, Mary Blair's style and color combinations became more distinctive.

THE BLAIR PARTY

The first group to leave Buenos Aires consisted of Lee and Mary Blair, Herb Ryman, and Jack Miller. Leaving by Pan Air on Saturday, 20 September, the Blair party flew to La Paz and explored the mountainous country of Bolivia and Peru for the next two weeks. Just as in Brazil and Argentina, the artists sketched, painted, and photographed profusely, recording the colorful sights of the region and seeking subject matter that might lend itself to animation. Here again, preparation paid off. Larry Lansburgh had suggested to Walt before the trip that a llama might make an ideal character: "As you know, the llama is not only part and parcel of the everyday life down there, but has a lot of possibilities for swell characterization in our medium because of its appearance and funny mannerisms." Llamas were plentiful in rural Bolivia, and Lee Blair filmed several of them, noting their haughty appearance and their habit of sitting down and refusing to budge when their loads became too heavy. Mary, meanwhile, haunted the Indian shops in the colonial section of La Paz, painting the colorful clothing and the goods on display, and buying some as souvenirs.

It was here too that the group had their look at Lake Titicaca and sketched the lake, the balsa boats, the people, and their dwellings in the surrounding country. The shots that appear in *South of the Border with Disney* showing the artists sailing on the lake in a small boat were taken on 23 September, when the party was ferried across a small channel to Ticuna. Their actual crossing of Lake Titicaca to Peru took place in the dark, the following night, on the steamer *Inca*. Arriving on the Peruvian side of the lake early on the twenty-fifth, the artists proceeded by train to Cuzco and traveled from there to other Peruvian cities, continuing to sketch markets, clothing, architecture, Inca ruins, and more llamas. The mountainous terrain of Bolivia and Peru represented by far the highest altitudes the group had encountered in South America, and several of them suffered from "altitude fever" during their visit.

OPPOSITE AND OVERLEAF: This girl and boy, painted by Mary Blair during the Blair party's visit to Peru, were later framed and displayed in Walt's home—the only Disney studio art ever displayed there.

On 3 October the Blair party was joined by Janet Martin and Larry Lansburgh, who had left the rest of El Grupo just before the group's ship sailed from Chile. Meeting the Lansburghs at the Lima airport, the Blairs took them to their hotel and, as Mary noted, "exchanged tales over cocktails." This party of six became the mavericks of the Disney group, working their way north through the interior of South and Central America and never encountering the rest of El Grupo until they all arrived at the Disney studio in Burbank. Although the Blair party represented only a third of the total group, this part of the journey was well documented because the party included two of the group's three 16 mm cameramen, Lee Blair and Larry Lansburgh. (Walt in the end appears to have shot very little 16 mm during the ship's voyage.) Their itinerary was not spontaneously improvised; thanks to the studio's advance work and the good offices of Pan Air, guides and representatives of government agencies were waiting for them at each stop to extend the same courtesies that the Disney group as a whole had enjoyed in Brazil and Argentina. Just as in those countries, their guides allowed the artists to bypass the tourist traps and to concentrate on the authentic culture of each land they visited.[22] At the same time, since the party included no celebrities of Walt's stature, they were spared many of his social and diplomatic obligations and could concentrate on their work.

On Wednesday, 8 October, the party moved on to Ecuador for a short stay. Here they visited handicraft markets, watched indigenous people producing pottery in their homes, and attended a specially arranged performance of indigenous music and dances. On Friday the tenth, on a flight from Guayaquil to Cristóbal, Panama, they were able to observe the complicated workings of the Panama Canal from the air. By chance, on the same flight, they were introduced to Pancho Arias—brother of Arnulfo Arias, the deposed president of Panama, whose path would cross that of the larger Disney party when they in turn reached Panama. Having arrived in Cristóbal, the Blair party toured the city and spent one day on a sketching and photographing trip on a chartered banana boat through the islands off the coast.

As the trip progressed, Mary Blair continued to paint incessantly, filling her portfolio with rich and varied impressions of South America. Her style continued to intensify as the party moved on to Guatemala for five days. The highlight of the

[22] Coincidentally, the Blair party had an added advantage in Lima: they were able to confer on local culture with Bill McFadden and Lyle de Grummond, two former Disney employees now working for Panagra in Peru.

mary blair

Mary Blair

Guatemalan stay was a motor trip (by way of the ruins at Antigua) to Chichicastenango, where the party sketched, painted, and photographed the colorful sights of the market. Here they found and purchased tiny, intricately detailed dolls representing regional types. An earlier itinerary had called for Walt's party to visit Chichicastenango and to stay at the Hotel Mayan Inn, which was owned by friends of the studio's Vern Caldwell. Now the Blair party simply occupied the rooms that had been reserved for Walt. A group of the hotel employees, still under the impression that Walt himself would be visiting, had prepared a special cake for the occasion, decorated with Mickey Mouse mouthing the words HELLO PAPA. The Blair party photographed the cake for posterity, then shared it with their young hosts.

From Guatemala the party moved on to Mexico. Although the first Disney Good Neighbor films would focus exclusively on South America, Mexico was a part of the studio's plans from the beginning. The Blair party spent five days in Mexico City, gathering survey material for future reference. Here they were taken in hand by José Soto, a sports writer for *El Nacional* who was a friend of Larry Lansburgh's from his polo trips to Mexico City. The Blair party was treated to a bullfight and to a special exhibition of *charro* roping and horsemanship, both of which they sketched and photographed. Mary produced a charming series of small paintings of Mexican children in various costumes and attitudes. The party took a special interest in the floating gardens of Xochimilco and, with an eye toward a possible film subject, painted and photographed the boats and the islands of flowers. Then, their suitcases and portfolios bulging and their minds reeling with the experiences of the previous two months, they boarded a Pan Air plane on Wednesday, 22 October, for the flight back to Burbank.

The children of Quito show off their pets for the Blair party.

THE BODRERO PARTY

Four days after the departure of the Blair party, on Wednesday, 24 September, a second group, consisting of Jim Bodrero, Frank Thomas, and Larry Lansburgh, left Buenos Aires to see a different side of Argentina. In the company of Carlos Uranga, a guide supplied by Pan Air, they flew to the city of Salta, the capital of Salta province in northern Argentina. Years later, Frank Thomas remembered Salta as "a tourist's delight because every building was old and had history in it, and the food was good." Here they attended a religious festival and held a press interview at the Palace Hotel. It was here too that they were introduced to Don Jaime Andalisio Gomez, the *ministro de hacienda* of the province (equivalent to the chancellor of the exchequer, or secretary of the treasury), who promptly saw to it that they were supplied with complete gaucho outfits.

In the morning the group left the city for Don Jaime's rancho, Estancia Pampa Grande, near Guachapas. The larger Disney group had already compiled voluminous material on gaucho culture in Buenos Aires, but the Bodrero party was seeking to meet and observe working gauchos here on the pampas, far from urban influence. They were installed as houseguests of Andalisio Gomez, whom Thomas described as "a little like Leo Carrillo. Sort of a broad, happy face, good laugh, a perfect host." The remote *estancia* was large and impressive, with numerous features including one that Thomas, an accomplished pianist, was quick to notice. "They had a grand piano in the chapel, because when you built an *estancia* in that region, you were everything. You were the judge, the jury, the priest, the peacemaker, the boss, everything, because there was nobody else around. And I guess it was his father, maybe, who had set it up, wanted a grand piano in the chapel. And he had to train two mules to walk in lockstep to carry it in, whatever it was, seventy-five miles, some long distance—where they would walk together over rough country, over rocks and no path to speak of, a little like crossing the plains in the covered wagons. And it always amazed me, and amazed Jaime a little too, that he could teach two mules to walk that way, you know, always left foot, then right foot, then left foot—because otherwise the thing would tip and throw them off balance and crash to the ground."

The party remained with Andalisio Gomez for three days, sketching and photographing scenes of gaucho life. On Saturday, 27 September, they accompanied a group of Andalisio Gomez's men on a condor hunt, even though the birds were endangered and protected by law. "They knew that they shouldn't kill off any more condors," said Thomas, but Andalisio Gomez's men made an exception—partly to provide a diversion for their special guests and partly because the birds had been killing their livestock. "If the condors couldn't get any carrion," Thomas said, one bird would descend and "grab a calf by the tail and pull on it" so that "the calf would bawl and its tongue would stick out," while another bird "would grab the tongue. And they'd have him by both ends, and it didn't take them long to kill him that way. It wasn't quite the same as wolves going after them or something like that, but it did account for one or two calves every year, I guess." The colorful episode of this condor hunt would be reflected in a Disney short—but only loosely, and not until three years later.

Returning to the city, the Bodrero party sketched and photographed local scenes, toured the city in a horse-drawn carriage, and visited such landmarks as the

Cárcel Penitenciara de Salta (the jail). Departing by plane on 30 September for Córdoba, they were grounded at Tucumán by bad weather.[23] Upon their belated arrival in Córdoba the next day, they were again met by newspaper reporters, for whom Bodrero and Thomas made several drawings. After a single day in Córdoba, which was devoted to an all-day *asado*, they flew on to rejoin Walt's party. The bulk of El Grupo having already arrived in Chile, the Bodrero party was the last remnant of the group to leave Argentina.

[23] The Blair party had been similarly grounded at Tucumán ten days earlier on their initial flight from Buenos Aires to La Paz.

Left to right: Larry Lansburgh, Jim Bodrero, Carlos Uranga, and Frank Thomas arrive in Salta.

THE DISNEY PARTY

One day after the departure of the Bodrero party, a third splinter group, consisting of Walt and Lilly Disney, Ted Sears, Norm Ferguson, and Webb Smith, left by Panagra to see yet another side of Argentina. Since Jack Cutting had already flown back to Rio de Janeiro, this left the Cottrells, John Rose, Janet Martin, and Chuck Wolcott in Buenos Aires to close up the Alvear Palace studio and attend to business details and final courtesies. Before leaving the city, Walt had given a final round of interviews and had written a special note of thanks to the two bilingual secretaries who had worked with the group in Buenos Aires: "The manner in which you have conducted our correspondence, business affairs and personal contacts has been nothing short of miraculous, considering the nature of 'EL GRUPO' that you have had to contend with."

The Disney party, with Pan Air's Doug Clark as a guide, flew to Mendoza in central Argentina. This party, with Walt as a member, inevitably received more high-profile publicity than the others and was more restricted as to movement. Just as in Rio and Buenos Aires, Walt was received by local dignitaries and educators at the Universidad Nacional de Cuyo, granted press interviews, and attended yet another all-day *asado* and rodeo at Los Arobles, an *estancia* in Tupungato. Mendoza was the heart of Argentina's wine industry, and during their stay the party was given a tour of the Giol and Arizu wine-making factories, described as "the two largest wineries in the world." On the morning of Saturday, 27 September, another special children's program of Disney shorts was shown at the Buenos Aires and Avenida theaters. This was a scaled-down version of the "chalk talk" program that had been presented in Buenos Aires: Walt and Norm Ferguson were both introduced to the audience, and Walt gave a short talk. Soon exhausting his Spanish vocabulary, Walt simply stood on his head on the stage, much to the delight of his young audience.[24]

Later the same day, the Rose party, having concluded their business in Buenos Aires, flew to Mendoza on their way to Santiago, Chile. Here there was some reshuffling of the two parties; Bill and Hazel Cottrell remained in Mendoza with Walt and his party, while Webb Smith joined John Rose and company on their way to Chile to prepare the way for the rest of El Grupo.

Despite the pressures of diplomatic and public relations obligations, the group was able to accomplish some survey work during their short stay in Mendoza. Still on the lookout for more gaucho material, Walt, Ferguson, and Ted Sears visited the home of Don Liborio Sosa, an eighty-five-year-old gaucho who maintained some of the older traditions of custom and dress. As Ferguson and Sears admired Sosa's clothing, saddle, and accessories, Walt filmed 16 mm footage that would later be seen in *South of the Border with Disney*. On the same afternoon, he and Ferguson visited a local English school. Walt later told a U.S. journalist that the class sang "Way Down Upon the Swanee River" for their visitors,

[24] This was the incident recorded in Rose's report and described by Walt in later interviews. In still later years, an eyewitness to Walt's visit to the Universidad de Cuyo, on 26 September, described a similar incident to Ted Thomas as taking place on that occasion. Virgilio Roig, a young student at the Universidad in 1941, remembered that Walt had made a personal appearance before the students and had made an unusual entrance. "He walked on his hands, with his feet up—but bent, not all the way up—and he walked to some chalkboards, jumped and he was standing. Immediately he put up his arms like this and said 'Hola, chicos,' of course with a very noticeable English [speaker's] accent." Roig also remembered Walt making several drawings of Mickey Mouse. It should be noted that, according to the studio's report, Walt's visit to the university took place at 7:00 p.m.

Ted Sears and Norm Ferguson (photographed by Walt) meet Don Liborio Sosa.

and the teacher explained to him that this was one of the methods used to teach English to the students. "'And you Americans should try and reciprocate,' the teacher told Disney. 'Very well,' he agreed. 'When I return to the States, I'll have our schools teach the children "Way Down Upon the Amazon."'"

On Monday, 29 September, Walt's party concluded their short visit to Mendoza and boarded a Panagra plane for the flight over the Andes to their next major stop: Santiago, Chile. The trip, over some of the most breathtaking mountain scenery in the world, made a vivid impression on Bill Cottrell: "On that flight we passed very close to Aconcagua, which is the largest mountain in the Western Hemisphere. It's over 22,500 feet high, a very impressive, rugged thing, and it seemed like we flew so close to it you could almost reach out and touch it. Of course we weren't that close, but it seems like it. . . . At the border of the two countries, Argentina and Chile, high up in the mountains, but still in kind of a valley, there's a big statue of the Christus, and this is supposed to bring eternal peace between the two countries of Chile and Argentina. When we flew over, maybe there's always snow up there, but the snow was very deep, you could see down there, and there was a weather station built on the side of a mountain there, opposite Aconcagua." The snow was deeper than usual because of a tremendous avalanche in August that had completely buried the Chilean mountain village of Caracoles. Rescue workers had immediately gone to the aid of the villagers, and two Chilean aviators, attempting to drop provisions for the rescue workers, had been caught in a downdraft and crashed in the snow. "This plane that we saw was nose down in the snow," said Cottrell. "The pilot and the co-pilot, I believe, were probably killed in that crash. The plane was still there, they couldn't get it out, and this was rather an ominous-looking thing to see."

In Santiago, Walt attempts a *cueca* to the accompaniment of Los Quincheros, in the background.

SANTIAGO

Although the Disney group had been asked to concentrate primarily on the "ABC countries"—Argentina, Brazil, and Chile—Brazil and, especially, Argentina had received the lion's share of their attention. This wasn't surprising, given the politics of the situation: Brazil and Argentina were large, volatile countries, swayed by the active courtship of Axis propaganda forces, while smaller, less powerful Chile was still resolutely neutral and would remain that way, even after the U.S. entered the war. Accordingly, El Grupo's visit to Chile lasted a total of one week, roughly a third of the time they had devoted to either Brazil or Argentina. But Walt's mission of course went far beyond the call of politics, and he and his party tackled their time in Chile with the same vigor and enthusiasm they had shown from the start of the trip. In Santiago there would be no gala opening of *Fantasia*, but in other respects the week played like a miniature version of the recent visit to Buenos Aires.

Just as in Brazil and Argentina, John Rose arrived in advance to pave the way for Walt, this time accompanied by a party that included Janet Martin, Webb Smith, and Chuck Wolcott. The Rose party landed in Santiago on Saturday, 27 September, and promptly established headquarters at the Carrera Hotel. Working as quickly as possible because of the tight schedule, Rose confirmed advance plans with local government and RKO officials, while Janet Martin coordinated her arrangements with representatives of the press. By the time Walt and his party arrived to a hero's welcome on Monday, 29 September, all arrangements were in place so that El Grupo could make the most of their week.

Several events of the Disney visit to Buenos Aires were echoed in Santiago. Here again a morning program of Disney shorts was presented for orphan children, with Walt, Norm Ferguson, and Ted Sears making a personal appearance. ("The reason I'm in on it," Sears wrote to his wife, "is that our artists are all in other cities—hope the kids recognize what I'm trying to draw."[25]) Here again Walt and other group members were treated to cocktail receptions and other social functions. Here too Walt was in demand for newspaper interviews, and was asked to speak on the radio. One notable occasion was the *Nuevo Mundo* broadcast on 30 September, sponsored by the Chilean-American Institute of Culture and broadcast by a special hookup throughout Chile. For this program Walt was interviewed by host Rafael Elizalde, and Chuck Wolcott, at the piano, played Disney music. One of the broadcast studio managers, a Frenchman named Robert Chalumeau, took the opportunity to demonstrate for Walt his special vocal trick: an imitation of a "duck's scream." When Walt responded with a laugh, Chalumeau was moved to write him a letter a few days later, offering his services in case any future Disney films should require the sound of a duck screaming.

[25] In fact Sears was an accomplished artist and had experience as an animator, but for the previous decade he had concentrated his talents on story work.

Just as they had been treated to numerous *asados* in Argentina, Walt and his group were invited to an all-day *aculeo* (country festival) in Chile. Here again the food was augmented by a rodeo and by a variety of musical entertainment, including a performance by Los Quincheros, a vocal quartet, and dancers who performed traditional Chilean dances. Walt, who had so often been dressed as a gaucho and asked to perform regional dances in Argentina, was now costumed as a *huaso* (Chilean cowboy) and cajoled into dancing a *cueca*.[26] This occasion was filmed in 16 mm, and the shots of Walt, taken at closer range than usual, are revealing.[27] Now over six weeks into his journey, undoubtedly tired and beset by business and production pressures, called upon to perform the same antics that have been expected of him at every other stop on the tour—Walt enters fully into the festivities and seems to be having the time of his life. When a guitar is thrust into his hands, Walt, who is no guitarist, awkwardly picks out a few chords and laughs as loudly as anyone at the resulting sounds. Asked to dance a *cueca*, which of course he has never seen before, he gamely attempts it with good-natured enthusiasm. His uninhibited spirit of friendly cooperation clearly has a disarming effect on those around him, and any cultural barriers instantly vanish. This is the Good Neighbor program at its best.

[26] The *cueca*, the national dance of both Bolivia and Chile, is a courting dance in ¾ time in which a couple mimics a rooster showing off for a hen. Special thanks to Christopher Caines for this information.

[27] We can be thankful these shots were made, but the identity of the cameraman remains a mystery; all three of the group's usual 16 mm camera crew can probably be ruled out. Walt, appearing in the shots, obviously didn't photograph them. Lee Blair was currently in Peru with the rest of the Blair party (as was Herb Ryman, another possible candidate). Larry Lansburgh, with the rest of the Bodrero party, arrived in Chile from Córdoba while the *aculeo* was in progress. That he immediately rushed to the site and began filming is possible, but unlikely, and the appearance of the shots is inconsistent with that of other material known to have been shot by Lansburgh.

Here, as elsewhere on the tour, the artistic and filmmaking communities eagerly welcomed Walt and his team. A Chilean counterpart to Ramón Columba was Jorge Délano, who was both a well-known cartoonist and Chile's foremost film producer. Délano was the owner and publisher of the magazine *Topaze*, in whose pages his caricatures often appeared. He served as El Grupo's principal guide in Santiago, and his son, also named Jorge, formed an attachment to Walt and several of the artists too. Among the events staged for the benefit of Walt and his party was a presentation by the national film group Industria Cinematográfica Nacional, where they were shown clips from one of Délano's upcoming films. John Rose later described it as a comedy about "the trials and tribulations of a Chilean debutante who suffered from 'B.O.'"[28] Another notable occasion was the founding ceremony of La Alianza de Dibujantes, a cartoonists' association formed as a direct result of Walt's visit, which promptly named him its honorary president.

With all its parallels to other stops on the tour, Santiago offered one unique and touching highlight. Chile had no real animation industry, but two young architecture students, Carlos Trupp and Jaime Escudero, had undertaken to produce an animated cartoon, financing it themselves. "They are just giving their work the finishing touches now," said the invitation extended to Walt, "and would be extremely honoured to have the King of Animated Cartoons view the work they have so far managed to get done, and even if it were possible to have Mr Disney visit their very rudimentary and humble work-shop." Walt and other members of the group did just that on Wednesday, 1 October, to the excitement of the aspiring young animators.

[28] Ted Thomas reports that the comedy *Escándolo* was currently playing in Chile and may have been the film shown to El Grupo.

Toward week's end the Bodrero party arrived from Córdoba and rejoined the others, and the Disney group began preparations for their departure from Chile. Once again there was general agreement that the Disney visit had been a resounding success. "Walt Disney has aroused more enthusiasm in Santiago than any other important visitor in the past two years," reported the CIAA's newsletter. "Every big Santiago paper carried at least two feature stories with pictures the day he arrived, one paper giving him half of the first page. His press conferences, visits to various institutions, willingness to give autographs, and general modesty have made him an exemplary visitor, reports say, especially because he makes no claims to be 'an ambassador.'"

On Friday, 3 October, Janet Martin and Larry Lansburgh left to join the Blair party in Lima, and the eleven remaining members of El Grupo boarded a special Pullman train for Viña del Mar, a famous tourist spot on the coast. After a brief stop there they arrived in Valparaíso on Saturday morning, 4 October. Amid a last-minute flurry of interviews, receptions, and general well-wishing, the travelers boarded the T.E.S. *Santa Clara*, a proud vessel of the Grace Line, which was affiliated with Pan Am on the west coast of South America, for the voyage back to New York.

Walt and Lilly, front and center, and other members of El Grupo pose for a group photo with their Chilean hosts. Jorge Délano, the younger, is in the branches of the tree at upper left.

Walt relaxes on the deck of the *Santa Clara* with Captain Parker.

THE VOYAGE HOME

"ELEVEN TIRED DISNEYITES SAFE ABOARD," John Rose cabled the home office, one day out of port. The passenger list for this voyage, besides El Grupo, included Peter Grace Jr., son of the Grace Line's owner, and his bride, who were on their honeymoon. The captain, Bligh Parker, USNR, the Disney party was told, was a descendant of the infamous Captain Bligh of HMS *Bounty* fame.

Walt, relaxing for the first time since the start of the trip, was in a reflective mood. "We're on the homeward lap," he wrote, "after two months of flying around the South American continent. We're tired looking at our own, and each other's, same two suits, and our bags are getting pretty shabby.

"Now that the majority of the mileage is behind us, we're beginning to gain a perspective on the trip. And all of us realize now that you certainly can't learn about countries from reading books, or from listening to other people tell you about their trips. Most of the things people told us about South America were based on personal opinions and not necessarily true. For instance, we all went to South America with raincoats and galoshes, on advice—mistaken, it turned out. They told us everybody in South America was late at meetings—so I got up my nerve to show up a half-hour late once, and everybody was there but me."

Although the party was homeward bound, its survey work was still not finished. As the *Santa Clara* sailed up the coast of South America it made periodic stopovers for transfer of cargo, and on several of these occasions El Grupo disembarked and continued their sketching and photographing activities. Their two-day stop in Lima (by way of Callao) was more extensive than that and, in fact, was comparable to the previous short visits to São Paulo or Montevideo. Walt's party arrived in Lima on 8 October on the heels of the Blair party, which had just left the city the same day, and Janet Martin had taken the opportunity to lay the groundwork for their visit just as at the earlier stops. "You should enjoy your stopover here," she wrote to Rose, "if you allow yourself time enough just to poke around and maybe take an hour's drive outside of town to see a ruin, if Walt would like to do that." She had taken pains to protect Walt by heading off the elaborate plans laid by the local Grace Lines representative, José Quimper. "He had everything all fixed up for Walt's visit to Lima to be one round of visits to fine arts galleries and meetings with Peruvian artists and everything Walt probably would like to duck. So I told him absolutely no—that Walt's time in port was so short that I knew he would want to have enough freedom to poke around for himself and make his own plans when he got here."

Among El Grupo's fellow passengers on the *Santa Clara* was a young girl named Patsy Bradley. Walt, Norm Ferguson, and Frank Thomas made these sketches for her.

As a compromise, Walt and his party were treated to a buffet supper at the Country Club Lima, where entertainment was provided by indigenous Peruvian dancers and musicians brought to Lima from the interior. Chuck Wolcott was immediately taken with the traditional melodies, played in the Inca five-tone scale, and transcribed some of them, which would be adapted later for use in *Saludos Amigos*. In addition to this supper Walt attended a cocktail reception, and spoke a few words of greeting on Radio Lima. The party stayed in the city overnight, and in the morning, just as in Argentina, Walt attended the founders' meeting of the Asociación Peruana de Expositores Filmográficos and signed the minutes. Other members of the party toured the city and visited artists' workshops and museums. Then the group returned to the ship to resume their voyage.

At a brief stop in Guayaquil, Ecuador, a few days later, Walt and company granted a press interview on board the ship, partly to help promote *Fantasia*, which had opened in Quito the previous day. When the ship reached Buenaventura, Colombia, members of the group were invited to take a cruise on a motor launch up the Dagua River. "So we all went on this cruise up the river with Peter Grace and his wife," Bill Cottrell recalled. "And it was a most exciting, marvelous trip, because we almost immediately got into the jungles there. And you could hear all these strange animals, sort of like in the movies—you know, all those sounds. And then the native Indians of this country would come up to our ship in their dugout canoes, because it was unusual for them, I guess, to see a big ship, a fairly good-sized ship like this in their river. It was like—I guess it was like the jungle cruise at Disneyland, on a bigger scale! And we were gone for several hours, up the river and then back again. And of course it was just the most wonderful thing to happen to us, because we felt very privileged in being invited to go on this cruise up the river. . . . And of course the verdant foliage, the trees hanging down in the river—it was really an exciting trip, I thought."

Like much of El Grupo's South American tour, the voyage of the *Santa Clara* was shadowed by wartime tensions. The ship's prow was emblazoned on both sides with large U.S. flags, brightly illuminated at night, and the crew was constantly on the lookout for enemy submarines. Cottrell recalled one night when "Captain Parker was talking to a group of us around the piano or something in the lounge, and was suddenly interrupted by a series of blasts from the ship's horn, which is a loud, frightening sound. And he said, 'Excuse me,' and then he ran out of the doorway to the deck and on up to the bridge, and we didn't see any more of him that night. So we never did find out what it was, but obviously it was something of some significance. Well, it was only speculation on our part: was it a submarine that they sighted from the bridge, or was it a small boat in distress, or what? We never did hear, we never knew, but because of the time, the war and so forth—you imagine a lot of things, you know."

The group's closest brush with wartime intrigue came in Panama. *Fantasia* was scheduled to open at the Eldorado Cinema in Panama City on 14 October, the same day the *Santa Clara* arrived at the Panama Canal. Walt's plans did not call for a personal appearance at the Panama opening, but F. S. Gulbransen, RKO's Panama representative, desperately wanted to build up the *Fantasia* premiere into a major social event like the openings in Brazil, Argentina, and Uruguay. Before the Disney party even left Chile, Gulbransen began bombarding RKO, the Disney home office, and John Rose with letters and telegrams requesting a personal appearance by Walt in Panama City. Rose tried to evade the question, then replied that Walt wanted to see the workings of the Canal and therefore would be unable to leave the ship and attend the *Fantasia* opening. But Gulbransen was not about to be brushed off so lightly. Knowing of Walt's interest in the operation of the canal, he arranged unprecedented permission for the party to disembark from the ship at the second chamber, where they would have an unobstructed view of the Miraflores locks in action. He cabled Rose: "THIS PERMISSION NEVER GRANTED BEFORE AND MR DISNEY WILL SEE OPERATION OF FIRST LOCKS IN DAYLIGHT AFTER THIS POINT IT WILL ALL BE IN DARKNESS AND HE WILL SEE NOTHING." And, of course, at that point Walt would be off the ship and it would be a relatively simple matter to proceed to Panama City for the *Fantasia* opening. Gulbransen had also chartered a special train to take the Disney party back to the Canal Zone after the opening so they could reboard the *Santa Clara* before it left the canal. In the face of such unshakable determination, Walt and Rose gave in and agreed to attend the Panama opening.

Gulbransen's strenuous efforts didn't end there: originally he had also arranged for Walt to be introduced to Presidente Arnulfo Arias of Panama. At the time he had no way of knowing that Arias, a Nazi sympathizer, was about to be ousted in a coup d'état. The pro-U.S. faction in Panama had been planning for some time to remove Arias from power, and when he left the country on 7 October to visit Cuba, they took the opportunity to stage their coup without bloodshed, seizing control of the government and arresting many of Arias's supporters, including several former cabinet members. By the time the *Santa Clara* sailed into the canal on 14 October, a new regime, headed by Presidente Ricardo Adolfo de la Guardia, was in power. Arias, meanwhile, had been apprehended in Havana and was on his way back to Panama, under guard, aboard the U.S. steamship *Cefalu*. Walt and his party, after attending the *Fantasia* opening at the Eldorado—which Bill Cottrell remembered as "a long, narrow theater on a terribly hot night"—enjoyed a motor tour of Panama City and then departed for Colón and their chartered train back to the ship. The train was compelled to back into the station at Colón, and El Grupo learned that it was just returning from another errand: transporting the heavily guarded Arias from the Canal Zone back to Panama City. "And they said to us, 'Don't sit near the window, there may be some shooting when you go through such-and-such a town,'" Cottrell recalled. "There's no place else to sit but by a window, on a train!"

On Monday, 20 October, the *Santa Clara* sailed into New York Harbor, where Walt Disney and his group were welcomed as returning heroes. Throughout his South American sojourn Walt had been surrounded by the press; now the U.S. press plied him with questions about South America. To the reporters he declared that Buenos Aires had "the cleanest subways I've ever seen" and that "I'd been warned of the Argentine audiences, told they were tough, that they'd hiss if they didn't like a scene. But they were wonderful." He similarly praised the artists and musicians they had met, and hinted at the beautiful Brazilian music that would be heard in his upcoming films. After two months of playing down his role as a goodwill ambassador, Walt continued to dismiss that aspect of the trip: "After all, friendship is something that you demonstrate by deed. You just don't talk about it all the time."

But there was no mistaking the fact that Walt's goodwill mission had been a tremendous success. Not only had El Grupo forged innumerable bonds of personal friendship in South America, but the general South American public had warmly embraced Walt and his films in no uncertain terms. Doug Clark, Pan Air's public relations chief in Argentina, commented on this, praising Walt's modesty, unfailing courtesy to the press, and general attitude of friendliness. He contrasted Walt's behavior with that of Bing Crosby, who was visiting Argentina at the same time: "While Walt had enhanced his popularity by being courteous to the Press, the opposite had been the case with Crosby, who had shunned the Press on all sides. Practical example: Local premiere of latest Donald Duck short was warmly applauded. Local premiere of Crosby's *Rhythm on the River* was given cold reception—some of the audience walked out halfway through."[29] Clark's summary of Walt's reception in Argentina could well be applied to the rest of South America: "The photographs of Walt in his gaucho outfit and the Argentine artists similarly attired were given wide publicity by the Argentine press, made the Argentine public conscious of the fact that Walt was making a genuine effort to capture Argentine folklore, led them to call him a real 'gaucho' (translation: real guy). . . . From the standpoint of fostering friendlier relations between the United States and Argentina, no visiting Hollywood personality has been so successful in his mission." As Vincent de Pascal commented: "Hollywood owes Disney the finest bunch of orchids in its pantry for a truly creditable job."

In short, even if the Disney studio had never produced any Latin American films at all, the 1941 trip to South America would have represented a major victory for the Good Neighbor program. But making movies was Walt's business, and in his eyes the project was just getting started.

[29] Although Crosby appears never to have crossed paths with the Disney party in South America, his tour coincided almost exactly with theirs, and he returned to New York on the same day.

Herb Ryman and Jack Miller on deck in the Canal Zone.

WALT DISNEY Goes South American
IN HIS GAYEST MUSICAL TECHNICOLOR FEATURE
SALUDOS AMIGOS
(HELLO FRIENDS)
Introducing JOE CARIOCA
THE BRAZILIAN JITTERBIRD
© W.D.P.
DISTRIBUTED BY RKO RADIO PICTURES INC.

2 SALUDOS AMIGOS

The members of El Grupo (except for Jack Cutting) returned to the Disney studio in Burbank gradually, in staggered groups, during the last two weeks of October 1941. The first to arrive was the Blair party, direct from Mexico City, along with Norm Ferguson, Ted Sears, and Webb Smith, who flew in from the East Coast. Other members of the East Coast contingent turned up in succeeding days. Walt himself, detained by business in New York and Washington, didn't arrive until Monday the twenty-seventh, while Chuck Wolcott traveled from New York to Detroit, his former home, by train and then drove his car back to California, arriving a few days after Walt. All were probably still tired out from their two months in South America, but there was no time to rest. Now the real work was to begin!

Janet Martin immediately set to work coordinating U.S. press coverage of the tour, cataloguing the hundreds of stills that had been shot, disseminating human-interest stories, and petitioning some of the artists for gag drawings depicting the group's experiences in South America. John Rose, besides preparing detailed expense and activity reports for the CIAA, launched a program of follow-up correspondence and survey by-products. By mid-December he had produced an eight-page booklet of suggestions for ancillary products inspired by the South American trip: a full line of books (aimed at both adult and juvenile audiences), comics, magazine features, toys, games, and other character merchandise. Some of Rose's more ambitious ideas, such as a lecture tour by Walt, never materialized, but many of his suggestions were adopted and became the backbone of an extensive merchandising program that continued for several years.

The main order of business, however, was film production, and this was Norm Ferguson's department. A "South American Unit" was established in wing 3A of the studio's Animation Building, and here Ferguson began the monumental task of sifting through the massive collection of visual and story material produced by the trip. The studio's contract with the CIAA called for a series of twelve one-reel cartoons, completed and released in groups of four, each film dealing with a specific country or region. This was a new kind of story development for the studio: along with the Canadian war bond films and other early wartime projects, this represented the studio's first attempt to transform propaganda or other "assigned" subject matter, dictated by outside agencies, into films that would retain the creativity and charm expected of a Walt Disney production.

Part of the challenge lay in the studio's intent, expressed in pretrip publicity, to work with Latin American artists in developing their Latin American productions. This concept became perhaps the most delicate aspect of the enormously delicate Good Neighbor program. It wasn't particularly problematic in the area of music; the studio did enjoy happy and fruitful collaborations with Ary Barroso and other songwriters and composers as the series progressed. But the *visual* aspect of the films was another

Domestic poster art for *Saludos Amigos* highlighted the Brazilian sequence of the picture.

story. The Disney party had socialized with numerous painters and cartoonists in South America, but few of those artists could be expected to integrate their styles with the standards of a Disney production, and the cause of international diplomacy would hardly be helped by bruised artistic egos. In the end, the studio entered into extensive dealings with only one South American painter—but that was plenty.

Although El Grupo had had only brief contact with F. Molina Campos during the tour, they had conferred extensively with his wife, Elvirita, and his agent, and had negotiated an agreement concerning the right to use his paintings in developing Disney's Argentine subjects. The agreement also made tentative provision for bringing Molina Campos and his wife to the Disney studio during production, and in the months immediately following the tour Rose began to explore that possibility. Roy Disney

Clockwise from left: Janet Martin, Mary Blair, Lee Blair, Frank Thomas, and Jack Miller as caricatured by their colleagues on their return from South America.

bridled at the idea of "employing" Molina Campos, since the CIAA had provided no budget for that expense, and in fact Rose agreed that there was little practical reason to bring Molina Campos to California, since the Disney staff had already acquired a number of his paintings *and* had observed and painted the Argentine landscape themselves. "The frank truth of the matter," Rose observed privately to Disney's New York office, "is that we don't *need* the guy at all—and that blunt fact applies also to all the other South American talent we had lined up." But because of Molina Campos's great popularity in his own country, the studio agreed to this diplomatic gesture. Molina Campos himself couldn't have agreed less with Rose's assessment; he was convinced that his presence was absolutely essential to the production of Disney's Argentine films. He and Elvirita arrived in California in March 1942 and took up residence in Hollywood, prepared for a long stay.

As Norm Ferguson, Ted Sears, and Bill Cottrell began the task of adapting their massive collection of inspirational material into individual film stories, they depended heavily on the story artists who had made the South American trip, gradually absorbing other studio personnel into the project as it progressed. They were also guided by practical considerations: the films were to be produced simultaneously in groups of four—the first group to be finished just as quickly as possible—and, while the tour itself had concentrated heavily on Brazil and Argentina, each group of films should cover a range of South American countries, avoiding any appearance of favoritism. There was of course a wealth of Brazilian and Argentine story material, but other countries that had received less attention would test the story department's resourcefulness.

For Argentina, the gaucho stories Ted Sears had suggested before the trip were made to order, and could now be enriched with the mass of gaucho lore and souvenirs the group had brought back from South America. Sears set to work adapting his original suggestions, and in short order had produced five new treatments, now leading off with "The Flying Horse." Brazil, meanwhile, was the land of the samba and the *papagaio*. Having acquired the rights to "Aquarela do Brasil," the artists began developing "Pan-American Symphonies" around that and other Ary Barroso music. Other story suggestions, some of them also incorporating Brazilian music, were concocted for the still-unnamed parrot character inspired by the *papagaio*. One idea called "Carioca Carnival," proposed for release in February 1943, would have involved a highly interactive relationship with local Brazilian agencies: "The music to be especially composed by Brazilian musicians, possibly on a competitive basis for first release through this picture. Publicity for competitive contest to be handled through the D.I.P. in Rio. Song plugging of winning selection could be made over the vast Byington radio chain just before carnival time in Rio, which would be the release date of the picture."[30] Other ideas suggested at this time included "Paulo Penguin," about a cold-blooded penguin who escapes from the South Pole to warmer Latin climes, and "Martingale," based on Helen Kirby's recently published horse story, to be set in either Chile or Argentina.

From this rich assortment of story material, Walt and Norm Ferguson selected the first four stories to be developed and produced.

[30] Albert Byington Jr., one of El Grupo's many contacts on the 1941 tour, was the head of a Brazilian media empire that included films, records, and broadcasting.

Lee Blair's story sketch for the opening scene was followed closely in the finished film.

LAKE TITICACA

The Blair party, from their visit to the Bolivian and Peruvian country surrounding Lake Titicaca, had brought back paintings and sketches of the landscape and of the haughty-looking llamas, who seemed potentially amusing cartoon characters. By late October 1941, barely a month after their visit to the lake region, two members of the party, Mary Blair and Jack Miller, were working to turn those sketches and paintings into a cartoon story about Donald Duck's encounter with a llama. Here, for the first time, the Disney Good Neighbor mission would become a cinematic reality: an established Disney character would be seen, not on his home turf, but in a specific Latin American setting. Norm Ferguson wrote to Walt: "Mary Blair and Jack Miller were working on Duck and Llama sketches with the thought that the Duck might be used as an archaeologist in a Bolivian or Peruvian setting. From what I have seen Mary has some interesting water color atmosphere sketches that look like possibilities for background handling. The story itself rests with the possibilities of gags we could get around the Duck and Llama."

The Duck's role was soon changed from archaeologist to tourist. As Walt later commented to the press: "In parts of Bolivia and Peru, some of our artists were so enchanted with the colorful dress and the life in general that they decided it would be a wonderful place for Donald Duck to flounder as a tourist—and that's just what he's doing." (Although the original concept for this story called for a Bolivian setting—the working titles were "The Bolivian Story" and "Donald in Bolivia"—it was adapted during production so that it could be identified with either Bolivia or Peru, the two countries that border Lake Titicaca. The narration in the finished film pointedly avoids mentioning either country by name, and tends instead to refer to the lake region as "the land of the Incas.")

The story became a clever satire on travelogues, with Donald as a traveler who sets out to see the lake country—rendered in accurate detail, thanks to the Blair party's research—and does everything wrong. The narrator introduces balsa boats; Donald examines one, can't resist yanking at a loose reed, and destroys the boat. A small boy is shown controlling a llama's movements by means of musical "commands" on a wooden flute; Donald has to try it himself, and his sour notes succeed only in annoying the llama. He sets out to explore the Andes on llama-back, and winds up clinging desperately to a wooden bridge suspended between two peaks, knocking the planks loose in his panic and watching them disappear into the gorge below. Donald's misadventures are played for comedy against the voice of the narrator (Fred Shields), who prattles on calmly with standardized travelogue narration. Sometimes the dialogue itself is the gag: as the Duck hurtles out of the sky, smashing into a native pottery market, Shields casually remarks on "the pottery market, where the visitor always drops in." At one point Donald even interacts with the narrator. As he clings frantically to the fraying ropes of the bridge, the full weight of the llama planted on his back, Shields cautions against undue exertion at high altitudes and advises the tourist to "remain cool, calm and collected." The exasperated Donald faces the camera and shouts angrily: "Shut up, ya big windbag!"

This use of the Duck in the studio's first cartoon story established a precedent that would influence many of the Disney Latin American films. By 1941 Donald Duck had surpassed Mickey Mouse in popularity, but there was another reason to use him in these pictures: his cranky, obnoxious personality. One of the prime considerations in producing the Good Neighbor films was to avoid any plots or gags that could possibly reflect badly on the Latin Americans themselves. By casting Donald Duck in this picture, the studio neatly avoided that trap. His appearance as an ignorant North American tourist—clumsily demolishing the balsa boat, ineptly trying to imitate the indigenous flute melody, ignoring the narrator's advice—guaranteed that he, the North American, would be the butt of all the slapstick gags (as he generally was in most of his other films).

Early in November Homer Brightman and Roy Williams were added to the story team. Brightman made a major contribution to the story: to the basic situation of the Duck-llama confrontation, he added the suspension-bridge sequence. In later years he described his inspiration to Milt Gray: "Mary Blair . . . had that nice watercolor painting of that rope bridge over the gorge. She was working on something about a little child and a clay pot. I just looked at that darned drawing for a long time, and I went to my room as quick as I could and got it down; it was ideal for the Duck and the llama, and it worked out funny. Walt laughed like hell when he saw some of this stuff." Brightman's sequence became the climactic section of the short, and Brightman himself soon became a fixture in the South American Unit, contributing story material to several of the other Good Neighbor pictures.

Other hands also contributed to the picture's development. Chuck Wolcott, who had transcribed traditional Inca music during El Grupo's stop in Peru early in October, found an immediate use for it in this picture. "I didn't have the pipes that they used down there, the reed pipes," Wolcott later told an interviewer, "but the strange thing about it is, they were handmade. And of course they were always made to fit the fingers of the man who was going to play them. So they weren't quite true. So some of the notes would be just a little off pitch. It was a strange thing to hear, but it lent a very piquant quality to the music, because they'd play—two of them would play, more or less, in thirds, sometimes they would get into fourths instead of thirds, and it would make a very peculiar sound. So I tried to figure out how to do it, and I finished doing it with two recorders, and it got the sound. It was close enough to the sound, and instead of having true thirds all the way through that particular melody . . . I used fourths mixed in with the thirds, and it came out very nicely." Wolcott's themes for this section were "Inca Princess," a lovely incidental motif, and "Llama Theme," the flute melody with which the small boy controls the llama's movements.

Another contribution came by an indirect route: Walt had suggested it for a different film. During a story meeting on the proposed 16 mm documentary film about the South American tour, Walt suggested adding some entertainment value: "What we need is some of the artists sketching . . . maybe the artist is sketching there where we talk about *siroche* [altitude fever] and he begins to feel the effect of the high altitude; it begins to show in his drawings." The gag was not used in the documentary, but was added to the opening of *Lake Titicaca*: as Shields warns of the effects of the high altitude, Donald, like several members of the Blair party, experiences an attack of *siroche* himself.

The relatively simple story for this picture was finished in short order, and by mid-December it was approved for production under director Bill Roberts. The Good Neighbor films had been designated a high priority at the studio, and the animators were cast with care. Milt Neil, one of the studio's "Duck men"—a pool of artists who specialized in animating Donald Duck—was assigned some key scenes in this short, including the Duck's introduction as a tourist, decked out in safari helmet and explorer's outfit, at the beginning. Milt Kahl, later to become one of Disney's elite "Nine Old Men," also animated much of the picture, including most of the llama's scenes. In Kahl's hands the llama (dubbed "Lulu" in some early story treatments, but nameless in the finished film) is not the "haughty aristocrat of the Andes" that the artists had encountered in South America. Instead this llama is simply a large, floppy, docile creature whose even temper contrasts with the Duck's irritable nature.

Frequently he/she is simply oblivious of Donald, or at most—as when goaded into a wild dance by the Duck's inexpert flute performance—regards him with mild annoyance. Kahl endows the character with a lumbering walk that nicely exaggerates the rolling motion of the wooden bridge during the climactic sequence.

Production of *Lake Titicaca* proceeded without incident through the spring of 1942.[31] The film represented a modest but promising beginning to Disney's Good Neighbor film program: reflecting the sights the artists had seen in Bolivia and Peru, it extended a hand of friendship to the people of those countries—and gave them some laughs, at North America's expense, into the bargain.

[31] The finished film differs from the planned version only in the excision of a few scenes. Walt, feeling that the story was moving too slowly, cut a handful of isolated scenes to tighten the pace.

A small boy plays flute melodies to control the llama's movements; and Donald, in Milt Kahl's original animation art, tries the same trick.

PEDRO

Pressed to develop and produce their first group of Latin American stories as quickly as possible, the studio didn't hesitate to make use of the ready-made story of P-T O-2-L (Petey O'Toole), the little mail plane. Bill Cottrell had taken an interest in adapting this story even before the South American trip, and upon his return to the studio he immediately set to work on it. El Grupo's one week in Chile had failed to generate a great amount of Chilean story material, but their airplane flight over the Andes into Santiago had had a serendipitous similarity to little Petey's flight in the story. The plot was quickly transplanted to a Chilean setting, and "Petey" became "Pedro." Joe Grant, one of the authors of the original story, shrugged off his part in the adaptation: "It just fit, because from the Rockies to the Andes was a short jump as far as we were concerned." By the end of October, Cottrell was at work on story development.

As developed for the Latin American program, *Pedro* is the story of a little plane whose father flies the mail route over the mountains between Santiago and Mendoza, Argentina (the route that Walt's party had traveled in late September). When his father is sick one day and can't carry the mail, Pedro takes his place, and brings in the mail after a series of adventures. The original Grant-Huemer story was ideally suited to this adaptation; it had even included a tall, forbidding mountain peak (known as the Old Man of the Mountain in one surviving draft and as Old Thunderhead in the other), which, with its penchant for violent storms that can wreck a small plane, had been the principal threat to Petey's mission. For this fictional mountain Cottrell substituted Aconcagua, the very real peak that had so impressed him on his own flight over the Andes. The plot, centering on the flight of the little airplane, afforded an opportunity for glimpses of the Chilean and Argentine landscape. The Grant-Huemer original had even included two of what would become the most fondly remembered gags in the finished film: the line about "a cold in your cylinder head," and the closing revelation that Petey/Pedro has risked his life to transport a single postcard.[32]

[32] In the drafts of "P-T O-2-L," both of these devices appear in chapter 8. The "cold in the cylinder head" line may seem only a throwaway line of dialogue, but apparently it was a studio favorite at the time; it was included in the *Saludos Amigos* trailer and was quoted by Walt in the December 1942 *Coca-Cola Hour* radio broadcast promoting the film.

The artists chosen to bring this story to life included some of the best animators in the studio. Fred Moore, long established as the studio's resident specialist in appealing, "cute" characters, was an obvious choice to animate the character of Pedro. As the narrator (Shields again) introduces Pedro on the sound track, Moore gives us our first glimpse of the little fellow: tiny propeller twirling, cap perched on head, "nursing" at a gasoline pump. Catching sight of the camera, Pedro grins broadly and wags his tail like a puppy. Moore's unmistakable touch continues throughout Pedro's preparations for his first big flight,[33] his awkward takeoff, the exhilaration of his flight through the mountains, his first terrifying glimpse of Aconcagua, and his safe descent into Mendoza and retrieval of the mail pouch.

[33] Disney enthusiasts will note that the line "The mail must go through," and some of the gags accompanying Pedro's takeoff, recall the 1933 Mickey Mouse short *The Mail Pilot*.

Ward Kimball, who had somewhat outgrown his late-1930s role as the impudent upstart of the studio by animating important scenes in the early Disney features, was also assigned

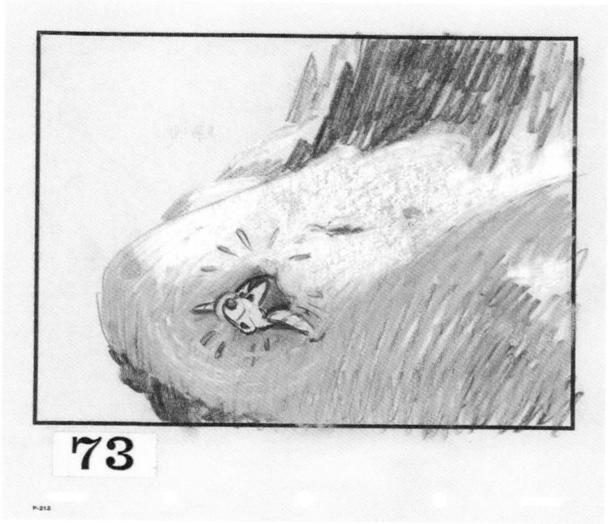

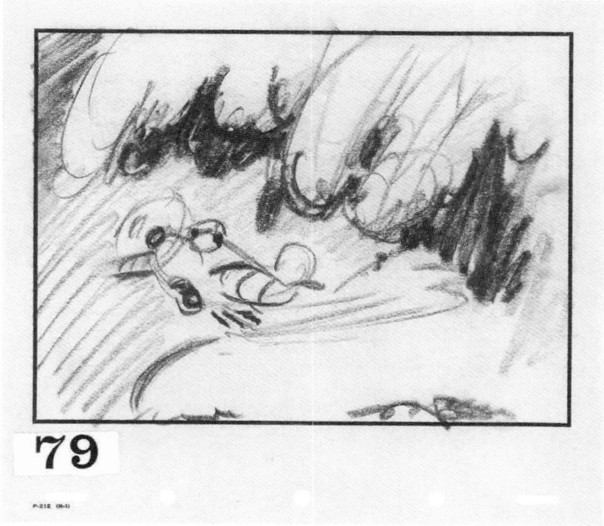

A fascinating set of *Pedro* story sketches—fascinating because they depict a scene, eliminated from the final film, that would have reflected the crashed plane El Grupo had actually observed in the Andes (*see* p. 61).

Little Pedro's personality is captured in Fred Moore's original animation art.

to *Pedro*. Aside from a few odd scenes early in the picture, his main contribution was the first part of Pedro's return flight from Mendoza, where the little plane's youthful high jinks and pursuit of a taunting condor carry him far off his course and into the vicinity of Aconcagua. Kimball's scenes exemplify the inevitable variations in different animators' handling of the same character: he *didn't* specialize in cute characters and his rendering of Pedro varies slightly from Moore's, but he clearly is following Moore's lead. His animation captures Pedro's youthful exuberance and cocky self-assurance—traits that, it might be argued, were also characteristic of Kimball himself.

Another legendary animator, Vladimir "Bill" Tytla, was assigned to *Pedro* at Walt's specific request. Tytla had made his reputation with his compelling animation of large, powerful figures—most famously the terrifying Chernobog in the *Night on Bald Mountain* segment of *Fantasia*—so it's not surprising that he was chosen to animate Pedro's father, the large mail plane. But more recently Tytla had proven his versatility when, cast against type, he had contributed some tender, touching scenes of the little title character in *Dumbo*. Perhaps for this reason he was also given a large block of Pedro's scenes, as the character fights his way through the storm, desperately trying to escape the malevolent clutches of Aconcagua. Tytla vividly captures the terror and drama of the sequence, but his rendering of Pedro, like Kimball's, is slightly at odds with the standard set by Fred Moore. One scene in particular, the remarkable 29-foot scene[34] of the exhausted Pedro giving up his struggle and slowly sinking back down into the chasm, is surprisingly and distractingly off-model. But Moore returns to animate Pedro's bedraggled but triumphant return to the darkened airfield, and the picture ends, as it began, with his animation of the beaming little plane.

[34] Because of the technical demands of their craft, Disney artists and technicians planned their scenes in terms of feet and frames of film, not minutes and seconds. At standard sound speed, 29 feet of 35 mm film have a running time of just under 20 seconds.

Ham Luske, a distinguished animator in his own right, directed *Pedro* and animated a few isolated scenes himself. The picture includes a number of subtle touches that may be missed on first viewing. The airfield's signal tower, with its windows drawn as large "eyes," registers its reactions to events by a simple movement of its "pupils"—a *Baby Weems*-style touch, achieving maximum expression with the simplest of means. The storm sequence, by contrast, is a technical tour de force, embellishing Pedro's wild flight with shattering lightning effects, multiplane shots, and live-action snow and rain doubled into the animated scenes.

As a crowning touch, the single postcard shown in Pedro's pouch at the end is addressed to "Jorge Delano"—the name of the Chilean filmmaker/cartoonist who had served as El Grupo's principal guide in Santiago, and also the name of his son.[35]

[35] Ted Thomas points out another detail that is missed by most viewers: the postcard is signed "Juan Carlos"—possibly a reference to Juan Carlos Alurralde, who had hosted Walt's party in Mendoza just before their flight to Santiago.

Upon release, *Pedro* met a mixed reception from audiences. Some viewers, confirming Fred Moore's sure touch with "cute" characters, were captivated by the little plane. The studio retained a fan letter to Walt from one New England moviegoer: "I have liked your other characters—but none so much as the new little Pedro, the plane. Please, please can't we see some more of him. Real soon. No kidding—he's wonderful. We're all crazy about him! . . . He's simply darling."[36]

[36] The studio produced no further pictures with Pedro, but this short may have influenced later cartoons built around anthropomorphized objects, such as *Susie, the Little Blue Coupe*.

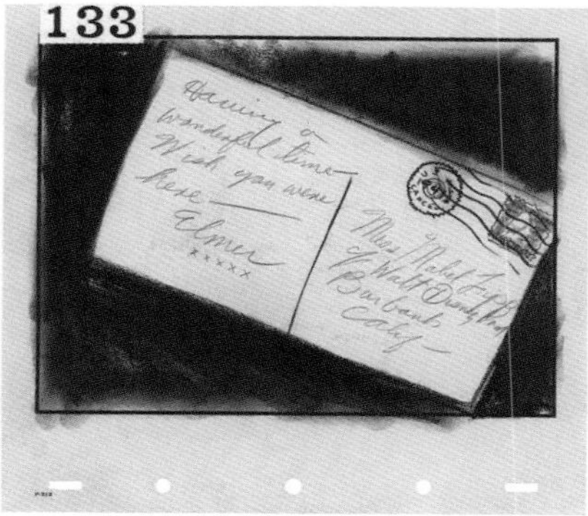

On the other hand, the story's universality—the very quality that had made it invaluable in the first rush of Good Neighbor production—became a mixed blessing when the finished film was shown in Chile. As early as December 1942 *Variety* reported: "There has been some criticism of this sequence, especially in Santiago, mainly on the basis that it doesn't show anything truly Chilean, but it's a kind of good-natured grousing." Bill Cottrell, who had put so much effort into *Pedro*, encountered the same sentiment on a studio trip in 1943. He wrote to Walt about a conversation with the wife of the RKO representative in Mexico: "She was born and raised in Chile, and gave me some very valid reasons why she was disappointed in *Pedro* as a representative subject of Chile. She brought up the Lake country of Chile, the farmlands, etc. as being typical . . . also the skiing, gauchos, dances etc." Proceeding to Cuba, Cottrell had been introduced to the U.S. ambassador's daughter. "She is a very interesting and intelligent young lady and it so happens that she was born in Santiago, Chile. Her mother is a Chilean. She had a similar criticism of *Pedro*, not as a picture, but as a representative subject. So I guess we'll have to do something about it."

Pedro's single postcard, as suggested in a story sketch (ABOVE) and as it appears in the finished film (RIGHT).

CAMPOS/938
de un argentino

EL GAUCHO GOOFY

OPPOSITE TOP: After working with the Disney studio, F. Molina Campos sent Walt this original painting of an Argentine gaucho.

OPPOSITE BOTTOM: El Gaucho Goofy cuts a somewhat less imposing figure in these four frames from the film.

The studio had *no* shortage of story material for films about Argentina. Thanks to the gaucho series inaugurated before the South American trip, and the wealth of gaucho material acquired during the trip itself, Norm Ferguson had his pick of numerous possible stories for the first Argentine short. A story known as "The Flying Donkey," which had been given a low priority when it was proposed earlier in the year, was selected from Ted Sears's list of story outlines as the first of the gaucho series to be produced. By late October Sears and a team of other artists were at work on story development. Thinking ahead, Ferguson also began laying the groundwork for future Argentine productions. He contacted director Jack Kinney to ask him to direct a followup to "The Flying Donkey," and this brought another discovery to light. "I have also found out," Ferguson wrote to Walt, "that he and Ralph Wright have developed a Goofy cowboy story that might fit in with our plans. Of course this is only a thought but they have it pretty well set up and it might be worth while looking at from that angle."

This was an inspired idea, for two reasons. Jack Kinney, a former animator, had made his directorial debut the previous year and had already proven himself a fast and reliable worker. Because the studio was under pressure to deliver its Good Neighbor films as quickly as possible, Kinney's speed and efficiency would be a valuable asset. He had recently launched what may remain his most memorable effort as a director: a series of "How To" shorts featuring Goofy. As Kinney's narrator, John McLeish, held forth in stentorian tones on the proper way to ride a horse or play a sport, Goofy would hilariously demonstrate the *wrong* way to pursue that activity. The third entry in Kinney's series, *The Art of Self Defense*, had recently been completed, and his current project, tentatively dubbed "How to Be a Cowboy," could easily be adapted to an Argentine setting.

Second, Goofy himself was an ideal character for such a film. Like Donald Duck in *Lake Titicaca*, he would automatically remove any possible sting from the slapstick gags in the picture. Ted Sears, in his earliest notes on the proposed gaucho series, had described the little gaucho's ineptitude at roping, riding, and so on, as "somewhat similar to the Goof in the *How to Ride a Horse* picture." He also acknowledged that such gags would have to be handled carefully to avoid offense. Casting Goofy himself as the would-be gaucho was the perfect solution; the audience already *knew* Goofy and *knew* that he would hilariously bungle any task he set out to accomplish. In addition, the revised story would open with the Goof explicitly shown as a North American cowboy, then "whisk" him away to Argentina, where he would learn gaucho lore and would clumsily attempt to imitate the real gauchos. Like all of Kinney's Goofy subjects, the film would deliver solid entertainment, but no one could possibly construe it as ridiculing the Argentines or the real gauchos.

Walt instinctively seized on this idea and began working closely with Kinney on the adaptation.[37] By mid-November 1941 "Goofy Gaucho" was listed among the South American subjects in active preparation, and early in December it officially started production. Kinney relied on the story

[37] Ferguson's first suggestion of the idea was made on 31 October 1941. Walt's desk diaries indicate that less than a week later, on 5 November, he met with Kinney to work on the adaptation. (The desk diaries also indicate that in mid-January 1942 Walt and Kinney screened an RKO short, *Gaucho Sports*, with an eye toward possible story material.)

At a studio screening, Molina Campos expresses his thoughts to Walt. To Molina Campos's left: Norm Ferguson, Frank Thomas, and Chuck Wolcott.

and animation unit he had already assembled for the Goofy series, and delivered his usual rapid-fire results. By the middle of December his picture had taken priority over "The Flying Donkey" as the studio's first Argentine release. This was no slight to the latter cartoon, and production on it continued apace—but there was room for only one Argentine subject in the studio's first Good Neighbor package, and it was clear that Kinney was, characteristically, about to deliver a top-notch picture in record time. By mid-March 1942 the bulk of the animation was completed.

Kinney's speedy work had an additional advantage: *El Gaucho Goofy* was essentially finished before F. Molina Campos could touch it. Molina Campos arrived at the Disney studio late in March, evidently expecting to take full charge of Disney's Argentine films. In line with the diplomatic aims of the Good Neighbor mission, he was accorded every courtesy: Walt and the staff met with him to discuss the gaucho series, he and his wife were entertained as El Grupo had been entertained in South America, and he lectured a studio audience on "Gauchos and Customs of the Argentine." But the artists who worked with him had strongly mixed reactions to Molina Campos. Some regarded him with amused tolerance. "He was a cocky little guy, he was cute," said Kinney. "He went down to the Ambassador [Hotel], to a dinner. He got up in the middle of the thing and announced himself. They were playing South American music, because of the group there, Freddy Martin's band. And at the end of it he applauded, and tipped his hat and held up his glass and said, 'F. Molina Campos, from the Argentine. *Saludos!*' And they all thought, who the hell is this guy, you know, and he sat down."

Learning that the studio's first Argentine short had been largely completed without his input, Molina Campos began to find fault with it. Frank Thomas chuckled as he recalled the artist's indignation over a sequence in which Goofy demonstrates traditional Argentine dances. "The horse sat down at the piano and was playing the piano. And Campos said, 'Oh, Mister Disney, you cannot do that, the horse, there are no fingers for the keys, he has a hoof, you know. I will show you in a drawing, the hoof cannot play more than one note, if any notes at all.'" Thomas stressed that the studio did make an effort to accommodate Molina Campos's painting style: "The way he staged things and the way he drew them, everything had a quaintness and a charm to it, which was what made them so popular. That and the fact that they were authentic, as far as the gaucho and his horse and his saddle and equipment, and all the things that he drew with it. So he was justified in thinking he was making quite a contribution, but there were other fellows from down there who said, 'Oh, gee, don't get connected with him, you won't be able to get rid of him!'"

Herb Ryman, on the other hand, remembered Molina Campos with profound respect and affection. "Our relationship grew into a warm and affectionate friendship," Ryman wrote in later years. "His thorough knowledge of and his enthusiastic reverence for the gaucho, along with a minute accuracy in depicting his way of life, aroused in many of us who worked with Campos a rekindled thirst for more information regarding these lonesome and romantic sons of the pampas. . . . This man's stark and sometimes brutal statement, and his intimate knowledge of his subject matter, express a basic primitive realism rather than what some may have referred to as a 'cartoony' or caricature approach. His authentic attention to detail and his endless varieties of types, both human and animal, give his work an impact that is reminiscent of a Doré or even a Daumier."

It was through Ryman's supervision of the *El Gaucho Goofy* background paintings that Molina Campos made his greatest impact on the Disney Latin American films. The backgrounds for the picture were specifically styled after the manner of Molina Campos's paintings, an influence acknowledged in the screen credits. In addition to Ryman's own firsthand experience and paintings of the pampas, the other artists studied Molina Campos's *Alpargatas* calendar paintings and followed his style. "So we used his backgrounds," Jack Kinney explained to Michael Barrier, "we used his low-horizon style. It made real good reading, because you could see your stuff playing. I always hated when these background guys would get so damned flamboyant with their backgrounds, and fall in love with the background, and the character would turn, and he'd lose a head or a nose or something. I like to see the damned things out there so you can read them. And I don't like anything playing here [holding his arms close to his body], I want their arms out here. They're ham actors, that's what they are, you know; let them be hams. Especially with the Goof; there was nothing subtle about him." To further mollify Molina Campos, he was invited to record the Spanish narration for the other Argentine subject, then known as "The Remarkable Donkey."

Building on El Grupo's experience in Argentina, Goofy prepares for a private *asado*.

In assembling story material for *El Gaucho Goofy*, Kinney drew heavily on the Argentine notes and sketches compiled by El Grupo. For all its entertainment value, the short packs more accurate South American detail per foot of film than most of the studio's other Good Neighbor productions. The sequences in which the Goof is outfitted with correct gaucho clothing, displays the bolas while sipping maté, and assembles the layers of his saddle are a virtual compendium of gaucho lore in cartoon terms. His demonstrations of folk dances are accompanied by the Chacarera, Malambo, and Palapala melodies supplied by Andrés de Chazarreta, the authority on Argentine music and dance who had helped El Grupo in Buenos Aires.[38] The *avestruz*, the Argentine ostrich, had been suggested as a film subject even before the South American trip. After observing, sketching, and filming the real thing, the artists continued to consider the gangly bird as a supporting character in various story treatments, and even as the star of his own picture, as late as 1943.[39] In the end, however, none of those stories were produced, and the *avestruz*'s supporting

[38] The film's cue sheet also credits Chazarreta with "La flor del pago," the ballad Goofy sings by the campfire in the same sequence.

[39] Ostriches, with their natural cartoony qualities, had appeared in earlier Disney pictures, including *Fantasia* and the short *Donald's Ostrich* (1937). In fact, the *avestruz* is a rhea and not a true member of the ostrich family. Thanks to Kenn Kaufman for clarifying this point.

A special Goofy model sheet prepared for this short.

role in *El Gaucho Goofy* remained his one appearance for Disney. Some of the faithfully observed details in the film are more subtle: the distinctive nest of the *hornero*[40]—another unsuccessful candidate for a starring short—can be glimpsed in several of the background paintings. (Another "hidden" detail in one of the backgrounds is an in-joke kidding Jack Kinney about his prominent nose. As the camera pans over a Texas landscape in the opening scene, the narrator rhapsodizes about the unspoiled prairie, "untouched and unsullied by the mercenary hand of civilization," while in fact we see the scenery overrun with billboards and oil wells. One of the billboards, barely visible as the camera pans by, announces: NOSE INN AUTO COURT/J. KINNEY, PROP.)

[40] The *hornero*, also known as the ovenbird, builds a mud nest that looks like an outdoor wood-fired oven.

Like Kinney's other Goofy subjects, this one relies heavily on Wolfgang "Woolie" Reitherman's expressive, loose-limbed animation of the Goof.[41] Reitherman's animation dominates the short, in fact, with solid support from Hugh Fraser and Harvey Toombs, both of whom are clearly following his lead. (Fraser also animated most of the *avestruz*.) The snubbing-post scene recycles some of Reitherman's horse animation from *How to Ride a Horse*, and the horse itself, although drawn differently from the horse in the earlier film, is essentially the same character—not Goofy's servant but his fellow clown and, if anything, more in command than he is. For the pursuit of the *avestruz* Kinney uses one of his favorite devices: the slow-motion sequence. As the narrator comments on "the grace and beauty of this light-footed creature in startled flight," the "slow-motion" camera reveals the ostrich as a clumsy, ungainly lummox, while Goofy and his horse, all bone-crushing bounces and flailing limbs, present an even more ridiculous spectacle.[42] The sequence ends with all three characters hopelessly tangled in the bolas. For transitions between sequences Kinney expands imaginatively on the device of transitional "wipes": Goofy and his horse are occasionally shoved to one side by the incoming scene or swept unceremoniously out of the old one.

[41] Wolfgang Reitherman, invariably known at the studio as "Woolie," is identified in the *Saludos Amigos* screen credits as "Wooly" Reitherman. Likewise, background painter Claude Coats is credited on-screen as "Coates."

[42] *How to Ride a Horse* had also featured a slow-motion riding sequence for similar comic effect. Instead of simply repeating the animation from the earlier film, *El Gaucho Goofy* offers an even more exaggerated version of the same action, climaxing when the Goof sits on his *espuelas* (spurs).

One of the first Good Neighbor subjects completed, *El Gaucho Goofy* is also one of the most entertaining. It offers a large dose of factual information, effectively packaged with an equally solid dose of laughter.

SANTA MARIA
Herb Ryman

AQUARELA DO BRASIL

If the first Argentine short had been produced quickly and with apparent ease, the first Brazilian short was just the opposite. The film that we know as *Aquarela do Brasil* struggled through a prolonged, arduous, and frustrating gestation period as the artists wrestled with problems of story construction. But their effort was justified; it resulted in a film of uncommon visual and musical richness.

That's partly because the film combines elements of what were intended as several different stories. To begin with, of course, there was the song "Aquarela do Brasil" itself. The song's sweeping popularity in Brazil, and the effort El Grupo had expended in acquiring the rights, dictated that one of the studio's first orders of business was to build a film around it. In this they had the enthusiastic support of the song's U.S. publisher, Southern Music, headed by Ralph Peer. Peer, an enterprising operator in the music business, had been quietly plying his trade for more than a decade, traveling to Mexico and South America and buying the U.S. rights to Latin American song hits. This had been a profitable enough enterprise in the 1930s, when Latin music enjoyed an increasing popularity in the United States, but two things happened at the outset of the 1940s that firmly established the soundness of Peer's practice. One was the Good Neighbor program itself, which backed the existing popular taste for Latin rhythms with the U.S. government's endorsement.

OPPOSITE: One of Herb Ryman's exploratory sketches for the new *papagaio* character.

ABOVE: José Oliveira, the voice of Joe Carioca, flanked by the two animators who would bring the character to life: Bill Tytla and Fred Moore.

The other was an extended dispute in 1940 between the radio networks and the American Society of Composers, Authors, and Publishers (ASCAP), the performing-rights organization that licensed the broadcast rights to the vast majority of American song publishers. For several months in 1940, ASCAP songs were simply not available to broadcasters, and some alternate source of music must be found. A new performing-rights group, Broadcast Music Inc. (BMI), was formed to fill the gap, and Peer cannily licensed his entire catalog to BMI. Suddenly Latin American music was everywhere on U.S. airwaves, and Peer was in an enviable position. "Aquarela do Brasil" represented a coup in itself for Peer; in 1939 it had been published in Brazil and Portugal by Ary Barroso's publisher, Irmãos Vitale, but Peer had promptly bought the rights for the rest of the world. By 1942 his anglicized version, retitled "Brazil" and fitted with new English lyrics by S. K. Russell, had already been recorded by some North American musicians (*see* Appendix B), but Peer knew that the song's exposure in a new Disney film would result in priceless exposure to a vast new audience. As the Good Neighbor program continued, Peer would continue to work closely with the studio, and other Southern Music properties would become international hits through their exposure in Disney films.

Before the trip, Bill Cottrell and Ted Sears had suggested a "Pan-American Symphony" consisting of "a ballet with South American music featuring the beautiful birds, butterflies and flowers of the country." Now "Aquarela do Brasil" emerged as the obvious musical foundation for such a film, and by the end of October 1941, Lee and Mary Blair were busily producing their own *aquarelas*—watercolors—of their Brazilian impressions. Norm Ferguson wrote to Walt that he was endeavoring to construct a film from these visual impressions, "making it a complete Effects Department job in the final animation, if possible. The question," he added, "seems to be as to when we will start thinking of the story to illustrate the music." Beautiful music and beautiful images would not be enough without some kind of plot structure to support them.

At the same time, Ferguson was working with Ted Sears to develop parrot stories for the *papagaio* series. Sears produced a list of story suggestions, along with a description of the parrot's developing personality as suggested in Brazil: "Papagaio is quite a comic and has a tendency to get into trouble through his own fresh remarks and actions. He is the type that will start a fight and then walk out leaving someone else to finish it. He is more carefree than Donald Duck, seldom loses his temper and when he does, his anger would take the form of clever criticism or insult. He is quick to take advantage of any situation—an opportunist. Papagaio is very musical and romantic." The comparison with Donald Duck was apt, and suggested that one of the parrot stories might incorporate yet another pretrip story suggestion: "Donald Duck Visits Rio." The eternally frustrated, temperamental Duck would make a perfect foil for the smooth-talking, happy-go-lucky parrot, and—as in *Lake Titicaca* and *El Gaucho Goofy*—would guarantee that all the laughs would be at the expense of the North American visitor, not the South American native. Advance publicity made the psychology explicit: "It's [Walt's] idea to make a series with Donald and the parrot. The parrot, of course, will be the victor in any fracas that arises. That's Walt Disney's good neighbor gesture."

More experimental parrot sketches by Frank Thomas.

The name Joe Carioca was applied to the parrot in story materials as early as November 1941, but only as a provisional suggestion. When Leo Samuels, of Disney's New York office, inquired in late December requesting permission to use the name in an RKO publicity story in Brazil, John Rose quickly replied in a telegram: "JOE CARIOCA ONLY TENTATIVE NAME OF NEW PAPAGAIO CHARACTER. NOTHING SET YET." When the parrot was officially christened, his first name was given alternately as either "Joe" or "José." Both names continued to be used indiscriminately throughout the character's tenure at the studio. In Brazil "José" was abbreviated, and the parrot quickly became known as "Zé" Carioca.

The parrot character takes shape as Joe Carioca.

The decision to combine all these elements—"Aquarela," Duck, and *papagaio*—into one film was apparently Walt's, early in November 1941. This inspired notion would result in a film that was much more than the sum of its parts: Donald Duck, as a surrogate North American tourist, would be introduced to Brazil by his colorful new South American friend, Joe Carioca, and would experience the same vivid kaleidoscope of colors and music that had so dazzled El Grupo on *their* visit.

Even after this decision had been made, the problems of story construction were just beginning. The challenge was to fit all this material into a single film without making it seem cluttered. The Duck-and-parrot story line carried with it additional business (such as a ride in a Rio taxi) and additional characters (including a female parrot and a menacing crow), all of which Walt ultimately trimmed away. Conversely, he and the other members of the team suggested a number of new ideas that were incorporated into the evolving story line. All these decisions were slowly, painstakingly hammered out in an interminable series of meetings. Walt's desk diary, a record of his daily activities, documents five major "Aquarela" story meetings in January 1942 alone.

Finally a deceptively simple structure was agreed on: the film would be driven by the tempo of Ary Barroso's music and would be keyed to the "watercolor" theme, beginning with a paintbrush that adorned the screen with lively visual impressions of Brazil. Barroso's composition is rather long[43] and slows to a lull in the middle, and this would be an ideal spot to break away and introduce the Duck and the parrot—both also provided by the paintbrush. At this point the film would insert yet another musical element, de Abreu's "Tico-tico," thus introducing *two* major Brazilian song hits to U.S. movie audiences in a single picture. Joe Carioca would endeavor to teach Donald Duck to dance the samba, and Barroso's "Aquarela" would return for a strong rhythmic finish. In February 1942—by which time the other three films were well on their way to completion—*Aquarela do Brasil* moved into production under the direction of Wilfred Jackson. "Jaxon" was one

[43] The original 1939 Brazilian recording by Francisco Alves was in two parts, beginning on one side of the record and continuing on the other (*see* Appendix B).

- JOE CARIOCA -
PROD. 2717
THIS MATERIAL IS THE PROPERTY OF
WALT DISNEY PRODUCTIONS
IT IS UNPUBLISHED AND
MUST NOT BE TAKEN
FROM THE STUDIO, DUPLICATED
OR USED IN ANY MANNER,
EXCEPTING FOR PRODUCTION PURPOSES,
WITHOUT WRITTEN PERMISSION
FROM AN AUTHORIZED
OFFICER OF THE COMPANY.
OK by DATE
NUMBER 72-7

Joe Carioca's design is officially established in the final model sheet.

of the studio's best directors, with a special knack for musical subjects; he had directed such brilliant shorts of the 1930s as *The Band Concert* and *Music Land.*

The task of introducing Joe Carioca to the screen fell to two of the same "star" animators who had worked on *Pedro*: Bill Tytla and Fred Moore. Joe's first appearance and his introduction to Donald, when he greets his famous visitor with an enthusiastic, back-slapping embrace, were animated by Tytla. In an animation lecture years later, fellow artist Marc Davis described Tytla's approach: "He's from New York and he was telling me about Italian or Latin people meeting one another on the streets in New York. There's lots of back-patting and slapping. These aren't gags, but they are gestures which relate to people. Anybody seeing Donald and the parrot meeting would be reminded of two Latin types they had seen." Wilfred Jackson had a particularly vivid memory of Tytla's method. "He worked me over, as I directed him," Jackson told Michael Barrier. "When the parrot was to pat the Duck's head up this way, Bill would pat my head up this way, to see what it was like to pat somebody's head. It was a workout to hand a scene out to Bill; he was a very intense person, he really got himself into things."[44]

When Joe sets out to introduce Donald to the sights of Rio, Fred Moore takes over his animation—and, once again, puts his unique stamp on the character. Joe's proportions change slightly, he becomes more compact, he demonstrates the samba with infectious joy, he

[44] This sequence includes another notable touch: when Joe first learns Donald's identity, he instantly breaks into a hopping action, one fist extended, the other swinging. Contemporary audiences would have recognized this belligerent action as Donald's trademark gesture, introduced in 1934 by animator Dick Lundy in the Mickey Mouse short *Orphans' Benefit*, the Duck's second screen appearance.

bubbles over with eager hospitality, and within minutes Moore has made the character his own. So distinctive was his touch that, when Joe Carioca made a return appearance in the studio's next Brazilian film, Moore was called on again to supervise his animation.

Although Donald Duck's design was well established long before 1942, a new model sheet was created for this picture.

As for Donald Duck—this time attired in his customary sailor suit, rather than his explorer's outfit from *Lake Titicaca*—his animation is shared by an assortment of artists. Some of his key scenes were assigned to two of the studio's resident "Duck men," Paul Allen and Milt Neil, while miscellaneous other scenes went to Tytla, Moore, and Les Clark. (As a result, the Duck's appearance changes slightly as he passes through the various animators' hands.) The anticipated conflicts, in which Joe would get the best of Donald, take the mildest possible form in the finished film. Joe, performing "Tico-tico," transforms his umbrella into a flute and Donald's hat into an accordion ("They [Brazilians] can get rhythm out of anything," Walt observed at one meeting), a feat the Duck is unable to duplicate. Later Donald takes his first drink of *cachaça* and, unaccustomed to the strong liquor, reacts violently, flames shooting out of his mouth. Joe calmly uses the flames to light his cigar.

Other animators too display their talents in *Aquarela do Brasil*. As Norm Ferguson had predicted, the "aquarela" sequences became a showcase for the effects animators. Joshua Meador had created some of the most striking effects in *Fantasia* and had contributed some isolated effects to two of the other Good Neighbor pictures; here, in the opening "paintbrush" sequence of *Aquarela*, he creates another landmark. His sequence is richly evocative: the animated paintbrush paints a palm tree, which becomes an exotic bird and flies away. A bunch of bananas, with the addition of a glob of black paint, becomes a flock of toucans snapping their bright yellow beaks like percussion instruments. Brilliant red paint, splashed on the screen in the shape of orchid petals, continues to run down in rivulets that form a pair of flamingos, which begin to samba. This is a fluid, sensuous, vibrant Brazil, pulsing with life, expressed as only the animated film can express it. The introduction of Donald Duck is equally imaginative: Meador's brush paints a stylized orchid, then a curious bee that begins to investigate it. Suddenly the petals snap shut, and the orchid, with the bee trapped inside, begins to shudder and shake violently—revealing itself as Donald, who continues his furious convulsions until the bee escapes from his mouth.[45]

Another effects animator, Dan MacManus (who had contributed some minor effects to *El Gaucho Goofy*), takes over the paintbrush when it begins to paint Joe Carioca. The brush remains an active participant in the sequence as it progresses, moving ahead of Donald and Joe to paint settings—a

[45] This is an appropriate introduction for Donald, whose history of confrontations with bees had been established in *The Band Concert* (1935), *Orphans' Picnic* (1936) and *Moose Hunters* (1937). Nothing further is done with the idea here, but it resurfaces after the war in *Bee at the Beach*, *Bee on Guard*, and other shorts.

staircase, a mosaic sidewalk, a café—just in time for the two characters to walk into them.[46] This charming "work in progress" device would be repeated after the war in *All the Cats Join In*, and the animated paintbrush would be used extensively in the studio's nontheatrical educational films—and, still later, would become a familiar sight in the animated openings of Disney's True-Life Adventure series of live-action nature films. As for MacManus himself, this was only the beginning of his connection with the Good Neighbor program. A native Mexican, he was fluent in Spanish and was called on as early as January 1942 to translate F. Molina Campos's letters and telegrams. This responsibility led to others, and MacManus was later pulled from the effects animation department altogether to play a determining role in the studio's educational films for Latin America.

[46] These and other scenes in this part of *Aquarela* were "wipe-off" scenes. Instead of completing his exposure sheet in the usual way, the effects animator would fill it out in reverse. The camera crew would start with the completed image on a cel and shoot the scene in reverse, progressively wiping off increments of the image as indicated in the exposure sheet. The same technique was used for similar scenes in other films, including relatively simple devices like the dotted lines that were sometimes seen snaking across maps and diagrams in the training or educational films.

The voice of Joe Carioca was provided by José do Patrocínio Oliveira, a versatile all-around performer known popularly as "Zezinho," who had come to the United States as a guitarist in the Romeu Silva band. Subsequently he had joined forces with the well-known group Bando da Lua, who were also in the U.S. accompanying Carmen Miranda, and in that capacity he had already appeared on-screen in some musicals for Twentieth Century-Fox. He too would continue to be associated with Joe Carioca in the character's subsequent appearances, and in later years he would himself be known by the professional name "Zé Carioca."[47] Another talented musician, singer-songwriter Aloysio de Oliveira (no relation), was chosen to sing Barroso's "Aquarela do Brasil" on the sound track. Jack Cutting later noted that Aloysio's commitment to sing in the picture conflicted with his simultaneous engagement in a New York show:[48] "Before he had done the work, he was called back east. Because he had assured me he would do the recordings, he flew back to Hollywood [at his own expense] in three days solely for the purpose of keeping his word." That integrity was rewarded; Oliveira was put on the studio payroll to serve as a consultant on future Brazilian productions. His vocal rendition of "Aquarela" in the film uses the original Portuguese lyrics. At Walt's request an English translation had been prepared, but it was not used. (The Southern Music edition of the song, simply retitled "Brazil" and published and widely recorded in the U.S., used an entirely new English lyric written by S. K. Russell.)

[47] Daniella Thompson points out that, although the word *carioca* denotes a connection with Rio de Janeiro, José Oliveira was a native of the state of São Paulo and therefore did *not* speak with a carioca accent.

[48] The New York show was Olsen and Johnson's *Sons o' Fun*, which had opened in December 1941 at the Winter Garden with Carmen Miranda featured in a prominent spot.

Additional delays and revisions continued to dog the production of *Aquarela do Brasil*. Studio production records indicate that Ward Kimball was assigned some animation that ultimately was not used in the film. They also reveal a major revision of dialogue in March 1942, after some of the dialogue recording and accompanying animation had already been completed. By June, however, the film was finished and ready for preview in Washington. Disney's first package of four Latin American shorts was officially complete.

OPPOSITE: Donald and Joe samba through a Rio landscape while the paintbrush is still creating it for them.

SALUDOS AMIGOS

Various stories have circulated over the years explaining how the four shorts came to be combined in a single feature. Surviving evidence suggests that the idea originally came from legendary motion picture producer David O. Selznick. Late in 1941 and early in 1942 Selznick wrote to Walt, and then to his former associate Jock Whitney, suggesting a feature-length "Walt Disney's Pan-American Follies." "The notion," he explained to Whitney, "was to do a feature with the biggest all-star cast in history: Mickey Mouse, Donald Duck, Dumbo, Pinocchio, Snow White and the Seven Dwarves [*sic*], Minnie Mouse, etc. . . . The further thought was to background the respective episodes with all of the countries of Latin America, or as many as you could crowd in." Informed by Whitney that Walt already had his hands full and that the CIAA was trying to target individual countries separately, with custom-designed short subjects, Selznick persisted: "Couldn't the shorts be so built that they could be all put together with very little additional work to make a revue?"

Filming pickup shots for *Saludos Amigos* "south of the border"—in Burbank. **ABOVE:** El Grupo boards a plane. **OPPOSITE:** F. Molina Campos pretends to show Norm Ferguson, Jim Bodrero, and Walt around "his" studio.

Coincidentally or not, that was exactly what eventually happened. A feature-length film was bound to command more attention and publicity—not to mention higher rentals—in all five of the countries covered than any short subject, no matter how brilliantly produced, could attract in any one of them. In addition, the same feature could also be released in the other Latin American republics that had not yet been addressed in the Disney Good Neighbor program. In April 1942 Roy Disney wrote to Francis Alstock, formally proposing that each group of four shorts be combined into a single package feature for release in South America. At this point he acknowledged that they might still be released separately in the U.S., and for months afterward that plan remained a possibility. Confusing and contradictory reports on the North American disposition of Disney's Latin American films continued to appear in the trade and popular press as late as August 1942. In the meantime, in May, Walt and his crew set about converting the first four shorts to a feature-length format.

The obvious way to tie the four shorts together was to use El Grupo's live-action 16 mm footage of their South American trip as connecting tissue. The shots had been intended for a nontheatrical documentary anyway, and the task of sifting through them to assemble the documentary had already started. Now some of them would be appropriated for theatrical use.

Unfortunately, even with the hours of 16 mm material the group had brought back, some needed shots were still missing. During the various flights around South America, no one had thought to film the artists boarding or traveling in the planes—but such shots would have obvious value in constructing a film continuity. The answer was to fake them in Burbank. Donning their traveling clothes, the members of El Grupo returned to the Burbank airport and, with Pan American's cooperation, were filmed boarding a Pan Am Clipper and "riding" in the interior. Similarly, to complement real shots of the roping and riding stunts of the gauchos in Argentina, the studio needed shots of the artists *sketching* the gauchos. Accordingly, Frank Thomas posed with Walt for a "reconstruction." Thomas recalled: "They found out, 'Well, gee, we need a shot here, a closeup of Walt with sky behind him, no trees, no buildings, just sky.' And at that time they hadn't built the hospital across the street from the studio. So they put us up on an apple box or something, and the camera was very low, and I was holding a sketch book and drawing and Walt was pointing out things to me." Other pickup shots depicted the other artists against similarly neutral backgrounds, along with such odds and ends as portfolios filling up with sketches, and a parrot (rented in Hollywood) that had supposedly helped inspire the character of Joe Carioca.

Since F. Molina Campos was to be acknowledged in connection with the *El Gaucho Goofy* segment, the decision was made to picture him on-screen as well. Molina Campos had not been present when the Disney party visited his Argentina studio in September 1941, but here again history took a backseat to showmanship. When Molina Campos arrived at the Disney studio in March 1942, he was filmed in 16 mm, in shirt sleeves, pretending to show Walt, Norm Ferguson, and other members of the group around his own studio. It was a simple device, but effective enough that generations of later viewers and commentators (including this one) have been convinced that they had seen Molina Campos hosting Walt and the gang in Argentina.[49]

[49] Along with these reconstructed scenes, the studio acquired outside stock footage of the Carnaval in Rio, which El Grupo themselves had not witnessed (not having visited Brazil during Carnaval season). The source of the Carnaval footage used in the film remains a mystery. By early May 1942 Walt and the artists were viewing rough cuts of unidentified Carnaval scenes, but inconclusive evidence suggests that the shots used in the feature were supplied by CIAA staff member David Hopkins. Late in May, Walt (passing through Chicago) wired Norm Ferguson at the studio: "HOPKINS ARRANGING FOR YOU TO VIEW SIXTEEN MILLIMETER RIO CARNIVAL STUFF LOOK IT OVER AND ADVISE YOUR DECISION." By late June the introductory scenes for *Aquarela do Brasil*, complete with the Carnaval, had been fully assembled.

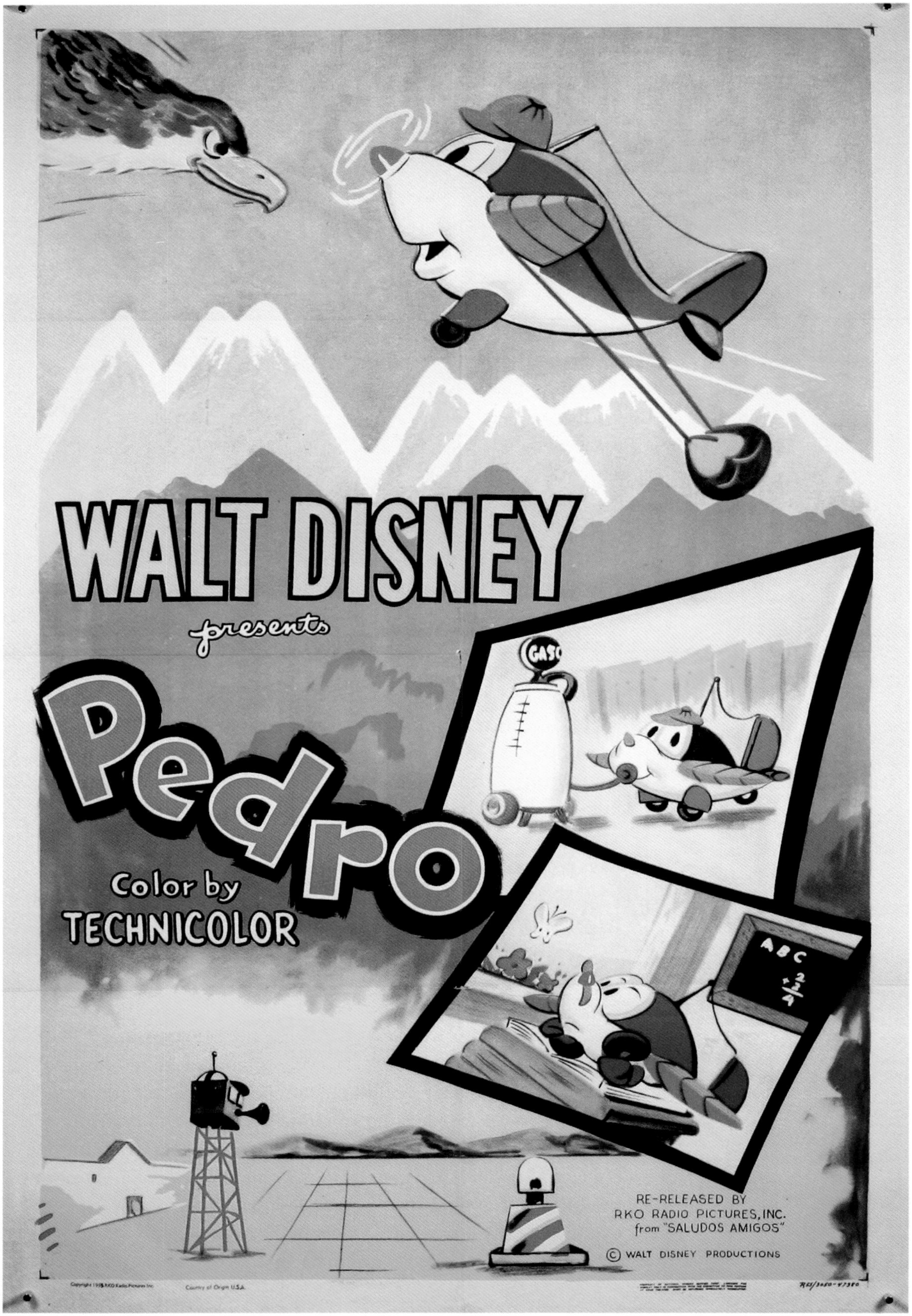
WALT DISNEY
presents
Pedro
Color by
TECHNICOLOR
GAS
ABC
RE-RELEASED BY
RKO RADIO PICTURES, INC.
from "SALUDOS AMIGOS"
© WALT DISNEY PRODUCTIONS
Country of Origin U.S.A.

Fred Shields, who had narrated three of the four short subjects, lent the feature a further unifying touch by narrating the connecting scenes as well. Interestingly, Walt seems to have been less than enthusiastic about Shields's work. "In Shields you haven't got a clever guy," he commented at one sweatbox session, "so you have to get your comedy out of the picture. Maybe we could get another guy for this narration and let Shields just do the shorts."[50] In the finished feature, however, Shields provided all the narration. For *El Gaucho Goofy*, which normally would have been narrated by Jack Kinney's usual standby, John McLeish, Shields simply read the narration in an imitation of McLeish's style. Alberto Soria, "Hollywood correspondent for numerous Latin mags," narrated the Spanish edition of the feature.

[50] "Sweatboxes" were the small projection rooms at the studio, so named in the earlier days at Disney's Hyperion studio when the rooms were not air-conditioned.

Records of the intensive screening sessions in May–June 1942 indicate that Walt and his team initially planned a feature film that would reflect the actual chronology of their trip: beginning in Brazil (*Aquarela do Brasil*), progressing to Argentina (*El Gaucho Goofy*) and Chile (*Pedro*), and ending in Bolivia and Peru (*Lake Titicaca*). At first glance this seemed a natural approach, but it would have meant beginning the feature with *Aquarela do Brasil*, the strongest of the four segments, and rendering the others anticlimactic. Walt, a born showman, would never have countenanced such an idea for long. By 20 May the running order of the segments had been exactly reversed, beginning with *Lake Titicaca* and ending with *Aquarela*. ("This is a much better order," Walt commented happily.) Because most of the shorts were already complete, discrete units, few changes were made to adapt them to their new feature-length format.[51] The opening scene in *Pedro*—the little plane skywriting his name to create a main title card (*see* page 23)—was now superfluous and was cut; instead the live-action scenes of El Grupo on tour segued into a closeup of a typewriter typing the opening words of the *Pedro* narration. By and large, however, the four shorts remained intact. The closing scene of *Aquarela do Brasil*, a glamorous cityscape featuring the flashing neon sign of the Cassino da Urca—where Walt and the artists had been entertained on their first night in Rio—now became the closing scene of the feature.

[51] In most cases the "adaptation" amounted to nothing more than cross-dissolving the opening and closing scenes of the cartoon with the surrounding live-action shots. *Lake Titicaca* discarded even that formality; although the camera department was asked to retake the last scene to eliminate the iris-out, the effect remains in the finished feature. On the other hand, as the opening segment in the feature, *Lake Titicaca* does ease into its cartoon material by alternating some of its introductory scenes with live-action shots of the artists' paintings.

The feature was given the title *Saludos*, and Chuck Wolcott composed an original song, "Saludos Amigos," to serve as its theme. This was the one original song in the picture, and the studio got considerable mileage out of it. Not only was the melody heard in varying arrangements throughout *Saludos* itself (including a rendition in the Inca five-tone scale to underscore the 16 mm Bolivian and Peruvian scenes), but it also received heavy radio airplay in programs publicizing the film, and later became the standard main-title music for many of the studio's educational films for the Latin American market. Like the genuine South American music acquired by the studio, "Saludos Amigos" was published by Southern Music.

OPPOSITE: Poster art for the reissue of *Pedro* as a short in 1955.

By July 1942 *Saludos* was essentially complete, and word began to spread that once again Walt Disney had created something unique and wonderful. *Hollywood Reporter* announced that Carmen Miranda had been granted a two-day leave of absence from the set of *Springtime in the Rockies* to serve as a "technical adviser" on the Brazilian section of the film—a gesture that, taking place so late in production, was surely undertaken mainly for publicity value. By the end of the month Walt was able to send an answer print of the feature (a preliminary version of the film with the color correction and sound snychronization completed) to Nelson Rockefeller in Washington. Rockefeller responded enthusiastically: "Thank you ever so much for sending the print of *Saludos* to Washington. It arrived on time and I showed it that night to the Bolivian Ambassador, the Minister of Finance, the Minister of National Economy and other guests. They praised it enthusiastically as did Mme. Martins, wife of the Brazilian Ambassador, who saw it later. . . . We all feel that *Saludos* is a great contribution to our program of inter-American relations and it quite exceeds our highest expectations."

This was apparently the first advance screening in the U.S., and it was followed by others throughout late 1942, including a private showing at the Museum of Modern Art in December for Central and South American consuls and other dignitaries. Everywhere *Saludos* was shown it met with the same delighted response, and the idea of releasing the four shorts separately in the U.S. quickly disappeared. The CIAA officials, elated by their good fortune, happily rewrote their original contract with Disney to accommodate three features in place of twelve shorts. Promotional events began to appear, among them a special radio broadcast of *The Coca-Cola Hour* in December, in which Andre Kostelanetz's orchestra previewed the *Saludos* music and Walt, Clarence Nash (the voice of Donald Duck), and Pinto Colvig (the voice of Goofy) publicized the film. It was on this broadcast that Walt, reflecting on current wartime conditions, spoke in words that have often been quoted since then: "I think up to now we have all been thinking of the barriers between the Americas: distance and different languages and different backgrounds. And now, rather suddenly, we see that these things don't matter. Our backgrounds are different, but our future, we know, has to be the same. The cowboy and the gaucho understand each other because both of them ride the plains as free men, not slaves. And Donald Duck and Joe Carioca will always be friends, I believe, because they're both grand independent spirits, meant for the pleasure of people who are not afraid to laugh. . . . While half of this world is being forced to shout 'Heil Hitler,' our answer is to say 'Saludos Amigos.'"

F. Molina Campos, who was still in Los Angeles when the feature was completed, responded to the finished version of *El Gaucho Goofy* with mixed signals. On the one hand, he continued to complain loudly to his influential friends over alleged offenses. "I tried to find a way of fixing [the film]," he wrote to Edward Reed, the U.S. ambassador to Argentina, "but . . . such was the conglomeration of errors that I asked that my name should on no account figure in the filming, if they insisted on doing it at all."[52] Two weeks later, after seeing an advance screening of

[52] This letter was quoted in a letter from Reed to Cordell Hull, U.S. secretary of state. Hull also received a letter from F. G. Klock of New York, taking up Molina Campos's complaint about the scene of Goofy "playing a guitar which is gaily decorated with colored designs," something that true gauchos, "real he-men," would never do. In the film, Goofy plays a plain brown guitar with no decorations.

Saludos (complete with his screen credit), he wrote Walt a note of hearty congratulations: "After witnessing yesterday the success of *Saludos* and the enthusiastic applause of the audience, you cannot understand how happy I am to congratulate you. . . . For you, Don Walt, the admiration and cordial affection of your friend, F. Molina Campos."

The world premiere of the film, under its Portuguese title *Alô, amigos*, took place 24 August 1942 in Rio de Janeiro. *Alô, amigos* opened simultaneously in five different Rio theaters and was a smash hit.[53] Dona Darcy Vargas, the Brazilian first lady, hosted the opening as a charity benefit, just as she had done with *Fantasia* one year earlier during El Grupo's visit. Because of its short running time of forty-two minutes (which would present a problem in all subsequent bookings), the Disney feature was presented with a full supporting program of newsreels and other short subjects. "That," reported one correspondent, "was stopped by audiences threatening to tear down the theater if they didn't repeat *Saludos*." Phil Reisman, RKO vice president, was present for the occasion and wired an excited report to the CIAA: "SALUDOS OPENED RIO NIGHT BEFORE LAST AT FIVE THEATRES TO ABSOLUTE CAPACITY BUSINESS AND THE ENTHUSIASTIC RESPONSE AND COMMENT FROM THE BRAZILIAN PEOPLE IS IMPOSSIBLE TO PUT INTO WORDS. MRS. VARGAS RECEIVED APPROXIMATELY FIFTEEN HUNDRED DOLLARS FROM THE OPENING NIGHT TOWARD HER PET CHARITY. WHOLE TOWN EXCITED AND PLEASED BEYOND WORDS WITH THIS BEAUTIFUL PICTURE."

[53] The theaters were the Plaza, Astoria, Olinda, Ritz, and Parisiense. These five theaters were a bloc that routinely presented the same program; *Alô, amigos* was preceded at all five theaters by *O fantasma de Frankenstein* (Universal's *The Ghost of Frankenstein*) and followed, at the end of its two-week run, by *Aventuras de Martin Eden* (Columbia's *The Adventures of Martin Eden*).

BELOW: Newspaper advertising for the film was tailored to individual markets. This Brazilian ad features Joe Carioca and "Aquarela do Brasil."

RIGHT: Walt with Ralph Peer, whose music publishing company, Southern Music, promoted the music in the Good Neighbor films.

Ralph Peer's sheet-music version of "Aquarela do Brasil" heavily identified the song with *Saludos Amigos*—although it featured the anglicized title, "Brazil," and the English lyrics by S. K. Russell, neither of which were used in the film.

This brilliant reception was doubly gratifying because the nature of the Disney Good Neighbor mission had undergone a dramatic shift. Walt had originally been approached by the CIAA to make films, not for Latin American audiences, but for those in *North* America. Like other Hollywood films produced at the behest of the CIAA, the Disney pictures had been conceived as vehicles to make U.S. audiences better acquainted with their neighbors to the south, and some publicity preceding the 1941 trip had suggested that the resulting films might not be released in South America at all. The experience of the tour, with the South Americans' outpouring of affection and admiration for Walt and his artists and pride in association with them, had served to reverse that concept. Now this first Disney feature was regarded as an offering, "a warm handshake for two" in the words of the title song, extended to South America. As *Variety* put it: "Audiences here [in Argentina], in Brazil and in Chile have been particularly interested in seeing their own native scenes and customs through the eyes of Disney and crew." The enthusiastic response of Rio audiences was evidence that this goodwill gesture was a tremendous success.

After a press preview in September, the Spanish edition of the film, *Saludos*, premiered at the Ambassador Cine in Buenos Aires on 6 October. This was another charity showing, hosted by Señora Castillo, the president's wife; the public opening took place the following night. Once again, the film scored a great success. "Walt Disney's *Saludos* looks like not only a strong potential goodwill builder," wrote the *Variety* reviewer, "but a potential box-office smash as well. . . . it is just as strong with the cash customers as with the hemisphere harmonists." J. R. Josephs, of the CIAA's motion picture subdivision, reported on the audience's enjoyment: "The sequences, particularly those dealing with Argentina, amazed the audience with their authenticity, their charm and their humor. The audience howled with delight at Goofy's sudden transfer from Texas to the pampa, and some of the slight resentment heard at the preview regarding Goofy's dance with his *caballo* seemed to have disappeared." "Goofy is not a gaucho with a Spanish hat who jumps through windows like Douglas Fairbanks," the magazine *Estampa* wrote approvingly, "but is a true gaucho wearing an old felt hat tilted over the forehead in any old way. He drinks maté according to our best traditions and, above all, he acts like a real gaucho. He is good-hearted, humble, respectful and shrewd. The Goofy short renders true homage to Argentina and is a result of sincere observation of the ranches of Argentina." *Saludos* played at the Ambassador for six weeks, and during that time Buenos Aires was the scene of a virtual Disney festival: *Pinocchio* was revived for four days at the Select Lavalle, and *Dumbo* opened in mid-October and played for several weeks, sometimes at multiple theaters. (When *Saludos* finally ended its run at the Ambassador, it was succeeded by a program that included Dante Quinterno's animated cartoon *Upa en apuros*—the Patoruzú short on which he had consulted with El Grupo, during their visit to Buenos Aires the previous year.)

The Argentine newspaper ads highlighted El Gaucho Goofy.

In September the decision was made to change the film's title to *Saludos Amigos*, corresponding to the theme song, before the U.S. opening. Prints of *Saludos* bearing the original title had already been shipped to South America, and for a time the film continued to be identified alternately by both titles. This caused some confusion and, in at least one instance, mild resentment. "I have seen Walter Disney's last picture here [in Argentina] and it also went to Uruguay," one correspondent wrote to the CIAA. "But, while in America they call it 'Saludos, Amigos,' in Spanish, here it is merely called 'Saludos' having cut off the 'Amigos.' Why? Why has the qualification 'Amigos' that means so much now been cut off?" This petty grievance, part of a larger complaint from Uruguay about having been left out of the feature ("Apparently we do not exist"), illustrates the enormously delicate diplomatic nature of the Good Neighbor program.

The official North American opening of *Saludos Amigos* took place Saturday, 6 February 1943, at Boston's Majestic Theater. The following week, on 12 February, it debuted in New York. Nelson Rockefeller had prevailed on the manager of Radio City Music Hall—at the time perhaps the most celebrated motion-picture theater in the world, where Disney shorts and features had enjoyed prestigious New York openings since 1933 —to host the opening of *Saludos Amigos*.[54] Instead the film opened at the Globe Theater in Times Square, sharing a bill with the National Film Board of Canada short *The Invasion of North Africa*. Walter Brooks, of New York, took issue with this decision and was moved to write a personal letter to Walt: "I deplore the booking of your excellent *Saludos Amigos* into the Globe Theatre. This is a fourth-rate house that catches all the 'skip-the-gutter' product on Times Square. It is sufficiently a resort for knee-nudgers and questionable characters that it is strictly avoided by audiences of women and children. It is the last place in town for a new and fine Walt Disney picture. Where is Nelson Rockefeller's pride in his own program?"

[54] In addition to his role as Coordinator of Inter-American Affairs, Nelson Rockefeller was still the president of Rockefeller Center.

The suitability of the Globe notwithstanding, *Saludos Amigos* opened to the same box-office success and rave reviews that had greeted it in South America. Howard Barnes of the *New York Sun* hailed it as "at once a potent piece of propaganda and a brilliant job of picture-making." "A delightful surprise is waiting for moviegoers who see the new Disney film," wrote Philip T. Hartung in *The Commonweal*. *Hollywood Reporter* opined that "it will do more to promote friendly understanding of South America in the United States than dozens of weightier tomes." And Jane Corby of the *Brooklyn Eagle* opened her review with the line "Now you'll like propaganda!"

That theme was repeated as *Saludos Amigos* continued to open around the country. Propaganda it may have been—and it made no attempt to hide its propaganda mission—but no one cared; it was also a delightfully entertaining *movie*. Utterly unlike any Disney film (or any other film) that had preceded it, it was nonetheless unmistakably Disney. Nor was the studio caught unprepared for this success; like earlier Disney favorites, *Saludos Amigos* generated a wide range of promotional merchandise, aimed at children as well as adults. For the children there were storybooks based on the individual segments: *Pedro* and *Donald Duck in the High Andes*.

But the feature was clearly designed for a more adult audience, and so was much of its related merchandise. Perhaps most obviously, *Saludos Amigos* served to introduce two major Brazilian hit songs to North American movie audiences, and the Disney studio became allied (not for the first time) with the popular-music business. In particular, Ary Barroso's "Aquarela do Brasil," now retitled simply "Brazil," gained a whole new popularity in the U.S., widely recorded and heavily promoted in connection with *Saludos Amigos*. Xavier Cugat, Jimmy Dorsey, and Fred Waring were among the artists who recorded the song—as were a young vocal trio, the Dinning Sisters, who would themselves become a part of the Disney Good Neighbor story a few years later. The other song, Zequinha de Abreu's lively instrumental "Tico-tico no fubá," had actually been heard in an earlier Hollywood film: MGM's remake of *Rio Rita*. The MGM *Rio Rita* reached U.S. screens in April 1942, nearly a full year ahead of *Saludos Amigos*. But the evidence suggests that this was not a deliberate effort on MGM's part to undercut Disney; "Tico-tico" slipped into the earlier film under benign circumstances, almost by accident, and was played briefly and without acknowledgment.[55] In *Saludos* the melody was featured much more prominently, and both the title and the composer were identified on-screen. (It's sometimes assumed that the Decca record album of the *Saludos Amigos* score, conducted by Chuck Wolcott, was recorded and issued during the film's domestic release. In fact, the Decca albums of both *Saludos Amigos* and *The Three Caballeros* would be recorded in tandem in 1944.)

Since 1934, *Good Housekeeping* magazine had featured a monthly Disney page in which new Disney shorts, and even some of the early features, were illustrated in picture and verse. Now these pages announced the forthcoming Good Neighbor pictures. *El Gaucho Goofy*, the first of the shorts to be completed, was illustrated in the magazine as early as June 1942. Later, coinciding with the domestic release of *Saludos Amigos*, the page was explicitly labeled "Mickey Mouse's Good-Neighbor Page" from December 1942 through May 1943. During this time the pages were given over to illustrations of the other *Saludos* segments as well as additional forthcoming shorts. One page, "José Carioca," was unrelated to any of the actual story material in *Aquarela do Brasil*, but served to introduce the cunning parrot in a story that took him, with Donald, to the top of Sugarloaf Mountain. Joe also achieved the distinction of starring in his own Sunday newspaper comic page. Written by Hubie Karp, penciled by Bob Grant and Paul Murry, and inked by Karl Karpe and Dick Moores, the "José Carioca" page first appeared in newspapers in October 1942 and ran for nearly two years.

Saludos Amigos itself, having scored such a success in the Americas, joined the other Disney features in overseas distribution. Opening in London late in 1943, it was hailed once again as "irresistible entertainment for all types of patron and a perfect gloom chaser for the war-weary." "The sum total," reported one trade paper, "is a jolly hour spent with a team who obviously enjoyed themselves and gladly let us share the fun." Having already been prepared in Spanish, Portuguese, and English editions, *Saludos* was now dubbed into other languages too as European distribution channels, previously crippled by the war, slowly began to reopen. By mid-1944 the film had been translated into Swedish, French, Russian—and, inevitably, Italian and German.[56] In later years, long after the Good Neighbor program had run its course, the film would be reissued and shown on television. And in 1955, reverting to the original plan, the studio would reissue all four segments separately as short subjects.

But even as *Saludos Amigos* was enjoying its first flush of success in the early 1940s, Walt and his artists had moved on to new projects. Their first Good Neighbor picture had scored an undeniable triumph, but there was much more work to do.

[55] Late in production of *Rio Rita*, almost as an afterthought, MGM made the decision to add the Brazilian Eros Volusia to its cast. Volusia was a distinguished young dancer who had created a distinctly Brazilian form of dance, fusing ballet with traditional folkloric dances—in Daniella Thompson's words, "the Brazilian Isadora Duncan." She had also appeared in an eye-catching photo on the cover of *Life* magazine's September 1941 issue. MGM, in a burst of Good Neighbor spirit, quickly decided to insert this Brazilian dancer into the vaguely Mexican setting of *Rio Rita*. In the film she performs an "authentic native dance," actually a medley of dances she herself had choreographed to a selection of tunes. One of those tunes happened to be "Tico-tico." Special thanks to Daniella Thompson, and to Ned Comstock of USC, for their help in assembling this information.

[56] The Russian translations of this and other Disney films were prepared by the Russian actor Leonid Kinskey, familiar to today's film enthusiasts from his roles in *Duck Soup*, *Casablanca*, and other classic films.

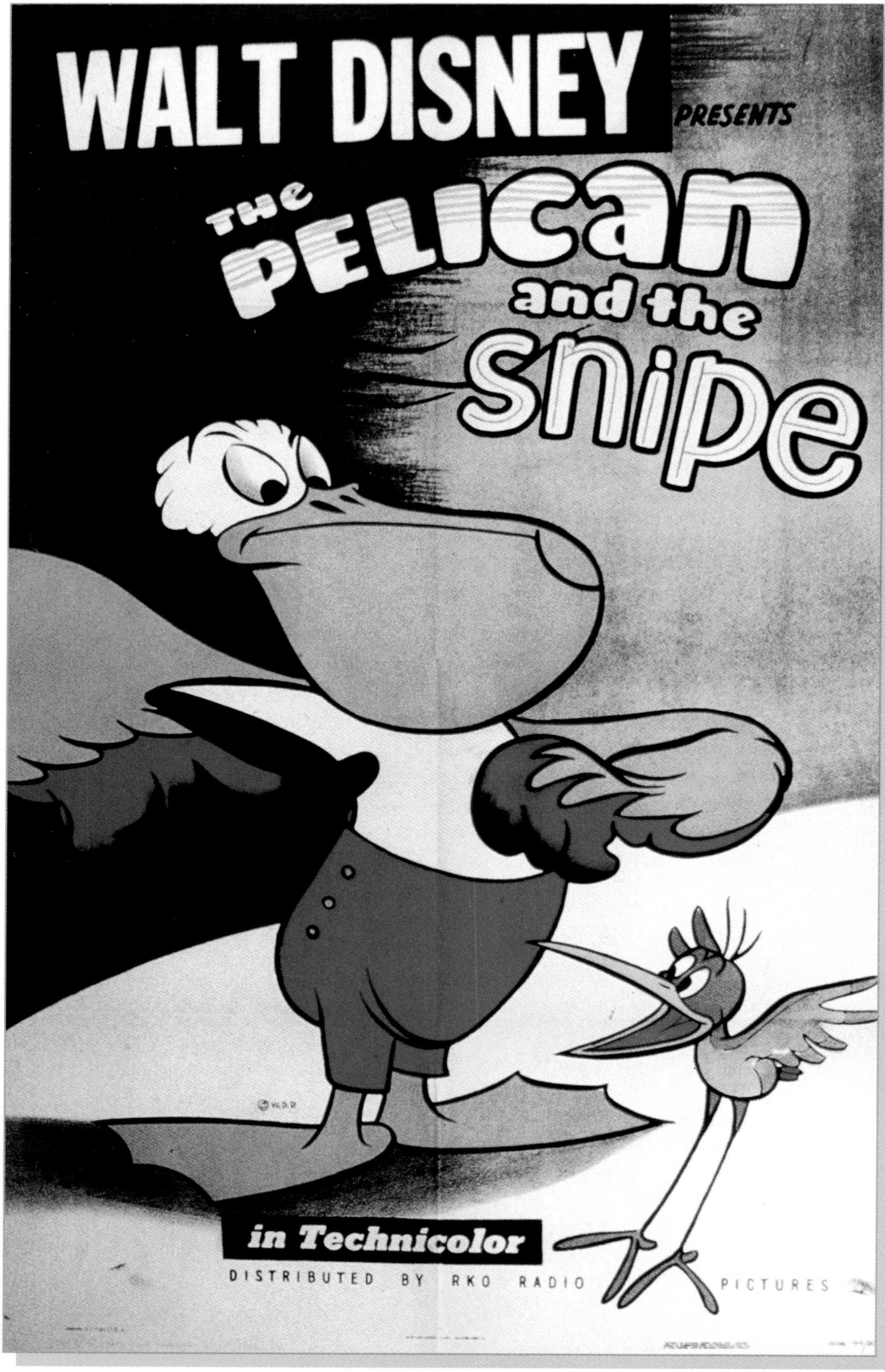

WALT DISNEY
PRESENTS
THE PELICAN and the SNIPE
in Technicolor
DISTRIBUTED BY RKO RADIO PICTURES

3 SELECTED SHORT SUBJECTS

El Grupo returned from South America in October 1941 bursting with ideas, and the newly formed South American Unit witnessed a creative explosion that produced dozens of story outlines. The stories that were selected for production and inclusion in *Saludos Amigos* were four of the best, but together they constitute only a fraction of the short subjects suggested and developed during those exciting, turbulent months. Of the many others, some were incorporated into other features, some evolved and were absorbed as story elements in existing outlines, and some were actually produced and released as shorts. And some, after considerable development and even active production work, were abandoned and never completed at all.

UNFINISHED FILMS

We can gain a fresh appreciation of the richly creative atmosphere of this time by looking at some of the ideas that—as entertaining and imaginative as many of them were—Walt could afford to abandon.

THE LAUGHING GAUCHO

OPPOSITE: Poster art for the Disney short *The Pelican and the Snipe*, released in 1944.

We've already seen that one of the story department's top priorities was a "gaucho series" incorporating the wealth of gaucho lore the artists had acquired in Argentina. In the end, only one of these gaucho stories was produced and completed: a story known at first as "The Flying Donkey," later retitled *The Flying Gauchito* and incorporated into *The Three Caballeros*. In late 1941, however, Norm Ferguson had every reason to think the gaucho series would continue, and even as production went ahead on "The Flying Donkey" he was planning a follow-up vehicle. The second outline in Ted Sears's list of gaucho stories was "The Laughing Gaucho," about a young Argentine boy with a laugh so shrill that it shatters glass. This troublesome talent causes no end of trouble for the boy until he decides to capitalize on it by going into show business—whereupon his voice changes, and his laughter loses its effect.[57] By early December 1941 Ferguson was working on this story with Ernie Terrazas, a story man of Mexican descent who would become more heavily involved in the Disney Good Neighbor program when it turned its full attention on Mexico.

Story development of *The Laughing Gaucho* (alternately known as *The Laughing Gauchito*) continued through January and February 1942. As the story evolved, the crew worked in a joking reference to the Alvear Palace Hotel, where their Buenos Aires studio had been set up, and recast the close of the story as a happy ending: the boy doesn't mind losing his glass-breaking powers—far better to accept his inevitable coming of age and grow into a man, a real gaucho. By early March Walt was reasonably satisfied with the story and it entered production under the direction of Jack Kinney, who was well

[57] There is evidence that this story idea may have preceded the 1941 South American tour. John Rose's notes from his cross-country U.S. trip, just before the tour started, include a list of items headed "TAKE UP WITH WHITMAN" (the Whitman Publishing Company in Racine, Wisconsin); one cryptic item on the list is "Discuss converting 'Laughing Lad' radio script into Gaucho short." As of this writing no further evidence has been found to clarify this point.

on the way to completing *El Gaucho Goofy*. Animation was assigned, once again, to Bill Tytla, together with Ollie Johnston and Frank Thomas. Although little animation was completed, *The Laughing Gaucho* remained under consideration for months. As late as October 1942 it appears in a CIAA report on Disney activities, and appears to have replaced *The Flying Gauchito* in the lineup of forthcoming Disney pictures.

Sometime after that, however, *The Laughing Gaucho* disappeared from Disney's plans. Why? It may be that Walt tired of the repetitive nature of the story, which mainly revolved around glass-breaking gags. As he commented at one story meeting: "We're going to have to go beyond just busting things up here."

Happily, the animation art was saved, and was unearthed a half century later by a production team preparing a special laser disc edition of *Saludos Amigos* and *The Three Caballeros*. By combining the surviving pencil animation with story drawings, the team was able to "reconstruct" *The Laughing Gaucho*. Thanks to their efforts, we can enjoy a taste of this uncompleted picture. Of the animators, Ollie Johnston is represented only by the opening scene, a 29-foot scene[58] of the gauchito riding a stick horse and chasing a chicken, pretending it's an *avestruz*. Bill Tytla contributes some animation featuring Don Vino, a comic drunk figure in the cantina, including one elaborate scene in which Don Vino—unaware that the chicken has perched on his head—tipsily prepares to drink a glass of wine, only to see it shatter just before he raises it to his lips.

[58] Just under 20 seconds.

The real animation "star" of this picture is Frank Thomas, the one current member of the animation staff to have made the trip to Argentina himself. Along with some Don Vino scenes of his own, Thomas animates the entire climactic episode in which the gauchito, facing an unresponsive theater audience, tries unsuccessfully to break a large mirror with his laugh. This sequence bears Thomas's unmistakable touch: the gauchito progresses from casual arrogance through puzzlement, embarrassment, annoyance, determination, and finally to outright anger when his laugh fails to break the glass. (Walt had suggested this as the comic essence of the sequence: "A guy madder than hell, trying to laugh.") Dissolving in tears of rage and frustration, the gauchito beats a retreat as the audience pelts him with vegetables.

In Frank Thomas's pencil animation, "a guy madder than hell" tries desperately to summon a laugh.

Although *The Laughing Gaucho* was never completed, it influenced one picture that was. Ted Sears, in his earliest notes on the gaucho series, had written of the continuing gaucho character: "He would not be a boy—sort of an ageless character like Chaplin." This story, however, specifically called for a young boy whose voice had not yet changed. Consequently it was framed as a flashback, narrated by the adult gaucho as he recalled his boyhood, and *The Flying Gauchito*—produced more or less concurrently, and featuring the same character—followed suit.

CAXANGÁ

One of El Grupo's discoveries in Brazil was a popular game called *caxangá,* played to the tune of a traditional song called "Escravos de Jó" ("Slaves of Job"). Seated at a table, two or more players slide or pass small objects to one another, following a rhythmic, circular pattern: now passing the object to the next player, now, on certain syllables, shuttling the item between one player's hands or tapping it on the table (both the lyrics and the motions have many variations). The game may be played with any small objects, but in the nightclubs of Rio, the Disney party invariably saw it played with matchboxes. The object of the game is to steadily speed up the tempo without disrupting the pattern—an increasing challenge to the players' dexterity. This picturesque pastime was suggested as a story element in several of the Brazilian film subjects, and the South American Unit tried at least three versions of a story built entirely around the game itself. Evidence indicates that they briefly considered a story with a cast of turtles, perhaps because of the game's resemblance to a North American "shell game." A "Production Progress" notebook compiled in late November 1941 for the benefit of the CIAA mentions a "Caxangá" film with turtle characters. And the following month, John Rose's long list of "Survey By-Products" proposes a merchandising tie-in with an anglicized name: "'Catch and Go,' the Turtle Shell Game."

From the beginning, however, Norm Ferguson and his team leaned toward a story with established Disney characters: Donald Duck, Goofy, and the new *papagaio* character who was evolving into Joe Carioca. In particular, a game requiring manual dexterity was made to order for Donald Duck, who could be counted on to fumble the matchboxes and to grow increasingly frustrated. Ferguson sent memos to Walt in October and November 1941 suggesting various ideas for the short, referred to variously as "Caxangá" or "The Match Box Song." At one point Ferguson made his own merchandising suggestion: the studio might tie in with the Diamond Match Company, and the latter might even want to adopt the Disney *papagaio* as its trademark. The song "Escravos de Jó" was in public domain, but in 1941 João de Barro had copyrighted a new *marcha* version (to be played in march rhythm), and this was the version El Grupo had heard in Rio. Back in California, Chuck Wolcott and Ted Sears further adapted this version by modifying the tune and adding an original verse and English lyrics. The resulting song, titled "Caxangá" and jointly credited to Wolcott, Sears, and João de Barro, was subsequently copyrighted by the studio.[59]

A tentative story was devised: Donald's heart is captured by a female parrot named Aurora (this character may have been based on Aurora Miranda, Carmen's sister, who would play a major role in one of the studio's later Brazilian films). Introduced to caxangá by Aurora and Joe Carioca, the Duck attempts to play it himself, with predictable results.

[59] João de Barro was a pseudonym for Carlos Braga, a well-known Brazilian songwriter who had conferred with El Grupo during their Rio visit and who continued to advise them as they moved forward with production. Apparently the final Disney version of the "Caxangá" song also included lyrics by Ned Washington but, according to Jack Cutting, Washington "was paid a flat sum" and did "not participate in royalties."

The game is framed as a competition between Donald and Joe, the winner to be rewarded with a dance with Aurora. This story was tentatively assigned to Wilfred Jackson in mid-April 1942, but before much of the animation had been completed, production was canceled and a different version started.

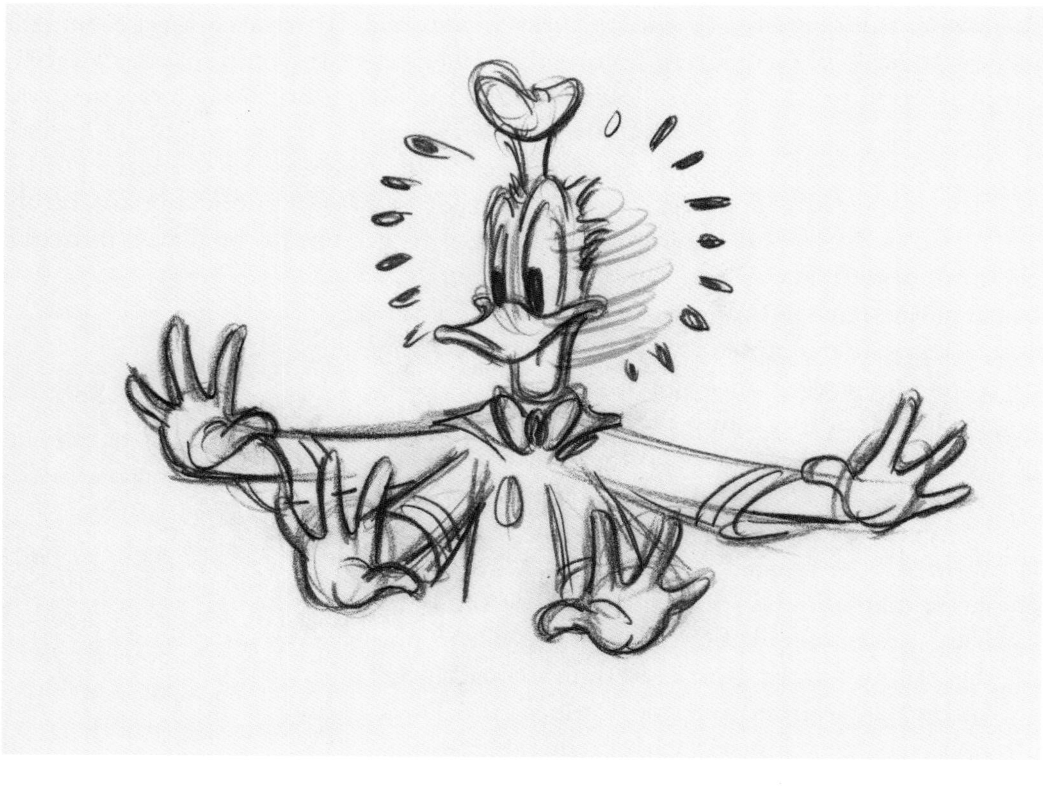

In the reworked version of the story, Donald tries his hand at caxangá.

This version was more fully developed. This time Donald, Joe, and Goofy are introduced playing caxangá, the Duck already frustrated and well on his way to a temper tantrum. (A novel device appears at this point: Joe speaks to Donald in Portuguese, with an English translation in a box at the bottom of the screen—whereupon Donald, replying in English, is also given a dialogue box. Characteristically, he soon comes to blows with his own dialogue.) Unable to master the game after hours of effort, Donald explodes in rage and stalks out. The rest of the short is built around the catchy caxangá melody: the Duck, trying to sleep, is unable to get the tune out of his head. A ticking clock, a dripping faucet, and other noises seem to pick up the rhythm. Donald tries counting sheep—and the sheep become matchboxes, pursuing him in his dreams. As the short progresses, Donald's nightmares become increasingly bizarre, always driven by that insistent caxangá rhythm. In the morning the sleep-deprived Duck stares wearily from his window at the Rio cityscape, only to see traffic and buildings continuing to jump to that same insidious beat.

Once again the story was brought to the brink of production: dialogue and music were recorded, pencil layout drawings were prepared, preliminary animation was roughed in. And, once again, production was halted and the idea of a "Caxangá" short suspended indefinitely. It was revived again briefly in 1944, this time with a different approach. Ferguson wrote to José da Rocha Vaz, one of the group's Brazilian contacts, asking for more information about the game: "We need history on the origin of it. The thought being that it might have possibilities for a symphonic treatment, starting with primitive handling and bringing it up to the present day." Rocha Vaz replied, after researching the question, that little was known about the game's origins. "The only thing we remember having told you [in 1941] was that the negro slaves here, while in prison, used to play this game as an entertainment, because of its easy rhythm. This is all we knew at that time and is still all we know now about this music."

Ultimately, apart from a short sequence in the nontheatrical *South of the Border with Disney* illustrating the game, no "Caxangá" film was produced by Disney. Donald's delightfully surreal nightmares in the most fully developed version of the story were reworked for the postwar short *Drip Dippy Donald* (1948), in which the Duck, trying to sleep, is plagued by a dripping faucet. *Caxangá* itself was forgotten until, like *The Laughing Gaucho*, it was "reconstructed" in 1995 for the *Saludos Amigos/Three Caballeros* laser disc set. Here, more than fifty years after its composition, the Disney "Caxangá" song was finally heard by the public. The original song, "Escravos de Jó," was played in *South of the Border with Disney* and was also used to underscore the live-action Carnaval scenes in *Saludos Amigos*. And one other vestige of this unfinished film survived in *Aquarela do Brasil*: Joe Carioca, sitting in the café, begins the reprise of Barroso's eponymous samba by tapping out the rhythm on a matchbox.[60]

[60] Daniella Thompson points out that the "matchbox" percussion represented in this scene is unrelated to the game of caxangá. It's more a reflection of 1940s society, when smoking was more common and matchboxes, readily available, were often pressed into service as impromptu percussion instruments. Today professional Brazilian musicians use metal "matchboxes" for the same purpose. Thompson also points out that, even though the word *caxangá* is used in the song, the game itself (especially in more recent times) is more apt to be known as "Escravos de Jó."

THE NEAR-SIGHTED OVEN BIRD

Another discovery of the 1941 South American tour was the Argentine *hornero*, a bird so named because of its unusual nest, constructed of mud and resembling the much larger clay *horno*, or oven. Early in 1942 Bill Cottrell and Homer Brightman began work on a story, "The Hornero Bird," based on this creature. Their story is framed as a romance in which the bird meets his mate, falls in love, and builds a home for his new family; this cannily allows for extensive nest-building scenes. The hero of the story is nearsighted, and in the climactic scene, while flying home, he mistakes a wineskin for his nest. His beak hopelessly jammed in the wineskin, the bird is at first unable to dislodge it, and eventually returns home roaring drunk. This story entered production in April 1942 under the direction of Ham Luske, and soon afterward was retitled *The Near-Sighted Oven Bird*. Sterling Holloway, whose unmistakable voice had been heard speaking for the Stork in *Dumbo*, was brought to the studio in June to record the narration, some of which survives today. Before animation could begin, this film too was scrapped.

Like *Caxangá*, however, the *hornero* idea persisted. Abandoned in mid-1942, the story was revived in November 1943. The following month it was announced that *The Near-Sighted Oven Bird* would take the place of *The Flying Gauchito* as a segment in the studio's second Good Neighbor feature. But this idea lasted only a couple of weeks; in January 1944 *The Flying Gauchito* was reinstated in the forthcoming feature. *The Near-Sighted Oven Bird* reverted to the status of a short and, in the end, was never produced at all. Perhaps as a consolation for the loss of his starring role, the *hornero* was granted three "guest" appearances in *The Flying Gauchito*.[61] And we've already seen that his distinctive nest can be glimpsed in some of the backgrounds of *El Gaucho Goofy*.

[61] Apparently there *was* a deliberate connection. While production of *The Flying Gauchito* was more or less complete in 1942, the exposure sheets indicate that the *hornero*'s close-up at the beginning of that film was substantially revised and retaken in January 1944, shortly after *The Near-Sighted Oven Bird* was dropped from the feature.

THE ANTEATER

Also known as *Pluto and the Anteater*, this story combined a distinctive South American animal with a familiar Disney story premise: Pluto's encounter with a strange animal. This device had been used successfully in several prewar shorts: *Mickey's Kangaroo* (1935), *Mickey's Elephant* (1936), *Mickey's Parrot* (1938). The studio's increasingly accomplished character animators had tested their skills in these shorts, relying on pantomime to express Pluto's cumbersome thought processes when confronted for the first time with a creature possessing some odd physical characteristic.

Here the odd creature was the anteater, and surviving story sketches indicate that the artists took varying approaches to the character. Slender in some sketches, tubby in others, sometimes adorned with a little goatee, the anteater's main physical characteristics are a large, bushy tail and, of course, his snout. His personality leans toward laziness and conceit, and he is seen happily demolishing whole communities of ants with careless aplomb. Other drawings depict his whimsical antics, such as hanging upside down from a vine by his legs and propelling himself along by blowing air through his ample snout. Just how Pluto was to get into this creature's domain posed a problem; one sequence of drawings simply has him wandering unannounced into the picture, sniffing the ground. The surprised narrator says, "Pluto! What are you doing here?" and orders him home. In an out-of-scale aerial view, Pluto plows straight through the Brazilian jungle, across the Gulf of Mexico, and back to the United States, where he hides behind the Rockies. But soon he reappears, ready to continue his losing encounter with the unflappable anteater.

This story may have been dropped because of its similarities to other Disney pictures. The gags built around the anteater's snout clearly recall the elephant's trunk in *Mickey's Elephant*, and in one group of sketches the anteater blows a series of bizarre bubbles like those in the "Pink Elephants" sequence in *Dumbo*. Most importantly, the studio had already started production on another Pluto-versus-strange-animal short that we'll examine presently: *Pluto and the Armadillo*.

The story artists tried a variety of approaches to the anteater.

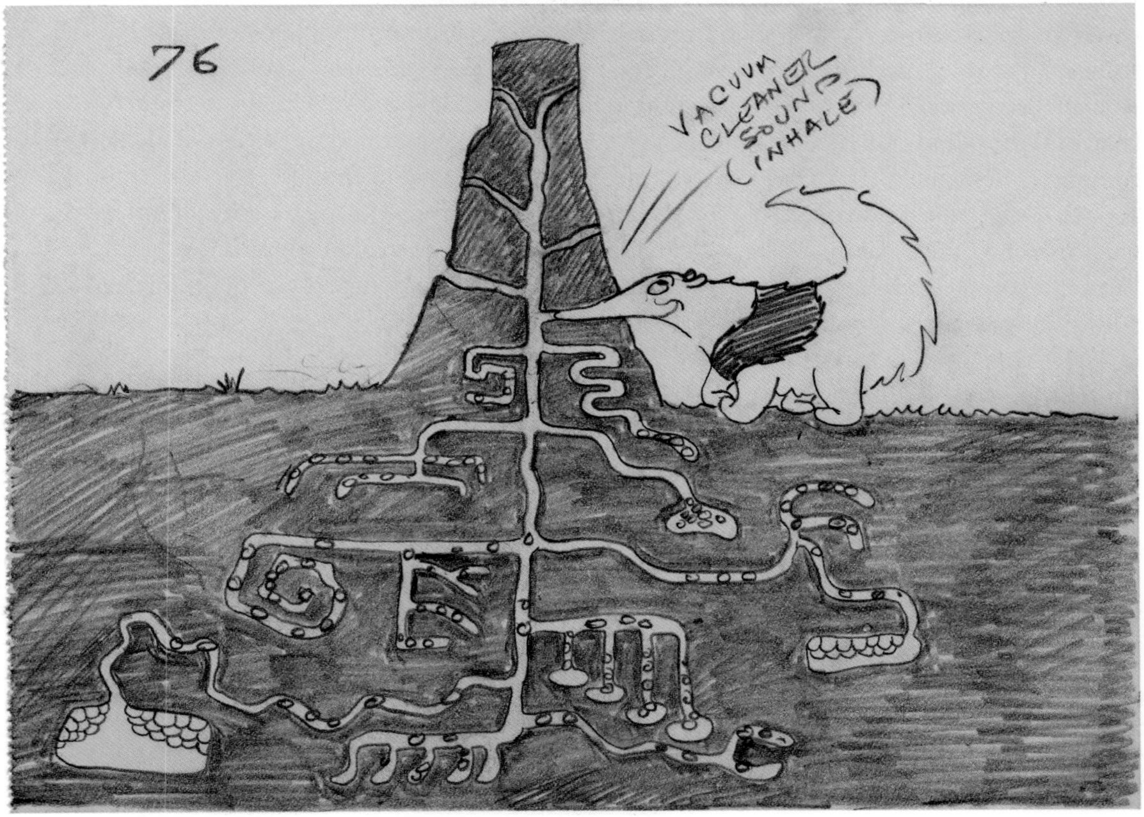

THE LADY WITH THE RED POMPOM

This title, which appeared on a list of tentative story ideas, was described as "based on Street Peddler's song" and may have been inspired by the peddlers who had so impressed Frank Thomas in Rio, singing songs about their wares and services. In April 1942 Jack Miller prepared a storyboard that, viewed today, is of interest mainly for its introduction of the zany, raucous Aracuan. This marks perhaps the earliest appearance of that character, who would make his explosive screen debut two years later in *The Three Caballeros*. Miller's sketches depict the Aracuan's pursuit of the lady of the title, whom he finds washing her clothes at a fountain, and his rivalry with three street peddlers—played by Joe Carioca, an unnamed toucan, and Donald Duck—who also come to court the lady. Later the "Red Pompom" song was also pitched in connection with the "Carnaval" story idea (*see* below). Apart from the storyboards, nothing came of these ideas.

A toucan character, who never appeared in any of the finished films, meets an early version of the Aracuan.

LA LOCA MARIPOSA

One of the great difficulties of the Good Neighbor program was a jealous rivalry among the Latin American republics; any special Disney attention shown to one country was apt to trigger resentment from another. In August 1942 Robert Bottome, of the Asociación Norteamericana de Venezuela, wrote to Nelson Rockefeller to warn of a potential public relations backlash in Venezuela, a country that El Grupo had not visited during their 1941 tour. The planned opening of *Saludos Amigos* in Venezuela, Bottome wrote, "might have just the opposite effect to that sought if the pictures are opened here with too much fanfare." On the other hand, a gala opening of *Saludos* might be a great success "if we could announce publicly at the same time, that Disney was going to do something similar on Venezuela, or even if we could say he was *thinking* of doing something on Venezuela."

To that end Bottome enclosed a story outline titled *Orquideas azules* ("The Blue Orchid"), based on a recent musical stage production that was itself based on Venezuelan folklore. The story told of the efforts of the animals and spirits of the jungle to repel an invasion by Man. Banding together, the spirits thwarted the invasion of their jungle by capturing a woman in the party and transforming her into a lovely blue orchid. This Bottome proposed as a possible basis for a Disney picture.

Rockefeller forwarded the material to Walt, who responded warmly: "I have read the synopsis of *The Blue Orchid* which I have found to be very fascinating. I would like to know more about this subject and would also appreciate information concerning the music of Venezuela, with the thought in mind of possibly including it in one of the forthcoming features on South America." But not all stories are ideally suited to animation, and although this story did prompt some story sketches, there's no evidence that the studio seriously considered a production of *The Blue Orchid*.

In these story sketches the *loca mariposa* confounds Donald with its transformations.

Instead, another Venezuelan story was tentatively started: "La loca mariposa." Intended for direction by Wilfred Jackson, this short was to depict Donald Duck as an entomologist hunting a *loca mariposa*, a crazy butterfly, to add to his collection. The story drawings indicate that the film was to begin with a straightforward exposition establishing the Venezuelan setting, with a map illustrating the Orinoco River, before launching into a whimsical sequence depicting fanciful butterfly life of the region: timeflies (which spread their wings to reveal clocks), eggflies (whose spread wings look like pairs of fried eggs),[62] and so on. The *loca mariposa* itself is drawn with segmented wings that can function as arms and legs and can also transform into an endless succession of other objects: at one point the creature allows itself to be caught in Donald's net, then changes its wings into a large pair of scissors and cuts itself free. In another sequence the butterfly discovers a picture of itself in Donald's book and is much taken with it, preening and posing for itself. Still other drawings depict the butterfly leading Donald into the clutches of a giant duck-eating plant that traps Donald in its tentacles, then toys with him and spanks him, all of which the butterfly finds hilarious. In the end the butterfly leads Donald into his own trap, and the picture ends with a large display of Donald Duck, captured by *la loca mariposa*.

This story was abandoned in June 1944. Again, it may simply have been dropped because of its similarity to another Donald-hunting-exotic-creatures short: *Contrary Condor*, completed and released earlier in the year.

[62] One caption proposed an in-joke: combining the eggs with Ham Luske.

FIESTA OF THE FLOWERS

One of the most curious of the unfinished Good Neighbor shorts came late in the cycle, in 1946, by which time the studio's Latin American initiative encompassed Mexico as well as South America. This short was to be based on the song "La feria de las flores," by Jesus "Chucho" Monge,[63] and was tentatively identified as "Flower Festival" or "The Flower Song" before being officially titled *Fiesta of the Flowers*. The plot is exceedingly simple: a dashing caballero rides to the Fiesta of the Flowers, finds and claims his fair lady, and rides away with her. What sets the story apart is its botanical cast: all the characters are loosely constructed of flowers. The short was to begin with slowly falling blossoms that gradually assume the form of a horse and its rider, which suddenly come to life and begin the action of the story. The caballero's trusty guns are a pair of elongated lilies, and his lady love is "the fairest rose" at the fiesta. Bob Cormack, whose previous Disney credits included art direction of the *Nutcracker Suite* segment of *Fantasia* (also with a cast composed largely of plant life), was assigned the direction of this potentially charming short.

The surprising thing about *Fiesta of the Flowers* was that it came so near completion before being abandoned. At least part of the sound track was recorded, and all the rough pencil animation completed, before the idea was dropped. Master animator Les Clark was initially assigned almost all of the action, but a succession of later memos reassigned many of his scenes to Paul Allen, Tom Massey, Jack Campbell, Marvin Woodward and, in one instance, Art Babbitt.[64] Animation took place mainly between October 1946 and early January 1947—but by mid-January *Fiesta of the Flowers* had been scrapped, perhaps partly because the Good Neighbor program was itself a thing of the past by that time.

[63] The studio had tentatively acquired rights to this number during production of *The Three Caballeros*. The *Caballeros* cue sheet, dated 1 December 1944, indicates an 18-second snippet of "La feria de las flores" at the end of "You Belong to My Heart" in the eighth reel. In fact, however, the final cut of the film differs from this description, and the last section of "You Belong to My Heart" bridges directly into "La Zandunga."

[64] Babbitt, of course, had been a key figure in the 1941 strike, and his brief reappearance at the Disney studio in the mid-1940s was merely a formality mandated by the National Labor Relations Board. His work on *Fiesta of the Flowers* was quite likely his last animation for Disney. John Canemaker points out that Babbitt was well suited to this assignment, having excelled in animating the mushrooms and thistles in the *Nutcracker Suite*.

THE SAN BLAS BOY

Another late entry in the Good Neighbor story campaign was this story by Del Connell about a little boy named Chico living in the San Blas Islands off the coast of Panama. In Connell's original outline, Chico disregards his mother's instructions and strays from his familiar fishing waters, gets lost, and makes his way back home by sailing his little *cayuca* through the Panama Canal. Later outlines, submitted in April and June 1946, augment this plot with an action episode: Chico's discovery of a giant swordfish and his attempts to escape from it, and capture it, during a frantic chase. After El Grupo's own trip through the Panama Canal in 1941, a picture featuring that location would have been a fitting Disney subject. But even apart from its late development, *The San Blas Boy* had other factors working against it. The addition of the swordfish and other business made the original, rather plain story much more cinematic, but as the plot became more exciting it also lost much of its original geographic and cultural focus—the reason for undertaking the project in the first place. In any case, the idea never progressed beyond the story-sketch stage.

Other unfinished Disney Latin American pictures included:

Llama Story. The llamas observed by the Blair party in Bolivia and Peru had suggested cartoon possibilities, and a llama character seemed destined to star in a film of its own until, as we've seen, it became a supporting player in *Lake Titicaca*. Later, Webb Smith, who had not been a member of the Blair party, worked on a story called "Chapito," which featured a llama and a little Indian boy. It was never completed.

Ostrich Story. The gawky, gangly *avestruz*, or Argentine ostrich, likewise seemed a born cartoon character, and several story ideas were suggested for him. Ted Sears was particularly keen on the character, and one of the gaucho stories he proposed prior to the 1941 tour was "The Ostrich Who Laid the Golden Egg." In March 1942, after the story for *El Gaucho Goofy* was well established, a separate story number was issued for "Ostrich Story," and Sears worked with Webb Smith and Herb Ryman on a short that would have featured both the ostrich and some *horneros*. Still later, the *avestruz* was tentatively slated for a brief appearance in *The Three Caballeros*. Ultimately none of these ideas came to fruition, and the character's supporting role in *El Gaucho Goofy* remained his one appearance for Disney.

Donald, Joe, and a lady friend enjoy a riot of color in a *Carnaval* story sketch.

Carnaval (or Carnaval Carioca). The vague idea of building a film around the Carnaval in Rio had preceded the 1941 tour, and took various forms afterward. Bill Cottrell proposed several variations on the theme, suggesting more than once that a "Carnival" film might be made along the lines of the 1935 Silly Symphony *Water Babies*. Because of the nebulous nature of the idea, elements of it cropped up in *Aquarela do Brasil*, *Caxangá*, and other Brazilian pictures, produced and unproduced. Surviving watercolor story sketches suggest an extended version of *Aquarela do Brasil*: Donald and Joe Carioca, resplendent in top hats and tails, enjoying the exotic night life of Rio. Donald, in the general hilarity, gets wrapped up in streamers, but mostly he appears dancing with a girl (similar to Aurora, in *Caxangá*, or the Lady with the Red Pompom) as in the earlier film. By late 1943 the studio had moved beyond these basic ideas but was considering an entirely new picture based on Carnival in various countries, Brazil among them. This idea would itself continue to evolve in other forms.

Chichicastenango. The Blair party had been vividly impressed by their experiences in Central America, and in 1942 Mary Blair made numerous sketches for a proposed film set in Chichicastenango. It never progressed beyond the story stage.

South American Horse Story. In 1939 the studio had bought the screen rights to Helen Kirby's recently published story *Martingale*, built around the career of a purebred filly. After the 1941 tour Ted Sears toyed with the idea of adapting the plot to a Chilean or Argentine locale, perhaps because of the importance of horses in those countries. The book "is a burlesque on society," Sears explained, adding that "we do not intend to follow the published story closely." The project acquired the generic working title "South American Horse Story." By February 1943 it had been discarded.

From the Disney studio's flourishing creative atmosphere in the wake of the South American trip, along with the ideas that became components of features and those that were scrapped altogether, several ideas emerged that were produced and released as short subjects.

PLUTO AND THE ARMADILLO

Along with the Bolivian llama, the Argentine *avestruz*, and the Brazilian *papagaio*, the Brazilian armadillo—with its peculiar armor-plated appearance and its habit of rolling itself into a ball when alarmed—had struck the Disney artists as a creature with distinct cartoon possibilities. Within a few weeks after El Grupo's return from South America, Norm Ferguson had assigned writer Harry Reeves to develop a story about Pluto's encounter with an armadillo. This idea, like the prewar cartoons mentioned earlier, followed a proven formula: the comedy would arise from Pluto's bewilderment at encountering an odd creature outside his experience. Story development proceeded smoothly, and by January 1942 *Pluto and the Armadillo* was ready for production. Clyde (Gerry) Geronimi, who had recently assumed direction of the Pluto series, was assigned to direct.

A handsome background painting from *Pluto and the Armadillo*. Note that the plane is part of the Pan American fleet.

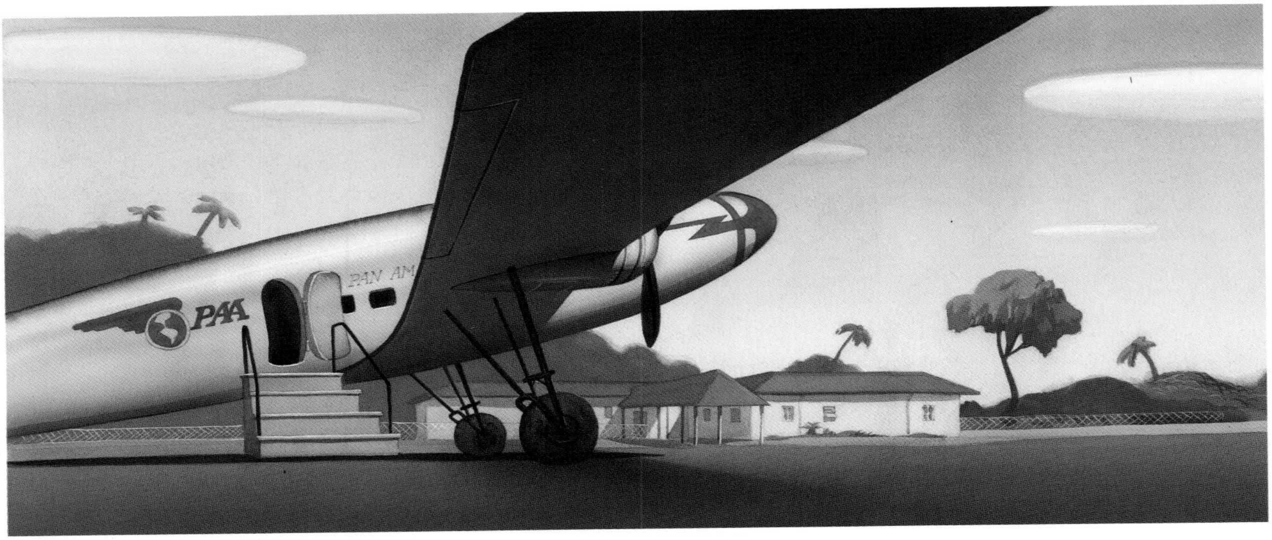

The meeting of the two title characters in *Pluto and the Armadillo*.

The story was simple enough: Mickey Mouse and Pluto, traveling by plane, make a brief stopover in Belém—just as Walt and his party had done in August 1941—and get out of the plane to stretch their legs. Pluto chases his ball into the jungle, and a nearby armadillo, alarmed at the intrusion, rolls itself into a ball. Pluto confuses the armadillo with his toy, and the resulting conflict and chase are resolved by film's end in a spirit of friendship. Charles "Nick" Nichols, who would soon take over the direction of the Pluto series himself, animated the bulk of the action, but key scenes were also taken by John Lounsbery and by Les Clark, who animated the armadillo's introductory scene. Although the cartoon was produced by Geronimi's regular Pluto unit, it benefited from the input of some of the South American Unit's principals: Lee and Mary Blair worked with layout artist Charles Philippi to key the Brazilian backgrounds, and Fred Shields, who had narrated *Saludos Amigos*, provided the narration.

Pluto and the Armadillo was absorbed into the Pluto series and was released in February 1943, shortly after the North American opening of *Saludos Amigos*. In its finished form this is an undeniably slight film, and has such a vague South American atmosphere that it could easily have been produced without any on-the-spot research. It has, however, at least one notable distinction: of all the Disney Latin American pictures, this is the only one featuring appearances by Pluto, Norm Ferguson's signature character, or Mickey Mouse, the studio figurehead.[64] Paul J. Smith composed the score, built principally around "The Armadillo Samba," a catchy instrumental theme for the armadillo. This was later published with both English and Spanish (!) lyrics.

[64] The two characters do make a *non*-featured appearance—one, in fact, "hidden" from all but the most alert viewer—in *The Three Caballeros*, as we shall see presently. And, as we'll also see, Mickey made a special appearance in connection with the studio's nontheatrical films; but this cameo was withdrawn almost immediately, and apparently does not survive today.

THE PELICAN AND THE SNIPE

One of the stories suggested as a "Pan-American Symphony" concerns a pelican living on top of a lighthouse. Bill Cottrell took a special interest in this idea after returning from South America. As he developed the story, it came to reflect both the Good Neighbor mission and the war: the lighthouse is located near a naval air base, and the pelican, prone to flying in his sleep, is in constant danger from the planes that practice air maneuvers and bombing runs every night. It is the pelican's friend, an unappreciated snipe, who stays awake every night and steers his companion out of danger. At the climax, caught in a narrow brush with disaster, the pelican finally comes to realize the sacrifices his friend has made for him. In early treatments the characters were given alliterative names: the pelican was first dubbed Percy (or Percival), then later renamed Pablo. The snipe was tentatively known as Sidney.

One advantage of this story was that, like *Pedro*, it was adaptable; it could be set in any country that had a seacoast. And, like *Pedro*, it was originally set in Chile; an early memo proposed a setting off the coast of either Viña del Mar or Valparaíso.[65] In

[65] El Grupo had, of course, visited both of those cities less than three months before.

The Pelican and the Snipe: a temporary rift between the two friends.

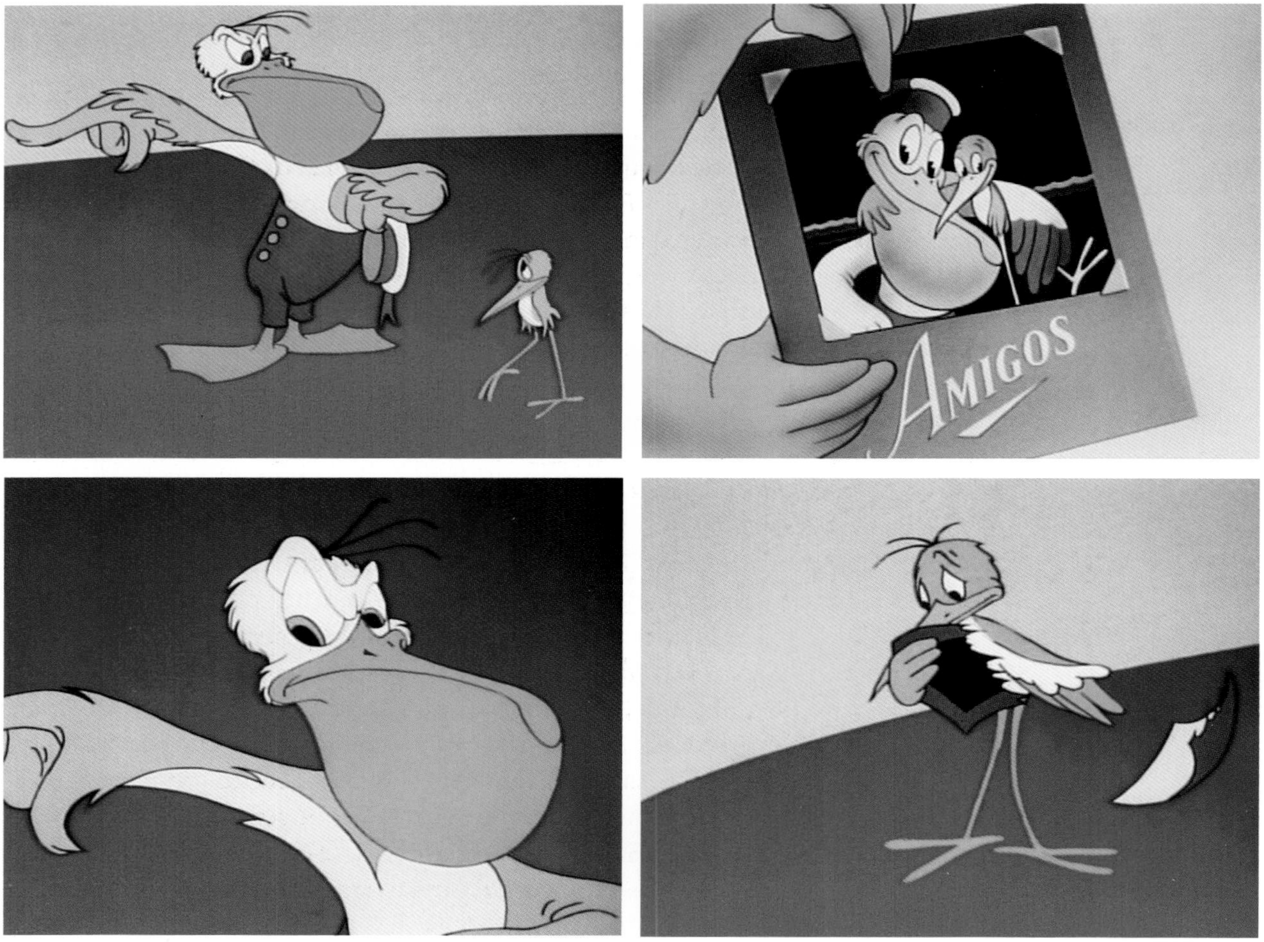

January 1942 the locale was changed to Uruguay, a country that had given Walt a rousing reception during the tour but had not yet been addressed in any of the studio's films. An elaborate nineteen-page script was prepared, illustrating each scene with tiny thumbnail sketches at the side of the page. This script reverses the climax of the earlier outline: instead of simply being rescued one more time, the pelican realizes his mistake just in time to save the *snipe* from danger. This is similar to the story that appears in the finished film, although the characters in the script are still named Pablo and Sidney. (Another departure appears as the story races toward its climactic moment: the pelican breaks character, faces the camera, and comments: "Exciting, isn't it?" This kind of self-reflexive gag would have been suited to a Tex Avery cartoon, but it was out of character for a Disney film and was not used in this one.)

In February 1942 the pelican and the snipe were renamed, respectively, Monte and Video, and the story assumed its final form. The film entered production under the title "Down Uruguay Way" but was retitled *The Pelican and the Snipe* six weeks later. As Cottrell's pet project, it was treated as a top-drawer production: directed by Ham Luske (who was currently well on the way to completion of *Pedro*) and animated by Ollie Johnston, Ward Kimball, and Luske himself.

And then, for reasons unknown, *The Pelican and the Snipe* was shelved for nearly a year. It next appears in Disney production documents in February 1943. By this time, with the experience of *Saludos Amigos* behind them, the studio was approaching the Good Neighbor project with further package features in mind, and a clear distinction was being drawn between the segments in those features and the films that were to be released separately as shorts. *The Pelican and the Snipe* was now designated as a short and, like *Pluto and the Armadillo*, somehow seemed to shift away from the core of the studio's Good Neighbor activities, losing much of its South American identification and becoming more generic. These shorts were designed primarily with all-around entertainment in mind, and any Latin American flavor became incidental. Even the production personnel were subject to change: a *Pelican* production memo observed that "It is not absolutely necessary that Chuck Wolcott write the music for this short. However, whatever musician picks up should check with Wolcott." And, in fact, the *Pelican* score was composed not by Wolcott, the studio's resident South American music specialist, but by Ollie Wallace.[66]

Completed late in 1943, *The Pelican and the Snipe* was released in January 1944.

It's worth mentioning, in connection with this short, another unfinished project known provisionally as "Pelican, Snipe and Octopus Story." This story was separate from *The Pelican and the Snipe*, perhaps intended as a sequel; a story number was issued in March 1942, after production had already started on *The Pelican and the Snipe*. The new story was assigned to Disney story veteran Roy Williams. No documentation of this project is known to survive, and Norm Ferguson noted in February 1943 that it had been discarded, its story material absorbed into *The Pelican and the Snipe*.

66 This is not meant to imply that Wallace was an inferior composer, only to make the point that he was not central to the studio's Good Neighbor project. Wallace was a distinguished composer in his own right, had recently written the hit song "Der Fuehrer's Face" for the film of the same title, and had earned an Academy Award with his music for *Dumbo*.

CONTRARY CONDOR

Perhaps the least likely of all the studio's Latin American productions, this short seems to have had nothing whatever to do with the Disney Good Neighbor project. Few of the artists or other creative personnel assigned to it were involved with the other Good Neighbor films; it was simply produced as one of the regular Donald Duck series by Jack King's Duck unit. Yet *Contrary Condor* (or one of the film's three other working titles) appears in correspondence between the studio and the CIAA as one of the studio's Latin American pictures. It's just possible that the story was based very loosely on the condor hunt that Jim Bodrero, Frank Thomas, and Larry Lansburgh had witnessed in Argentina in September 1941, but that seems highly unlikely. Evidence suggests, instead, that the similarity was strictly a coincidence, that someone at the studio simply noticed this short's South American setting and, as an afterthought, volunteered it to help satisfy the studio's commitment to the CIAA. (The working title "The Colombian Condor"—of the film's four titles, the one with the most conspicuously Latin American flavor—was assigned in June 1943, four months after the start of production.)

The story for *Pluto and the Armadillo* had grown out of the artists' observation of armadillos in Brazil. The condor story, instead, originated as most short-subject stories did, with the director's story crew.[67] The film does open by establishing its Colombian setting, and proceeds with mysterious footprints climbing the Andes. But when the Duck makes his first appearance, he's yodeling and wearing a vaguely Tyrolean outfit—an introduction reminiscent of the opening sequence of *Alpine Climbers* (1936), suggesting a European setting more than a South American one. This intrepid explorer is not hunting condors; he merely wants a condor egg for his egg collection (another echo of *Alpine Climbers*, and perhaps an influence on the unfinished *La loca mariposa*). The mother condor returns and catches him raiding her nest, so Donald pretends to be one of her newly hatched chicks. The rest of the short consists of the Duck's efforts to keep up his deception, to fend off the attacks of the real condor chick, who is his jealous "sibling," and to escape.

Studio records suggest that this picture was produced without incident; the most troubling aspect of the film seems to have been selecting a title. The final title, *Contrary Condor*, was assigned one month before the film's release in April 1944.

A background painting suggesting the lofty locale of *Contrary Condor*.

[67] Two Production Management memos suggest that Carl Barks, still on the threshold of his legendary comic-book career, worked on the story for this short. Barks *had* been a member of King's story crew, but Michael Barrier, who has documented Barks's career, points out that Barks had left the studio on 6 November 1942, the Friday before the first of these memos was issued. Barks may have contributed to the *Contrary Condor* story, but it's far more likely that the Production Management office simply continued to record his name as part of King's unit out of habit. In any case, Barks's own records of his story work for the studio make no mention of this short. Harry Reeves, the other writer mentioned in the memos, remained at the studio and probably did work on *Contrary Condor*.

CLOWN OF THE JUNGLE

As we'll see in chapter 5, the studio's second Good Neighbor feature, *The Three Caballeros*, introduced yet another Brazilian bird: the Aracuan. In line with the 1940s cartoon trend toward wild, zany characters, the Disney Aracuan was uncontrollably crazy, zipping around at high speed as he defied the laws of logic and nature. After *The Three Caballeros*, the character made return appearances in two later Disney films, *Blame It on the Samba* and this short. *Clown of the Jungle* can be considered a by-product of the Good Neighbor project, returning one of its distinctive characters to the screen and exploiting his inherent entertainment value.

Known at first by the working title "Feathered Frenzy," this picture was another entry in the Donald Duck series. This time Donald is seen as a wildlife photographer in the South American jungle, photographing exotic birds—until confounded by the irrepressible, madcap antics of the Aracuan. Director Jack Hannah takes advantage of the jungle setting of his earlier Duck picture, *Frank Duck Brings 'Em Back Alive* (1946), reusing some of the layouts and backgrounds from that picture. The animators include several of the artists who had worked on the bona fide Good Neighbor films—Bill Justice, Josh Meador, Hal King—and the Aracuan's first appearance, abruptly bursting into the lush jungle landscape, recycles animation from *The Three Caballeros*.

Clown of the Jungle remains a fast-paced and entertaining short, and little more. It's essentially a Daffy Duck–Porky Pig cartoon, with Donald in the role of the hapless victim.[68] Like *Contrary Condor*, the film is marginal to the Good Neighbor project. Meanwhile, even as these theatrical films—Disney's stock-in-trade—were being produced, more explicitly Latin American–themed activities were leading the studio into new and unexplored territory.

[68] Strictly speaking, it could be seen as a loose remake of *Donald's Camera* (1941), which in turn bears a certain resemblance to the earlier Warner Bros. short *Elmer's Candid Camera* (1940). Later, in Disney's *Hold That Pose* (1950), Goofy would take his turn as a "wildlife" photographer (in a zoo).

Donald pursues his losing battle with the Aracuan in *Clown of the Jungle*.

STUDIO EQUIPMENT CO

4 FILMS FOR THE AMERICAS

Walt Disney was not a total stranger to nontheatrical filmmaking in 1941, but it was an unfamiliar arena for him. Even the Disney productions that had fallen outside the studio's regular cartoon series—such as *Mickey's Surprise Party*, produced for the 1939 World's Fair—had usually been presented in a theatrical setting. With the onset of World War II, that situation changed forever. Immediately upon the United States' entry into the war, the Disney studio was contracted to produce a series of Armed Services training films and other war-related pictures. And the Good Neighbor mission—in addition to inspiring *Saludos Amigos* and other theatrical productions—led the studio into a program of nontheatrical films, for distribution in 16 mm throughout the Americas, that was far more extensive than anyone could have foreseen.

SOUTH OF THE BORDER WITH DISNEY

When El Grupo returned to New York from South America in October 1941, Walt lost no time in tackling many different activities at once. One of those activities was the 16 mm documentary on the South American tour that he had agreed to produce for the CIAA. Before returning to California, he met with Kenneth Macgowan in New York to discuss the project. Macgowan seems to have had an exceedingly modest vision of the film. Two months earlier he had issued a call for 16 mm film of Latin American countries, "taken by stars, directors, writers and others," and promised: "All footage borrowed will be returned promptly after [Macgowan's] organization edits and runs off prints." Clearly Macgowan had nothing more ambitious in mind than simply releasing the raw travel footage through nontheatrical channels. In fact, while El Grupo was still in transit on the *Santa Clara*, John Rose had received a telegram advising him that Francis Alstock was planning to surprise Walt with a special dinner in Washington and to show the 16 mm film there, releasing it soon afterward.

Rose, of course, showed the telegram to Walt immediately, and immediately Walt vetoed both the dinner and the quick release of the 16 mm pictures. The idea of a documentary had caught his enthusiasm, and he had something very different in mind. After discussing his concept with Macgowan, he flew back to Burbank and started work on a four-reel film that would have the full production polish of any of his theatrical releases. As Rose articulated it, "What we have in mind is a production worthy of release under the Disney name, and a radical departure from the usual type of travelogue." The documentary would not be completed until a full year later, several months after the completion of *Saludos Amigos*.

The first order of business was to screen, organize, and catalogue all the 16 mm film shot in South America. This in itself was a major undertaking. "I had never shot a camera before," said Larry Lansburgh, one of the three principal 16 mm cameramen on the tour, "and Walt gave me this camera and said, 'Shoot, I want to get everything, I want to see everything.' And he said, 'Get closeups, go in there and get closeups.'

OPPOSITE: Walt lines up a 16 mm shot on the studio sound stage.

And so, wherever we were, I got closeups of the gauchos' hands braiding the rope, I got a closeup of the ostrich feet running. And when we came back we went into the projection room and we ran all the footage I had done. And he said, 'Larry, you have to have establishing shots. You have to know where you are!' And that's when I realized, in editing, you move into the closeup after you establish. It was a great lesson to me, in editing."

Even with the hours of footage the group had brought back, important parts of the story were missing. In particular, there was a major gap in the group's Brazilian coverage. Before leaving Brazil, Lansburgh had turned over thirty-two magazines of exposed Kodachrome to the Eastman Kodak representative in Rio, with explicit instructions to send the film to Hollywood for processing. Instead the film had been sent to Kodak's home office in Rochester, New York. Then, after processing it, Kodak had inexplicably tried to ship it back to Rio—on a plane that crashed in San Juan Harbor, Puerto Rico, en route to Brazil. All of the plane's cargo, including the Disney film, was lost. "Such scenes as Walt greeting the President of Brazil and other distinguished personalities in Rio which were included in the lost footage could never be duplicated," Rose lamented. "Other scenes, such as the Survey group of some 15 Disney artists sketching and sight-seeing in various situations around Rio, could not be duplicated unless we incurred the expense of sending the whole gang down on location again."[69]

Kodak, mortified at its mistake, offered to replace the missing footage with generic travel scenes of Rio de Janeiro. The Disney studio did use not only this outside footage but more of the same from other sources. Lacking general-interest views of Buenos Aires, the studio obtained some from the travelogue *By Air to Argentina*, produced by Moore-McCormack Steamship Lines. Similar shots of Montevideo were borrowed from the National Geographic Society's documentary *Buenos Aires and Montevideo*. Both Moore-McCormack and National Geographic were acknowledged in the opening titles of the finished film, in gratitude for this help.

Then there were the scenes staged by the Disney crew in Burbank. We've already noted the scenes representing F. Molina Campos's Argentine studio, and the miscellaneous shots of sketching artists, faked in Burbank for *Saludos Amigos*. That was only the beginning; some of the same shots and many more like them were used in the 16 mm picture. Ultimately, only a part of the film we know as *South of the Border with Disney* was actually filmed *by* the Disney group *in* South America. The new pickup shots ranged from odd individual reaction shots to elaborately constructed sequences. At a series of story meetings and sweatbox sessions, fine-tuning the continuity of this film as carefully as that of a theatrical short, Walt devised and directed these fictitious sequences. One concerned a hotel "studio" in Rio de Janeiro, similar to the one that had actually existed in Buenos Aires. "Have the studio in Rio," Walt commented at one meeting, "no one knows whether we had one or not." The "studio" was actually a set constructed on Disney's live-action stage. Re-dressed, the same set became Molina Campos's studio for the scenes representing Argentina.

[69] Actually Walt's meeting with Presidente Vargas was also documented in the *Cine jornal Brasileiro* newsreel, albeit in black and white.

Filming the horse gag for *South of the Border with Disney*. Roy Williams as the customs officer, with Norm Ferguson, Mary Blair, Walt, and an unidentified extra.

South of the Border is thus roughly analogous to the Disney feature *The Reluctant Dragon* (1941), which had offered a part real, part fanciful tour through the Disney studio. Genuine Disney artists appear on-screen in *The Reluctant Dragon*, alongside Frances Gifford, Alan Ladd, and other Hollywood actors *cast* as Disney employees. If this fakery violates our concept of documentary truth today, it's important to remember that an entirely different "documentary" aesthetic existed in the film business in 1941. In producing "manipulated" versions of the truth in these films, Walt was simply building on the practice of the great documentary filmmakers, from Robert Flaherty to Merian C. Cooper and Ernest Schoedsack, who had not hesitated to include staged or faked scenes in their classic films. Moreover, Walt was an instinctive showman and made no bones about it. *The Reluctant Dragon* was intended primarily for entertainment, not for documentary realism. And *South of the Border* does offer authentic scenes of El Grupo's 1941 tour—enclosed in an entertaining package.

As if to call attention to his role as a showman, Walt staged several outright comedy scenes in order to enhance the film's entertainment value. One of these depicted Norm Ferguson drawing pictures of his signature character, Pluto, for a group of eager children. As the requests multiply and he tries to keep up with the demand, Ferguson appears more and more exhausted—and so does Pluto. Another openly staged sequence was the ending, with Roy Williams cast as a harried U.S. customs officer, exasperatedly digging through the piles of artwork and South American souvenirs brought back by the travelers.[70] As he removes Walt's gaucho saddle and numerous accessories from one bag, Williams complains: "You might as well have brought the horse!" Instantly, thanks to a breakaway suitcase and a carefully staged camera angle, a real horse's head, wild-eyed, seems to emerge from the same suitcase.

[70] Williams, at this time a ten-year veteran of the studio, could be cast in this role because he was not yet a familiar face to viewers—as he would become in later years through his television appearances as "The Big Mooseketeer" on the *Mickey Mouse Club*.

A third comedy sequence, filmed but not included in the finished picture, was "the umbrella gag." At one meeting Walt had suggested a sequence that would depict, in humorous terms, the group's difficulties with the language barrier, perhaps showing them trying to order food in a restaurant. "Maybe one of the guys wants a steak with mushrooms—The waiter speaks three languages but unfortunately he does not know English—we go through the whole thing and finally the guy draws a picture [of a mushroom]—the waiter smiles and goes off and we say something about 'a picture is often worth a thousand words'—Then here comes the waiter—we just see him standing with a big smile on his face and there you see what he brought—it's an umbrella!" This scene was filmed with Lee Blair, Jack Miller, and Herb Ryman as the hapless customers and Dan MacManus as the waiter. Although it was omitted from *South of the Border with Disney*, the gag continued to circulate within the studio and finally surfaced in written publicity. We find it in, of all places, the *Time* magazine review of *Saludos Amigos*, recast with Chuck Wolcott and exactly reversed. According to this version, Wolcott "tried to explain to an Argentine innkeeper that he wanted to borrow an umbrella by drawing one. The innkeeper nodded, soon returned with a broiled steak and mushrooms."

Early in 1942 the staff sifted through the 16 mm footage of the tour, selecting the best shots to be used in the documentary. The selection process was more or less complete when, in mid-spring, the decision was made to combine the first four theatrical shorts into *Saludos Amigos*. Now those "best" 16 mm shots were quickly appropriated to serve as a linking device in the theatrical feature. Some producers might have jumped at the chance to milk the same footage in two different productions, but Walt repeatedly warned against duplicating too much of the *Saludos* material in the documentary. At one meeting he articulated the problem: "The trouble is we selected stuff for the 16 mm, then used it all on the package and now we need to get new material, stuff we discarded before." The staff resumed their review of the raw film, searching for fresh material, with the happy result that much more of El Grupo's travel footage was preserved for posterity. Some shots, such as the Rio sidewalk scenes, appear in both films—but *South of the Border* also gives us such exclusive gems as the children of Colonia presenting Walt with a bouquet, the Chazarreta dance troupe in Buenos Aires, Ferguson's and Ted Sears's encounter with eighty-five-year-old gaucho Don Liborio Sosa in Mendoza, the Blair party braving the winds of Lake Titicaca in a small sailboat, and Market Day (and the young hotel workers' presentation of the Mickey Mouse cake) in Chichicastenango.[71]

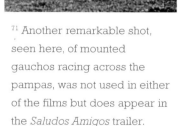

[71] Another remarkable shot, seen here, of mounted gauchos racing across the pampas, was not used in either of the films but does appear in the *Saludos Amigos* trailer.

The studio had agreed to a budget for this four-reel documentary that was roughly equal to the cost of a single one-reel cartoon. Not surprisingly, costs soon became an issue—but here again, creative solutions were found that allowed Walt to save money without compromising the quality of his film. He had pictured a documentary that would include animated sequences, but animation was the single most expensive part of his filmmaking operation. The solution: the documentary would use animated scenes from the theatrical films—not in their finished, inked and painted form, but

as cleaned-up pencil animation. In this form *South of the Border* gives us unusual sidelights on Goofy's snubbing-post gag from *El Gaucho Goofy*, Fred Moore's charming scenes of a dancing Joe Carioca and of Pedro the little airplane "nursing" at a gas pump, Les Clark's introductory scene of the armadillo in *Pluto and the Armadillo*, and other morsels of animation.[72] One sequence, introducing "Caxangá," includes still drawings of Donald Duck's attempt to play the game, made for a film that was never completed.

[72] These were probably originally intended as "previews" of the theatrical films, but most audiences saw the documentary only after the theatrical films had already been released. The exception was a Frank Thomas scene from *The Flying Gauchito*, which was produced concurrently with *South of the Border* but was not released until it became part of *The Three Caballeros* much later.

Musically too the documentary is economically produced but benefits from its family connection to other Disney films. Chuck Wolcott recorded several instrumental arrangements of his *Saludos Amigos* title song for use in the documentary, setting a precedent for the reuse of the song in many of the other nontheatrical films. Another original Wolcott song, "Mexico," was used for instrumental underscoring of the Blair party's Mexican footage, two years before theatrical audiences heard it performed in *The Three Caballeros*. Ed Plumb composed an original *gato* (an upbeat gaucho song-and-dance form celebrating life, dance, and drinking) that was used to accompany the Argentine dancers. And some miscellaneous scenes were tracked with existing music from other Disney films; general-interest shots of Buenos Aires, for example, were underscored with an instrumental passage of Frank Churchill's "I Bring You a Song" from *Bambi*.

Norm Ferguson, Bill Cottrell, Mary Blair, and Jack Cutting perform a round of caxangá for the camera.

In October 1942, a full year after the studio had started working on it, the documentary was essentially complete and was approved for negative cutting. Even then, the film's title remained in doubt. The original working title, "Walt Disney Sees South America," had failed to account for the Central American sequences and had been changed to "Walt Disney Sees Latin America"—which, in turn, was rejected by the CIAA as unsatisfactory and perhaps even offensive. Only in March 1943 was the title officially changed to *South of the Border with Disney*. (The English title, that is; *see* Appendix A for the Spanish and Portuguese titles, which translate as *Through the Lands of America with Walt Disney*.) Early plans had called for Walt himself to narrate the documentary, which would have given it even greater interest. Late in production this idea was dropped, and the film was instead narrated by actor Art Baker, who would also narrate *Victory Through Air Power*.

CIAA officials, having waited for this film far longer than they had expected, were delighted with the end result and happily proceeded to distribute it through their nontheatrical channels. Herb Golden, of the CIAA staff, even tried to interpret the Disney contract as giving the CIAA the right to distribute the film theatrically in 35 mm, a notion the studio was quick to discourage.[73] It's true that, in terms of theatrical production values, *South of the Border with Disney* is hardly in the same class with *Saludos Amigos*—but on its own terms, as an informal record of the 1941 South American tour and immediate post-tour activities, it was and remains an engaging and fascinating document. And it was only the beginning. By the time the CIAA began to distribute *South of the Border with Disney*, many more nontheatrical Good Neighbor films were in production at the Disney studio.

[73] Golden expressed his ambitions in two letters to his West Coast associate Jack Leighter in November 1942. Jack Cutting, perhaps having got wind of the scheme, wrote to the Dunningcolor company—the lab contracted to process the 16 mm prints—warning that no 35 mm prints were to be made "without first securing written permission from the Walt Disney Studio."

Walt himself took the initiative in this venture. *Hollywood Reporter* announced in January 1942 that "Walt Disney has volunteered his personal services to the Jock Whitney motion picture division of the inter-American affairs committee, and will produce special educational and other cartoon subjects for the committee at cost, as well as devote 50 percent of his time without recompense to all phases of inter-American work." Walt's personal sacrifice notwithstanding, this new and unfamiliar direction had two immediate appeals for him: the new CIAA contract would help keep his studio doors open during the financial crisis imposed by the war, and—perhaps equally important in Walt's eyes—it would allow him to work on something new and different. Another purely pragmatic consideration had a bearing on the contract itself: the CIAA had an increasingly strong mandate in the area of educational and health-related activities in Latin America. Nelson Rockefeller, maneuvering to keep his agency afloat in turbulent wartime Washington, had had to concede some activities in order to protect others. As the war effort continued, control over propaganda (or "information") was increasingly seen as the province of other agencies, while the CIAA was not only permitted but encouraged to expand its efforts on behalf of health and educational activities in Latin American countries—what was now known as the agency's Basic Economy division.

Consequently, more financial support was available to Disney for nontheatrical film production than for the theatrical propaganda pictures the studio had originally been contracted to produce. An ambitious new nontheatrical production program emerged at the Disney studio. Staff writer Robert Spencer Carr, assigned to research possible story ideas for the nontheatrical pictures (both for the CIAA and for other agencies), produced a thirty-seven-page document listing his suggestions.

Carr's ideas were divided into categories: "Direct Propaganda," "Indirect Propaganda," and "Training Films." The Direct Propaganda ideas did lead to some Disney productions,[74] but it was the Indirect Propaganda series, principally a series of health- and agriculture-related subjects to be distributed in Latin America, that caught the enthusiasm of both Walt and the Coordinator's staff. After consulting with the CIAA principals for their reaction to individual ideas, Walt again took the initiative: he plunged into production of a series of "sample" films to show what his studio could do in this unaccustomed field.

[74] These ideas focused on direct attacks on Hitler ("Hitler the Anti-Christ" was one title) and on the military might of the United States and its allies. One of the first goals of the CIAA film program had been to counteract Axis propaganda, which alleged that the U.S. and its allies were weak and would fall to Hitler's war machine, with demonstrations of military prowess. The Disney studio did produce a famous series of propaganda cartoons for the CIAA—*Der Fuehrer's Face*, *Education for Death*, *Reason and Emotion*, and *Chicken Little*—but, because of their lack of Latin American orientation, those films are not covered in this book.

THE WINGED SCOURGE

Of the various kinds of nontheatrical films produced by the studio for the CIAA, the series on health care would prove by far the most successful. One of Bob Carr's suggestions along this line had been a series on "Public Enemies": insects that carried diseases. One of these was the mosquito, and in particular the anopheles mosquito, the agent of malaria. Carr proposed a short that would demonstrate techniques for fighting this pest and slowing the spread of malaria. The CIAA responded enthusiastically to this idea, and by the end of February 1942 Walt had assigned "The Mosquito and Malaria" to writer Norm Wright for preliminary work.

In Frank Thomas's original animation, Dopey goes after the "winged scourge" with insecticide.

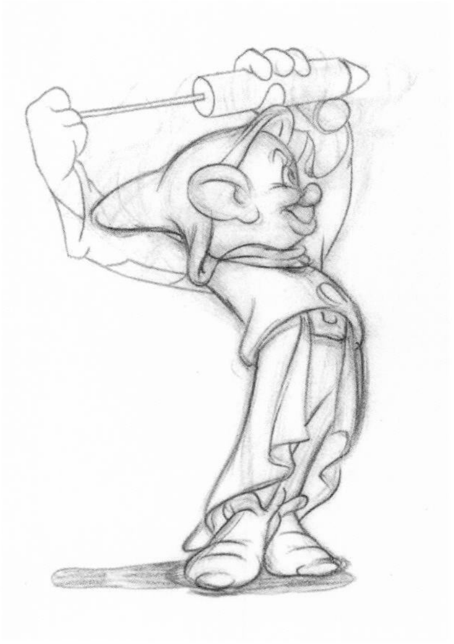

Story development proceeded slowly, because this was a new kind of story work, combining the entertainment expertise of the Disney studio with the propaganda and education aims of the CIAA. The CIAA was, effectively, part of the story team. Formerly a Disney story crew had answered only to the director and Walt himself; now their ideas had to be checked with Washington. To facilitate this process, the CIAA began sending specialists to California to work directly with the Disney story crews. In April 1942 Dr. Edward C. Ernst, acting director of the Pan American Sanitary Bureau, and Assistant U.S. Surgeon General Dr. E. R. Coffey were dispatched to Burbank to lend their assistance on the health-care series. This included "The Mosquito and Malaria" and four other titles under consideration.

For "The Mosquito and Malaria" a two-part structure was devised. The first part would be deadly serious, explaining the devastating effects of malaria and demonstrating, with animated diagrams, the method by which the anopheles mosquito spread the disease. Then the narrator would ask for "six or seven volunteers" from the audience to help fight the mosquitoes—and would be answered by the Seven Dwarfs, from the studio's first feature-length film, *Snow White and the Seven Dwarfs*. The Dwarfs would then demonstrate, in a more lighthearted vein, techniques for combating the mosquitoes. Walt, mindful of his mission, was determined not to let the Dwarfs' scenes overwhelm the film's message. "The only reason to bring in the dwarfs," he warned the story crew, "is to add a little interest; when you begin to get into gags and impossible things, you're not accomplishing the job we're supposed to do—show in a simple way how to get rid of mosquitoes." He stressed that the prevention techniques should be shown simply and directly: "If you make it look like a tremendous job, they'll say, hell, I'll take the mosquitoes."

In June 1942 a group of eleven CIAA shorts, their storyboards approved, moved into production simultaneously. Directors were assigned to each of them (the "Mosquito and Malaria" director was Bill Roberts), but the entire group was under the general supervision of Ben Sharpsteen, who had been one of the top Disney directors during the 1930s and was now assuming a more administrative role at the studio. Norm Ferguson, supervising director of *Saludos Amigos*, continued to supervise the theatrical Good Neighbor productions; but as nontheatrical film production began to increase, much of it came under Sharpsteen's control.

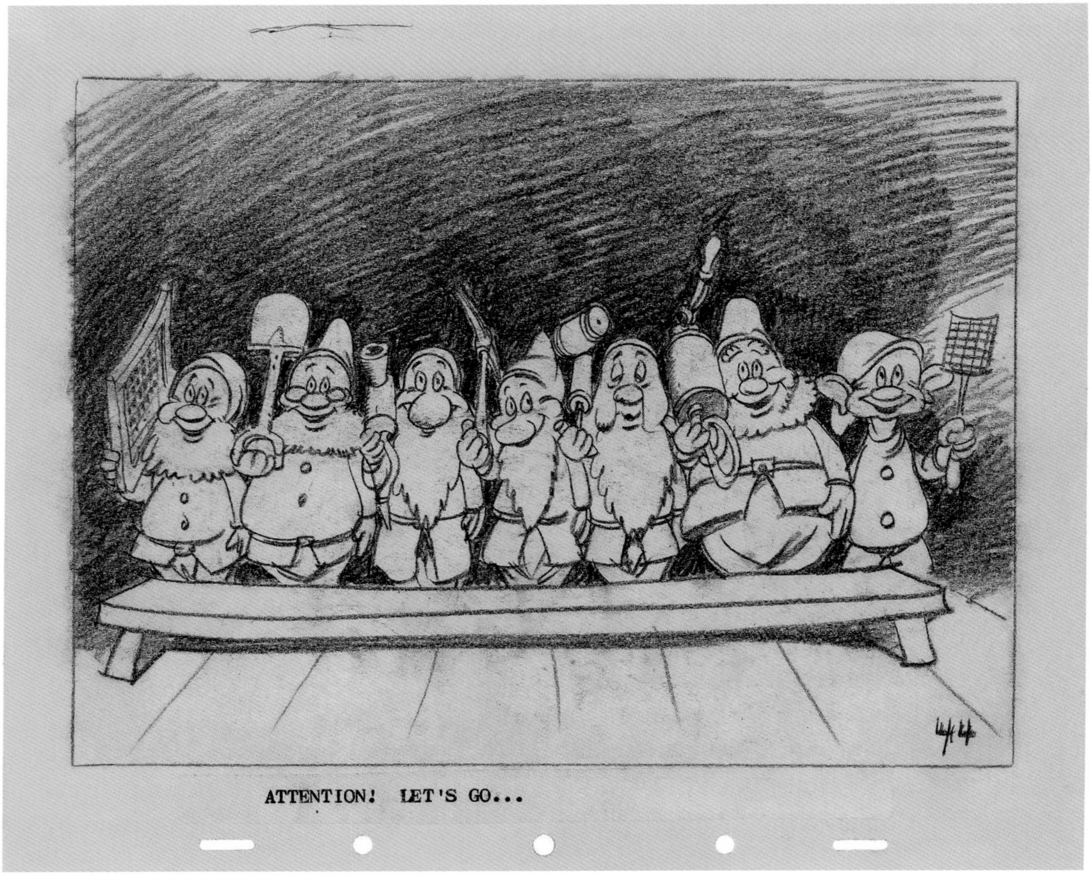

In a story sketch, the Dwarfs volunteer for duty.

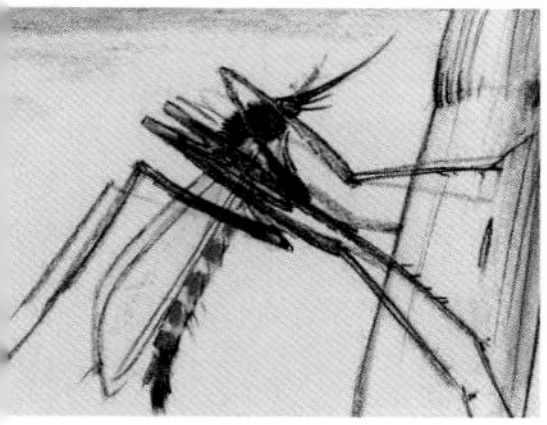

ABOVE: A story sketch of the malevolent mosquito.

RIGHT: A frame from the finished film.

The first of the health films to be completed—"The Mosquito and Malaria," now retitled *The Winged Scourge*—refreshingly demonstrates Walt's principle: combining solid factual information with proven entertainment techniques. One of the challenges in producing these pictures was to achieve the customary production polish of a Disney film on the limited budgets approved by the CIAA, and with these "sample" films, Walt was anxious to prove that such a feat could be accomplished. *The Winged Scourge* meets the challenge imaginatively; like *South of the Border with Disney*, it makes ingenious use of the resources of the Disney studio. The single most expensive ingredient in a Disney production was full character animation, and *The Winged Scourge* uses that ingredient sparingly but effectively. The first half of the film, illustrating the menace of the mosquito, employs some simple animation, but holds the eye mainly by other means: camera movement, atmospherically painted backgrounds—and the haunting appearance of the mosquito itself. The malevolent mosquito has a long history in American animation, going back as far as Winsor McCay's disturbing *How a Mosquito Operates* in 1912. Subsequent nightmare images of mosquitoes appeared in such films as Pat Sullivan's *Felix in Hollywood* (1923) and Max Fleischer's *There's Something About a Soldier* (1934).[75] *The Winged Scourge* builds on this collective imagery, and culminates in an unforgettable image of its own: the farmer's hut menaced by a towering, horrific mosquito that puts even McCay's bulbous monster to shame.

Full character animation is reserved for the film's second half, in which the Seven Dwarfs demonstrate prevention techniques: cutting weeds and draining stagnant water to remove the mosquitoes' breeding grounds, screening and protecting their home to keep the pests out. Although it's mildly jarring to see the Dwarfs, who seem to belong in the Black Forest, draining swamps and sleeping under mosquito netting, this section makes its point *and* enhances the film with a touch of lavish production. Walt demonstrated his commitment by assigning some of his top artists to the project; much of the Dwarf animation was done by Milt Kahl and Frank Thomas. Ollie Johnston later opined that Kahl's animation of the Dwarfs had "much more subtlety" than that by the original artists in *Snow White and the Seven Dwarfs*—high praise indeed. Thomas animated some extended sequences featuring Dopey, redesigning and transforming the character in the process.

One of Thomas's Dopey scenes aptly illustrates the ingenuity behind the CIAA films. The Dwarfs' mosquito-exterminating activities are set to an instrumental rendition of Frank Churchill's "Whistle While You Work," tracked directly from the music previously recorded for the housecleaning sequence in *Snow White*. One scene in the feature had depicted a deer, loaded down with dirty laundry, getting tangled in the clothes hanging

[75] Walt himself came closest to these images in a 1934 Mickey Mouse cartoon, *Camping Out*, in which Mickey and his friends on a camping trip are plagued by an organized swarm of mosquitoes. The *Camping Out* mosquitoes are pesky and relentless, but at least retain their normal size. One of the gags in *Camping Out*, a detachment of mosquitoes attacking a flyswatter and unraveling it down to the handle, is coincidentally repeated in the lighter second half of *The Winged Scourge*.

from his antlers, underscored by music with a percussive "stumbling" effect. In *The Winged Scourge* Thomas matches that musical passage with a scene of Dopey repeatedly stamping the floor, trying to kill a mosquito. The fit is so perfect that the music seems tailor-made for the animation, rather than the other way around.

By late January 1943 *The Winged Scourge* was completed, and Walt was able to screen it in Washington for Francis Alstock and an invited group of journalists and science writers. The film was received with enthusiasm, and Walt was encouraged to go ahead with further production. Although some observers, as we shall see, would find fault with *The Winged Scourge*, the overall response was gratifying. By mid-1944 Russell Pierce, of the CIAA's motion picture division, could report to Jack Cutting that "Our records show that *The Winged Scourge*, one of the most popular films, has been shown 2,531 times to a total audience of 440,177" in the United States and "2,390 times to a total audience of 1,109,186" in Central and South America. "This might indicate," he added, "that people in the other American republics are more enthusiastic about the films than people in the United States, but bear in mind that in the other American republics we have many outdoor showings where two, three and four thousand people are present, whereas, distribution in the United States is to audiences which rarely total more than 150." In addition to its intended Latin American audience, *The Winged Scourge* proved popular with other viewers. In 1943 the Australian Legation requested prints to be shown in Australia. And Walt noted that the U.S. military had also requested prints: "Malaria, it seems, is almost the No. 1 health problem of our armed forces."[76] Today *The Winged Scourge* remains the most popular and best remembered of all the nontheatrical Disney films for the CIAA.

[76] As if to corroborate this statement, Chuck Jones later directed two malaria-related pictures—*Private Snafu vs. Malaria Mike* and *It's Murder She Says*—in Warner Bros.' Private Snafu series, produced exclusively for the U.S. armed forces.

THE GRAIN THAT BUILT A HEMISPHERE

Along with the health-care series, the studio proposed a series of films on agricultural subjects. The first of these, produced simultaneously with *The Winged Scourge*, was a film with the working title "Corn and Corn Products," which promoted hemispheric solidarity by depicting corn as an agricultural common bond between the Americas. The studio's agricultural subjects would generally receive far less support from the CIAA than health-related subjects, but this film was different—perhaps because of the influence of Vice President Henry A. Wallace, who was one of Nelson Rockefeller's most powerful allies in the maintenance and support of his agency's program. Wallace was a former secretary of agriculture, had a strong interest in agrarian politics, and in particular was convinced that corn truly *was* the bond between the Americas (he had himself pioneered in the development of new hybrid strains of seed corn). A film on the subject was assured of the Coordinator's enthusiastic support.

Simple but powerful animation by Bill Tytla for *The Grain That Built a Hemisphere.*

In February 1942 Walt assigned "Corn and Corn Products" to writer Leo Thiele for development. This film was apparently conceived on an ambitious scale; early cost estimates project it as a two-reel subject running between 1,500 and 1,800 feet (in terms of

[77] This would have given it a running time somewhere between 17 and 20 minutes.

35 mm footage).[77] As Roy Disney pointed out, "This footage is nearly the equal of three of our regular short subjects." CIAA officials loved the idea behind the film but balked at the cost, and in the early summer of 1942 the studio agreed to scale down the idea and produce it as a standard one-reel film (although the finished product, with a running time of over ten minutes, is still a very full reel).

As with *The Winged Scourge*, story development of "Corn" proceeded slowly because of the need to check factual details with the CIAA office in Washington. In this case Dr. Earl N. Bressman, director of the CIAA's agriculture division, spent two weeks at the studio in the spring of 1942, working with Disney artists on "Corn" and several other agricultural stories. After returning to Washington he continued to weigh in on the script, lending his own expertise and also conferring with government consultants to verify the accurate depiction of such details as pre-Incan corn pots.[78] The picture moved into production on 1 June 1942, simultaneously with *The Winged Scourge*, and like that film was directed by Bill Roberts. Production of "Corn" was an uncommonly slow and difficult process, however, plagued by frequent interruptions and revisions. Even the final title, *The Grain That Built a Hemisphere*, was not assigned until the last minute. By late December 1942 the short was tentatively complete, and the cutting department started negative cutting—then suspended it because some scenes were still being revised and reshot!

The film that emerged from this grueling production is still ambitious, packing into its one-reel length a capsule history of the development of corn in the Americas, a brief account of corn's botanical makeup and cultivation techniques, and an indication of the many by-products derived from corn. Visually it's a handsome production, and like *The Winged Scourge* is carefully assembled for maximum visual effect from economical means. Here again much of the story is carried by charts and diagrams, and information in these scenes is conveyed by held drawings, sliding cels, color changes, camera movement, and other cost-effective techniques. Original character animation in this picture is mostly the work of Bill Tytla, here assigned the animator's most difficult challenge: animating the human figure. Tytla shines in the early historical section of the film, depicting the early Indians' discovery of corn and the development of the plant by Maya, Aztec, and Inca civilizations. These scenes arguably represent Tytla's most important contribution to the Good Neighbor project. He had earlier created solid, workmanlike animation of Pedro and Joe Carioca, characters that fell outside his unique artistic strengths, but *The Grain That Built a Hemisphere* bears out, in a modest way, John Canemaker's description of Tytla as "animation's Michelangelo." This is no *Night on Bald Mountain*, to be sure, and Tytla is clearly being reined in by economic considerations—but it's doubly remarkable that, even with these restrictions, he invests his indigenous characters with a simple strength and dignity. This applies especially to an elegant image of a character rolling corn, which appears at film's beginning and recurs periodically throughout. The film also includes brief "guest appearances" by animators Frank Thomas and Milt Kahl.

[78] As late as September 1942 Bressman was corresponding with the studio's Bob Carr about the distinction between contour plowing and terracing. The discussion led Carr to abandon his idea for a film on "Contour Plowing," but Bressman's information about terracing found its way into the Inca sequence in *The Grain That Built a Hemisphere*.

But *The Grain That Built a Hemisphere* also benefits from animation recycled from earlier Disney films, a procedure that was then known at the studio as "salvage." When Tytla's aboriginal Indian goes hunting he flushes a covey of quail, and shoots his arrow at a deer—both originally animated for *Bambi*. Even more remarkable is a complete extended sequence, depicting a flock of barnyard animals stampeding to enjoy a meal of corn, lifted bodily from the 1938 Disney short *Farmyard Symphony*.[79] And the corn by-products depicted in the last sequence include guns and bombs for the war effort, in scenes similarly taken directly from the studio's recent Donald Duck short, *The New Spirit*, produced at the government's request to support the federal income tax.

Finally completed in January 1943, *The Grain That Built a Hemisphere* was shown in Washington along with *The Winged Scourge*. It was the enthusiastic response to these two shorts by the CIAA that paved the way for more nontheatrical production at the studio. And *The Grain That Built a Hemisphere* achieved another distinction: crossing the "nontheatrical" boundary, it was nominated for an Academy Award as the best documentary short of 1942.

[79] The alert viewer will note, in the midst of this sequence, a scene *not* taken from *Farmyard Symphony*: a steer, growing bigger and more muscular as he eats from a trough, turns to stare in surprise as cuts of meat are outlined on his side. This scene was animated by Frank Thomas in the style of the rest of the sequence, and in appearance is consistent with the other scenes.

WATER—FRIEND OR ENEMY

Hard on the heels of *The Winged Scourge* and *The Grain That Built a Hemisphere* came another health film, with the working title "Water Supply." This subject was enthusiastically endorsed by the CIAA because it was sorely needed. Charles Morrow Wilson of the Coordinator's staff, an authority on Latin American medicine, enthused: "it is a sound exposition and I do not know of any way to approach such a broad subject more effectively. The water situation in Latin America is very bad—and has been for centuries." But the resulting film, retitled *Water—Friend or Enemy*, is often overlooked today, overshadowed by more dynamic and entertaining films in the same series.

The approach adopted by the writers was a direct address to the audience by the "Spirit of Water." "I am water," announces the narrator (Fred Shields again) at the film's opening, expounding on the life-giving properties of water, then showing how man has polluted his own water supply, his words all the while illustrated by the images on-screen. Skulls appear in the water to symbolize the disease lurking there; place settings around a family table disappear to represent the needless deaths caused by contaminated water. The film moves on to charts and diagrams showing methods of treating water, constructing sanitary wells, and other prevention techniques. Here the visuals become more abstract: clear water in a cutaway view of a well turns red when tainted by a red area of pollution that has seeped in through the ground. After demonstrating prevention techniques, the short ends on a positive note as the water becomes pure, healthy, and life-giving once again.

This film, like its predecessor, employs some "salvage": it begins and ends with a waterfall originally animated for the 1937 Silly Symphony *Little Hiawatha*.[80] But Hiawatha himself does not appear in these scenes, nor do any other characters. Aside from

[80] The narration in the opening and closing sequences is also similar to that in *Little Hiawatha*, written in a cadence that vaguely recalls Longfellow's in the original poem.

a few perfunctory scenes illustrating the use of water—mostly close-ups of hands, and other generic views of the human figure animated by Bill Tytla—there is no bona fide character animation in all of *Water—Friend or Enemy*. The film conveys its information clearly and professionally, but with none of the added entertainment value that gives such life to *The Winged Scourge* and *The Grain That Built a Hemisphere*. This is no accident; *Water* is a deliberate effort to try an alternate technique, a directly educational film *without* entertaining frills. And, in fact, authorities on Latin American culture would later endorse this approach, though some of them would find fault with the film's presentation of facts. From today's perspective, the real problem with *Water—Friend or Enemy* is that it makes little impression on the viewer. The subject is water, but the film is very dry.

As if triggered by the U.S. release of *Saludos Amigos*, an explosion of Latin American-related activity occurred at the Disney studio during the early months of 1943. If the studio's Good Neighbor program had previously been traveling on a single track, it now took off in many directions at once. The theatrical production program continued to build in exciting new ways; Walt and his artists embarked on further research trips to Mexico, Cuba, and other countries; the *Saludos* by-products continued to multiply and took on a life of their own, leading to such unfamiliar activities as a Mexican poster contest sponsored by the studio. And the nontheatrical film program, fueled by the CIAA's enthusiastic response to Walt's first sample films, shifted into high gear. Walt decided to delegate some of the responsibility for this initiative to Bill Cottrell and Jack Cutting. Production of the nontheatrical films would still be overseen by Ben Sharpsteen, but in terms of determining the program's overall direction, developing story material, and coordinating the studio's work with that of the CIAA, Cottrell and Cutting (under Walt's supervising eye) became a two-man "educational department." Both men had been at the studio for more than a decade, both were erudite, literate, and well traveled, and both had been part of the original El Grupo on the 1941 South American trip. Cutting had the additional advantage of his familiarity with Latin American cultures, and in fact continued his work of supervising the foreign-language editions of Disney's theatrical films even as he took on this new challenge. For the next two years the Cottrell-Cutting team would lead the studio, and the educational film itself, into unexplored territory.

Their commitment to, and the studio's support for, this new program was evident in one of their first acts: an international "Seminar on Visual Education" to be hosted by the studio later in 1943. This would be a summit meeting bringing together Disney artists and members of the CIAA staff from Washington, *and* an international panel of educators and scholars recruited by the CIAA. Throughout the spring of 1943 Cottrell and Cutting laid ambitious plans for the seminar. By uniting the resources of the world's best animation studio with the educational expertise of a handpicked group of international scholars, they were aiming at nothing less than the ultimate realization of the ideals of educational film. As Cottrell and Cutting prepared for the seminar and for the production work that would follow it, they sought ways to develop further their health-care and agricultural film series.

The primary focus of the seminar, however, was a third category of film production: films promoting literacy. Coincidentally, the Disney studio had already taken some tentative steps toward an unrelated literacy project, based on Dr. Ivor Armstrong Richards's "Basic English." Richards, a Harvard educator, had developed his system as a way of teaching non-English speakers a functional knowledge of English, and from 1942 to 1943 the Disney studio had worked with him to produce a film or films explaining his method.[81] The films were never completed, but in the meantime the growing problem of adult illiteracy in Latin American countries had become a concern of the CIAA. This gave rise to one of the most ambitious aims of Disney's nontheatrical film program: in place of Dr. Richards's English-teaching agenda, this project would teach adult Spanish- or Portuguese-speaking illiterates to read and write their own languages, through the medium of film. As early as December 1942 Francis Alstock had tentatively authorized a film with the working title "The Advantages of Reading and Writing," and as the seminar's target date in late spring 1943 approached, story artists worked to prepare "Reading and Writing" storyboards that might serve as a springboard for discussion by the seminar attendees.

As if that were not enough, Cottrell and Cutting took off for another survey trip, this time to Central America. For several weeks in March and April 1943 they toured Guatemala, Costa Rica, and El Salvador, with additional stops in Mexico and Cuba. Their schedule was carefully coordinated with those of Walt and other staff members, so that they were able to lend their assistance on other Disney projects and cement diplomatic relations with some of the studio's contacts in Mexico and Cuba. (It was during this trip that Cottrell learned about the negative reaction of some native Chileans to *Pedro*; *see* page 81.) The main purpose of the trip, however, was to confer with government and educational leaders in the Central American countries, solicit their suggestions for the forthcoming series of films, and observe existing educational techniques. "In Salvador we went to the very humblest type of schools—both municipal and federal," Cutting reported to Walt partway through the trip. "We examined the copy books of the students and talked with their teachers. We find the educational facilities very poor in these places. In many schools there is such a lack of funds that there are not simple text books available for the students, and most of the class work is done in copy books, and lessons are explained and written on a blackboard. . . . We visited clinics and talked to many doctors. We also made a point of seeing as much as we could of the poor sections of the cities and observed conditions in their markets. The more we see these things, and the more we talk to the doctors, the more convinced we are that simple and elementary subjects on personal hygiene and nutrition would be among the most valuable items of education for large masses of people. We do not

[81] Dr. Richards's system, which reduced the English language to eight hundred basic words, was already being used in schools both in the U.S. and abroad, and Richards had demonstrated its efficacy by publishing a Basic English edition of Plato's *Republic*. His system attracted some attention in the press; *see*, for example, Lincoln Barnett, "Basic English: A Globalanguage [*sic*]," *Life*, 18 October 1943, pp. 57ff, which includes a photo of Richards next to a Disney storyboard and implies that the Disney film has already been completed. (This brought at least one letter to the studio from a Northwestern University professor who wanted to use the film in his classes.) Although the film was never completed, a rough black-and-white demonstration reel was made in 16 mm and shown in various venues, including the 1943 seminar.

feel that the original subject 'The Advantages of Reading and Writing' should be put aside, there is much to be said of subjects to be used in the classroom, but we cannot help emphasizing the importance of the health subjects."

THE SEMINAR ON VISUAL EDUCATION

Returning to the studio with a wealth of new information, Cottrell and Cutting set to work in earnest finalizing the details of the seminar. **Dr. Enrique S. de Lozada**, a special adviser on the CIAA staff in Washington, flew to California to confer with them. De Lozada was a native of Bolivia, a former member of the Bolivian diplomatic corps, and an acknowledged authority on Latin American education, with a special interest in the literacy problem. His interest had, in fact, become downright proprietary; unknown to the Disney staff, he had engaged in a political struggle for control of the seminar and the literacy film series. Kenneth Holland, director of the Science and Education division of the CIAA, had been tentatively appointed to lead the seminar, but de Lozada had actively campaigned to take over that post. Finally de Lozada trumped Holland by going directly to Nelson Rockefeller and asking, and receiving, written authority to lead the seminar. During the seminar proceedings and much of the film production that followed, de Lozada would virtually become a member of the Disney staff, helping to determine the direction of the literacy series. The dates for the seminar were set, and invitations were issued to the participants. These included:

Eulalia Guzmán, a prominent educator and supervisor of primary schools in Mexico City, who had been introduced to Bill Cottrell and Walt on their visit to that city the previous December;

Doris Warner LeRoy, consultant to the CIAA's motion picture division, who—as the daughter of Harry Warner and the wife of Mervyn LeRoy—provided the committee with one of its direct links to the Hollywood filmmaking establishment;

Dr. Frank C. Laubach, a Congregationalist missionary who had already attracted international attention by taking his original literacy system to other countries;

Dr. Luis Martínez Mont, inspector general of Guatemala's Department of Education;

Dr. Reinaldo Murgeytio, founder and director of the Indian Normal School in Ecuador;

Dr. Calixto Suarez of Cuba, director general of Havana's municipal educational system;

Dr. Victor Sutter, director general of the Health Department in El Salvador;

Father Luis Alberto Tapia, chaplain of the Bolivian army;

Dr. Hernane Tavares de Sa of Brazil, a professor at the University of São Paulo and a member of the Faculty of Philosophy of São Bento;

Charles Thomson, chief of the Division of Cultural Relations in the U.S. State Department;

Dr. Mildred J. Wiese, a U.S. author and consultant who had been active in the Adult Education program of the Works Progress Administration (WPA); and

Dr. Arthur Wright, president of the Southern Education Foundation, which worked for the education of African Americans in the southern United States.

Walt, front row center, poses with the seminar attendees.

In addition to these main participants in the seminar, other notable guests were in attendance. These included Nelson Rockefeller; Dr. Peter L. Spencer of Claremont College; and the distinguished Mexican cinematographer Gabriel Figueroa Mateos, remembered today for both Mexican (*María Calendaria*) and U.S. (John Ford's *The Fugitive*) films. Participating Disney staff members included Bob Carr, who had suggested many of the nontheatrical film subjects; George Stallings; and of course Cottrell and Cutting themselves.

The Seminar on Visual Education was conducted at the Disney studio over a period of eleven days in late May and early June 1943. The second floor of the studio's Shorts Building was transformed for the occasion, providing offices, conference rooms, and projection facilities for the attendees.[82] Out-of-town visitors were put up at the Knickerbocker Hotel in Hollywood, and were transported to and from the studio each day. The opening of the seminar on Tuesday, 25 May, was marked by an appearance by Nelson Rockefeller, the guest of honor. Rockefeller addressed the attendees in Spanish, expressing his support and that of Vice President Henry Wallace for the proceedings and his hopes for the resulting film program. Over the next ten days the guests toured the Disney studio and learned how animated films were made, took field trips to Los Angeles public schools and observed existing visual education techniques, discussed their own educational theories and ways of translating their principles onto film, divided into subcommittees to tackle individual aspects of the project, and strove for a consensus on the proposed literacy series.

One key activity was the screening of the studio's already-completed educational and propaganda films. This was done mainly to acquaint the visitors with Disney techniques and the possibilities of the animated film, but the Latin American viewers' responses to the early health-care subjects were illuminating in their own right. While generally delighted with the films, they also made comments revealing cultural barriers between the Disney artists and Latin American audiences, barriers whose existence had never occurred to the artists in the course of production. These revelations would influence the production of later health-care films.

[82] The Shorts Building, located across the street from the southeast corner of the Animation Building, was made up of two existing structures that had been physically transported from Disney's Hyperion lot when the studio moved to Burbank in the late 1930s. The two edifices had originally been joined to the two wings of the Hyperion animation building, which itself had been built in an L shape. When reassembled at Burbank, they were not joined at right angles but aligned in a straight line.

The Winged Scourge, for example, though it was almost universally admired, drew some criticism. In creating the first section of the film the artists had depicted the mosquito's victim as a farmer, living in what they imagined as a typical farmer's house. According to Dr. Murgeytio, however, by Latin American standards the dwelling in the film was that of a wealthy landowner. "He said that in Latin America people of some means knew how to defend themselves against the disease, and were able to do so. It was the under-privileged masses who, through their ignorance and utter destitution, fell prey to the scourge." Another point of sharp disagreement was the element of entertainment. Some attendees appreciated the use of entertaining scenes and characters to help make the films' points, while others found them distracting and felt that a more serious, straightforward presentation would be more effective for Latin American audiences. By the latter standard, *Water—Friend or Enemy* should have been an ideal production. But *Water* had problems of its own. Its scenes depicting the spread of contaminated water, symbolized by the color red, were singled out by Dr. Martínez Mont. "For the Latin mind," he observed, "the red color used in the picture does not give the impression of sorrow and death. Black is used by us for this purpose. Contaminated waters in Malaria districts are called 'aguas negras.' To use red to indicate contaminated waters, far from giving the desired impression of death, gives the impression of life and joy."

(At a writers' conference later the same year, Disney artist Karl Van Leuven made a similar comment but suggested that yellow should have been used instead. He added another cross-cultural observation: "In the same picture the effects of the contaminated water were graphically illustrated by showing a dinner table that is suddenly vacant, then dissolving to a row of coffins. This is very effective for us. But for people whose religion teaches them that death, as God's will, is a good thing, that it frees you from the sufferings of the world and sends you to a glorious life in the hereafter, for a people who have holidays in death's honor, it is a misplaced emphasis. The thing they fear far worse than death is sickness, sickness that lets you live but keeps you helpless, unable to work, a drag on your family.")

As the seminar continued, other guiding principles were established. One question posed to the group was whether animation or live action would be a more effective medium for educational films. At first the delegates' responses were divided between the two, but as discussion continued, proponents of live action were forced to admit that shots of people living in one culture would be ill-suited to represent those of other cultures. Animation, with its ability to simplify and universalize, gradually emerged as the preferred medium. "The argument was clinched when it was pointed out that in Latin America the Disney characters have already tremendous popularity and goodwill. It would be helpful to capitalize on this goodwill and popularity."

Another Disney strength was highlighted when, once again, the *Baby Weems* sequence was exhibited for the attendees. "The group was especially interested in the fact that, without actual animation on the screen, an impression of movement and pace was created through the sound track. It was suggested that educational films might avail themselves of this resource." The impression of pace in *Baby Weems* is, of course, sustained by means other than the sound track—including camera movement and *some* limited animation—but the point that had aroused so much comment in 1941, that a story could be produced with such economy and still maintain the Disney standard of quality, now became doubly significant. Nontheatrical films for the CIAA would have to be produced on limited budgets, and the cost-cutting techniques pioneered in *Baby Weems* would become crucial as the series continued.

One question at issue was the subject matter of the literacy films. Even before the seminar started, it had been recognized that the potential audiences for these films might need additional motivation to learn to read: "You want to teach them to read things they are interested in." Because of the need for health education in so many Latin American countries, the seminar guests agreed that the literacy films might be constructed around words and sentences teaching basic lessons in health care. The student would learn to read and, at the same time, would reinforce important principles of health and nutrition; two worthwhile goals would be accomplished at once, and the resources of the Disney educational film program would be consolidated for maximum effect.

On Friday, 4 June, the seminar concluded with general meetings and reports from the various subcommittees. Final recommendations were submitted for the impending film program, and the help of several attendees was enlisted on an ongoing basis. With a new understanding of the challenges before them, and a newly formed network of consultants and specialists to assist them, Cottrell and Cutting returned to work on nontheatrical films for the Good Neighbor program.

HEALTH FOR THE AMERICAS

Of the various kinds of nontheatrical films produced by the Disney studio for the CIAA, by far the most successful group was a series on health care. In addition to the "sample" films, several of these had been started before the seminar, but lessons learned during the seminar would influence production of the shorts as they moved forward. Cottrell and Cutting also drew on other resources. Captain Ryland Madison, of the CIAA staff, was installed at the studio as the official "technical adviser" on the health films, participating in story conferences and advising on technical details. Madison was a member of the USA Medical Corps, and he in turn called on the expertise of other specialists. One of these was Charles Morrow Wilson, another CIAA staff member, who visited the studio in July 1943. Wilson was an authority on agronomics and the author of numerous books including *Ambassadors in White*, an account of American tropical medicine. Wilson reviewed the films that had already been produced and consulted with the writers and artists on storyboards for the upcoming films. Thus fortified with input from Madison, Wilson, and other outside authorities, the studio proceeded with its health-care series.

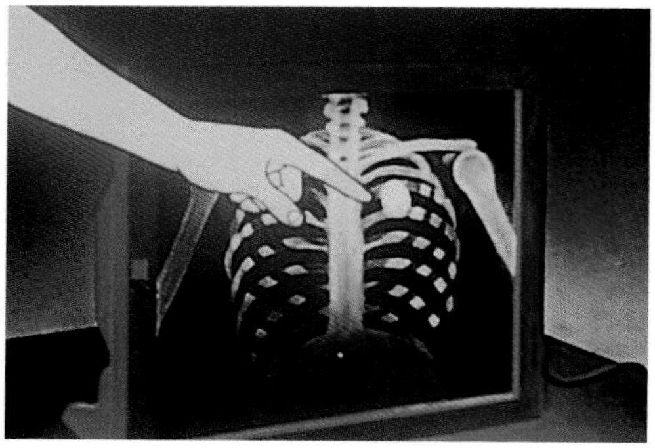

An X-ray reveals the presence of disease in one of the health films, *Tuberculosis*.

Factory-worker corpuscles manufacture munitions in *Defense Against Invasion.*

DEFENSE AGAINST INVASION

This little gem really belongs with the three "sample" films produced prior to the seminar; it was started simultaneously with them and was produced along the same lines. But *Defense Against Invasion*, more elaborate than the other three films, was produced more slowly and was not completed until the summer of 1943. This was yet another idea taken directly from Bob Carr's list of story suggestions: "A simple analogy between the principles of vaccination and the principles of defense against invasion. . . . We show antibodies actually repelling 'landing parties' of fierce smallpox germs." In March 1942 this idea was assigned to writer Norm Wright. Later, when Jack King took over direction of the animated segments of the film, Carl Barks and Jack Hannah joined the story team. Collectively, these artists expanded on Carr's idea. The inside of the human body was pictured as a city, with the blood vessels as "roads" on which the "workers" (blood corpuscles) transported goods from one "factory" (organ) to another. The germs became an invading army of slithering, spiderlike creatures, representing not just smallpox but any disease. The "workers," strengthened by vaccination, engaged the invaders in battle and protected the "city." In the finished film this visual metaphor would become quite elaborate, with richly detailed animated sequences, especially in the climactic battle. This luxury was perhaps made possible by the live-action framing story, in which four boys visiting a doctor's office were told the story of vaccination to calm their fears. The live-action scenes, shot in a mere four days late in 1942, accounted for over half the footage in *Defense Against Invasion*, helping to offset the expense of the animated scenes. Even so, this became the most expensive of all the nontheatrical CIAA films produced before the seminar.

By using red as the color of the corpuscle "workers," the studio avoided the criticism that had been leveled at *Water—Friend or Enemy*; here the color associated by Latin American cultures with life and vitality was, happily, used to symbolize the life force. This time, however, the choice of the color red was criticized for a different reason. "Advised at every step by government experts, Disney is keeping his pictures as close to scientific truth as possible," reported *Fortune* magazine. "But occasionally a minor point is yielded for the sake of drama or clarity. Actually, of course, it is the white corpuscles that put up the body's resistance to disease germs. But because most people think of blood as red and because red is a good fighting color, Walt and his men held out for red as the color of the corpuscle soldiers, and got their way against the mildly scandalized experts."

This same written account reveals a major change that was made, and unmade, during story development. The studio's original plan, *Fortune* tells us, "was to compare the body to a walled city. But on second thought it was realized that a walled city would be totally unfamiliar to rural Latin Americans. So, without changing the plot, the body will probably become a fairy-tale castle. The doctor explains that the castle walls are easily breached (by scratches), and there is one big gateway (the mouth) for entry of supplies." This article, published in August 1942, reflects the status of the story a few months into development. In the end, for whatever reason, the fairy-tale castle was abandoned, and the community in the film is simply a modern city.

It's not generally recognized that *Defense Against Invasion* represented another kind of technical experiment for the studio. Since Walt's first foray into color film production in 1932, all the Disney studio's color films had been produced in three-strip Technicolor. The three-strip process, a significant improvement on earlier color film processes, reproduced a full range of lush, vibrant colors, but it was expensive and difficult to use. A three-strip Technicolor camera literally employed three separate strips of 35 mm film and was very large, cumbersome, and unwieldy, especially for live-action filmmakers.[83] In the early 1940s, in an effort to accommodate those filmmakers, Technicolor introduced an alternate system called Monopack. This was, essentially, a 35 mm color-reversal process: it was a single strip of film that could be used in any standard motion-picture camera, the resulting picture converted by Technicolor to its three-strip format and processed in the usual way. The quality of the color suffered somewhat—the range of colors was narrower, and the multiple printings heightened the contrast and grain—but the ease and portability of a single-strip system made it a highly attractive option for filmmakers. Technicolor encouraged all the major studios to try the Monopack system in their current productions, and the Disney studio tried it in one film: *Defense Against Invasion*. The film's use of both animation and live action made it an ideal test case, and since it was to be distributed in the form of 16 mm Kodachrome, the absence of a full range of Technicolor hues would be less noticeable.[84] Walt's reaction to the process can probably be gauged by subsequent events: after this one experiment, the Disney studio never used the Monopack system again.

The finished film, if less familiar than *The Winged Scourge*, has nevertheless become a cult favorite among later generations of animation enthusiasts. The live-action scenes are adequate, but *Defense Against Invasion* really sparkles in its animated sequences. Character design in these sections is simple but effective: the corpuscles are shown as charming, faceless little red blobs, waddling purposefully about their business, while the germs invading the "city" are slithering four-legged creatures with menacing eyes, and occasionally voracious mouths, but no other features. No one artist dominates the animation of these characters. Top effects animator Josh Meador divides the bulk of the scenes with Marvin Woodward, Judge Whitaker, and Hal King, with key scenes also taken by Milt Neil and Paul Allen, both of whom had worked on *Saludos Amigos*. Brief as they are, the animated sequences abound in striking and imaginative visuals. In one scene an invading wave of black germs washes over city buildings, splashing high in the air like an ocean wave. During the climactic

[83] For Disney and other animation studios, an easier option was available. By the late 1930s the Disney studio had adopted a *successive-exposure* camera which exposed each frame in triplicate, recording all three color values separately on one strip of film. The resulting negative was "skip-printed" in the Technicolor printing process, transferring each color value, in turn, to a separate matrix by printing every third frame. Obviously this system was useful only for stop-motion photography; live-action producers were still obliged to use the mammoth three-strip camera.

[84] Since the camera positive and the Kodachrome prints used essentially the same process, one might have expected that the prints would be generated directly from the original. Surprisingly, that's not the case: Technicolor followed its usual procedure and generated YCM matrix negatives from the original, then used them to produce a Technicolor print, which was then converted *back* to Kodachrome. Special thanks to Scott MacQueen for all of this Technicolor information.

battle, a retreating germ is hammered by a corpuscle who pounds away at a "Chicago piano," a keyboard instrument with gun barrels mounted on the back.

Clearly, Walt and his artists put special effort into *Defense Against Invasion*—which makes its initial reception all the more disappointing. The consensus was that the film was *too* imaginative and would not be understood by its intended audience; Charles Wilson flatly stated: "*Defense Against Invasion* would go way over the heads of the Latin American people." There's no evidence that the film was used extensively in the CIAA program. Russell Pierce of the CIAA, writing to Jack Cutting in mid-1944 to report on the record numbers of Latin American viewers who had already seen the other preliminary films, added: "*Defense Against Invasion*, at present, has not been approved by the Department of State." The film survives today, however, as a brilliant example of the art of educational animation.

TUBERCULOSIS

Following the Seminar on Visual Education, production of nontheatrical films for the CIAA began in earnest along two parallel tracks. One of these, following the recommendations of the seminar, was a series that combined basic health care with reading lessons. We'll examine those films presently. In the meantime the studio also embarked on a separate series called "Salud para las Americas," or "Health for the Americas." This was a series of one-reel shorts dealing in a direct, no-nonsense way with more specific health-care issues. In July 1943 the CIAA authorized production of three of these pictures, all on topics of special relevance to Latin America. A unit under the supervision of Ben Sharpsteen was established to produce the series. The director was Jim Algar, another former animator, and the principal writer was Norm Wright. Retta Scott, the animator best remembered today for her scenes of the vicious hunting dogs in *Bambi* (and one of very few female animators in the industry during this era), painted backgrounds for the health films.

The unit first tackled a film on tuberculosis, which had been in tentative development as early as February 1943. The CIAA endorsed this idea with special warmth because it was especially needed, as Charles Wilson commented: "Tuberculosis is the Number One enemy of Latin America, and it is, unfortunately, getting worse all the time." (Wilson continued to counsel the unit as they developed the story, weighing in on such details as changing the word *tubercular* to the more medically accurate *tuberculous*.) In its finished form, *Tuberculosis* announces a dramatically different tone for the health series. It offers a stark contrast with the "sample" films produced in 1942: in place of the lushly crafted entertainment of *The Winged Scourge* or *Defense Against*

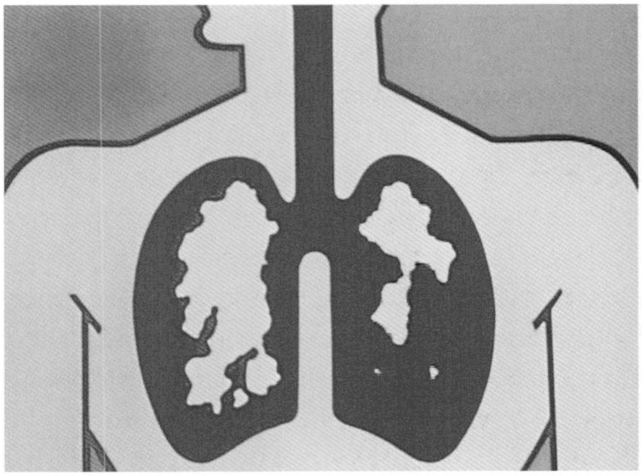

Tuberculosis **illustrates, in a severely plain visual style, progressive damage to the lungs.**

Tuberculosis: The patient is isolated in a separate room to recuperate.

Invasion, it features a lean, spartan visual style—charts, diagrams, held drawings, and extremely limited animation.

Walt took an active hand in this no-frills style. Instead of brooding over the rejection of his entertainment-with-education approach, he quickly adapted to the suggestions of Wilson and the seminar attendees: these films were meant to teach, in the simplest and most direct way possible, and elements of entertainment might be only a distraction. Always pragmatic, Walt knew that the health films would be distributed on 16 mm and exhibited in the field under less than ideal conditions, and directed his staff to design them accordingly. At one meeting he urged the artists to key their designs with simple, bright colors—"like a comic strip, not the subtleties we get into *Bambi* or something like that. That is for first class projection. These things have to be transparent enough to come through with poor projection."

In developing a script for the tuberculosis film, the writers suggested such working titles as "The White Plague" (one of the euphemisms for tuberculosis). They initially suggested opening the film with the introductory scene from the 1937 short *Don Donald*, in which a sombrero-wearing Donald Duck makes his entrance riding a burro and strumming a guitar. In new animation, the Duck would proceed to introduce a framing story about a couple, José and Dolores, whose family is stricken by TB. The writers felt that the audience's sympathy for these characters would enhance their vicarious education about tuberculosis, its causes and effects, and appropriate preventive and curative measures. It was Walt who vetoed all of this introductory material, telling his team that they should use the footage to convey the film's message without delay. "Walt stressed his feeling that there was a job to be done and that we can't try to tell a story. He suggested that if it were necessary that they be entertained, a Donald Duck could be run after the picture. He feels that if the films on the body are handled properly, the people will be interested in them, in seeing what goes on inside themselves, and it could be made more interesting by animation."

The animation in *Tuberculosis* was assigned in a way that reflected Ben Sharpsteen's own experience at the Disney studio. In the early 1930s Sharpsteen, as one of the more experienced animators on the staff, had often been assigned a large block of scenes that he would redistribute among the younger "apprentice" artists. Animating some of the scenes himself, he would assign others to the junior animators and work with them on their individual scenes. Now, since *Tuberculosis* was to include no detailed character animation but would include occasional action (boiling water, a flickering candle, a book's pages turning) that would be categorized as effects animation, the entire assignment was turned over to effects specialist Josh Meador. In turn, Meador distributed scenes among other artists on his effects crew: Jack Boyd, Ed Aardal, John Reed, and Sandy Strother. Retta Scott, in addition to her background paintings, contributed some still paintings of vegetables and other foods.

The finished *Tuberculosis* announces the new direction of the "Health for the Americas" series: if clear, simple, uncluttered instruction is required, *Tuberculosis* delivers the goods. It represents, in fact, the radical extreme, with a visual style far more severely plain than in any of the succeeding films. But that simplicity clearly accomplishes its educational purpose. The film begins by offering a simple comparison between human lungs, attacked by tuberculosis germs, and a pair of leaves being eaten away by parasites. Methods for guarding against the disease and caring for the patient are conveyed with unmistakable clarity. Attendees of the seminar had endorsed animation for its ability to simplify and universalize, and there is no sign of Donald Duck, José, or Dolores here, only extremely generic characters who can stand in for all cultures. (Their coughs on the sound track were supplied by sound-effects chief Jim Macdonald and by Violet Bayerl of the studio's ink and paint department.) No music is heard, apart from an instrumental "Saludos Amigos" under the main titles, and a stirring Paul Smith march to accompany the closing scenes.

Tuberculosis was completed by mid-July 1944 and was delivered to the CIAA in August. The following spring, some retakes were made, a new narration track was recorded, and the film was issued in a revised version. The change was slight but fundamental: in the 1944 version a woman contracts tuberculosis when exposed to the coughing of an infected shopkeeper. The 1945 version eliminates the shop and the shopkeeper, and the woman (now named Marie in the English edition, Maria in the Spanish) is infected with the disease while visiting her sick mother. Prints of both versions apparently remained in circulation, and are held today by various archives. As we've seen, constant revision of the CIAA films during production was a common practice, but *Tuberculosis* is apparently the only one that survives today in two distinct finished versions.

CLEANLINESS BRINGS HEALTH

Concurrently with *Tuberculosis*, the studio tackled a subject designed to show that personal cleanliness was essential to good health. Under the working title "Personal Cleanliness," this idea was authorized by the CIAA in July 1943 and was initially developed as a story by Winston Hibler, who, like Jim Algar, would later play an important role in the studio's True-Life Adventure series. Here again, the writers suggested story material designed to shore up the film's educational function with entertainment value. Charles Wilson's August 1943 letter sheds some light on this material. While generally enthusiastic about Hibler's treatment, Wilson noted, "a rather theoretical point is brought up that man's first experiments in cleanliness were probably instinctive precautions against parasites rather than accidentally falling in the water. My own suggestion is that unless the writer is pretty sure of his authority for this falling in the river theory, the whole thing had better be left out." And, just as with *Tuberculosis*, Walt jettisoned much of the story material anyway, and even shelved the picture briefly. It was reactivated early in 1944, stripped to the basics. The finished picture is a simple comparison between the Clean Family and the Careless Family (in the Spanish version, respectively, "la familia de Juan" and "la familia de Pedro"). The slovenly lifestyle of the Careless Family leads to sickness and misery, while the Clean Family is healthy and happy. (This is the latest illustration of a principle Walt had used as early as 1922 in *Tommy Tucker's Tooth*, a dental-care film: a "good" character who does something properly, contrasted with a "bad" one who doesn't, and suffers for it.)

The Clean Family, or *la familia de Juan*, is introduced in *Cleanliness Brings Health*.

Considering this simplicity, the animation in *Cleanliness Brings Health* is substantially richer than that in *Tuberculosis*. As an exemplar of the animated film it's still a long way from *Saludos Amigos*, but compared to its immediate predecessor it's almost luxurious. That's partly because of a heavy use of salvage. This film borrows background paintings and generous helpings of animation from *Water—Friend or Enemy*: a child being bathed in a river, clothes being washed. There are also two animal scenes from *Farmyard Symphony* (1938). Ed Aardal's scene of a woman washing her hands, animated for *Tuberculosis*, was reused here and would recur in most of the subsequent health films. And as the series continued, the studio would accumulate a virtual stock library of these salvage scenes, which could be reused indefinitely in similar subjects.

In addition to all this recycled art—and, in a sense, thanks to it, since salvage eased the strain on the CIAA's tight budgets—*Cleanliness Brings Health* boasts some original character animation by Harvey Toombs and Murray McClellan. This enlivens the proceedings considerably, and even allows for some modest gags. The child of the Clean Family, helping his father plant corn, pauses to eat one of the kernels. The point about keeping livestock out of the house is made comically by a curious pig that repeatedly wanders into the Careless Family's house and is pulled out by a giant hand representing the narrator. This original animation is necessarily simple, in keeping with enforced economy measures, but ingeniously effective—as in a scene of the Careless Family's lazy son, drawn so that only his arm moves as he scratches himself. (As if to endorse the effectiveness of this scene, director Jim Algar uses it twice.) The animation concludes with one final, humble luxury: a group portrait of the Clean Family, with the child dancing (and momentarily stumbling) into place—animated by one of the studio's top artists, Ollie Johnston.

During the seminar, Dr. Victor Sutter of El Salvador had criticized *Water—Friend or Enemy* for its emphasis on the placement of toilets, pointing out that eighty percent of rural Latin Americans *had* no toilets and that films on the construction of toilets would be more to the point. *Cleanliness Brings Health* duly devotes some screen time to the building of a latrine. The proceedings, and the need for them, are depicted tastefully, but directly and without mincing words. The child of the Careless Family, which has no latrine, contributes to the cycle of disease by walking into the cornfield and reemerging a few seconds later, adjusting his pants. As construction of the Clean Family's latrine is outlined, their son bounds into the half-finished structure and prepares to use it—then looks up, sees the camera, and reacts with embarrassment. Walls of thatched straw are quickly wrapped around the structure to afford him some privacy.

One other feature of this picture merits comment: the animated paintbrush that paints the characters and objects on-screen. This idea was borrowed from *Aquarela do Brasil*, but in that film it had been a thematic device inspired by Barroso's song. Here it's cannily used to supply some movement in otherwise static scenes, sustaining the audience's attention. As Disney's educational film activities continued, the animated paintbrush would become a familiar sight.

INFANT CARE

The third subject authorized by the CIAA, tentatively titled "Infant Care and Feeding," was designed to convey the importance of prenatal and infant care, and especially the benefits of a healthy diet. Like its two predecessors, this picture was jointly developed by the Disney team and outside specialists. This time Captain Madison arranged for Major Einor H. Christopherson, a child-care authority consulting in Brazil for the CIAA, and his wife to visit the studio to consult with the story artists. Christopherson confirmed that such a film was needed in Latin America to help combat the high infant mortality rate, and made numerous other comments and suggestions. The goat-milking scene is a direct result of his input; Christopherson was concerned over the reluctance of rural Latin Americans to use goat's milk. Conversely, he also steered the artists away from such cultural gaffes as unlikely children's furniture: "I have never seen a high chair. They have very little furniture, if any."

Once again Walt's inclination was to keep the story as simple as possible. Norm Wright had considered an approach like that of *Cleanliness Brings Health*, demonstrating the right and the wrong way to care for an infant. Walt instinctively rejected this idea, feeling that the negative example was unnecessary. "I don't see any reason for it, that you should need the other side at all. The positive seems to be it." Like the other health pictures, *Infant Care* adopts a simple, direct approach to its subject and doesn't flinch at such scenes as a cross-section of the womb or a mother breast-feeding her child. Smallpox vaccination, the subject of *Defense Against Invasion*, is here briefly promoted again, and a passing reference to the success of vaccination in the United States is deliberately inserted in response to the CIAA's request for subtle U.S. propaganda in the nontheatrical films.

As the studio's health-film salvage library continued to grow, *Infant Care* availed itself of more scenes borrowed from previous productions. The hand-washing scene from *Tuberculosis* is back again, along with another useful device from that picture: a book whose pages turn, revealing a succession of scenes. This page-turning action, animated by Jack Boyd, was an ingenious economy measure; combined with a simple camera wipe, it could be used repeatedly, imparting a sense of luxury to what was essentially a series of transitions from one static drawing to another. Jim Algar was pleased with it: "One turning page and a set of about 20 drawings serves the whole picture." Walt saw another advantage: "The idea of these things being in books ties in well with the reading [films]."

Infant Care also benefits from another kind of salvage: a musical score that is mostly taken from the sound track of *Dumbo*. (The music in question is appropriately borrowed from the scenes of Dumbo with his mother: primarily the instrumental tracks from Frank Churchill's lovely lullaby "Baby Mine," along with Ollie Wallace's incidental cues that immediately precede that song in the feature.) Because these preexisting recordings obviated the need for new recording sessions, a special waiver from the musicians' union was required for the right to use them in *Infant Care*.[85] This established a precedent that was followed in most of the succeeding health films.

[85] The waiver was granted on the grounds that this was a nontheatrical film and would not be shown commercially.

The picture was almost completed when, at a screening of the Technicolor composite print in the spring of 1945, Walt noticed a painting error in the closing scenes and commented on the "albino baby" at film's end. Even in a rigorously economical picture like this, Walt was not about to let such a mistake go uncorrected. The offending scenes were repainted, and *Infant Care* was delivered to the CIAA without the albino baby.

By late summer of 1944 the animation of *Infant Care* was complete, and the requirements of the first health-film contract with the CIAA had been satisfied. The literacy films (*see* page 156), produced concurrently, were also essentially complete. In the meantime the CIAA, moving quickly to preserve this momentum, had proposed a new contract calling for four additional health-care films. The contract was quickly executed, and even as the first entries in the "Health for the Americas" series were working their way through postproduction, the studio was embarking on new ones.

HOOKWORM

The first of these four stories was one that had actually been kicking around the studio for some time. Bob Carr's 1942 list of story ideas on health-threatening "public enemies" (including the anopheles mosquito) had included one about the hookworm. "It may be a tough job to create an entertaining . . . short about the hookworm," Carr acknowledged, "but Disney artists who have endowed other worms, snails and similar vermin, with charm and personality, will be able to make Herr Hookworm a scheming menace, beaten in the end by modern medicine." His suggestion was adopted, and preliminary story work began under Leo Thiele's supervision during the spring of 1942.

Careless Charlie, the star of *Hookworm*, has seen healthier days.

Walt was evidently intrigued with the idea. "Take the hookworm," he told one journalist. "He's supposed to be a villain. But by the time you get the little fellow going awhile, you begin to like him."

By late summer the picture had been abandoned, for reasons unknown, but the research and story material was retained at the studio and sporadic attempts were made to revive the project. Intentionally or not, Carr had hit upon a subject of special interest to the Rockefeller family. Three decades earlier John D. Rockefeller Sr. had launched an earnest campaign to combat the danger of hookworm in the United States. The Rockefeller Foundation's efforts had included funding of a short film, *Unhooking the Hookworm*, which was widely exhibited in schools and other nontheatrical venues.[86] Now, in the early 1940s, Nelson Rockefeller's agency was predisposed toward the same cause. In November 1943 Captain Madison urged the Disney studio to resume work on its hookworm picture, promising the support of George C. Dunham, a veteran of the Army Medical Corps who had now become the assistant coordinator at the CIAA. "It would be worth developing to the extent of sacrificing something else a little," Madison commented. "General Dunham feels it is a big thing." Within a few weeks the production had been reactivated, and when the CIAA's new four-picture contract was proposed in early summer of 1944, the hookworm subject became the first of the series. Jim Algar, who had directed the earlier "Health for the Americas" reels, was assigned direction of this one as well.

[86] The menace of hookworm in the rural southern U.S. had originally been brought to Rockefeller's attention in 1909 by Dr. Charles W. Stiles, a specialist who had researched the problem. Produced in 1920 by Coronet Pictures, a division of Educational Pictures, *Unhooking the Hookworm* proved such an effective teaching tool in the U.S. that it was translated into several languages and distributed in other countries, including some in Latin America. Prints survive today in the collections of the Rockefeller Archives Center and the National Archives and Records Administration. Special thanks to Carol Radovich and to Rick Prelinger for providing this information.

But *Hookworm* emerged as something very different from the earlier health pictures. The plain, austere look of *Tuberculosis* had been gradually leavened as the element of entertainment began to work its way back into the series, but *Hookworm*, allowing for the CIAA's tight budget, has a far more lavish look than any of its predecessors. Perhaps because the story work had originated in 1942, simultaneously with *The Winged Scourge* and the other "sample" films, *Hookworm* delivers its message in a package built for entertainment. The film centers on a character who, as we'll see shortly, had already been introduced in the literacy series: a farmer with a floppy mustache and a generally comic appearance. In the literacy films this character had been identified as Ramón, but in the English versions of *Hookworm* and other health-care films Ramón became Careless Charlie.

The early scenes immediately set the tone with casual, folksy narration by Art Baker and "guest" animation by Ollie Johnston, more extensive than his single scene in *Cleanliness Brings Health*. The opening sequence introduces sick Charlie, who looks at a picture of his healthy former self and doesn't recognize it. These and other key scenes, animated by Johnston, serve to set Charlie's character, which is then animated in the balance of the picture by other artists. The film continues along these entertaining lines: the narrator describes the vicious hookworm, and then can't find Charlie—frightened by the description, Charlie has hidden in a tree. The narrator (represented again by a giant hand) brings Charlie back to earth by erasing the branch he's sitting on, whereupon Charlie plummets comically to the ground. The film presents another lesson in latrine construction, but this time couched in cartoon gags: Charlie, carrying the stakes and thatched straw to the latrine site, trips on a rock and falls, and the materials fly into the air and simply land in place. The hookworms, animated by John McManus as faceless monsters, are morbidly fascinating—in particular a horrific close-up of one worm, fastened to an intestine wall, voraciously gulping down huge quantities of blood—but because the focus of the film is on Charlie, the pitfall that had concerned Walt, making the worms too sympathetic, is avoided. All this is accompanied by a lively musical score, tracked from earlier films, in particular a jaunty walking theme from the 1937 short *Pluto's Quin-Puplets*. In short, *Hookworm* is, far more obviously than its "Health for the Americas" predecessors, a Disney cartoon.

INSECTS AS CARRIERS OF DISEASE

Another health-threatening "public enemy" identified on Bob Carr's 1942 list was the housefly. "This should be much easier to put over than the hookworm," Carr noted. "The Fly can be made into a mischievous, dirty little character, who enjoys giving free rides to germs, and loves to walk in butter."[87] This suggestion was immediately adopted, and "The House Fly, Public Enemy No. 1" underwent extensive story development during the spring and summer of 1942.[88] Like "Hookworm," however, it had an uncertain status at the studio. Production was suspended, resumed, and suspended again between 1942 and 1944.

[87] Of course, (more or less) sympathetic houseflies had already been depicted in such Disney films as *Snow White and the Seven Dwarfs* and the 1937 Mickey Mouse short *The Worm Turns.*

[88] Captain Madison, writing in August 1943, objected to the phrase "Public Enemy No. 1" because that distinction had already been accorded the mosquito in *The Winged Scourge.*

The 1944 CIAA contract brought this housefly story out of limbo by proposing a new film, combining the fly with two other pests: the mosquito and the louse. The resulting story, "Insects as Carriers of Disease," was developed during the summer of 1944, and preliminary storyboards were presented to the CIAA committee at a meeting in Washington in mid-August. Here the story department's ideas collided with those of the agency's medical consultants. The story crew, Ed Penner and Ernie Terrazas, had proposed an approach that gave the insects strong, malevolent personalities and depicted them as villains who deliberately plotted their disease-carrying assault against human victims. The literal-minded medical consultants quickly rejected this approach, pointing out that in real life the insects had no logical reasoning power, and asked the studio to rework the story and depersonalize the insects. Captain Madison took the studio's part, protesting that such changes would "quite completely emasculate the entire picture." But the medical consultants stood their ground, arguing that a strong film could still be made with a more scientifically accurate premise.

A letter from one of the consultants, Dr. Janet Mackie, reveals something of the original story ideas that would be eliminated from the finished film. "I have looked at the story boards again," she wrote, "and it seems that it would take very little alteration in text and practically none in the pictures to put the conversation into the mouth of the narrator instead of the mouth of the insect. . . . For example: #s 11–23. The fly speaking, 'Yes, my friends, Ramon is a fool. He thinks I cannot harm him. Why, *I* am one of the world's great disease carriers! Of course, Ramon helps me. He allows his yard to become fouled with garbage and animal filth. It is in filth like this that I live and breed . . . etc.' could be changed to the narrator speaking, 'Yes, my friends, Ramon is a fool! He thinks the fly cannot harm him. Why it is one of the great disease carriers . . .

etc.'" In the end the studio did agree to the requested changes, and the revised story was ready for production by mid-September.

Assigned to the direction of Bill Roberts, *Insects as Carriers of Disease* became the most polished of the four new health subjects. The insects of the title were depersonalized, as the consultants had requested; and, like *Hookworm*, the film compensated by centering its attention on Ramón—or, as he had now been renamed, Careless Charlie. Once again the film benefited from a "guest appearance" by a top animator: Ward Kimball supplied rough animation of Charlie in the film's opening scenes. Harvey Toombs followed through on Kimball's work and continued to animate Charlie's key scenes throughout the rest of the picture. Kimball's influence is clear: Charlie, introduced at the dinner table, chews his food in a comical manner emphasized by his floppy mustache, and Toombs maintains a consistently loose approach to the character in succeeding scenes. The film's ingenious twist is to reduce Charlie to the size of the insects, so that these seemingly harmless pests (animated mostly by Al Coe and John Reed[89]) are revealed as monstrous creatures. Without personalizing the insects, without giving them voices or attributing rational motives to them, this device effectively establishes them as malignant enemies and lends weight to their disease-spreading activities. The mosquito had, of course, already been treated in *The Winged Scourge*, and two scenes from that picture are salvaged here. By and large, however, *Insects as Carriers of Disease* maintains a high standard of original animation, and a handsome look that compares well with some of Disney's contemporary theatrical productions. By contrast with the other health films, their musical scores cobbled together from existing tracks, this one even boasts an original score by Paul Smith, complete with a character theme for Careless Charlie.

[89] Both Coe and Reed also contributed isolated scenes of Charlie.

PLANNING FOR GOOD EATING

Another title suggested on the CIAA's new list was "Nutrition," a subject of great concern in rural Latin America.[90] By late December 1944, Dan MacManus, whose multiple roles in the Good Neighbor project were expanding to include story work, had produced a preliminary script. MacManus's outline suggests a contrast between a healthy character who follows a balanced diet, and an unhealthy one who eats only corn and beans—a continuation of the good character/bad character device used in such earlier pictures as *Cleanliness Brings Health*. This script was submitted to the CIAA and, again, elicited a request for changes. Between the agency's suggestions and further work by the Disney story department, the story was overhauled. The finished film discards the contrasting-character idea and returns to Careless Charlie and his family, who embody *both* sides of the issue: at film's beginning they subsist on a substandard diet of corn and beans; by the end of the reel they have upgraded their diet and are healthy and happy. MacManus had also suggested a model diet made up of four food groups; in the finished film these are reduced to three, the fruits and vegetables combined in a single category.

[90] Jack Cutting and Bill Cottrell, on their survey trip through Central America, had noticed the problem of malnutrition and had suggested a film to address it as early as February 1943, but nothing further came of the idea until the CIAA office suggested it more than a year later.

Direction of the film was assigned to Gerry Geronimi, who had recently directed several sequences in *The Three Caballeros*. Initially developed as the second title on the current health-film contract, "Nutrition" was delayed in production and was actually the last of the four subjects to be completed. Geronimi lamented that, because the picture was given a low priority at the studio, it was repeatedly delayed to allow for work on other films. (Even after the animation had been completed the delays persisted, and Geronimi wrote plaintively to Sharpsteen that "a lot of cels have been painted by Eric Hansen and are just lying around and will probably crack if they are not put through Production Camera soon."[91])

[91] Eric Hansen had also painted backgrounds for the picture.

These factors are reflected in the finished picture, which has a much less lavish look than *Hookworm* or *Insects as Carriers of Disease*, reverting to a style that recalls the earlier health films. A look at the animation crew reveals why: virtually the entire film is animated by *two* artists. Not for this film a contribution from visiting royalty like Ollie Johnston or Ward Kimball; practically all of the character animation is the work of Harvey Toombs. Toombs was a skilled animator and had worked on some of the studio's most distinguished features, but here he relies on an extremely simple, cartoony style. The balance of the visuals is contributed by effects animator Andy Engman, and consists mainly of diagrams or static paintings of the food groups. There's still room for a certain element of humor—the ox in the opening scene looks resentful until the paintbrush finally supplies him with a tail; Charlie, preparing to take a bow for the improvement in his family's health, is unceremoniously shoved out of the picture so his wife can receive the credit—but the overall style of the film is far more austere than that of its immediate predecessors. The music, once again, is liberally tracked from earlier pictures. (A short "march" theme from *Insects as Carriers of Disease* is used, three times, to underscore scenes of Charlie chopping wood. Another sequence, illustrating growing vegetables and their beneficial effect on healthy bones, is accompanied by the title character's theme from *Bambi*.)

In the summer of 1945, during production of "Nutrition," the CIAA contacted the studio to request a title change. The new title, they suggested, should be "It is Easy to Eat Well." Sharpsteen felt this was an awkward title, and later wrote back to the CIAA suggesting something simpler like "Eating for Health." The agency, in turn, rejected that idea but responded with a list of alternatives: "Improved Rural Nutrition," "Easy Eating for Farm Families," "Good Food for Small Farmers," and "Good Eating Is Easy." Sharpsteen agreed to the last suggestion on their list: *Planning for Good Eating*. (The Spanish edition retained the agency's original suggestion: *Es facil comer bien*.) At this stage the CIAA also questioned whether this film belonged in the "Health for the Americas" series at all, since it seemed to focus more on agriculture than on health. Nothing came of this query, and the finished film retains its "Health for the Americas" introductory title.

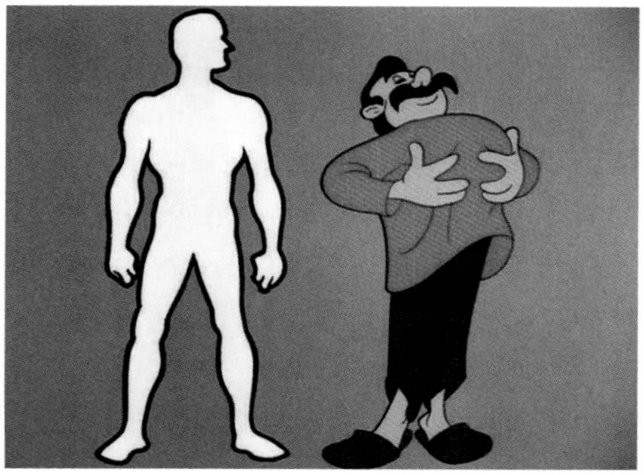

Careless Charlie strikes a healthy pose in *Planning for Good Eating*.

ENVIRONMENTAL SANITATION

The final subject for this CIAA contract was "Environmental Sanitation." Like *How Disease Travels*, which had already been completed (and which we'll consider in connection with the literacy films), this subject took the concept of hygiene from the personal to the community level, showing how a town or city could maintain a clean, healthy environment for its citizens. Having been suggested by the CIAA staff, the preliminary story outline was developed during the summer of 1944, simultaneously with *Insects as Carriers of Disease* and *Planning for Good Eating*—and, like those outlines, was roundly criticized by the agency. Submitted to Washington in late September, the preliminary script brought a quick response from Dr. Janet Mackie: "We had in mind a much broader range in presentation of the care of a whole city than the present script provides. This script has too much emphasis on the care of an individual home and not sufficient on the care of the city as a whole. If the two cannot be combined we should prefer the theme to be a panorama of the care of the city. The artists could make a beautiful picture of the ideal city on the lines of the film 'Water, Friend or Enemy' emphasizing the fact that the ideal city must have proper sanitation. Clean swept streets, tidy houses, ample safe water, wastes safely carried away for proper disposal are an essential part of this picture. . . ."

The revisions were effected, again, by Dan MacManus. In later years MacManus told Milt Gray: "I took environmental sanitation, which can be a pretty dull subject. And I wrote it with the idea that the narrator was a nice, feminine voice, like a mother. She said, 'I am the city, and the inhabitants are my children. Today it's a very beautiful city, but it wasn't always that way, it used to be this way'—all the bad things they were doing in sanitation, and what they had done. We had to be careful not to preach, not to lecture, but just tell a nice little story about how beautiful things are today because they did this and that and the other. They could take a hint from that. Awareness films, to make them aware of what could be done. Ben [Sharpsteen] said, 'Do it in a romantic way.' What do you mean, 'do it in a romantic way?' Anyway, I submitted it, and that's what they wanted."

Even after the submission of MacManus's script in December 1944, revisions continued for several months. The "nice, feminine voice" he had suggested was replaced by a standard male narrator (Art Baker). Sanitation practices at the community level were still unfamiliar material for the story artists, and the CIAA experts weighed in with numerous suggestions for changes: "The pump handle should be omitted from the drawing and the word 'well' eliminated from the script. . . . It would be advisable to show a row of houses lying close together with an ordinary row of latrines in the back. This would suggest crowded conditions and, at the same time, show how this problem can be met even though a sewage system has not been installed . . . Wash boards are not used

Safe water is provided in a community reservoir in *Environmental Sanitation*. (Black-and-white frame enlargement from a color film.)

to any extent in Latin America." By mid-March 1945, the story was tentatively finalized and production had started under the direction of Graham Heid.

Coincidentally or not, the resulting film is produced, as Dr. Mackie had suggested, very much along the lines of *Water—Friend or Enemy*. "I am a city," Baker announces at the opening, much as Fred Shields had opened the earlier picture with the words "I am water." As before, the narrator continues to carry the continuity of the film, the visuals serving simply as an illustration of his words. And, as in the earlier film, there's virtually no character animation at all. Some moving figures are shown from a distance or represented by close-ups of hands, but movement on the screen is maintained largely by effects animation (flowing water, flickering candles), dissolves, and camera movement. In fact, some of the animation that does appear is salvaged from *Water*. (One Bill Tytla scene, depicting a woman's hands bathing a small boy in the water, is transplanted from a river in the earlier film to an indoor bathtub in this one!) The salvage doesn't end there: on a technical level, much of *Environmental Sanitation* is assembled from spare parts. Besides the recycled animation, most of the music is, once again, tracked from *Bambi*, *Saludos Amigos*, and other earlier films. All in all, the economy of production and the simplicity of treatment suggest a return to the bare basics of *Tuberculosis*, where the "Health for the Americas" series had started. As if to make it official, Ed Aardal's hand-washing scene from that film returns for one final appearance. In spirit, if not in strict stylistic terms, the series has come full circle.

READING FOR THE AMERICAS

At the end of the Seminar on Visual Education in June 1943, a consensus of agreement had been reached on several broad topics. One was that the medium of animation (as practiced by the Disney studio) was uniquely suited to combat the problem of illiteracy in Latin America, especially if reading lessons could be built around subject matter that was also of interest to the same audiences. The seminar attendees also agreed that a comprehensive literacy-film program would include films in three categories: *motivation* films, which would inspire illiterate adults with a desire to learn; *teaching* films, which would accomplish the actual work of teaching the students; and *teacher training* films, which would acquaint teachers with techniques for using the films effectively in the classroom. The teaching films were recognized as the spearhead of the program and would be produced first. The seminar's recommendations also allowed for supplementary materials, such as pamphlets, illustrated with scenes from the films, that would reinforce both the health and agricultural lessons of the films and the vocabulary used in them.

As the seminar attendees dispersed, a team was formed to begin preliminary work on the films. In addition to Bill Cottrell and Jack Cutting, the team included Dr. Enrique S. de Lozada, who had exercised a leadership role during the seminar and who now assumed a similar role over the proposed literacy series. De Lozada's government duties called for his return to Washington at the end of the seminar, but two of his staff members, Dr. Hernane Tavares de Sa and Doris LeRoy, remained at the studio to represent him. Kenneth Holland, of the CIAA's Science and Education division, was named as a member of the team. Two of the more outspoken members of the seminar group, Dr. Mildred Wiese and Eulalia Guzmán, were also retained as consultants. Together this group set out to put the seminar's recommendations into action.

Jack Cutting methodically set to work framing guidelines for the teaching films, seeking economical production methods that would allow the studio to deliver the films for a reasonable price. In mid-June 1943 he wrote to Francis Alstock, outlining a plan for a series of nine one-reel films "produced in black and white, using the simplest types of characters and backgrounds possible. The supplementary materials will likewise be made inexpensively." Cutting estimated that such a series could be produced for as little as $200,000. He also suggested experimenting with alternative forms, such as filmstrips, which had been discussed at the seminar and were far easier and more economical to produce than motion pictures. He felt that filmstrips might, in some cases, take the place of motion pictures in the teaching series, or at least might be included among the supplementary materials.

Bill Cottrell, meanwhile, worked with Mildred Wiese on tentative development of two film stories for the literacy project. One was a sample teaching film, "Plant Soy Beans with Corn," which would teach beginning vocabulary words built around an agricultural theme. The other was a motivation film, based on the preseminar proposal "The Advantages of Reading and Writing." Now known as "Learn to Read and Read to Learn," this was conceived as a color film featuring Donald Duck and Joe Carioca. Comments from a meeting just before the seminar reveal that this picture would have been roughly similar to the two Donald Duck income-tax films already produced by the studio: "For example the duck is indicated to be someone with intelligence but because he can't read he gets himself into a lot of jams. After he has had some bad moments he gives up and says, 'Oh, what the devil!' Then the parrot, who represents a suave, educated type, gives him some object lessons in knowing how to read and write."

As they proceeded with these activities, Cutting and Cottrell were careful to check their ideas with Walt—who, according to Cutting, "was very enthusiastic about their possibilities"—and, by mail, with de Lozada. It wasn't long before de Lozada responded. Returning to the studio late in July, de Lozada made it clear that he took the literacy films, and his part in them, very seriously. The project was on the wrong track, he announced, and three major changes must be made to rectify the problem.

First, the films must be developed from the beginning in Spanish, not in English. The earlier health-care films had been produced in English; then Spanish and Portuguese editions had been made simply by recording new sound tracks in the appropriate languages. The production team had assumed that the literacy films would be produced in the same way and, indeed, the earliest plans for the series had called for English, Spanish, and Portuguese editions of all the films. This would allow for distribution in all of the Americas (since, after all, the problem of adult illiteracy was not unknown in the United States either). This idea, de Lozada informed the team, was naive; because Spanish and Portuguese are essentially phonetic languages and English is not, the methods for teaching English would be useless when applied to the other languages. "Furthermore," Cutting noted, "we believed we had to make

English teaching films in order to placate persons in our Government who have charge of appropriating funds for such programs as this. Enrique informs me that we're quite mistaken about this; in other words, that it's perfectly all right to concentrate all our efforts, first, on the Spanish part of the program."

Second, de Lozada took exception to the idea of producing the films in black-and-white and with limited quantities of animation. "Eliminating color and personality animation from this project is a serious handicap," he wrote. "The advantage of Disney films, as a teaching instrument, is their simultaneous use of animation, color and sound. . . . It will not be possible to sustain the interest of adult illiterates unless we employ all the devices in the Disney bag-of-tricks. I'm sure that Disney will be in accord with this. He no doubt agreed to black and white solely in the interest of simple and inexpensive production." Cutting had indeed proposed economy measures only to make the project more financially feasible in the eyes of the CIAA, but de Lozada insisted that economy must not be a consideration in the literacy program. To eliminate the full benefit of Disney style from the films would undercut their effectiveness, and if color and character animation cost more money, more money must be found.

Third, and perhaps most daringly, de Lozada insisted that the story work done to date must be scrapped and that Cutting and Cottrell must go back to basics—and back to the field. "I don't believe the solution is to bring Latin American educators to the Studio as advisors," he wrote, "this is vicarious living. I contend that Disney personnel should be put in direct contact with the problem in the field so that while working on the problem they will be able to absorb the psychology of the audience they are trying to reach." The survey trip Cottrell and Cutting had already made through the Central American republics for this project the previous spring, de Lozada maintained, was not enough. Now he proposed another field trip. This time a studio group led by Cottrell, Cutting, and de Lozada himself was to travel to Mexico, observe actual adult literacy classes in progress, absorb teaching techniques currently in use, and start new storyboards from scratch while still in the field. "We plan to study adult illiterates in various environments, making visits to rural homes, urban slums, isolated mountain areas, etc. We will observe their work and living conditions, their family life, visit their churches, their places of recreation, etc. The advantage of our doing this is that the writers and artists who create the lessons for the screen will gain a true understanding of the problems which adult educators and illiterate pupils face. They will see conditions under which the films will be used, and will be better able to determine the content which will be of greatest usefulness."

De Lozada's demands illustrated his commitment to the literacy series and his high ambitions for it. They also exacerbated the friction that had been developing within the literacy team and that would ultimately undermine the project. Cottrell and other staff members were uneasy over de Lozada's memo, which had been written while both Walt and Roy were in New York, away from the studio. Cutting, on the other hand, was more sanguine about de Lozada's views and inclined to agree with them. In a memo to Walt, Cutting defended de Lozada: "The recent discussions with Enrique de Lozada, and the attached memorandum, have been the subject of considerable concern to members of the production department and even Bill Cottrell. I am certain that many believe that memo, and my participation in discussions with Alstock and de Lozada, constituted some kind of a commitment which compromises the Studio. . . . Some have the impression that de Lozada is assuming the role of producer. I honestly believe that nothing is farther from his mind. The idea of the literacy program originated with de Lozada and his great personal enthusiasm is apt to be misunderstood."

Whatever Walt, Roy, or other Disney personnel may have thought of him, de Lozada's bid was successful: both the studio and the CIAA approved the new field trip. A tentative itinerary was established for September–October 1943, and a miniature El Grupo was formed for the occasion. Besides Cutting, Cottrell, and de Lozada, this group included Mildred Wiese; unit manager Erwin Verity; story men George Stallings, Dan MacManus, and Graham Heid; and a bilingual secretary, Blanca Palacios. MacManus, a native of Mexico, was fluent in Spanish and had already assisted with odd translation jobs for the Good Neighbor films. Heid, in addition to his work in the story department, had experience in direction and was a capable photographer. He would divide his time in Mexico between story work and documentary photography of the project. With Cutting, Verity, and Blanca Palacios as an advance party, this group flew to Mexico City in September 1943 to begin what would become a difficult and contentious survey trip.

For the task of teaching literacy from the screen was a monumentally complex and difficult undertaking, far more so than either the CIAA or the Disney studio had realized at first. To begin with, the seminar had demonstrated that there were multiple methods of teaching reading, some of them fundamentally opposed to one another. Two leading systems were in use in 1943. One was the *global* method, which focused on teaching the student to recognize complete words, phrases, and even sentences. This was the method currently favored by most educators in the United States. The opposing candidate, the *phonetic* method, focused on teaching the student to recognize the letters and permutations of letters that represent the sounds of vowels and consonants, before proceeding to develop more complex ideas from those basic components. Within these two broad categories were a variety of subdivisions, along with maverick methods like Dr. Richards's "Basic English" or the technique of Frank Laubach, who had used his own literacy system to teach the peoples of many countries, some of them Latin American.[92] The seminar group had agreed to adopt an exhaustive approach, considering *all* of these methods and perhaps developing a teaching technique that would combine the best elements of several of them.

In Mexico, however, El Grupo soon learned that educators strongly favored the phonetic method, especially for teaching adults. This was partly because Spanish itself, unlike English, is basically a phonetic language. Mexican teachers were not required to adhere to any one system, and some used the global method to teach classes of children, although, as Cutting noted, "all agreed that this system is not practical in Spanish for the instruction of adults."

[92] Laubach had been invited to the seminar and had offered a presentation on his teaching system, but, like the "Basic English" demonstration reel, it had been roundly criticized by the professional educators in attendance.

Compounding this conflict of methods was a conflict of personalities within the group. Mildred Wiese, her expertise in adult education notwithstanding, proved to be a public relations liability because of her blunt, often tactless, manner with strangers. "Unfortunately," Cutting wrote after one encounter with local teachers, "Wiese displayed lack of tact in her questioning, which made some of us, as well as the teachers, uncomfortable. . . . She has an unfortunate faculty of presenting questions in a manner that is quickly mistaken for criticism, and it was plain to see that these teachers were put on the defensive by her attitude." Wiese was also an outspoken advocate of the global method of teaching literacy, and was inclined to disregard any and all claims for the phonetic method. In her work with Cottrell on "Learn to Read and Read to Learn" and "Plant Soy Beans with Corn," she had taken pains to build her initial reading lessons around the global method, despite the recommendations of the seminar. Now the "Learn to Read" storyboards and supplemental materials were taken to Mexico, where Wiese insisted on presenting them as samples of progress to date on the Disney literacy project.[93] This brought her into direct conflict with Eulalia Guzmán, the Mexican instructor who had participated in the seminar and who was an equally passionate advocate of the phonetic system of education. The more the Mexican educators endorsed the phonetic method, the more Wiese insisted on the global method. An uneasy personal tension continued to build within the group, even threatening to drive a wedge between longtime friends and colleagues Cottrell and Cutting.

[93] The storyboards were presented in the form of a "Leica reel," a device developed at the Disney studio in the 1930s to simulate a film's continuity on-screen by means of still drawings. This presentation was supplemented by a "Learn to Read" pamphlet, which Wiese had prepared with MacManus's help.

As for de Lozada, the man responsible for the trip in the first place, he was nowhere to be found. It had been understood that he would precede the group to Mexico and would make all necessary contacts and arrangements for the observation of reading classes; in fact, he did neither. El Grupo found themselves in Mexico City with no advance groundwork, no CIAA literacy experts apart from the problematic Dr. Wiese, and no contacts with schools or individual teachers. Moreover, unbeknownst to the Disney staff, they had planned their trip just on the eve of the national vacation period for Mexican schools. Practically every school in the republic would be closed for the next ten days![94] Fortunately, thanks to Cutting's and Cottrell's resourcefulness and the Mexican contacts established on previous Disney expeditions, they were prepared to take matters into their own hands. With the assistance of Alejandro Buelna Jr., head of the Department of Tourism, they contacted Mexico's top education officials and asked whether an adult-education specialist might be hired to convene a special literacy class in some smaller village, recruiting students from among the locals. After some discussion, this arrangement was made. The teacher was Inspector of Rural Schools Juan A. Pina, who had considerable experience teaching poorer adults. For a location, Buelna suggested Fortín de las Flores, in the state of Veracruz. This

[94] The exception was the state of Morelos, which was changing its academic schedule. One education official suggested that the group might set up headquarters in Morelos and observe classes at a school in Cuernavaca. But El Grupo was hoping to observe classes of absolute illiterates, and Cuernavaca proved unsuitable for their purposes: too modern, too sophisticated, too many tourists.

beautiful little town and its neighboring communities were far enough from Mexico City to be relatively untouched by city sophistication; and although Fortín was something of a tourist spot, its economy was driven by agricultural and textile workers. It also boasted an excellent hotel, whose owner, Antonio Ruiz Galindo, likewise owned a nearby plantation and could supply students for the class from among the plantation workers. Ruiz Galindo was inclined to help El Grupo in any way he could, for he had a special interest in the literacy problem, and in bettering the lives of the peasant classes in general.[95]

[95] Buelna apparently took special pride in Fortín de las Flores. His department had earlier cooperated with the CIAA in producing a 16 mm short, *A Town in Old Mexico*, narrated by Orson Welles, which devoted some footage to neighboring Puebla and Orizaba but also featured some lovely shots of Fortín. The theatrical short *Land of Orizaba*, released in 1942 as part of MGM's FitzPatrick TravelTalks series, had also included some shots of Fortîn and of the Ruiz Galindo hotel itself.

Proceeding to Fortín and establishing a combination school and "studio" at the Hotel Ruiz Galindo, El Grupo—augmented by Eulalia Guzmán and two of her colleagues, Guadalupe Cejudo and Estela Soní—belatedly began their survey work.[96] Despite the professional demeanor of all concerned, personal tensions continued to seethe beneath the surface. Shortly after their arrival in Fortín, they were visited by Buelna and none other than Francis Alstock, who learned for the first time that de Lozada had failed to make an appearance. "Mr. Alstock was sore as hell," wrote Erwin Verity. "Moreover he admitted that the Coordinator's office had failed to provide us with the cooperation as planned. He also stated that if Enrique did not show up . . . he would give the studio complete authority to make these films as per our own judgment." De Lozada did arrive in Fortín two weeks later, in early October, by which time the improvised literacy class was well established and in progress. Meanwhile, El Grupo had other problems to contend with. It had been anticipated that Dan MacManus, as a native Mexican fluent in Spanish, could surmount the language barrier and help the group communicate with the illiterate adults in the class; but MacManus was an upper-class Mexican who had lived in the United States most of his life, and was unable to establish a rapport with the poorer classes. Luckily Blanca Palacios, the bilingual secretary, was better able to communicate with them. Graham Heid had been expected to divide his time between story work and photography of the region, but his photographic activities were hampered by incessant rain.

[96] Guadalupe Cejudo was the supervisor of schools in Mexico City; Estela Soní was the director of Escuela Cristobal Colon.

Despite all these problems, the literacy class was formed and was soon meeting on a daily basis. "We have learned," Verity wrote, "that even the regular Government adult illiteracy classes run spasmodically, so numerous are the problems connected with assembling a group of adults, so our experimental classes are no different than any others. The illiterates in general are not anxious to learn to read and write—they feel that they don't have time, consequently they must be compelled to attend, or they must be inspired. Later we hope to inspire in them a desire to learn, through our pictures, but for now our attendance results from direct orders from the owner of the plantation, Señor Ruiz Galindo, and in one instance, the local police force.

"In most cases, these men have been working from sunrise till almost sundown, or time for the class. They are very tired and they don't hesitate to tell the teacher that they're very sleepy. In this respect they are an ideal group for the experiment, since this is probably typical of most illiterate groups, and we must produce films that stimulate interest and a desire to learn, if the program is to be successful. The Coordinator's office plans to show these films at night in local plazas, using sound trucks, after the people have completed their daily work, so we must plan the films on this basis."

Cutting was impressed with Professor Pina: "He is of Indian extraction, is a cultivated man of considerable poise. His way of handling adult illiterates impresses everyone. Special note should be made of the way in which he speaks to the class, the language he uses, and the way he phrases his talks." Cutting left the group early in October to return to California and resume his duties as head of the studio's "Foreign Department," and this served to ease his strained relations with Cottrell. By the time Walt—visiting Mexico to gather survey material for a theatrical picture—arrived in Fortín in mid-October for a visit, the class was running more or less smoothly and the staff were gathering the data for which they had come. Of course Walt had been apprised of their problems to date, and in a hectic series of meetings he did his best to resolve those problems before taking his departure. El Grupo remained in Fortín until early November, then returned to Burbank to start from scratch on the literacy film series.

The series was still being planned on an ambitious scale, and still in accordance with the recommendations of the seminar. That is, the reading films should be built around subjects already of interest to the illiterate audiences, and should include both *motivation* and *teaching* films. At story meetings in November 1943, Walt described his vision of the motivation films in sweeping terms: "Keep stressing the intellect. That is a good basis. When you can read, the sky's the limit—you're unlimited in what you can do. You can make that interesting and humorous." The series would begin with basic health-care principles like those already addressed in earlier pictures, and progress to subjects on economic and social betterment—always with an eye toward words or sentences that could be used in the reading program. Then one or two teaching films would be produced with the material in each motivation film, reinforcing both the ideas and the reading skills being taught. Specific numbers fluctuated from time to time, but the plan most often mentioned in interoffice correspondence called for twenty motivation films, with two reading lessons based on each one—a total of *sixty* one-reel films.

Clearly, it would be a challenge to produce such a high volume of films, accomplish the educational function that had been planned for the films, *and* stay within the CIAA's tight budgets. The studio decided to test the plan with an initial series of seven pictures. In December the CIAA approved production of two health-care pictures, similar to the concurrent Health for the Americas entries, tentatively titled "The Human Body" and "What Is Disease," along with two teaching films based on the material in each one. These films would be produced, not individually, but more or less simultaneously as a single unit. Animation and other art would be designed, not for individual films, but to be used repeatedly within the series; and production costs for *all* the pictures would be pooled. In this way the studio hoped to maintain standards of quality but, at the same time, to keep the series economically feasible. Finally, the contract called for a third health film, tentatively called "The Transmission of Disease." Assuming the first six pictures were found satisfactory, this one would provide additional material for the next group of teaching films.

Unfortunately, the conflict over teaching methods in the literacy series had still not been resolved. Some members of the team had been convinced by their experience in Mexico that the phonetic method should be adopted. "Let us not be forever Yankees with patronizing airs," Cutting had written to Walt before leaving Mexico. "The Ministry of Education in Mexico is using the method they are, for instructing adults in reading, not because they are living in the Dark Ages and are ill-informed about so-called modern methods, but because they have found that definite results are achieved by the work they are doing. With due consideration for the global method, we cannot wait to see whether or not Mexico will one day accept it as a system for teaching adults. To be practical, we must get on with the project and, to do this, we must do our best to adapt for the screen the method that has proved its success in Spanish-speaking countries." Enrique de Lozada, who had exercised such influence over the literacy project, had advocated the phonetic method from the beginning.

But de Lozada had assumed a less prominent role in the project since the Fortín de las Flores debacle. Mildred Wiese, the leading proponent of the global method, had by contrast become more powerful. Wiese's formal contract with the studio expired in January 1944, but by virtue of her strong connection with the CIAA, she remained firmly ensconced in the literacy program. The debate over teaching methods in the Disney films now became essentially a turf war between Wiese and Eulalia Guzmán, who had participated in both the education seminar and the Fortín workshop, and who now continued to champion the phonetic method.

Saddled with this none-too-promising working arrangement, the studio embarked on the first entries in its combined health/literacy series. By late January 1944 preliminary storyboards had been prepared for the new series, and the first film, *The Human Body*, had tentatively started production. At this point Guzmán and her colleagues, Guadalupe Cejudo and Estela Soní, were invited to the studio to work with the rest of the group. A general meeting of all production personnel was held on 19 January. Guzmán was asked for her reaction to the storyboards, and the transcript of the meeting is dominated by her response—rambling, long-winded, ambiguous but vaguely dissatisfied with the plan to date. Production of *The Human Body* faltered in its tracks after this meeting, then resumed within a week. But Guzmán continued to quarrel with Wiese, with MacManus, and with a new CIAA representative who had been added to the group: Nelson Rockefeller's cousin Eleanor Clark. Erwin Verity, the unit manager, noted: "It looks as if these people never will agree on the exact teaching method to use, and the content of each subject. The Producer has set a deadline of March 10, 1944 for last minute changes requested by technical advisors." After finishing her work, Guzmán returned with her colleagues to Mexico, but continued to send long, rambling letters, voicing her discontent over the literacy series in English that was not always clear but was always emphatic. Walt himself was usually the recipient of these epic epistles.

Thus conflicted, the studio strove to produce its contracted seven films.

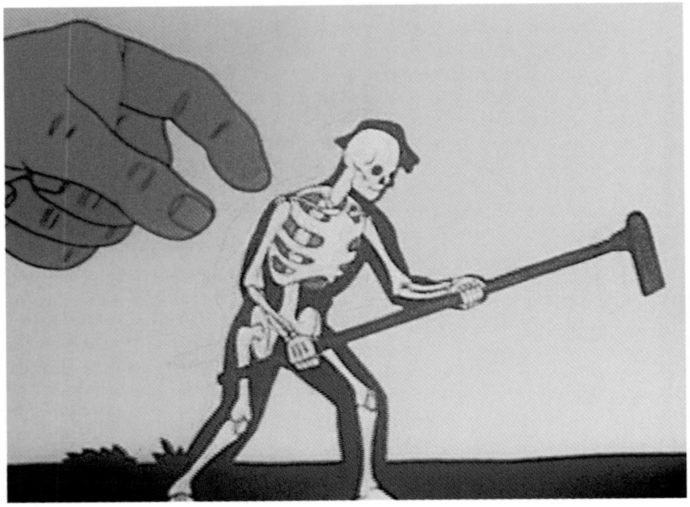

The narrator's hand removes the body's skeleton to illustrate the importance of strong bones.

THE HUMAN BODY

Produced by Ben Sharpsteen's unit, which was concurrently producing the Health for the Americas series, *The Human Body* and the other motivation films are simply additional entries in that series. The opening titles announce as much, backed again by the instrumental "Saludos Amigos" theme. *The Human Body* starts by establishing a main character, then systematically robbing him of each of his possessions—his livestock and his home—to make the point that the most valuable possession of all is his healthy body. The character and his surroundings are drawn in an extremely simple, generic style, similar to that in the simplest of the other health films, which has two advantages: economy of production, and a universality that can represent multiple cultures at the same time. The character's eyes are dots, his hands an interesting stylistic compromise. Disney characters such as Mickey Mouse had traditionally been drawn with three fingers per hand, but that principle had sometimes been abandoned, as with Snow White and other human characters, who were drawn more realistically with four fingers. (The nontheatrical CIAA films, departing from traditional Disney style, treated the principle flexibly in other instances too.) The hands of this leading character are usually drawn with a "mitten" effect, sometimes with the forefinger delineated. (When all the fingers are delineated, he has three per hand.)

Proceeding at a leisurely pace, and even allowing for a few mild gags, *The Human Body* continues to make its points simply but effectively. The importance of strong bones is illustrated when the character performs a simple hoeing action, then is silhouetted to show the skeleton inside his body, still hoeing away. When the skeleton is removed, the silhouette flops baggily to the ground. The workings of the lungs, heart, and circulatory and digestive systems are similarly outlined. The film's severely simple style is offset by an interesting bit of salvage at the introduction: this film not only borrows the *idea* of the animated paintbrush in *Aquarela do Brasil*, but actually recycles the background painting and animation from that film.

LA HISTÓRIA DE JOSÉ

The teaching films, like the motivation films, were produced under the general aegis of Ben Sharpsteen's unit. They were made under a loose arrangement by which Dan MacManus, who had done most of the story development, shared direction responsibilities with Graham Heid.

As Mildred Wiese developed a script for the first teaching film, she was at first guided by Walt's vision of a sweepingly inclusive series. In December 1943 she submitted a script titled "El hombre tiene intelegencia": in January 1944 this was simplified to "Este es el hombre." By the time of the first completed teaching film, the concept had evolved into an extremely simple basic lesson built around the main character in *The Human Body*, now named José. The lesson, couched in the global teaching method, endeavors to teach the audience to read the sentence *José es un joven sano* ("José is a healthy young man").

Taking its cue from the health films, *La história de José* opens with titles announcing a new series, Lectura para las Americas (Reading for the Americas), again backed by the "Saludos Amigos" theme. The concept of "salvage" is largely irrelevant in discussing these films, since virtually all the animation in them was *designed* to be reused in multiple films. The still drawings of José and his chickens, pig, and hut, already seen in *The Human Body*, dutifully reappear in *La história de José*—this time as illustrations in a book, whose turning pages are taken from Jack Boyd's animation in *Tuberculosis*. José's body collapses again when the skeleton is removed, and the cycle depicting his hoeing action is repeated extensively to illustrate the idea of the *joven sano*.

Yet not all of the film is dominated by character animation—even simple character animation, recycled from other films. In fact, there's an ingenious concentration on finding any device *but* character animation to hold the audience's attention: held drawings, sliding cels, effects animation, color changes, sound effects. The camera plays a part too, trucking in or out and occasionally wiping between scenes. (Surprisingly, much of the footage in the teaching films was shot on the multiplane crane—not to create an illusion of depth, the multiplane's usual purpose, but to eliminate the cel shadows that would have been doubly distracting against the teaching films' flat, solid-color backgrounds.) Much screen time is devoted to vocabulary words, and the shapes of the letters are dramatized with simple animation, stretching the letters out of shape and then snapping them back into place. Interest is given to moving accents and other elements with sound effects: the word *sano* is disposed of and zooms off the screen with a "whisk" sound, the dot on the small *j* jumps up and down with a ringing-bell effect, and the small words *es* and *un* are introduced with a drumroll. (In their use of such devices, the Disney reading films anticipate celebrated educational-television programs such as *Sesame Street* by a good two decades.) When the audience is asked to read words from the screen, a chorus of voices reads them on the sound track, presumably to help the real audience overcome their self-consciousness. The narrator rewards these vocal readings with positive reinforcement: "*¡Bien, muy bien!*" and other words of praise.

Repetition of vocabulary words in *La história de José*.

JOSÉ COME BIEN

This second reading film builds on its predecessor, and on *The Human Body*, by teaching two new sentences: *José come bien* and *Este joven come bien*. The same words are then shuffled to produce other sentences. The effect, as planned, is cumulative—*José come bien* reinforces both the student's reading skills and one message of the motivation film: José is healthy because he eats well. The first teaching film relies heavily on an animation cycle from *The Human Body*, depicting José's hoeing action; this second one dwells on another scene from that picture, José sitting at a table and eating.

Here again, however, the film is made up of varied visuals other than character animation. Much of the running time of these teaching films is dominated by repetition of vocabulary words on the screen, supplied not by animators but by Harvey Orr of the studio print shop. The effect of movement in these scenes is simulated by changing the color of the words as the students read them aloud, a form of "animation" that can be accomplished quickly and easily on the camera crane. Simple effects animation reinforces the reading lesson with mild humor: the word *come* (eats) is isolated on the screen, whereupon the *c* chews on the *o*. Later, the narrator encourages the class to find the phrase *come bien* in successive sentences on the screen. White underlines are drawn under the words, then burn away like fuses with a quick explosion effect.

WHAT IS DISEASE?/THE UNSEEN ENEMY

Originally known by the working title "What Is Disease?", this film was tentatively renamed "The Unseen Enemy" (a phrase referring to disease-carrying germs) during production. Unlike other such retitling cases, this one was never completely resolved, and prints survive today bearing both titles. The copyright title is *El enemigo invisible*.

This second of the motivation films can be traced to one of Bob Carr's story suggestions in February 1942, which he had called "The Enemy Within": "What a germ is. Where it comes from. How it lives inside you. How it harms you. How you can kill it with soap, boiling water, disinfectant—and sunshine." For this picture the studio devised a new leading character—a farmer, but very different from the leading character in *The Human Body*. That farmer (José in the teaching films), although drawn simply, was an idealized, handsome figure. This farmer is an out-and-out cartoon character, who will come to be known in the health films as Careless Charlie; in the reading films he'll be identified as Ramón. In this, his first appearance, he's identified simply as "you," a surrogate figure standing in for the audience. This character has a dumpy body, an eternally bemused expression, and droopy black hair and mustache.

A housefly magnified to horrific proportions in *What Is Disease?*

(His mustache is something like Geppetto's in *Pinocchio*, and sometimes stretches and flops for comic effect, as when he chews his food.) *The Human Body* had featured an animation cycle in which José vigorously hoed his field; this character has a hoeing cycle too, but his action is loose and comical.

Thanks partly to this cartoony character, *What Is Disease?* is more entertaining than its predecessor. The farmer, informed by the narrator that he is being stalked by his worst enemy, panics and tries to run away, but the narrator stops him and explains that this enemy is microscopic, adding an explanation of the microscope for good measure. The farmer is shown how the germs can enter his body—through impure drinking water, contact with flies and other insects—and their effect on his body is compared to a large tree destroyed by tiny parasites. The farmer kneels beside a stream and drinks water from it, and a cutaway view of his body shows the germs going to work on his digestive system. Finally, basic prevention principles are explained: food coverings, windows for fresh air, mosquito netting. The importance of building a latrine rather than depositing waste in a cornfield, soon to be detailed in *Cleanliness Brings Health*, is briefly alluded to in this picture.

Here again, full character animation is supplemented by production tricks that help to sustain movement on the screen by economical means. The scenes of the doctor and the microscope are made up entirely of still drawings and sliding cels. One microscopic view of germs is accomplished by painting the germs on two cels and moving them at varying speeds beneath the camera for a bilevel effect. Adding to the general production polish of this film is a liberal use of salvage: *What Is Disease?* benefits from animation and backgrounds created for other films. The ubiquitous hand-washing scene from *Tuberculosis* is back again; scenes of water boiling in a kettle or carried in a dipper are taken from *Water—Friend or Enemy*; the anopheles mosquito injects her germs into the bloodstream in scenes from *The Winged Scourge*.

LA HISTÓRIA DE RAMÓN

This teaching film distinguishes the new leading character by giving him a name: Ramón. The key sentence taught in this film is *Ramón toma agua mala* ("Ramón drinks bad water"), and most of the animation is taken from *What Is Disease?*, particularly the key scene of Ramón dipping water from a stream and drinking it. The repetition of this action is lightened by variations: Ramón stopping to look at the water before he drinks it, the cutaway view of his internal organs, and occasionally a reversal of the drawings so that he faces in the opposite direction. (There's also a waterfall, originally animated for the 1937 short *Little Hiawatha*, which we've already seen recycled in *Water—Friend or Enemy*.) In addition, José, the character from the earlier reading films, makes a return appearance to demonstrate the proper way to treat water to

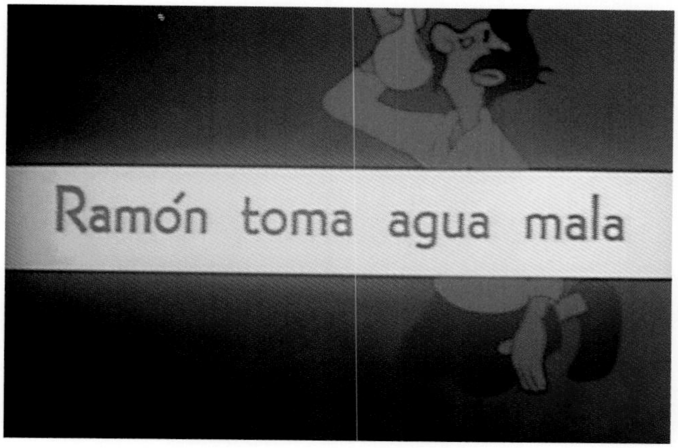

Illustrating a vocabulary-building sentence, Ramón drinks bad water.

make it safe for drinking. This is a return to the good character–bad character device used in *Cleanliness Brings Health*: here José drinks good water, remains healthy, and looks good, while goofy-looking Ramón drinks bad water and gets sick.

As in the other teaching films, clever devices are used to maintain audience interest during the instructional scenes. The accent on *Ramón* stretches like a rubber band, then pops back into place; the squirming germs from *What Is Disease?* form the word *mala*; the submerged skull representing *agua mala* is filmed through distortion glasses that lend an appropriate feeling of watery movement to the scene. Later there's a device we haven't seen before: a rectangular "iris" effect is used to isolate varying scenes on black within a single frame. The audience is then encouraged to match a vocabulary phrase with the picture that represents it.

RAMÓN ESTÁ ENFERMO

The second teaching film based on *What Is Disease?* follows naturally on the first: we've seen Ramón drinking bad water, and now *Ramón está enfermo* ("Ramón is sick"). José makes another return appearance in this film and continues to set a good example, leading to further sentences: *José toma agua buena* and *José no toma agua mala*. The image of Ramón drinking from the stream is reprised again, this time supplemented by that of the stricken Ramón, flat on his back. At the end he recovers, and the film ends with his comic hoeing action. In addition to these and other scenes from *What Is Disease?*, this film reuses the kettle of boiling water from *Water—Friend or Enemy*.

The still drawing of the supine Ramón, lying on a pillow and covered with a blanket, is one of the continuing creative devices used to sustain interest in the instructional scenes. It's used to illustrate the word *enfermo*, and slides off the screen when its function is finished. Later the same drawing is seen standing upright, and falls over with an impact effect as the word *enfermo* squeezes to one side to get out of the way. The similarity between *es* and *está* is stressed visually: the letters *es* emerge from the longer word. The word *no* slides back and forth, perhaps to suggest a head shaking. The narrator asks the audience to identify the word *está* from three available choices including *agua* and *bien*; he tries them one by one as the viewers say no, and picks the correct one last. One transition from one set of vocabulary words to another is done over a spinning pinwheel design; one set of words recedes, then the other advances toward the camera.

HOW DISEASE TRAVELS

In the story conferences following the Fortín de las Flores survey trip, Walt had advocated a teaching program that would start with basic, individual health care, then progress to community, regional, and then universal subjects. "These people know man and nature, and after a certain foundation is built there, go into other things in the outside world. . . . So, instead of just teaching them to read here, we will be giving them a foundation, a background, for the things which will follow." The story originally known as "Transmission of Disease" is a first step in that expansion: *What*

Is Disease? had dealt with sickness on an individual basis; this story takes it to the community level. One sick person is seen infecting others in the community when his germs are spread by insects, by improper waste disposal, or by simple human contact. The danger of leaving human waste in a cornfield and the importance of building a latrine are stressed, although construction of the latrine is shown in less detail here than in *Cleanliness Brings Health.* (We've already seen that these and the other health films were produced simultaneously and, in fact, story development of *Cleanliness Brings Health* was temporarily shelved in January 1944 while the same story crew worked on this subject.)

Interestingly, the more entertaining style introduced with the character of Ramón in *What Is Disease?* is abandoned here. Instead *How Disease Travels* reverts to the simplified style of *Tuberculosis* and other earlier films, with one character who resembles the plain design of "José." Even when a man is shown kneeling and drinking out of a stream, *How Disease Travels* resists the temptation to recycle Ramón's drinking scene, but substitutes its simplified basic character performing the same action. Whatever the reasons for this stylistic decision, it allows for the reuse of a large block of animation from *Tuberculosis*—not only the hand-washing scene, but the entire episode of the coughing grocer and his infected customer, and scenes of the coughing family in their beds. (Here the disease is not specifically identified as tuberculosis, only as a generic respiratory ailment.)

THE PROLOGUES AND EPILOGUES

As the literacy and health films neared completion, the CIAA stepped in with one more ill-fated suggestion. The idea apparently originated with Richard C. Rothschild, who saw initial plans for the series in the spring of 1944 and volunteered his opinion that a valuable opportunity for political self-promotion was being wasted. In a later letter he made his priorities clear: "There is too little evidence of the fact that this invaluable information is made available through the good offices of the United States Government. . . . It would seem to me . . . that the series, in addition to doing its major job of educating the people on the subject of health, should sell a little merchandise, if you know what I mean."[97] His meaning was, indeed, all too clear, and the suggestion came to the Disney studio in April 1944 in the form of a directive from the CIAA. By this time the literacy films and some of the health films were nearly finished, but Fran Alstock, Gerald Smith, and Eleanor Clark came to the studio to urge some kind of revision. The solution: a series of prologues and epilogues, to be attached to the films, announcing: "To contribute to the health and prosperity of the Americas, the people of the United States present this film." That this would entail additional time and expense was not important; the CIAA was prepared to absorb the cost.

There's no direct record of Walt's reaction to this campaign of blatant self-advertisement, but a later editorial by a Mexican

[97] Rothschild apparently made his original suggestion in conversation with Eleanor Clark in the spring of 1944. This quote is from a letter written to Wallace Harrison more than a year later. By that time the prologues and epilogues had already been produced, tacked onto the films, and hastily cut again after their disastrous reception. Rothschild, unaware of these developments and seeing a screening of the films in New York *without* the additional material, was simply concerned that his valuable advice was being ignored.

HI NEIGHBORS!
HERE IS A VERY INTERESTING AND USEFUL BOOK WHICH TELLS ALL ABOUT - -
- - OUR BIG FAMILY OF NATIONS OF THE AMERICAS, BUT DO YOU KNOW THAT THERE ARE MANY PEOPLE TO WHOM - -
- - THIS BOOK MEANS NOTHING -- PEOPLE WHO CANNOT READ?
I KNOW -- I WAS ONE OF THEM, BUT I'VE LEARNED TO READ -- HOW?
WELL, YOU SEE, THE GOVERNMENT OF MY COUNTRY, THE UNITED STATES, WITH THE AID OF EDUCATORS OF THE AMERICAS, HAS MADE PICTURES TO TEACH US TO READ.
THAT'S THE WAY I LEARNED. THIS FILM CAN HELP YOU TO READ, TOO.
-- WOULD YOU LIKE TO SEE?
THE
HUMAN BODY

In these remarkable storyboard drawings, Mickey Mouse is pressed into service to help the government "sell a little merchandise."

journalist claims that he objected to it. In any case, the studio agreed to the plan, and production started immediately on the prologues and epilogues. To vary the presentation, a prologue was prepared for the first and third of the reading films, and an epilogue for the second and fourth. An alternate prologue was produced for several of the health films. To soften the offense, the studio made a remarkable concession: the prologue to the reading films featured none other than Mickey Mouse—the studio's figurehead, and a character who had been almost completely

[98] We've already noted his appearance in the short *Pluto and the Armadillo* and, as we'll see in the next chapter, he makes a "hidden" appearance in *The Three Caballeros.*

absent from the Latin American films to date.[98] Surviving story materials indicate that Mickey couched his appeal in the most diplomatic language possible: "Do you know that there are many people to whom this book means nothing—people who cannot read? I know—I was one of them, but I've learned to read—how? Well, you see, the government of my country, the United States, with the aid of educators of the Americas, has made pictures to teach us to read. That's the way I learned. . . ." These scenes would surely be fascinating today, but unfortunately no prints appear to have survived.

The contracted films completed, the CIAA set out to test them in the field. An elaborate plan was laid to show the films in the summer of 1944 to illiterate Spanish-speaking audiences, both in the United States and in Latin America, and to monitor the results. Assuming a reasonable success, the Portuguese versions would also be tested in Brazil. The CIAA duly provided 16 mm projectors for the showings, and dispatched operators to accompany the testing groups. The U.S. showings were entrusted to Mildred Wiese, who did her best to recruit audiences in Southern California and New Mexico. The Latin American testing trip, encompassing Mexico, Honduras, and Ecuador, was made by a handpicked group including Dr. Ismael Rodriguez Bou, professor of educational psychology at the University of Puerto Rico, and Dr. Antonio Rebolledo, head of the Department of Modern Languages at Highlands University in Las Vegas, New Mexico, along with Ryland Madison and Eleanor Clark. The only Disney representative on this trip was Dan MacManus.

The film program for this experiment consisted of *The Human Body*, *What Is Disease?*, and the four teaching films,[99] along with assorted other CIAA productions: *Tuberculosis*, *The Grain That Built a Hemisphere*, *The Winged Scourge*, and even *Chicken Little*. The reading films were supplemented by a booklet prepared at the studio, *José and Ramón*, which contained homework exercises based on the lessons in the films. To balance the educational films with an element of pure entertainment, the programs also included *Saludos Amigos* and several recent shorts from the Goofy series: *The Art of Skiing*, *The Olympic Champ*, *How to Swim*, and *How to Fish*. The tests were conducted scientifically, by showing the teaching films to one group of students while a professional teacher taught the same set of vocabulary words to another group, then tabulating and comparing the test results. Beginning in Mexico in August 1944, the team tested this program on a group of young Mexican army conscripts, private and public schoolchildren in Guadalajara, and mixed audiences in El Salto and Tonala. Proceeding to cities in Honduras and Ecuador, they tested the same program on audiences there.

[99] *How Disease Travels* was presumably being reserved for the next phase of distribution. In any case, it was still not completed when the testing program began in August 1944.

What was the result? According to the CIAA, the films were wildly successful. "I am very happy to be able to report that both the Health films and the Literacy films have been successful far beyond our expectations," wrote Captain Madison before leaving Mexico. "As a result of the few preliminary showings which were made in Guadalajara, we have been swamped with requests that the films be made available for showings throughout Jalisco State. . . . Señor Aleman, the ranking member of President Ávila Camacho's cabinet, was extremely pleased with the pictures and has requested that we make them available to him in 35 mm form, so that they can be shown in the commercial theaters in Mexico."

The testing group's voluminous report, filed with the CIAA in December, expanded on this glowing account. The students, they reported, received the health and literacy films warmly and actually preferred them to the entertainment films. The report described one woman in Mexico who responded eagerly to one of the reading pictures: "She began to anticipate the narrator at the second showing of the film, and gave the words at the top of her voice. Shortly thereafter the remainder of the class began to catch on to the lessons and tried to shout her down. The net result was a reading class of some 40 women all shouting back at the screen as lustily as possible." Another woman confessed to the testing group: "You know, I just love Ramón. I think he's such a dear, sweet man, but I am very upset because last night I went home and dreamed all night about José. I must be in love with him." In El Salto, the students nominated two spokesmen to give speeches of appreciation and thanks to the testing team on the night of the final class.

But there was another side to the story. Eulalia Guzmán, still stinging from her treatment at the hands of the CIAA's representatives, was waiting for revenge. She got her opportunity when Carlos Denegri, a reporter for the Mexico City newspaper *Ultimas noticias*, attacked the literacy films for their global teaching technique—singling out the three Mexican teachers who had permitted such a "caricature" of Spanish. "Let's make it clear: It is not Walt Disney's fault. The entire fault must rest with our three so-called supervisors who should have reported to our authorities, when it was still time to do so, of the poor teaching technique of these pictures." This was enough to unleash Guzmán's fury. Her blistering rebuttal appeared in *Ultimas noticias* two days later: "The lessons were prepared and submitted by us, not merely supervised, and they are the lessons which, changed and ruined afterwards by Mesdames Wiese and Clark, are now appearing on the screen. Consequently, we refuse to accept the responsibility for the pedagogic outrages committed in the lessons." This was only the beginning; Guzmán launched a campaign of letters to other newspapers, continuing her attack on the films. "'José is a healthy young man. José eats well. José is healthy because he eats well,' etc. Nobody knows who José is and no one cares whether he is healthy or whether he eats well; and the truth is that many illiterates probably do not eat well, not because they may not know how to do so, but because they can't, because they are very poor. And then resentment may be strengthened against social injustice while these people are seeing the film. Of course, this reaction does not have anything to do with the process of learning except in that it interrupts the process through the emotional deviation of the attention."

Although Guzmán later came to regret her smear campaign against the films, her arguments had touched a nerve. Other journalists began to take up the cry: "It is true that we cannot produce pictures with the attractiveness of those of Walt Disney, but can we not produce a more modest piece of work? . . . May the education of Mexico be carried out now and always by her own people!" Interestingly, such editorials consistently took pains to exempt Walt himself from criticism, but the very idea of the literacy program now prompted a sudden wave of resentment. Herbert Cerwin, of the U.S. embassy in Mexico City, wrote to Nelson Rockefeller: "They do not question our superiority as industrialists, as business administrators, as technicians, as dentists or doctors—they admit it, even if they dislike us for it. But now, their big brother to the north is coming to teach them their own language. That is just rubbing it in too much." The prologues and epilogues, boasting of the United States' generosity in producing these films, only made matters worse, and Dan MacManus hurriedly removed them from the films to minimize the damage. Reports from Honduras and Ecuador were guardedly positive, but by November it was clear that Mexico had soured on the idea of *any* U.S.-produced literacy films, no matter how well made. The embassy's official report observed in understated tones: "It is therefore recommended that no effort be made to promote the use of these films in Mexico unless a request for them should be made by the Mexican Government. It is believed that this is unlikely."

The CIAA did not immediately abandon the literacy program at this turn of events, but they entered into a period of bureaucratic inaction that amounted to the same thing. Captain Madison and Eleanor Clark returned to Washington and, despite the firestorm in Mexico, recommended that the agency proceed with the literacy-film program. There followed a round of meetings, discussions, recommendations, and memoranda, long on planning but short on action. Dan MacManus continued to participate in these activities, but the Disney studio was not otherwise involved. The completed films were shown to literacy experts at Columbia University and the University of Chicago, panels were formed, appointments were made, and—in effect—nothing happened. Finally, in June 1945, Dr. J. J. Osuna, of the CIAA's Inter-American Educational Foundation, was appointed director of the Adult Literacy Program. Osuna declared that insufficient thought and discussion had been devoted to the film program and suggested a conference of educators to discuss it. When Eleanor Clark pointed out that such a conference had already been held two years earlier at the Disney studio, that it had produced a specific list of recommendations, and that the José and Ramón films were the direct result of those recommendations, her objections were brushed aside.

The Conference on Community Education in Latin America with Special Reference to Literacy was held in Washington on 21 and 22 July 1945. The list of attendees is revealing. Eleanor Clark and some other members of the 1944 Latin American testing group were present, but Enrique de Lozada was conspicuous by his absence, and neither MacManus nor any other Disney representative attended the meetings. In fact, only two members of the film industry were present: Warner Bros. producer Jack Chertok,[100] and Harold Evans, formerly of ERPI Films. The presence of an ERPI (Electrical Research Products, Inc.) executive was a clear indication of the trend in the agency's thinking; since the early 1930s ERPI had been notorious for a series of tedious,

[100] Perhaps coincidentally, Chertok had recently produced a film with a plot centering on the importance of education: the Warners feature *The Corn Is Green*.

cheaply made classroom films, far below the Disney standard of quality. From this attendance list and from the conference's recommendations, it's not difficult to read between the lines: the CIAA, wanting professional results but unwilling or unable to fund professional budgets, was drifting away from the idea of working with the Disney studio at all.

The final nail in the literacy-film program came in December 1945 in a memo from Kenneth Holland, who was now president of the Inter-American Educational Foundation. Holland's language made it clear that the CIAA had cooled considerably toward motion pictures. The previous year, the Latin American testing group had compiled a mass of test scores and statistics to suggest that the Disney literacy films had been approximately as effective as human instructors in teaching illiterate students to read. (Dan MacManus, a member of the team, felt the films were *more* effective than the teachers.) Now Holland interpreted the same data to indicate that the films, while a useful teaching aid, could never take the place of qualified teachers; moreover, they were too expensive. "It is obvious from the experience of the Motion Picture Division with the literacy films prepared by the Disney studios that the Foundation does not have sufficient funds to finance an extensive literacy motion picture program. . . . There are not, therefore, sufficient funds available to carry out the project, even had the results of the testing program been favorable to the films."[101]

And so the Disney literacy project, which had begun with such high ideals and such enthusiastic commitment from the CIAA, fizzled out less than two years later—a victim of budget restrictions, conflicting educational theories, bitter personal rivalries, cultural antagonism and, in the end, bureaucratic indifference. Of all the Disney Good Neighbor efforts, this was the one that ultimately failed—a noble gesture, destroyed by politics.

[101] By this time the CIAA was on its last legs anyway and would have been unable to fund an extensive series of films under any circumstances; see chapter 6.

THE AMAZON AWAKENS

Although a number of films on agricultural subjects had been planned, beginning with *The Grain That Built a Hemisphere*, most of them, lacking that film's cachet of vice presidential endorsement, were abandoned before they reached production. The agricultural subjects suffered none of the controversy or other internal problems that plagued the literacy series; it was simply that individual films on agricultural topics were, again and again, judged less urgent than the health-care pictures. One of the abandoned projects was "Trees and Tree Products." Another, "The Ever-Normal Granary," was intended to explain the benefits of the grain-storage system of its title, already in use in Paraguay. Considerable work was expended on this subject, and detailed storyboards made up by writer Leo Thiele, before the CIAA decided in August 1943 that an ever-normal granary film simply wasn't needed as much as some of the other subjects.

Another proposed film, "The Soy Bean," actually reached the stage of production before being dropped. Story work started as early as February 1942, and Walt apparently took a personal interest in the project. His eyes twinkling, he told one journalist: "We're going to call this one *The Mighty Mite*, or *There's Jack In That Beanstalk.*" Here again, storyboards were assembled and reviewed by the CIAA on one of Walt's trips to Washington in July 1943. (The story material also circulated within the studio; recall that one of Mildred Wiese's suggested literacy films in mid-1943 was titled "Plant Soy Beans with Corn.") The expert advice of several of the CIAA's consultants was solicited and incorporated into the storyboards. In September 1943, however, this project too was shelved and never revived.

The animated opening of the film stressed the theme of the Amazon Basin as the fabled El Dorado sought by Spanish explorers.

At least one of the projected agricultural films *was* produced, completed, and released. But in the process, it grew and evolved into something completely unlike its original conception—or any of the other Disney Good Neighbor films.

From the beginning of the studio's South American story work, Walt had stressed the importance of including the Amazon River in any account of Brazil. At one of the early story meetings on *Aquarela do Brasil* he urged, "Don't overlook the Amazon—do something showing the immenseness of the river. . . . Show Rio as a big city—Bahia for its quaintness—move on to the Amazon, covering it in some fashion so as not to insult them." The finished version of *Aquarela* was a paean to all of Brazil, but tended to focus on Rio. Bahia later became the subject of a separate follow-up film, as we'll see presently. Meanwhile, the next reference to the Amazon turned up in Bob Carr's February 1942 list of nontheatrical story possibilities. Among Carr's suggestions were "Rubber in Brazil," about the work of Henry Ford and others in building up the rubber industry that had become so vital to defense efforts, and "Awakener of the Amazon," about the work of John James in developing other agricultural production in the Amazon region. These and other ideas were combined in a single picture provisionally titled "The Amazon Basin." Elmer Plummer, assigned the subject, compiled a voluminous notebook of research material on the Amazon region, along with a film treatment. In June 1942, along with *The Winged Scourge*, *The Grain That Built a Hemisphere*, and other films, *The Amazon Awakens* started production.

Like the Amazon itself, however, the film continued to absorb new material and gather momentum as it went along. Originally envisioned as a one-reel animated picture, like the other nontheatrical films then in production, the film soon grew to encompass live action as well. The scope of the film changed dramatically too; now, instead of focusing on one or two aspects of the region, the film would encompass the entire epic sprawl of the Amazon Basin and the burgeoning industries there. Today, of course, this subject appears in a very different light. Perceptions have shifted radically in the intervening decades, and today those proud visions of airports and industry clearing away acres of jungle land have become an environmentalist's nightmare. But in 1942 Nelson Rockefeller was concerned with strengthening the unity of a hemisphere at war, with promoting the American republics' pride in themselves and one another, and stressing the part each one played in the strong defense of their common cause. A film depicting the harnessing of natural resources in the Amazon Basin would be helpful in promoting that message. Accordingly, the Disney studio went to work to produce such a film.

To provide the live action, the studio contracted with Herbert E. Knapp, an adventurer-filmmaker who had already worked with the CIAA's motion picture division, shooting 16 mm film in South America. Knapp had recently completed *Latitude Zero*, a two-reel documentary on Ecuador that was later retitled *Down Where North Begins*. He had then contracted with the CIAA to shoot raw footage of Peru, which the agency edited into three separate films. When Ben Sharpsteen contacted him early in 1943 about working on the Disney Amazon film, Knapp was still in Lima. He readily agreed to undertake the assignment, traveling with his wife, Gertrude, who compiled the shot identification data along with hundreds of pages of reference notes on the region and dutifully mailed them to the studio.

The Knapps' journey down the Amazon was an adventure in itself. Just the trip from Lima to the Peruvian town of Iquitos, the first major filming site, occupied nearly a week. Overland travel, through winding waterways and over mountain passes, was an arduous and time-consuming proposition; but, with wartime restrictions on air travel, transportation by plane was almost equally difficult. Luckily Knapp had a close contact with the Rubber Development Corporation, and was able to find space on their cargo planes for occasional unscheduled flights within the Amazon region. Arriving in Iquitos late in April 1943, he set to work. Despite heavy rains he filmed the waterfront, and the cultivation of barbasco, chicle, tagua,[102] and quinine. He also shot footage of Iquitos College and the surrounding territory—including areas so remote that, in one village, he "spent afternoon and evening (by request) explaining to the Prefect and various other officials who Walt Disney is." Yet in another spot along the river, described in the film's script as one of "the remotest villages," Knapp found and filmed the town band's bass drum, decorated with a crude painting of Donald Duck.

[102] Barbasco is a tree from which the indigenous peoples of the Amazon extracted a poison used to stupefy fish; chicle is a tree whose gum was used as the basis for chewing gum until the 1960s (hence the brand name Chiclets); the tagua is a palm whose nuts yield a carvable "vegetable ivory."

By 1943, Donald Duck's fame had spread as far as the remote Amazon jungle.

For the next four months the Knapps continued their trek down the Amazon, sometimes traveling by boat along the river itself, when boats were available, but more often relying on the occasional short flight. Exploring the major tributaries, Knapp filmed Manaus, with its cultural institutions, rubber tapping and curing activities, and experimental agricultural

colony Boa Vista; the two-million-acre Ford plantation, with its self-contained workers' community and sophisticated farming techniques; and assorted scenes of river and jungle wildlife in between. Whenever he reached a spot that had mail service, or was able to make an arrangement with one of the Rubber Development pilots, Knapp would send his latest shipment of exposed Kodachrome to Sharpsteen, along with letters detailing his progress to date. These shipments sometimes followed a circuitous route before reaching the United States, and it soon became clear that sending the film on one of Rubber Development's own flights to Miami, then forwarding it to the studio, was faster and more reliable than trusting in regular air mail. In August the Knapps arrived in Belém, near the mouth of the Amazon, where they filmed the great harbor and the civic and architectural landmarks of the city—scenes similar to those El Grupo had shot in Rio two years earlier.

ABOVE AND BELOW RIGHT: **Other animated portions of the film charted the Amazon region, and depicted future industrial expansion in the territory.**

In September, having received and processed all of Knapp's footage, the studio set about assembling it into a finished film. One of the first considerations was the picture's running time; clearly there was far too much raw material to be crammed into a standard one-reel film. Walt asked and received authorization from the CIAA to expand on the original plan, and in November he wrote to them that *The Amazon Awakens*, first conceived as a one-reel picture, would now be produced in *four* reels—about the same running time as that of *Saludos Amigos*—without a corresponding increase in the budget. Unfortunately this was the last picture to be produced on the studio's then current nontheatrical contract with the CIAA, and some of the earlier pictures on the same contract (*Defense Against Invasion* in particular) had run over budget. *The Amazon Awakens* was obliged to absorb the cost overruns. As a result, this four-reel film was produced for *less* than had been budgeted for it as a one-reeler.

This was not accomplished without certain economy measures, some of which are visible on the screen. Walt, unhappy with some of the animation that had been done for the film, eliminated it; and the limited quantities of animation that remain—rudimentary scenes of the geography and early history of the Amazon region, a diagrammatic demonstration of rubber-tree bud grafting, and closing scenes depicting the future—are done in an extremely

simple style, reminiscent of *Tuberculosis* and some of the other health films.[103] Thanks to another agreement with the musicians' union, the entire musical score of the film is tracked from earlier Disney films, particularly *Saludos Amigos*. The main title music is Ed Plumb's "Song of the Grain," borrowed from the opening sequence of *The Grain That Built a Hemisphere*, while shots of municipal Iquitos are underscored by Frank Churchill's "I Bring You a Song" from *Bambi*. A gaggle of amateur musicians, strumming listlessly at their instruments, are accompanied on the sound track by a spirited rendition of "Tico-tico," and scenes of Belém—the city where Walt had first heard Barroso's "Aquarela do Brasil" in August 1941—are underscored by that melody.

[103] Most of the studio's nontheatrical films were produced in 35 mm, from which a 16 mm reduction negative was made. Perhaps to maintain an image quality consistent with that of Knapp's 16 mm live action, the animation in *The Amazon Awakens*, including the multiplane scenes, was filmed in 16 mm. (Also like the live action, the animation was filmed in Kodachrome, a reversal process similar to the 35 mm Monopack Technicolor that had been used for *Defense Against Invasion*.) The original prototype of the multiplane crane had been built for a full-size 35 mm three-strip Technicolor camera in the 1930s; now, for this film, that same towering structure supported a relatively tiny 16 mm camera.

Mindful of their mission, the studio endeavored to depict the Amazon Basin as a land of unlimited potential, the fabled El Dorado that Spanish explorers of the sixteenth century had sought in South America. In this they were sometimes hampered by Knapp's footage, some of it excellent, some merely adequate. The strain of forcing his shots to fit their concept is sometimes evident. The narrator, describing the idyllic life of the Ford plantation workers, announces, "Their children are given every opportunity to develop into healthy, happy individuals"—while, on the screen, a pair of dour children scowl at the camera. In fact, the CIAA, having commissioned this optimistic portrayal of the Amazon Basin, began to have second thoughts when they viewed the first cut of the picture. Gerald Smith of the CIAA staff, viewing the film in March 1944, felt that perhaps the "El Dorado" idea was overplayed. Erwin Verity, the unit manager, privately grumbled: "His point is well taken in that we realize perfectly well that there are crocodiles, swamps, malaria, and other tropical diseases there; but the basic idea or reason for making the picture was to build up the Amazon Basin itself." Francis Alstock, on his first viewing, declared: "*The Amazon* is the best documentary film I've ever seen" and urged a rush order of prints in time for Pan American Day, 14 April—then abruptly changed his mind.

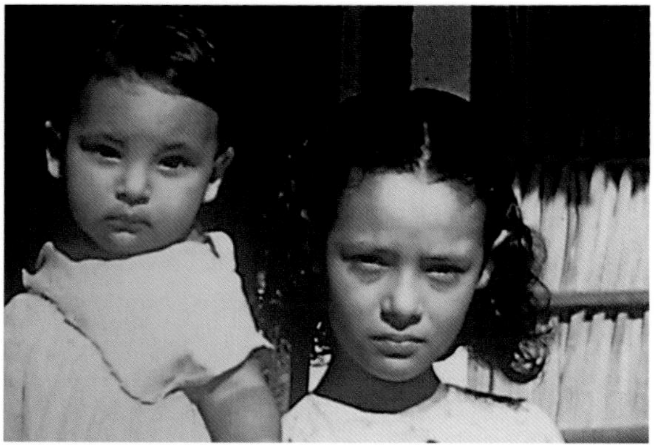

Two "healthy, happy individuals" of the future at the Ford plantation.

The studio had done its job too well; *The Amazon Awakens* presented a *too* idealized portrait of the Amazon and its possibilities. The CIAA staff were reluctant to ask for changes in the visuals (perhaps realizing that any changes would cost additional money), but asked that the optimistic glow of the narration be toned down. Russell Pierce of the CIAA did write to request the elimination of one of the closing scenes, a futuristic skyscraper borrowed from *The Grain That Built a Hemisphere*. "All who reviewed the picture were critical of this shot as even the wildest dreams would not envision such a structure. . . . We would like you to delete the skyscraper. The general idea back of the changes was that people must understand that it is a tough pioneering job." The skyscraper was eliminated, and Sharpsteen worked with Pierce to revise the closing narration, tempering its optimism with an acknowledgment of the hard work still to be done in the Amazon region. Even then, the CIAA hedged on *The Amazon Awakens*. Their approval of the English version was finally issued in October 1944, while approval of the Spanish and Portuguese editions was still withheld. "As a matter of fact," Pierce wrote, "it will probably be necessary to cut the Spanish edition to two reels and highlight the Spanish speaking countries bordering the Amazon Basin. You can readily understand that the other countries would not be interested in the long version which plays up Brazil."

Thus handicapped by a variety of factors—a meager budget, a tight schedule, the limits of Knapp's coverage, and conflicting directives from the CIAA—*The Amazon Awakens* represents something less than Disney's best work. Yet the following February, when the agency publicly honored the producers of its nontheatrical films, the Disney film specifically singled out for praise was *The Amazon Awakens*. More importantly, this film pointed the way for future Disney production. The method used to produce *The Amazon Awakens*—engaging a cameraman or camera crew to shoot raw footage in the field, then applying Disney production expertise to assemble that footage into a polished documentary film—became a virtual blueprint for the method used to produce Disney's theatrical documentaries, principally the True-Life Adventure and People and Places series, beginning just a few years later. (As if to suggest the coming of the True-Life Adventures, *The Amazon Awakens* includes a short passage on the colorful wildlife of the Amazon.) The Knapps would continue their Disney connection by working on further projects for the studio, including several entries in the People and Places series during the 1950s. The narration for *The Amazon Awakens* was written by Winston Hibler, who would lend both his writing skills and his distinctive voice to the later documentary series.[104] This modest travelogue, unremarkable in itself, becomes fascinating when we consider its making and the role it played in Disney triumphs yet to come.

[104] The narration in *The Amazon Awakens*, although written by Hibler, is (like that in some of the health-care films) read by Art Baker.

In addition to all these nontheatrical films for the CIAA, many others were started but never completed. It's worth noting, in particular, a separate series of live-action shorts that Disney was to produce for the agency's Basic Economy division. This plan originated in the summer of 1944, just as the field testing program for the literacy films was getting under way. It called for a series of simple one-reel films on specific agricultural subjects, such as irrigation and soil maintenance and conservation, and health topics, including food preparation and the symptoms and treatment of individual diseases. These films were to be distinct from the studio's other series, filmed in 16 mm in Central and South America, presumably because live action could be produced so much more quickly and cheaply than animation. The subjects and shooting scripts were to be supplied by the CIAA, the films to be produced by the

Disney studio. If plans for the individual films were not ambitious, the overall scope of the series was; at one point the plan called for as many as thirty-four films. The CIAA writers duly provided their list of topics, and in September–November 1944 Ben Sharpsteen and Captain Madison made yet another survey trip through Central and South America to set more definite plans.

Production commenced in the summer of 1945 with the gathering of a production crew in Peru. Captain Madison was on hand to represent the CIAA, and Dan MacManus, who by now had all but abandoned animation for his more specialized role in the Good Neighbor program, was appointed as field director of the films. Herbert and Gertrude Knapp were engaged again for the camera detail. This group convened in Lima, Peru, in July 1945 and proceeded to Iquitos, the same city where Herbert Knapp had filmed much of *The Amazon Awakens* two years earlier, to begin shooting. Production continued busily for several months; Roy Disney noted in early November that the studio had received 10,000 feet of exposed film to date.[105]

[105] This would have amounted to more than four hours of raw 16 mm footage.

The live-action series was apparently undone by one of the same factors that had derailed the literacy series: the CIAA's tight budget, coupled with the Disney studio's refusal to compromise on quality. Madison wrote to the CIAA in November 1945, recommending, "with greatest reluctance," that the proposed list of thirty-four films be reduced to nineteen. Better to complete part of the plan, Madison reasoned, than to abandon it altogether. (One of the health subjects that Madison considered expendable was "Care of the Newborn," but because MacManus and the Knapps had already filmed all the necessary shots for this picture in Tingo Maria, Peru, he suggested that it might be salvaged anyway.) Then, at a meeting with CIAA officials at the end of the month, Roy Disney announced that the budget proposed by the Coordinator would be sufficient to produce twelve films. Kenneth Iverson, CIAA general counsel, and Francis Alstock endeavored to raise the guarantee to at least fifteen, but Roy stood firm. Iverson considered the possibility of retaining the raw footage and farming out production to a cheaper producer, but in the end the series was dropped altogether.

Over a period of four years, the Disney studio had produced an amazing variety and abundance of nontheatrical films for the CIAA. But that was no sign that the studio's theatrical production for the Good Neighbor program was diminishing. On the contrary, it was stronger than ever.

OPPOSITE: Filming a scene for *Saludos Amigos* and *South of the Border with Disney* on the soundstage. Mary Blair looks on while Jack Cutting practices the samba with instructor Pilar Ferrer, of São Paulo. Chuck Wolcott is at the piano.

WALT DISNEY'S
miracle musical FEATURE
The Three
Caballeros
in technicolor
featuring
PANCHITO
JOE CARIOCA
DONALD DUCK
and
in the flesh,
AURORA MIRANDA
of Brazil
CARMEN MOLINA
of Mexico
DORA LUZ
of Mexico
© W.D.P.
RELEASED THROUGH RKO RADIO PICTURES, INC.

5 THE THREE CABALLEROS

The completion of *Saludos Amigos* in the summer of 1942 brought a marked change in production of the studio's Good Neighbor films. Ecstatic early reactions to *Saludos* made it clear that combining the individual short subjects into feature-length package films was not only a viable option, but a far better strategy than releasing them into the limited short-subject market and letting them fend for themselves. A feature had greater visibility and could be promoted as an *event*, in a way that short subjects could not. Accordingly, in June 1942—even before the South American openings of *Saludos*—the studio issued a production number for a picture known at this point as "South American Group Number 2." The individual shorts for this package were still regarded as separate entities, and in fact two of them were already in production; this new production number merely provided for the interstitial material that would *connect* the shorts in a single feature.

"South American Group Number 2" was eventually completed, two and a half years later, as *The Three Caballeros*. Along the way, it went through a remarkable evolutionary process. What is sometimes not understood today about *The Three Caballeros* is that, structurally, it's exactly the same thing as *Saludos Amigos*: four Latin American–themed short subjects combined in one feature-length film. The difference is that, unlike *Saludos*, it was *planned* as a feature almost from the beginning. That two-and-a-half-year gestation period allowed the studio to disguise the film's structural skeleton, easing the transitions between segments, and to develop the scope of those segments far beyond that of individual one-reel films. In the process, *The Three Caballeros* was transformed into something utterly unlike *Saludos Amigos*—or, for that matter, any other film before or since.

Despite the working title, it was predetermined that this second package would include not only South American material but also a segment on Mexico. Mexico had been included in the Disney Good Neighbor plans from the start; six members of El Grupo had spent several days in Mexico City on their way back from South America in 1941, sketching and photographing their impressions. In August 1942, based on those visual records, and in particular Mary Blair's paintings, a Mexican subject titled "La Piñata" started tentative production. The trade press reported that the story crew had "completed research of the music, traditions and romance of old Mexico and have woven them into a story for Technicolor production." In fact, however, the studio's Mexican research was just beginning. By the time story work started on "La Piñata," plans were already circulating for a Disney trip to Mexico—not merely a quick visit by a few unannounced emissaries, but a full-fledged goodwill tour like the South American trip the previous fall.

The request for this visit came, not from Walt or any of his staff, but from the Mexican government, and in particular from Miguel Aleman, the *ministro de gobernación* (minister

OPPOSITE:
Poster art for the domestic release of *The Three Caballeros* in 1945.

for the Mexican equivalent of the British Home Office, responsible for immigration, law and order, civil defense, etc.). Robert Hastings, legal counsel for the CIAA, traveled to California to discuss the request with Norm Ferguson and Jack Cutting. Ferguson wrote to Walt: "We impressed Hastings with the fact that we do not have to go to Mexico to make this Mexican subject as from those Mexicans who have seen the storyboards, all indications are that we are on the right track. Consequently you would be going down there through the insistence of the Coordinator's office." Roy Disney, in fact, actively opposed the trip on the grounds that it would unnecessarily aggravate the studio's manpower shortage. But Walt's visit to South America had proven a brilliant success for the Good Neighbor program, and the CIAA prevailed on him to make a similar gesture in Mexico, agreeing that they would absorb the cost of the trip.

As it turned out, there would be not one but several visits to Mexico by Walt and/or members of his staff. The single tour of South America in 1941 had lasted two months and had been well publicized; by contrast, the studio made numerous smaller-scale and lower-profile visits to Mexico. Each one of these trips, however, involved intensive research, planning, and coordination—like the 1941 tour, but on a miniature scale.

The first trip, in December 1942, lasted approximately two weeks. Walt assembled a miniature El Grupo for this excursion, including several veterans of the original group along with some new faces: writers Ernie Terrazas and Homer Brightman, layout artist Ken Anderson, top animators Eric Larson and Fred Moore. As before, much of Walt's time was consumed by diplomatic functions—including a meeting with President Manuel Ávila Camacho of Mexico—while other members of the group concentrated on individual artistic assignments. Terrazas and Anderson made a side trip to Morelia and Pátzcuaro, visiting the beautiful lakes where fishermen plied the waters with butterfly-shaped nets; Mary Blair and Brightman visited Ixtepec and sketched the colorful Tehuantepec costumes; others visited Taxco and the pyramids near Mexico City, sketching, painting, and shooting a 16 mm record of their visit.

Two Mexican government officials helped to ensure the success of this visit. One was Alejandro Buelna Jr., head of the Department of Tourism, who took a special interest in Walt and El Grupo and made every effort to play the hospitable host. Under his supervision Walt met the president and other dignitaries, and attended a bullfight, a pistol tournament, and a *charro* festival. Buelna also arranged private parties and banquets for the group. In succeeding months, whenever any member of the Disney staff had a question or a problem involving Mexico, "Alex" was the man with the answers. A member of his staff, Clarence de Lima, also took a personal interest in the Disney group and expedited their visits to the people and places they needed to see. Learning that Bill Cottrell and Jack Cutting were involved in the beginning stages of a literacy project, de Lima took special pains to introduce them to a Mexican educator who could surely assist them: Eulalia Guzmán.

Contrary to Ferguson's expectations, the December 1942 trip did yield useful story material for the Mexican film. Among the sights El Grupo witnessed during their visit were Las Posadas (the Christmas festival) and a *torito* (a small boy dressed as a little bull, with strings of firecrackers attached), both of which would appear in the finished version of *La Piñata*. And Walt's comments to the press during this trip reveal another development already in progress: a new character who might symbolize Mexico as Joe Carioca had already represented Brazil. "Disney has a new creation in mind, typifying the national character of Mexico," reported *Población*. "This is to be represented on the screen by a peripatetic, swaggering little rooster." "Six months from now, más o menos," another correspondent wrote optimistically, "whimsy's newest swashbuckling gallant, El Señor Gallito, is due to spring in all his radiant habiliments upon the screen-loving public from Walt Disney's California studios." In the end, of course, the production would take far longer than six months, and the "little rooster" would change considerably before reaching the screen.

Walt and his party returned to California two days before Christmas, carrying hundreds of sketches and paintings, 3,500 feet of 16 mm film[106], and stacks of phonograph records by Mexican musicians. Walt praised his Mexican hosts to the press, just as he had praised the South Americans the previous year. "Mexicans in every walk of life are 100 per cent behind the United States and the Allies in the war," he said. "I was greatly impressed with the progressive attitude of all the Government officials we met. They are doing grand things for the Mexican populace and they all desire a closer bond between our peoples."

[106] This amounted to more than an hour and a half of film.

Following this very public visit to the Mexican capital, members of the Disney staff made two relatively quiet trips there in the spring and summer of 1943. The first of these, beginning in mid-March, was undertaken primarily for the purpose of recording Mexican music on 35 mm optical tracks. These recordings were made at the CLASA studio, one of Mexico's leading production centers. Disney sound man C. O. "Sam" Slyfield was a key member of El Grupo on this trip, working with Chuck Wolcott and the distinguished Mexican composer, conductor, and arranger Manuel Esperón. A prominent Mexico City radio station, XEW, further cooperated by supplying some of its top performers for these sessions. The trip did generate additional survey material (notably from a side trip by Ernie Terrazas and Homer Brightman to Veracruz), but the music recordings were its chief objective. Although hampered by a labor dispute between two local unions representing the radio musicians and the studio musicians, the sessions produced some valuable recordings that served to audition both songs and potential on-screen performers for *La Piñata*. In addition, care was taken to produce recordings of a quality that might be suitable for production. As each day's recording was completed, the exposed film was rushed back to California. There it was immediately processed and reviewed by the Disney staff, who wired their report back to El Grupo for reference.

A gag shot from the Mexican trip in spring 1943: Norm Ferguson and Chuck Wolcott pose as members of a mariachi band.

The follow-up trip, occupying eight days in July 1943, was a more concentrated "audition" session. By now Norm Ferguson and his crew were starting to narrow down their choices of performers and, again with Manuel Esperón's help, acetate recordings were made at XEW of some of the best singers. Dancers and other potential on-screen performers were subjected to further auditions, some of them performing several times for El Grupo, and "screen tests" of the top contenders were filmed and taken back to the studio in California for review. By the end of July, the live performers who would appear in *La Piñata* had been chosen.

Meanwhile, production was going ahead on the other segments of the package feature.

THE COLD-BLOODED PENGUIN

During the summer of 1941, as the first Disney tour group was preparing for its visit to South America, the story department had prepared a list of advance story ideas. One of the "Tentative Alternate" titles on the list was "Paul, the Peculiar Penguin," apparently inspired by the discovery that penguins actually do inhabit some coastal areas of South America. The story concerned a penguin who hates cold weather and escapes from his polar home to a warmer Latin American climate. Like "P-T O-2-L," the story of the little mail plane, this was a generic plot without ties to any specific country; the list of story outlines suggested that it might represent "Brazil or any other S.A. country in the tropical belt."

OPPOSITE: Early story sketches depict a "cold-blooded penguin" who looks quite unlike the character in the finished film.

Upon El Grupo's return from South America, Bill Cottrell took an interest in the penguin story and began to develop it. The locale of the story was changed; now the penguin would sail up the west coast of South America, as El Grupo had done. "We would like to feature definite places," Ted Sears wrote, "such as the Straits of Magellan and any port of interest in Chile." Development of the story became largely a matter of inserting South American locations that the penguin hero would observe along the coast. Among other locations, Sears suggested that Quinta Bates—a well-known hotel where the Blair party had stayed in Arequipa, Peru—might be depicted in the film, simultaneously acknowledging that the picturesque Arequipa "happens to be 100 miles inland." In the end the Arequipa idea was discarded, while the few locations depicted in the film were restricted to places, such as Viña del Mar and Lima, that do lie reasonably close to the coast. (The exception was Quito, Ecuador, which is also hundreds of miles inland. In the film, Quito is matted as if seen through the penguin's telescope, and the image prominently features a railroad train climbing a steep mountain grade—probably representing the Ferrocarril Guayaquil-Quito, the railway that formed Quito's link with the coast.) For the penguin's final destination, Cottrell suggested the Galapagos Islands, which lie directly on the equator and which do have a penguin population of their own.[107] "Pablo Penguin" moved into production late in February 1942 under the direction of Bill Roberts, who was nearing completion of his previous Good Neighbor assignment, *Lake Titicaca*. In April the new film's title was changed to *The Cold-Blooded Penguin*.

[107] Of the seventeen recognized species of penguins, the Galapagos penguin is the only one with a range extending as far north as the equator. (Special thanks to Kenn Kaufman for this information.) In 1960 the Disney nature short *Islands of the Sea* would bring live-action Galapagos penguins to the screen.

Now as long as Paul can remember he has always wanted to go to the South Seas.

This unlikely Latin American subject draws some of its entertainment value from an unrelated Disney tradition. Penguins, with their comic appearance and waddling walk, had always been a natural subject for animated cartoons, and they had previously been featured in more than one Disney film. A notable example (though not the first) was the 1934 Silly Symphony *Peculiar Penguins*, for which live penguins had been brought into the studio so that the animators could study their movements. The result was a delightful depiction of the cartoon penguins' movements, caricatured, but rooted in nature. The "star" animator of *The Cold-Blooded Penguin*, Milt Kahl, draws on that tradition in establishing Pablo's character. Little Pablo, miserable in his Antarctic home and asking only to be warm, is an appealing character, and part of his appeal comes from his toylike appearance and movement. Kahl accentuates his comic walk with accessories attached to his feet in his earliest attempts to leave home: snowshoes, skis, and finally hot-water bottles.

The other main character animator, Harvey Toombs, builds on Kahl's key scenes and animates additional Pablo scenes, clearly following Kahl's lead. But Toombs also offers original contributions of his own, including the early scenes of Pablo's fellow penguins in the Antarctic. (Disney artists frequently caricatured each other, and two of Pablo's friends in these scenes—a tall, gangling penguin and a short, stocky one—appear to be caricatures of, respectively, Jack Campbell and Ham Luske.) Josh Meador, continuing to stretch the boundaries of effects animation, provides such

The silhouetted figures of Mickey Mouse and Pluto on the bucket seem strikingly obvious in this *Cold-Blooded Penguin* background painting. In the finished scene, the movement of the animated characters draws most viewers' eyes away from this detail.

The finished version of Pablo, taking extreme measures to keep warm on his trip north.

unusual "effects" as a melting igloo and the aerial views of Pablo's boat hugging the coastline. (For one long shot of Pablo standing night watch on his voyage, Toombs supplied the first drawing and the scene was subsequently animated by Meador. In the finished scene Pablo himself remains motionless, while the action on-screen is carried by the lapping water, the smoke puffing from his stove, the gently flapping sail.) More conventional effects, such as rain and splashing water, are the work of Ed Aardal and of Dan MacManus, who would later play such a major role in the studio's literacy series.

To the Disney enthusiast, *The Cold-Blooded Penguin* offers numerous other details of interest, some of them "hidden" as private in-jokes. To begin with, the film includes two bits of animation borrowed from earlier Disney films. One of the early scenes, depicting an anonymous penguin diving into the water, was taken from the aforementioned *Peculiar Penguins*. To this action, originally animated by Ham Luske, Toombs added the splash that freezes in midair. In another scene Pablo fails in his first attempt to hike north, rolling back down the hill and gathering snow until he becomes a giant, destructive snowball. For this scene Roberts used the snowball drawings created by Cornett Wood for a similar scene in the Donald Duck–Goofy short *Polar Trappers* (1938).[108] One scene in the opening sequence is a gag showing penguins at the "beach," shoveling snow as if it were sand. In the foreground, unnoticed by most viewers, is a child's beach bucket, decorated with silhouetted figures of none other than Mickey Mouse and Pluto. Finally, the musical score offers a subtle joke saluting the Good Neighbor mission. As Pablo sets off on his ocean voyage, he's accompanied by a melody that North American viewers undoubtedly recognized as "Over the Waves"—perhaps unaware that it had originated as "Sobre las olas," by the nineteenth-century Mexican composer Juventino Rosas.

[108] Coincidentally, *Polar Trappers* was another short featuring penguins.

Production of *The Cold-Blooded Penguin* proceeded uneventfully through the summer and fall of 1942. The English narration was provided by Sterling Holloway, who was enjoying increasing prestige at the Disney studio. In the finished film he not only received screen billing (as he had not in *Dumbo* or *Bambi*) but was identified on the sound track as "Professor Holloway." Interestingly, of all the scenes in this short, the only ones requiring extensive retakes were the static views of the sun in the equatorial sky. That dimly seen nimbus of raging flames, circling the sun with a palpable sense of heat, was achieved early in 1944 (long after the rest of the short had been completed) only through extensive experiments with diffusion, distortion, and multiplane levels.

Although most Disney films of this period were heavily promoted by publicity tie-ins, *The Cold-Blooded Penguin* received an unusual amount of such exposure, beginning well before the film was released. Perhaps because the lineup of the package feature was still in flux, a "Cold-Blooded Penguin" page appeared in *Good Housekeeping* in April 1943, nearly two years before U.S. audiences saw the film in theaters.

THE FLYING GAUCHITO

In the summer months preceding the 1941 South American tour, a number of story ideas had been suggested for the proposed gaucho series—and, of those suggestions, the story then known as "The Winged Donkey" was not considered a top choice. That it was singled out for production after the group's return from South America may owe something to the possibilities it offered for horse-racing scenes. "Horse racing is a top sport, not only in the big population centers but in smaller communities as well," Larry Lansburgh had pointed out to Walt as early as May 1941. "And especially now since South American horses have won big money on our tracks up here, horse racing is even more glamorous to the average South American." Ted Sears had made a similar point, suggesting a gaucho story "built around a race, since races take place in every town whenever a group of ranch hands congregate." Both of these independent observations were made before the "Winged Donkey" idea was suggested.

Another factor in this story's selection may have been the impact of *Fantasia* in South America in 1941. The Beethoven *Pastoral* segment of *Fantasia* had been a favorite in South America, and some of the impromptu cartoons El Grupo had drawn in Argentina featured "centaurettes" and other characters from the *Pastoral*, recast with gaucho trappings. For this Argentine film they created a winged donkey that resembles a combination of two equine characters from the *Pastoral*: the little flying horse seen in the opening sequence, and the donkey-unicorn that serves as a steed for Bacchus. As if to underline the similarity, they included a scene in which the flying donkey hovers in midair, munching blossoms from a tree, just as one of the little Pegasus characters had done in *Fantasia*.

Whatever the reasons for selecting this story, it was in active development within a few days of El Grupo's return to the studio in October 1941. In time it would become the only film in the proposed gaucho series to be completed and released.

The premise of the story was simple: a tall tale told by the gaucho about his adventure with the flying donkey. During the early development of the gaucho series, varying concepts of the leading character had been considered. It was on his return from South America that Sears had suggested: "The little Gaucho (whose name will be decided upon later—probably 'Panchito') will be a character with a vivid imagination. Each story will open with Panchito in a different atmosphere and some small incident will give him the excuse to go into one of his fanciful tales." These wild adventures would feature such phenomena as an ostrich that lays a golden egg, a pair of "magic bolas," a singing horse. In this first story the gaucho would discover a winged donkey, would capture and tame him as a pet, and would entertain visions of winning fabulous sums of money in the races—until something went wrong.

And *The Flying Gauchito*, as the story was eventually retitled,[109] also reflects other evolutionary stages of the gaucho series. We've already noted the studio's concern over depicting Latin American cultures in a humorous way: how to avoid the appearance of ridicule? Casting Goofy in the role of *El Gaucho Goofy* was one way to deflect the problem; Goofy

[109] By the time story development started in October 1941, "The Winged Donkey" had become "The Flying Donkey." The story entered production in December as "The Remarkable Donkey." It was officially rechristened *The Flying Gauchito* in April 1942.

A model sheet establishing the appearances of the two leading characters in *The Flying Gauchito.*

was already established as a bungler *and* as a North American, so no offense could be taken. The new character in the gaucho series, Sears had originally suggested, "would not be a boy—sort of an ageless character like Chaplin." Because this "ageless character" was to be the butt of slapstick gags, Sears added, "In order to steer away from any thought of ridicule, it might be possible to show another character doing the gaucho actions in the correct manner in contrast to the little comedian." But, as we've already seen, the uncompleted *Laughing Gaucho*—whose production overlapped the production of this story—offered a better solution. The *Laughing Gaucho* story required a character who *was* a small boy, because his voice changed in the course of the plot. Consequently the story was told as a flashback by an adult gaucho, looking back on his boyhood adventures, and this became the format for the rest of the gaucho series as well. The boy who appears in *The Flying Gauchito* is the same character who would have appeared in *The Laughing Gaucho* and other films in the series, and his role in the slapstick gags is harmless and inoffensive.

Most of the Disney Good Neighbor films included input from the artists who had gone to South America in 1941, but *The Flying Gauchito* features an unusually strong concentration of El Grupo. Personally directed by Norm Ferguson (who supervised other directors on most of the shorts), its credits include Larry Lansburgh as assistant director, Jim Bodrero as the story director, and Herb Ryman as both layout artist and background painter. In addition, Frank Thomas, the one current member of the animation staff to have gone to South America and observed the real gauchos, dominates the animation of the picture. Thomas had recently animated another little boy, the title character in *Pinocchio*, but in his hands the gauchito becomes an entirely separate and distinct character. Thomas's opening scenes establish the gauchito as an appealing little boy, but never cloying; instead he's independent, resourceful, and just the slightest bit temperamental. He displays fierce determination in capturing the donkey, and even bridles occasionally at the interference of the narrator—himself, as an adult![110] Other major sections of animation are assigned to Ollie Johnston (including preparations for the race and the first part of the race itself) and Eric Larson (the gauchito and donkey by the campfire and the last part of the race), but the character of the gauchito unmistakably belongs to Thomas.

[110] This is a vestige of another of Sears's early suggestions, that the gaucho might occasionally contradict or argue with the narrator. In the finished picture the gauchito has no dialogue, but he occasionally glares at the narrator in annoyance or rejects his advice.

Larson, for his part, uses his well-known skill with birds and animals to advantage. Besides contributing a large amount of the horse-race action, Larson animated key scenes of the flying donkey and the little hornero. His introductory scenes establish the donkey's personality—quick, graceful, engagingly mischievous—and afford the hornero, whose own starring short was never completed, the consolation prize of a "guest role" in this picture. (The first of the hornero's three appearances, a sleepy early-morning close-up, was reanimated by Larson in January 1944, long after the bulk of the short was substantially complete.[111] The hornero's third appearance amounts to a deus ex machina at film's end: the boy's deception in winning the race, nearly successful, is undone when the donkey reveals its wings by flying to the top of a pole to get a better look at the hornero and its nest.)

[111] As reanimated by Larson, this scene may reflect a trace of the hornero's unfinished short, *The Near-Sighted Oven Bird*: the yawning hornero emerges from his nest, walks to the end of his perch and falls off, then hurriedly scrambles back onto the perch.

As one of the first Latin American stories developed at the studio, *The Flying Gauchito* was originally planned as the Argentine entry in the first package of Good Neighbor shorts, which meant that it would have appeared in *Saludos Amigos*. Its place in that package was taken in mid-December 1941 by *El Gaucho Goofy*, but work on *The Flying Gauchito* continued apace. Most of the animation was completed during the summer of 1942, and at that point the short was shelved to await the next package feature. But even during that interim, *The Flying Gauchito* continued to evolve. The scenes in the town, featuring prerace

The gauchito and his steed, preparing for the race, encounter a lack of peer respect.

festivities, games, and a montage of musical instruments, were animated (mostly by Larson and by John Sibley) in late 1943 and early 1944—long after the other scenes had been completed. Other details in the race were likewise revised as the studio continued to fuss with details. As late as December 1943, Larry Lansburgh ordered a retake of the scene in which the gauchito and donkey cross the finish line. In Larson's original animation, the spectators in this scene had worn sandals. The finished scene, re-inked and repainted, depicts the characters properly shod in *botas* (gaucho boots).

Like the four individual sections of *Saludos Amigos*, with which it was concurrently produced, *The Flying Gauchito* was reissued separately as a short in 1955.

BAÍA

A lively moment from the "Os quindins de Yayá" number. José Oliveira, who provided the voice of Joe Carioca, appears on-screen in this shot, playing the "pencil tambourine."

The first two segments in *The Three Caballeros* (*The Cold-Blooded Penguin* and *The Flying Gauchito*) differ from the last two (*Baía* and *La Piñata*) in obvious ways, but the most striking difference is one of *scope*. The first two pictures, started during the initial surge of production activity following the 1941 South American trip, were conceived and produced as discrete one-reel cartoon shorts. In other words, they were more or less interchangeable with the four segments in *Saludos Amigos*, which were produced at the same time. *Baía* and *La Piñata*, on the other hand, both entered story development in mid-1942, at the time *Saludos Amigos* was taking shape as a feature. As it became increasingly clear that the studio's Good Neighbor shorts were likely to be absorbed into feature-length package films, a corollary became equally clear: there was no reason to restrict them to the usual format of cartoon shorts. A feature-length setting was a virtual invitation to break the old precedents and try new ideas in these films. And if there was one producer in early-1940s Hollywood who loved to break precedents and try new ideas, it was Walt Disney.

By the spring of 1943, Walt's brother Roy had also taken an active interest in revising the concept of the Good Neighbor films. Noting an article in *Variety* about the studio's new group of Latin American short subjects, Roy wrote to the publicity department: "It is a mistake to talk of these sequences as short subjects. This may have been the trade paper's language, but we should all guard against calling these short subjects. Instead it would be better to refer to them as Mexican sequence, Brazilian sequence, Cuban Sequence, etc., all woven together into a musical feature. Referring to these pictures as a group of shorts creates terrific sales resistance because it lessens people's appreciation of the subject and belittles the entire picture and immediately sets up a value in the exhibitors' minds of 4 times the short subject price." By March 1943, then, for a variety of reasons, it was clear that the second Latin American feature would be something substantially different from *Saludos Amigos*.

The studio's first Brazilian picture, *Aquarela do Brasil*, had been by all accounts a brilliant success, and a follow-up was clearly indicated. El Grupo's visit to Brazil in 1941 had produced a wealth of research and story material on all regions of the country, including the northeastern coastal state of Bahia. In the story development of *Aquarela*, an attempt had been made to incorporate all this material. Walt's comments at one early meeting had included the following: "We come to Rio on the map—then get shots around Rio—from Rio we go to Bahia. Don is in Rio—then in Bahia with the parrot. From the point where we find Donald and the papagaio in Bahia we are into the Samba rhythm. . . . In Bahia we have the fruit market and flower stuff. . . . Show Rio as a big city—Bahia for its quaintness—move on to the Amazon, covering it in some fashion so as not to insult them." In the end, even a film as rich as *Aquarela* could not contain all this material, and the only location explicitly featured in the finished version was Rio de Janeiro. Now the second film would focus on Bahia. The studio was musically prepared for such a picture, having negotiated the rights to Dorival Caymmi's lively samba "Você já foi à Bahia?" (Have You Ever Been to Bahia?). Also earmarked for the picture was "Os quindins de Yayá," a second song by the composer of "Aquarela," Ary Barroso.

Embarking on story development, the studio soon found itself in the midst of an unexpected debate over the spelling of "Bahia." In the early 1940s, Portuguese spelling was in an active state of flux, and production of the studio's new Brazilian picture coincided with the 1943 Orthographic Reform negotiated by Brazil and Portugal.[112] This initiative called for the virtual elimination of some letters from the Portuguese alphabet and changed the spelling of numerous words, including geographical names. "Before the streamlining of the Brazilian language, the name was spelled 'Bahia,'" Jack Cutting explained in a memo to Norm Ferguson in 1944. "Subsequently the 'h' was dropped, and an accent added to the 'i.' This new spelling seemed to displease the people of Baía in particular, because without the accent the word means 'horse stall.' Nevertheless the modern dictionaries show the word spelled without an 'h', and when Assis Figueiredo [of the DIP, the Brazilian propaganda department] was here a year or so ago, he himself pointed out that it was incorrect for us to have Bahia spelled with an 'h' in the picture." This remained a touchy diplomatic question; Cutting also noted that a storm of protest from prominent Bahians had forced the government tentatively to concede the original spelling, and that the next Carnaval had celebrated that event with a song, "Bahia Has Its 'H' Again." The issue remained volatile during succeeding decades and, in fact, has never been entirely resolved to this day, but over time the older *Bahia* spelling has once again come to be accepted as the standard. In the 1940s, however, the Disney studio bowed to what was then the prevailing consensus of opinion, and in its film *Bahia* remained *Baía*.

[112] This was not an isolated event; Portugal had adopted an orthographic reform as early as 1911, and the first Orthographic Accord had been approved by both Brazil and Portugal in 1931. There would follow the Convenção Ortográfica Luso Brasileira, adopted in 1945 by Portugal but not by Brazil, and numerous other laws and proposals aimed at reducing the orthographic divergences between the two countries. Special thanks to Daniella Thompson for all this information.

During the summer of 1942, a story was tentatively assembled for *Baía*. At this point, along with the proposed gaucho series, the studio was still thinking in terms of

The train arrives at the Bahia station—with spelling corrected for the mid-1940s.

a papagaio series, and *Baía* was conceived as a second picture featuring the papagaio—that is, Joe Carioca, who had scored a great success in *Aquarela do Brasil*. The original story outline is simple: Joe is introduced standing on a stage and speaking directly to the audience, extolling the beauty of Bahia, "the romantic part of my country." His speech is interrupted by the crazy antics of the Aracuan, a mischievous bird who grabs Joe's cigar, fills the screen with smoke rings, and generally disrupts the proceedings. Attempting to ignore these distractions, Joe invites the audience to come with him to Bahia on board a fanciful little train. Despite the further mischief of the Aracuan, who draws multiple alternate railroad tracks in chalk so that the cars scatter all over the screen, the train does arrive at its destination. The story culminates in romantic scenes of Bahia, where Joe dances a samba with a lovely *baiana*—who is ultimately revealed as the Aracuan in disguise. This relatively simple outline would have fit neatly into a self-contained one-reel short, much like the other Good Neighbor pictures that had already been produced. The story was approved, and the studio submitted a synopsis to the Production Code Administration office of the MPPDA (Motion Picture Producers and Distributors of America) for review in September 1942.

By that time, however, Walt was already restlessly exploring ways to expand the idea. *Saludos Amigos* was about to make an impact on the U.S. popular-music market by introducing two South American hit songs on North American screens, but for his next film Walt was seeking native performers to appear on-screen, introducing the native music. The Hollywood live-action studios, initially slow to catch on to the Good Neighbor idea, had by now embraced it and had begun to produce cinematic salutes to Mexico and South America, featuring appearances by prominent Latin American performers. None of these performers was better known than the Brazilian bombshell Carmen Miranda, who had already appeared in three features for Twentieth Century-Fox and established herself as Brazil's liveliest export. The value of her name was such that in July 1942 Walt engaged her as a "technical adviser" on the Brazilian material in *Saludos*, simply for the publicity value. Within three months he had taken a considerably bigger step on behalf of his next picture: he approached Carmen's younger sister Aurora to appear on-screen in *Baía*. Aurora Miranda was herself no stranger to show business; in Brazil she was as famous as Carmen and had sung on radio and in the movies. In the U.S. she had appeared onstage in Earl Carroll's revues, billed simply as "Aurora."[113] She filmed a screen test at the Disney studio in October 1942, singing Barroso's "Os quindins de Yayá," and was found more than satisfactory. The studio contracted with her to appear in the film, and the story crew began working on a way to combine her performance with the cartoon material that had already been planned. Their solution to this problem led to what would become the most celebrated feature of *The Three Caballeros*.

[113] She would also receive screen billing as "Aurora" in Universal's *Phantom Lady*. Filmed late in 1943, after the completion of her work for Disney, *Phantom Lady* was nevertheless completed and released nearly a full year before *The Three Caballeros*. By the time *Caballeros* appeared on theater screens, Aurora Miranda was being identified by her full name.

Combination scenes—scenes in which animated characters and live-action performers appear together on-screen, appearing to inhabit the same world—have made periodic appearances throughout film history, each time hailed as something new. In fact, the device is nearly as old as animated cartoons themselves. As early as 1916, movie audiences could see cartoon characters Bobby Bumps and Dreamy Dud interacting on-screen with their cartoonist creators. These artists were followed by Max and Dave Fleischer with the Out of the Inkwell series, Walter Lantz with Dinky Doodle—and, beginning in 1923, Walt Disney himself, who found his first commercial success with the Alice Comedies. The mixture of real and cartoon worlds was nothing new; what did change was the increasingly elaborate nature of the illusion, and the increasingly complex technical means used to achieve it. In the earliest Out of the Inkwells, it was a simple matter to substitute a still photograph for a painted background so that a cartoon character would appear to be walking through the real world. Later films became far more sophisticated, creating a convincing illusion that Max Fleischer and KoKo the Clown, or Walter Lantz and Dinky Doodle, really were sharing the same space. Walt Disney appears to have been intrigued from the beginning with the possibilities of this effect, and devised special technical challenges for himself even in his earliest Alice Comedies. *Alice's Wild West Show* (1924), for one example, is filled with ingenious devices to show Alice (Virginia Davis) convincingly inhabiting a cartoon world. With the coming of sound, combination scenes continued to appear sporadically, and continued to raise the bar for intricate interactions of live and cartoon figures. A special Disney sequence produced as an insert for the Fox feature *Servants' Entrance* (1934)

In this rare production still, Aurora Miranda plays a scene with the rear-projected Donald and Joe.

showed that Walt's delight in complex technical challenges was just as strong as it had been a decade earlier.[114] And other producers also continued to produce occasional combination scenes; as late as 1940 the Warner Bros. cartoon studio had produced the ambitious combination short *You Ought to Be in Pictures*.

These varied and delightful films all had one thing in common: they were produced in black and white. Combination scenes in *color* added a whole new dimension of technical difficulty to the challenge. If the lighting and color temperature of animated characters were not precisely coordinated with those of the live-action elements, the illusion would be destroyed (as latter-day films, produced by less exacting filmmakers, have demonstrated all too often). In *Fantasia* Walt had teasingly hinted at the possibility of color combination scenes by including a scene in which Mickey Mouse ran on-screen to shake hands with Leopold Stokowski—but the event was cannily staged in silhouette, reducing the technical challenges to a minimum.

As the expanded version of *Baía* began to take shape, however, Walt took a renewed interest in exploring the full possibilities of combination scenes in color. Aurora Miranda wouldn't simply appear as a guest star; she would enter into the animated world on the screen and interact with Donald Duck (who had now been added to the story) and Joe Carioca. Throughout late 1942 and early 1943, the Disney technical staff worked to meet this challenge. Earlier black-and-white combination scenes had usually been accomplished by some kind of matte process; for these color scenes the studio decided to use a process screen—the rear-projection device that had long been used in live-action films to provide a moving background behind actors who

[114] The Disney contribution to *Servants' Entrance* was a Janet Gaynor dream sequence in which the animated characters were intricately juxtaposed with their live-action surroundings.

were actually being filmed on a sound stage. For *Baía*, after carefully planning and timing the scene, the artists would prepare the animation element first. Then, on the studio's live-action stage,[115] the animation would be rear-projected on a translucent process screen while Aurora, standing before the screen, was filmed playing her part of the scene. The camera would record both Aurora and the animated characters in a single image.

[115] At this time—since Disney was still primarily an animation studio—there was only one full-size soundstage on the lot. In later years more stages were constructed, and this original building became known as "Stage 1." In 1942, because the smaller dubbing stages were known as Stages A, B, and C, the larger structure was identified as "Stage D" or, more often, simply as "the live-action stage."

This may sound like a simple procedure; in fact it was anything but. By December 1942 the action for the combination scenes had been tentatively worked out, and an exhaustive series of experiments began, testing the process "plates" (the term for the film rear-projected on the screen) with endless combinations of lenses, lights, screens, exposures, and color balances. In January 1943 the studio engaged the prominent Technicolor cameraman Winton Hoch as a consultant and conferred with him at length on the special problems involved in these scenes, and on maximizing their effectiveness in Technicolor. Hoch's advice was carefully recorded and led to modifications of the equipment and methods in use—and to more tests, some of them shot by Hoch himself.[116] The basic procedure was difficult enough: Aurora, performing before the screen, obviously had to be lighted—but, also obviously, this meant she couldn't stand too near the screen, or the lights would wash out the rear-projected image. Accordingly, she was required to stand at a distance of six to ten feet from the screen. The cameraman, obliged to keep both Aurora and the screen in focus, was compelled to stop down his lens in order to maximize depth of field. This in turn meant that the lights, already intense for the requirements of Technicolor, must be made even more powerful in order to achieve adequate exposure. As a result, for any given process scene, Aurora was standing (or, for "moving" shots, walking on a treadmill) under blinding and intensely hot lights, "interacting" with characters who were actually at least six feet away. For some scenes it was possible to ease the heat problem by slowing the action slightly and shooting at 20 fps, but the process scenes were still very hot work. And the technical problems didn't end there. "This all had to be figured out mathematically, and [Aurora's] movement had to be exactly choreographed for her, by me, to work with the animation which she was being photographed with, before she ever did it," layout artist Ken Anderson explained decades later to Milt Gray. "Then she had to be completely rehearsed to do it exactly that way . . . That had to be lined up with a camera, and we had the added difficulty of a 'hot spot.' If the camera was exactly centered on the screen, the projection light would cause a burnout, right in the middle. That was a difficult thing to get over. The rear projection screen is a tremendous problem."

[116] Hoch had a previous connection with the Disney studio, having filmed the Technicolor live-action sequences in *The Reluctant Dragon*. After the war he would return for other productions.

By mid-May 1943 the technical crew had tentatively solved most of these problems and was finally ready to shoot Aurora's musical number. "Os quindins

OPPOSITE: One of Mary Blair's costume sketches for Aurora Miranda's appearance in *Baía*.

O.K.
Bahiana costume for Aurora Miranda

de Yayá" was filmed over a period of three weeks in May and June, with occasional delays as the cartoon action was revised and the animators scrambled to finish new process plates. Ray Rennahan, another legendary Technicolor cameraman, shot the number.[117] In these scenes Aurora appeared not only with the rear-projected Donald Duck and Joe Carioca, but also with fellow human performers—including the distinguished Brazilian musical group Bando da Lua. The six members of Bando da Lua had come to the United States with Carmen Miranda to accompany her in her stage performances. They also had already appeared on-screen with Carmen in her Fox musicals, so this appearance with Aurora amounted to a show of familial support—doubly so since one of the band

[117] Rennahan, like Winton Hoch, had an existing Disney connection; he had worked with the Disney studio in producing its earliest Technicolor cartoons in 1932, and was concurrently shooting the live-action sequences in *Victory Through Air Power*. (Because Disney's live-action stage was not fully soundproofed, the *Victory Through Air Power* unit had no defense against the noise from the nearby Lockheed aircraft plant and was forced to shoot its scenes at night. *Baía*, with its prerecorded sound track, presented no such problem.) Rennahan's crew included another veteran cameraman, Dave Kesson, whose credits included a long collaboration with director Marshall Neilan in the silent era.

members was José Oliveira, the voice of Joe Carioca.[118] Aloysio "Luis" Oliveira, who had sung "Aquarela do Brasil" in *Saludos Amigos*, also appeared on camera in this number as the guitar-playing *malandro* who temporarily diverts Aurora's attention. Dance director Billy Daniels assembled a troupe of twenty-two dancers (featuring himself) who also appeared in the number.

118 Twentieth Century–Fox took a proprietary attitude toward Bando da Lua, considering them part of the package in its contractual arrangement with Carmen Miranda. Consequently the Disney studio was obliged to "borrow" the band from Fox, with the express stipulation that neither the name of the band nor the names of any of its members could appear in Disney publicity. John Canemaker points out another show of familial support: Aurora Miranda made her Disney screen test in October 1942 wearing one of Carmen's dresses.

This extended live-action sequence marked a turning point in the production of the second Latin American feature. The Disney studio was the unquestioned world leader in the making of animated cartoons, but its wartime activities had brought about an increasing focus on live-action production as well, and Walt seemed to revel in this show of versatility. *Hollywood Reporter* remarked on the new development in April 1943, noting that the Disney studio had five "flesh troupes" at work in addition to its regular cartoon staff.[119] The exhilarating new blend of live action and animation in *Baía*, in particular, generated a high level of excitement at the studio. Attempting to shield this innovation from imitation, the studio conducted its process-screen experiments in relative secrecy. At the same time teasing stories began to appear in the press: "Air of mystery surrounds a closed set at Walt Disney's studio. All that is known is that he has in process of development a new and revolutionary exploit in live action for his cartoon pictures." Walt himself was more intrigued than ever with the new effects, and his enthusiasm would lead to still more elaborate experiments as production continued.

119 In addition to the *Baía* crew, three live-action units were working on military and industrial training films. The fifth "troupe" consisted of Herbert and Gertrude Knapp, who were then in Peru preparing to film *The Amazon Awakens*. Curiously, the article made no mention of *Victory Through Air Power*.

OPPOSITE: The combination scenes required extraordinarily detailed planning at the story-sketch stage.

Meanwhile, the story crew was also continuing to expand *Baía*. The developing scope of the picture allowed new latitude to the story artists, among them Mary Blair. Mary's role in the Good Neighbor program had continued to grow since her seminal work on *Aquarela do Brasil*. For *Baía* she designed the little train that transports the audience to Bahia. This whimsical little train, painted in bright pinks, oranges, and yellows, achieved a mild celebrity within the studio. Mary's visual concept was transferred to the screen intact, as she later wrote to Ross Care: "Only on the little train sequence did I feel that it was really my own artwork and my style." In fact, however, Mary's stamp is everywhere on the film. Her eye for visual style, combined with her growing wealth of knowledge of Latin American cultures, made her indispensable for the live-action portions of the film as well as the animated sequences. She contributed preliminary costume designs for "Os quindins de Yayá," and amateur 16 mm footage taken during a publicity

BELOW: One of Mary Blair's original pastel sketches of the little train.

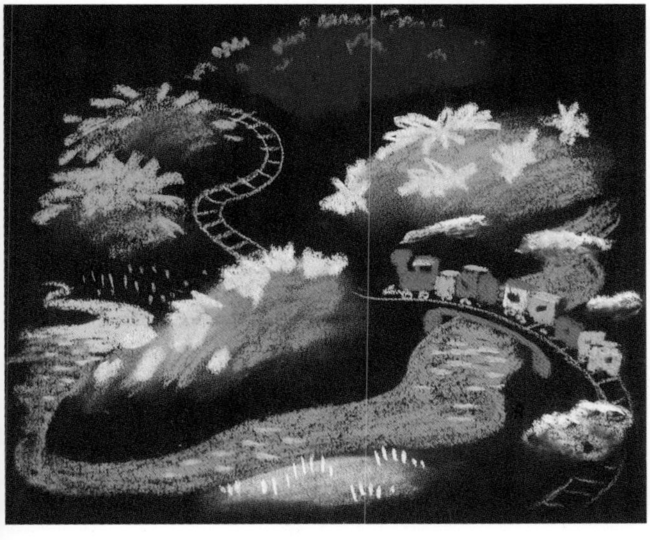

Using Herbert Knapp's reference footage of São Salvador as a guide, the artists produced scenes that were both atmospheric and authentic.

still session reveals Mary acting in a supervisory capacity, posing Aurora Miranda and the other dancers and arranging details of their costumes for the camera.

In August 1943, *after* the sumptuously detailed Aurora Miranda sequence had been shot, still another new sequence was added to the picture. To underscore their depiction of Bahia as "the romantic part" of Brazil, the artists dipped yet again into the song catalogue of Ary Barroso for the lovely "Na baixa do sapateiro." This sensuous, elegant samba had been written in 1938 (predating "Aquarela do Brasil") as an ode to the city of São Salvador, the capital of the state of Bahia, and in particular to Baixa dos Sapateiros (Shoemakers' Hollow), a street, formerly a cobblers' district, that divided two distinct neighborhoods in the city. In the early 1940s a long period of industrial development was just beginning in Bahia, but the area was still celebrated for its colorful history and charming colonial architecture. While Rio de Janeiro was seen as an exotic modern city, Salvador was pictured as a romantic land of fiery sunsets and picturesque eighteenth-century cathedrals.[120] In order to give their picture visual authenticity, the studio sought additional reference material on the region. Unit manager Jack Dunham, learning that Herbert Knapp was about to complete the filming of *The Amazon Awakens*, wired him in Belém and asked him to remain on the Disney payroll, filming additional 16 mm material in and around Salvador, "SHOWING SHIPS, FORTS, ETC. STREET SCENES, BAIXA DO SAPATEIRO, ROMANTIC SHOTS, SUNRISES, SUNSETS, BOMFIM, ELEVATOR, TERRACES, ETC." Dunham advised Knapp to "SPEND AT LEAST TWO WEEKS COVERING [THE]

[120] In 1942 Orson Welles and his crew had photographed some black-and-white footage in Salvador (itself also sometimes known as Bahia) for the ill-fated *It's All True*.

ASSIGNMENT." Knapp accepted the assignment and, working with his footage as a guide, the artists would produce one of the most visually striking sequences in the film.

At the same time, studio lyricist Ray Gilbert was penning English lyrics for the song. The studio had used Barroso's other songs, "Aquarela do Brasil" and "Os quindins de Yayá," with their original Portuguese lyrics,[121] but "Na baixa do sapateiro" would be heard in the new film as the English-language song "Baía" and would score a tremendous new worldwide success.

[121] "Aquarela do Brasil" had been published in the U.S. as "Brazil," with new English lyrics by S. K. Russell, but these had nothing to do with the film, or with the original lyrics. Similarly, after the release of *The Three Caballeros*, "Os quindins de Yayá" would be published as "Angel-May-Care," with new English lyrics by Ervin Drake.

Throughout the late summer and fall of 1943 the studio continued to fuss with the finishing touches on *Baía*, changing details of the cartoon action, producing new scenes to bridge the gaps between sequences—and tinkering further with the combination scenes, which, as amazing and charming as they were, still failed to satisfy Walt's quest for perfection. The technical crew had done a stellar job, but there was no denying a certain softness in the rear-projected animation—perhaps inevitable, considering that the production camera was shooting the process screen from an average distance of twenty-five feet. Further refinements were needed, and they came from the man who had become one of the studio's resident technical wizards: Ub Iwerks. To Disney enthusiasts, Iwerks is well known as the star animator who had played a crucial role in launching Mickey Mouse in the late 1920s. After breaking away and running his own animation studio for a time during the 1930s, Iwerks had returned to Disney in a new role as a specialist in effects, his real passion. One of his innovations was a miniature process screen, which was used in *Baía*. Animated scenes in the picture—scenes featuring straightforward cartoon action *without* any live action—were shot in the usual way, then rear-projected on Iwerks's miniature screen and reshot, so as to match the appearance of the combination scenes.

But Iwerks had also been seeking a way to improve the combination scenes themselves. The process screen, besides producing a soft cartoon image, was also restrictive: it offered a way to film live actors standing in front of animated characters, but no way to put the animated characters in the foreground. In mid-1943, Iwerks unveiled an exciting new device that would make just such an effect possible. This was a two-head optical printer that allowed great flexibility in matting and combining visual elements from two different strips of film. Previously, filmmakers trying to combine two images in one had been hampered by the need to shoot and reshoot matte elements in multiple exposures on the same strip of film, creating a progressively grainier image, as well as by the difficulty of maintaining perfect alignment among the matte elements in the face of minute degrees of film shrinkage and other factors. Iwerks conquered both problems with an innovative "aerial" printing system. His new printer featured a projector head that optically projected one element onto another image in a second head, the combined image being simultaneously shot by the camera. This meant that complicated matte combinations, which previously would have required multiple steps, could now be shot in a single exposure; and that the operator could view the scene at all times as it progressed, adjusting the matte elements as needed.[122] Using the Iwerks printer, animated characters could be inserted in a live-action scene at the filmmakers' discretion, with relative ease and with no softness, grain, or distortion.

This exhilarating development constituted the breakthrough Walt had been looking for, and during late 1943 and early 1944 it was used to embellish *Baía* with even more intricate effects than before. Parts of "Os quindins de Yayá" that had been filmed in the spring of 1943 as straight live-action shots were now reshot to depict Joe Carioca and Donald Duck observing the action from the foreground. Building on the same principle, one part of the dance sequence was now augmented with a surreal montage of animated percussion instruments and colorful abstract shapes. All these innovations, layered into the film as they became available, combined to transform *Baía* into a far richer visual experience. Those original process scenes, filmed with such difficulty and at such great expense, remained in the film, now combined with newly enhanced visuals. The cumulative effect was dazzling. By now the film had clearly outgrown its original synopsis, and a revised version was submitted to the MPPDA in December 1943.

[122] My understanding of the Iwerks printer has been aided immeasurably by conversations in 2003–2004 with Don Iwerks, Ub's son, and Bob Broughton, who operated the machine in the 1940s. Special thanks to both of them. The printer itself, long preserved by Don Iwerks, is now in the possession of the Walt Disney Family Foundation.

Undimmed by the passage of time, *Baía* remains a delightful experience. In the finished film the song "Os quindins de Yayá" is preceded by three other sequences, all of them animated at a later date, in the spring and early summer of 1944. The first sequence is, in effect, the opening lecture by Joe Carioca that had been planned from the start, now modified to fit the overall structure of *The Three Caballeros*. Joe delivers his remarks, not to the camera, but to his old friend Donald Duck—and since the four segments of *The Three Caballeros* had been framed as a series of birthday gifts to Donald, this is a miniature Joe, emerging from a pop-up book on Brazil. Most of the short sequence was animated by Fred Moore, preserving the unique stamp he had put on Joe's character in *Aquarela do Brasil*.[123] "Have you ever been to Bahia?" Joe asks Donald—promptly interrupted by the Aracuan, who appears on cue, snatches Joe's cigar, runs crazily around the perimeter of the frame, then escapes the confines of the film itself, bouncing past the frame line and the sprocket holes into the blackness beyond. The aracuan is a real Brazilian bird (correct Portuguese spelling: *aracuã*) whose raucous cry and habit of congregating in unruly flocks have earned it a place in the country's folklore as a maker of mischief. On-screen, the Aracuan in this film is Disney's closest parallel to the zany, frenetic characters, such as Daffy Duck and Woody Woodpecker, who burst forth from other cartoon studios in the early 1940s. He's fueled by a lively traditional "Aracuan" song, arranged here

[123] For the record, one long (nearly 35-foot, or 23-second) close-up of Joe is jointly credited to both Moore and Les Clark. The Aracuan's antics are animated by Eric Larson.

The Aracuan, who becomes in this film an incorrigible troublemaker.

[124] Daniella Thompson, who provided the information on both Almirante and the Aracuan, points out that Brazil's Civil Code allows any songwriter to adapt an existing public-domain composition and copyright the adaptation as his or her own. This provision has led to competing versions of the same song, and created some problems for the Disney studio when traditional songs, used in the films, were subsequently copyrighted.

by Henrique Foréis Domingues, the Brazilian cultural personality better known as Almirante.[124]

Joe does his best to ignore this nuisance and resumes his tribute to Bahia, which leads to the next sequence. "Na baixa do sapateiro," now rechristened "Baía," is one of the musical and visual highlights of the feature. The song itself, one of Barroso's most haunting melodies, is a gem, performed here by Nestor Amaral, chorus, and orchestra with delicacy and taste. Visually the sequence is a stunning tour de force by Josh Meador, surpassing in some ways Meador's brilliant work in *Aquarela do Brasil*. Bahia in this film is a rich montage of jungle foliage, village rooftops and Baroque cathedral towers, orchids blooming by quiet pools and distant sailboats moving on the bay, all backed by a vivid, blood-red sunset sky. Two doves animated by John McManus soar languidly through this dreamlike world. Enchanting in themselves, the visuals are also subtly keyed to the music: dewdrops ruffling the surface of the pool, or reflections shimmering in the shell of a cathedral bell, are synchronized to chimes in the orchestra. The overall effect of the sequence is captivating; small wonder that the song achieved a new level of world popularity after being showcased in this lovely film.

Roused from his reverie, Joe launches into the third sequence, a continuation of the first, by resuming his theme: Caymmi's "Have You Ever Been to Bahia?" (The English lyrics in the film were written by none other than Norm Ferguson. To Ferguson's other

Lost in a romantic moment, Joe Carioca sings of the beauty of Bahia.

accomplishments as animator and director, we can add the title of lyricist.) Now the film shifts gears and becomes lively again. Joe splits into four parts and sings harmony with himself, performing instant costume changes to appear as four *baianas* (today's viewer has the bizarre impression of seeing four miniature parrots dressed as cigar-smoking Carmen Mirandas), then as four *malandros*. Donald hasn't been to Bahia, and, as it turns out, neither has Joe. Joe produces a handy mallet and smashes the Duck down to his own miniature size, and the two dash back into the book to board the little train, which is just leaving for Bahia. Mary Blair, in addition to designing the train itself, painted the backgrounds for this sequence, preserving her flat, posterlike design of jungle flora against a solid black background. The train, animated by Les Clark and Marvin Woodward, puffs jauntily along through this child's landscape. Its bright Day-Glo colors are vivid against the black setting; its wheels are disembodied discs (with one square wheel at the end), sliding apart or squeezing together as the locomotive reacts to obstacles in its path. These include the Aracuan, who impishly

After drawing multiple sets of tracks for the train, the Aracuan, characteristically unconcerned, plants himself in its path.

draws a maze of alternate tracks on the screen (he holds a pencil, but it produces white chalk lines against the black background) so that the train splits up and all the cars go careening off in different directions. But it's a harmless mischief; the train is reconstituted in time to arrive at the Baía station. All this is set to the strains of a spirited musical theme, "Flauta e pandeiro" (Pandeiro and the Flute; the pandeiro is a hand drum), performed on the flute by its composer, Benedicto Lacerda.[125] This is a performance worth noting, recorded in September 1941 at the Carmen Santos studio in Rio during El Grupo's visit to Brazil—the one recording from that session to be used in a finished film.

Now the stage is set for "Os quindins de Yayá." Aurora Miranda, as Yayá, is given a teasing introduction, her (animated) shadow visible on a wall before she enters the scene. Donald is instantly smitten with Aurora, elbowing Joe aside in his eagerness to pursue her, and overcome with murderous jealousy when she displays any romantic interest in one of her human suitors. His attraction to her is easy to understand—Aurora sparkles in these scenes with a lively, vivacious charm—but this is, nevertheless, a curious shift in the Duck's character. From the time of his introduction in 1934, Donald Duck had been defined mainly by his short temper, a trait sometimes augmented by laziness or by a streak of mean-spirited mischief. His two appearances in *Saludos Amigos* had done little to alter that basic prototype (although, in *Aquarela do Brasil*, he had been swept up in the general spirit of Good Neighbor friendliness). Now, placed in an unfamiliar setting, he reacts in an unexpected way: he's driven by his libido rather than his temper. This is an odd development, and it will become more pronounced as *The Three Caballeros* continues.

The blend of animation and live action, so lovingly crafted and refined over the course of more than a year, continues to delight viewers today. Fred Moore, who had dominated the animation of the earlier sequences, contributes some key scenes here too, but other scenes are parceled out more or less evenly to other animators—John Lounsbery, Ward Kimball, Eric Larson, Les Clark, Ollie Johnston—probably as a response to the exigencies of production in early 1943, when a large quantity of process plates was required in short order by the live-action unit. Wonders multiply: first Aurora greets Donald and Joe and sings to them; then Donald, in a fit of jealousy, goes after Nestor Amaral with Joe's mallet, succeeding only in conking himself; and finally Aurora (back to camera) rewards Donald's devotion with a kiss. In one nicely understated moment, the animated Joe Carioca and the live José Oliveira (who provided Joe's voice) appear together on-screen. With the percussion montage the proceedings become even more surreal, including one nightmarish moment when two male dancers, squaring off as if for a fight, are suddenly transformed into two animated fighting cocks and back again. By the finale the mood has become thoroughly delirious, and Aurora's spell is enough to set the very buildings of Bahia dancing to the rhythm of Barroso's infectious samba.

[125] One result of the Portuguese orthographic reform was the altered spelling of some personal names. The musician known as *Benedicto* Lacerda in the early 1940s is now called *Benedito* Lacerda.

In Ward Kimball's original animation, the caballeros sing their title song. Note the timing chart at the right, indicating placement of intermediate drawings in the arc of the action. (These charts were commonly used by animators; *see* the similar charts in the drawings on p. 262.)

LA PIÑATA

By the time serious story development started in August 1942 on *La Piñata*, the Mexican segment of the new feature, its Brazilian counterpart *Baía* was already under way. As production continued on both films over the next two years, they would become inseparably linked—partly because they would be seen in tandem in the feature, partly because many of the same artists worked on both films. Development and production of *La Piñata*, always a few steps behind that of *Baía*, would be heavily influenced by the evolving Brazilian segment, and by the lessons learned in producing it. And just as *Baía* had taken advantage of its package-feature setting and had quickly outgrown the normal limits of a one-reel cartoon short, so *La Piñata* continued the expansion process, finally emerging as a far more lengthy, complex, and innovative film than anyone could have envisioned at the start.

The earliest description we have of the original story, as Walt explained it to the press during the December 1942 Mexico City trip, is modest enough. As visualized at this point, the film was simply to depict Donald Duck's celebration of Christmas along traditional Mexican lines. After observing Las Posadas, the holiday festival that El Grupo had witnessed during their visit, the Duck was to be presented with a piñata and instructed in its use. Breaking open the piñata, he would release a flood of "gifts," which were the sights and sounds of Mexico: colorful locations such as Pátzcuaro and Xochimilco, exciting customs such as bullfights. The idea of a rooster character representing Mexico was a late addition to this story outline and was only slowly absorbed into it. Press accounts of the Disney visit to Mexico City conflict on this character; "Señor Gallito" appears in some of them but not in others. (The rough synopsis given above is taken from *Caminos del aire*, which made no mention of the character. In this version the task of explaining the piñata and other Mexican customs to Donald was entrusted to Joe Carioca.) Even at the studio, as late as February 1943, Norm Ferguson could report to Walt that Homer Brightman and Ernie Terrazas were "reworking 'La Piñata' using the Charro rooster as a basis."

By midsummer 1943 the rooster character was firmly planted in the story and had been christened Panchito. In July an official synopsis was registered with the MPPDA: in this version the story begins with the breaking of a piñata, which unleashes a shower of Mexican gifts—and Panchito. The rooster enthusiastically greets Donald and Joe, although his wild behavior scares both visitors out of their wits. An exuberant slap on the back from Panchito knocks Donald completely out of the frame, where he becomes tangled in the sound track. Panchito sets up two full-length mirrors so that his reflections can join him in singing a Mexican song (unspecified). Like the original synopsis of *Baía*, this description reflects only a fraction of the content that would ultimately appear in the finished film. This time, however, the studio was clearly aware that this was only a partial outline. The synopsis is deliberately open-ended: Panchito ends by promising his guests that "I will show you Mexico with the magic sarape." In all likelihood the studio registered this synopsis only to protect the story material for the opening scenes of *La Piñata*, and carefully avoided revealing what would come next.

For by July 1943 many of the eye-popping combination shots for *Baía* had already been filmed, the technical crew was at work embroidering those scenes with more spectacular effects, and Walt was not about to produce *La Piñata* without more of the same—even more elaborate and spectacular, if possible. Between December 1942 and summer 1943, Walt and other staff members had visited Mexico City to audition performers who would appear in *La Piñata* as Aurora Miranda had appeared in *Baía*. These auditions were, in fact, quite extensive. Among the performers considered for *La Piñata* were Trío Calaveras, a vocal trio who billed themselves as "los reyes del folklore mejicano" and who had coincidentally appeared in Chile while El Grupo was there in 1941; Chucho Martínez Gil, a tenor popular in both Mexico and South America; the Hermanos Domínguez Marimba Orchestra, "the best marimba band in the world," headed by Alberto Domínguez, composer of the international hit songs "Perfidía" and "Frenesí"; and numerous other solo, duo, and trio acts.

Panchito the rooster in a typically exuberant moment.

Through these auditions, the studio selected a performer to supply the voice of their new charro rooster character: the popular stage performer Paco Miller. At first glance Miller seemed a perfect choice for this role: he was an accomplished singer, he had a large and enthusiastic following in Mexico, and one of his specialties was ventriloquism, so character voices were nothing new for him. His casting in the role of Panchito had been confirmed by late August 1943, when Walt was invited to Mexico City to receive the Aguila Azteca, one of the country's most distinguished honors to non-Mexican civilians.[126] As part of the festivities, Walt participated in a radio broadcast with Miller and Clarence Nash, the voice of Donald Duck. The radio script, prepared in Spanish at the studio, depicted an encounter between Donald and Panchito in Mexico City. Walt was photographed presenting Miller with a large figure of Panchito.

[126] Two other Hollywood filmmakers received the Aguila Azteca at the same ceremony: MGM studio chief Louis B. Mayer and veteran travelogue producer James FitzPatrick.

It's important to remember the social context in which these activities were taking place. If charity begins at home, Rockefeller's Good Neighbor program was facing an uphill battle simply in countering ethnic prejudice against Mexicans on the home front. South America was distant enough from the U.S. that it could easily be portrayed in the mass media in exotic, glamorous terms. Mexico, bordering directly on the southwestern United States, including California, was a different story. An uneasy racial tension, fueled by direct contact, had been brewing in the most heavily populated U.S. cities for several decades, and it found a particularly ugly outlet in the wartime atmosphere of the early 1940s. The infamous "Zoot Suit Riots," capping more than a year of escalating hostilities, erupted in the streets of Los Angeles as gangs of U.S. servicemen openly attacked Mexican neighborhoods on the night of 3 June 1943—one day before the end of the international Seminar on Visual Education at the Disney studio, and in the midst of story development on *La Piñata*. Clearly, the cause of hemispheric unity had a long way to go. The efforts of Walt and his staff on behalf of the Good Neighbor program, exercising special care to create a motion picture that might truly help to cement good relations between the U.S. and Mexico, take on added significance against this backdrop.

The studio's selection process in Mexico City eventually narrowed the field down to the two human performers who would be featured on-screen in *La Piñata*. One of these was Dora Luz, a lovely, petite radio singer at XEW who had auditioned for El Grupo earlier in the summer. In August 1943 she was selected to appear in the film, and the studio began negotiating for her services. Some consideration had been given to filming the Mexican live action at a Mexico City studio, but because the combination work in *Baía* had proven so complicated, Walt and his staff opted to minimize their technical difficulties by bringing the Mexican performers to the Disney studio in California. By the end of August Dora Luz had arrived in Burbank, ready to begin work.

The studio had also determined to hire a dance trio that might demonstrate traditional regional dances of Mexico. During the early summer months of 1943, two such groups were under serious consideration: the Hermanos Pastor and the Trío Mixteco. In July the studio selected the latter trio, a family group consisting of José and Vicente Molina and their sister Carmen. Informed of their selection, the Molinas happily began packing their trunks for the trip to the Disney studio. In the end, however, only one member of the trio would appear in *La Piñata*. José Molina, the older brother and leader of the group, was prevented from entering the United States—by an act of governmental bureaucracy that was hardly calculated to advance the Good Neighbor cause.

Dora Luz, the Mexican singer who appears on-screen in *La Piñata*.

The matter began with what seemed merely an annoying inconvenience: the Molinas, contacted in mid-July to come to the Disney studio, were unable to leave Mexico City immediately because of some little problem concerning José's draft status. Upon investigation, the studio learned the problem: José was registered with the *United States* draft—and was considered delinquent. Why? In December 1942, attempting to enter the U.S. for a professional engagement, he had been stopped at Laredo, Texas, and forced to register for the U.S. draft. The Mexican consulate had previously assured him that this was unnecessary, but his protests fell on deaf ears; he would not be allowed to enter the country without registering. Resigned, José signed the registration papers, continued his journey, and thought no more about the matter—until he received a letter in May 1943, ordering him to report to the U.S. Selective Service for his physical examination. Having ignored the letter, he was now considered delinquent. This should have been a simple matter to clear up, since José was a Mexican citizen and was already registered with the Mexican military—but there were more complications. Technically, in fact, José *wasn't* a Mexican citizen; he had been born in Chile while his parents were on a theatrical tour. As a member of a Mexican family, he had always considered himself a Mexican citizen, but had never bothered to complete the naturalization process. His military standing was no help either: the Mexican War Department refused to endorse him because his service—raising and training carrier pigeons—did not qualify him as an active member of the armed forces. Moreover, he had made his ill-fated 1942 visit to the U.S. with a passport that mistakenly identified him as a Mexican citizen, and was now considered to have misrepresented his citizenship. In short, a second visit to the U.S. to appear in *La Piñata* could involve very serious consequences for José Molina.

Instead of performing with her brothers, Carmen Molina appeared in *La Piñata* as a solo dancer.

As letters and phone calls flew between Clarence de Lima, of the Mexican Department of Tourism, and Disney unit manager Dan Keefe, this bureaucratic snarl became progressively more tangled. The Molinas, believing at first that the matter would be quickly resolved, asked the studio to wait for them until they could all travel together. The studio agreed to a short delay in production. By mid-August, however, when a month had gone by with no sign of a resolution, it was agreed that Carmen and her younger brother, Vicente, would proceed to the Disney studio to begin preliminary work on their sequences in the film, and José would follow whenever he could. Carmen and Vicente arrived in Burbank during the last week of August, along with Dora Luz and Paco Miller. But the weeks dragged by, and José's problem seemed no nearer a solution. Finally, early in October, the combined efforts of the Disney studio, the CIAA, and the Department of Tourism succeeded in obtaining a Mexican passport for José, along with a permit allowing him to leave Mexico for a limited time to work in *La Piñata*. Walt arrived in Mexico City, on a trip combining several matters of studio business (including his visit to Fortín de las Flores to check on the literacy group), just in time to learn of this breakthrough. "One of the first things Walt asked when he got off the plane," de Lima wrote to Keefe, "was—'Clarence, what about Molina?' I was glad to be able to reply that José had his papers all in order and was ready to leave whenever word was received. Walt said he couldn't believe it, but I showed him your wire received yesterday morning and then he showed extreme pleasure and gratification." But that joy was short-lived. The U.S. government was promptly notified of José's new status—and replied that it made no difference. José was still considered a delinquent registrant in the U.S. Selective Service, and still subject to prosecution if he attempted to enter the country.

At this point the Disney studio bowed to the inevitable. During the course of José's legal battles, Carmen and Vicente had not been idle in Burbank. Along with Dora Luz, they had worked with the production team, posed for publicity stills, and appeared in special stage presentations in honor of Mexico's Independence Day, 16 September. In addition the studio had filmed a Technicolor screen test of Carmen, who proved a charming screen personality in her own right. Trío Mixteco's stage act included a variety of group dances, along with a few solo turns by Carmen. Now the studio was faced with the delicate task of eliminating the trio from their film and substituting Carmen as a soloist. It must have been a bitter disappointment for both José and Vicente—but, for the sake of their sister, they gallantly stepped aside. Carmen Molina would appear in *La Piñata* as a solo dancer.

Besides auditioning singers and dancers for *La Piñata*, the studio had been seeking Mexican music for the score. The songs of Ary Barroso and other Brazilian composers had proven an invaluable asset to Disney's Brazilian films; now the studio turned to the catalogue of the distinguished songwriter Agustín Lara, who enjoyed as great a popularity in Mexico as did Barroso in Brazil. During the 1930s Lara's songs had achieved great success in Mexico, on records (recorded by Lara himself as well as other singers) and in films, including the landmark Mexican talking picture *Santa* (1931) for which Lara had written the title song. They had also crossed international boundaries, being heard in films produced in Hollywood (Paramount's *Tropic Holiday*, 1938) and in Argentina (*Melodías de América*, 1942). For *La Piñata* the Disney studio selected Lara's recent hit "Solamente una vez." Outfitted with new English lyrics by Ray Gilbert, "Solamente una vez" became "You Belong to My Heart."[127] This would be the song performed by Dora Luz and, like Barroso's "Baía," it would enjoy a new level of international success after its exposure in the Disney film.

[127] Almost concurrently, another Lara standard, "Granada," would be sung (with its original Spanish lyrics) by Carlos Ramírez in MGM's *Two Girls and a Sailor* (1944).

Another song featured in the picture came from Manuel Esperón, the multitalented musician who had worked with El Grupo in conducting their Mexico City recording sessions in the spring and summer of 1943. Two years earlier, Esperón had written the title song for the Mexican film *¡Ay, Jalisco, no te rajes!* (1941). This modest picture, a model of a popular genre, the *comedia ranchera*, had scored a tremendous hit in Mexico and had established its star, Jorge Negrete, as "the quintessential Mexican singing charro."[128] Esperón's song had shared in that success and had become successful in its own right, widely recorded by popular singers; in time it would become a traditional favorite in Mexican culture. Now, in the most striking musical transformation in any of the Disney Good Neighbor films, the song's cultural identity took on an added dimension by replacing Ernesto Cortázar's original Spanish lyrics with new English lyrics, again by Ray Gilbert. "¡Ay, Jalisco, no te rajes!"—originally a song of embattled regional pride—now became "The Three Caballeros," a song expressing the film's theme of hemispheric unity. This would become the song that Panchito the rooster would sing in *La Piñata*; and, of course, ultimately it would lend its title to the

[128] Negrete's subsequent success included an appearance in one Hollywood film, Hal Roach's *Fiesta* (1941), in which he was billed as "George" Negrete and sang three songs.

package feature. Thanks to this inspired invention, the three caballeros—the South American parrot, the Mexican rooster, and the North American duck—became an unmistakable symbol of the Good Neighbor policy in action. Standing together, the three caballeros *were* the Western Hemisphere. And the song made it entertainingly clear that, standing together, they made an unbeatable team.

Along with these and other, more traditional Mexican songs, the film offered one original studio composition. Chuck Wolcott's romantic "Mexico" had actually been composed shortly after the 1941 South American trip; an instrumental recording can be heard on the sound track of *South of the Border with Disney*.

As various Disney groups visited Mexico during 1942 and 1943, they continued to witness new facets of Mexican life and culture, and the story content of *La Piñata* continued to grow. Both the Blair party (in October 1941) and Walt (in December 1942) had attended bullfights in Mexico City, and throughout most of 1943 a bullfight sequence was planned for *La Piñata*. The studio obtained amateur 16 mm footage of bullfights to be used as visual reference material, and made a concerted search for radio recordings of professional bullfight announcers to use as a guide in recording the sound track. In the finished film, the only bullfight scenes were in the brief *torito* sequence at the end. Another sequence, planned from the beginning, would have featured the lovely floating gardens of Xochimilco. The Blair party had shot extensive 16 mm footage at Xochimilco during their 1941 visit and had followed up with inspirational sketches for a suggested film (glimpses of both can be seen in *South of the Border with Disney*). Tentative story development continued through 1942 and 1943, and when work started on *La Piñata*, the Xochimilco story was absorbed into it. In August 1943 the sequence was assigned to Jack Kinney, one of the studio's top directors. "Xochimilco, as you probably know," Kinney recalled years later, "is a very popular lake outside of Mexico City, where they have lots of floating ponds with trees, huge trees, growing out of them. It was a little love story between a little Mexican boy

Story sketches from the discarded sequences. **BELOW:** A romantic moment from "Xochimilco." **OPPOSITE:** Farmer Pulido on shaky ground in "Paricutín."

and a little Mexican girl. She picked out these flowers and put them in her hair, and he was singing to her. It was cute as hell."

Another story idea was born unexpectedly of an important event that occurred in Mexico after *La Piñata* had already started development. On 20 February 1943, after two weeks of earthquakes that had rocked the state of Michoacán in western central Mexico, a fissure suddenly opened in what had previously been a farmer's field, spewing ashes, rocks, and, eventually, lava. Within a few short days, as the eruptions continued, it was clear that this was rapidly becoming a major volcano. Eventually named Paricutín,[129] after a village near its base that was completely buried in lava, the volcano partially engulfed other towns and villages as well, and at its peak of activity rained ash on Mexico City, two hundred miles away. Bill Cottrell and Jack Cutting, visiting Mexico in March in the course of their survey trip through Central America for the literacy project, took part in a special airplane flight to Paricutín and viewed the crater from the air. Cottrell was much taken with the spectacle and afterward wrote to Walt, suggesting a film about this natural wonder: "The idea for the short would be based on the very brief history of this volcano. A Volcano is Born—less than two months ago that place was a cornfield—then one day rumblings were heard, etc. etc. Today the crater is over 600 feet high—smoke and lava and rocks and flame shooting thousands of feet in the air—Explain how volcanoes work by cross section animation, etc. Gad, it's sensational (the Krakatóa idea). You can release it with *Victory Through Air Power*—It's a bomb shell—it's dynamic. All right, Cottrell, that's enough. I thought of that idea when I saw it in *Life* magazine and have already discarded it."

[129] Today the name is usually accented differently: Parícutin.

The studio did in fact start work immediately on a Paricutín film, and began by following another of Cottrell's suggestions: trying to obtain quality 16 mm color footage of the volcano for live-action scenes in their finished film. Clarence de Lima, who was already acting as a go-between in the Disney negotiations with singers and dancers for *La Piñata*, attempted to bargain on the studio's behalf with cameramen in the area. For a time the leading candidate was Ralph Gray, a semiprofessional cameraman from the U.S. who had traveled to the volcano within a week of the first eruptions and had secured hundreds of feet of spectacular day and night shots. The advantage of Gray's film, as de Lima explained, lay in its timeliness: "He was able at that time to get some wonderful shots because he had clear, unobstructed views, plenty of sunshine, little or no dust and ash in the air to becloud the shots." Unfortunately Gray was demanding a small fortune for even a preliminary viewing of his film, so the studio looked elsewhere. An attempt to contract with a local cameraman for new footage, late in July, also failed—partly because of inclement weather, partly because the air in Michoacán was by now saturated with volcanic ash. In time, 16 mm shots of Paricutín were purchased from two sources: Charles B. Beery, a travelogue producer in Minneapolis, and Harry Wright, residing in Mexico City, who also supplied some of the bullfight footage the studio had been seeking.

In addition to this live-action element, the Paricutín film was to tell the volcano's story in cartoon form. The animated sequence, like "Xochimilco," was assigned to director Jack Kinney. More than four decades later, Kinney recalled: "Now 'Paricutín' had a little story about the farmer who was farming his land . . . And we had the name of the guy, the farmer gave his name, and he was planting his seed. And you see him tilling the soil in his sarape and Mexican hat and whatnot, but one seed, the seed would not stay planted. And Señor So-and-so said, 'I'll see that you stay in the ground,' so he tamped like hell on the thing, and all of a sudden it erupted, and that became Paricutín. And pretty soon Farmer Whatever-his-name-was had a garden on the side of a volcano!" The real farmer's name was Dionisio Pulido, and his remarkable story had been publicized both in Mexico and in the U.S. The Disney studio planned to acknowledge him on the screen and made an effort to involve him directly in exhibition of the film. "If now we could secure . . . [Pulido's] permission to use his name and story and experience in the picture," production manager Dan Keefe wrote to de Lima, "we have planned what you and Alex [Buelna] will agree is an interesting publicity stunt to follow it up. At the time of the opening of the picture in Mexico City, Walt Disney, in the presence of yourselves and others, would like to present Señor Pulido with a beautiful new sombrero to replace the one that he lost in the volcano and which, you will discover when you see our picture, is still bobbing up and down in the smoke of Paricutín."

Throughout 1943, work continued on all these varied story ideas, all of them still considered segments of the ever-expanding project that was *La Piñata*. Of them all, the combination live-action–animation scenes featuring Dora Luz and Carmen Molina retained the greatest claim on Walt's attention, and remained the principal focus of production. Dora Luz, as a singer, had been engaged simply to sing "You

Story sketches for Carmen Molina's appearance in the Zandunga sequence. The production stills show Carmen on the set (LEFT) before a blank process screen and (RIGHT) with a process plate rear-projected on the screen.

Belong to My Heart," so her scenes were relatively simple to shoot. Under Chuck Wolcott's supervision she recorded the song in September 1943, then was filmed in Technicolor a few weeks later, lip-syncing to playback. By 10 October she was back in Mexico, "singing the praises of Walt and of everyone of the Studio to high heaven," as de Lima reported. "Never had anyone been so kind and gracious to her as all of you were." Carmen Molina's scenes were more complicated, not least because the filmmakers had been expecting a trio and were now compelled to devise new scenes for a solo dancer. In the finished film Carmen would perform three numbers—the Lilongo, Zandunga, and Jesusita—and filming of these scenes stretched through February of 1944. But *none* of the live-action scenes in *La Piñata* presented the excruciating ordeal that had marked the combination scenes in *Baía*. Having learned their lesson in producing *Baía*, the production team avoided using the process screen this time around. Some process plates were provided as backdrops for Carmen's dances—waving flowers for the Zandunga, marching cacti for the Jesusita—but now that the Iwerks optical printer was available, it was much easier and more effective to use the printer for any intricate interactions between live and animated characters. Iwerks's special-effects crew, galvanized by the limitless possibilities suddenly placed at their fingertips, were inspired to create ever more dazzling effects with the printer. "It was exciting because it was brand new," recalled operator Bob Broughton, "and what we were doing had never been done before. I remember the excitement of that." In the case of Dora Luz singing "You Belong to My Heart," the crew simply shot a straightforward performance of the song, leaving the cartoon elements to be animated and doubled in months afterward. (The shots used in the film were close-ups of Dora against a neutral background, but the crew also filmed the number with alternate settings, costumes, and angles, including some full-length shots. Some of this material can be seen in the *Three Caballeros* trailer.) For other sequences, such as the Carmen Molina dances,

Iwerks's department worked carefully with the story department and the live-action crew to devise their visual pyrotechnics.

Other material for the film was sought from various sources. During Walt's visit to Mexico in October 1943 to check on the literacy group, he commandeered the unit's production manager, Erwin Verity, for a side project. "Shortly after Walt's arrival in Mexico City," Verity wrote, "I was given the assignment of photographing all of the signs of the prominent night clubs. Not knowing any Mexican union regulations for photographers, and realizing that Walt wanted the job done as quietly and inconspicuously as possible, I hired a cameraman and completed the job in one night. . . . We used, in all, two 100-ft. rolls of special 16 mm Kodachrome stock."[130] Verity filmed a half dozen nightclub signs, along with other views of Mexico City, but oddly—like the bulk of El Grupo's 1941 Brazilian footage—his film failed to arrive at the studio.

130 This would have yielded five or six minutes of raw footage.

Along with Carmen Molina and Dora Luz, who were prominently featured in *La Piñata*, the studio engaged numerous other Latin American performers. These included:

Carlos Ramírez, an operatic baritone under contract at the time to MGM, where he was being heavily promoted. Ramírez was actually a native of Colombia, not Mexico. On the strength of his memorable performances of "Te quiero juste" in *Bathing Beauty* and of Agustín Lara's "Granada" in *Two Girls and a Sailor*, the Disney studio engaged Ramírez to sing in their film. *Hollywood Reporter* announced that Ramírez would "voice the part of one of the caballeros, and sing 'Mexico,'" but in fact his sound track performance of Wolcott's "Mexico" was his sole contribution to the Disney film. It was recorded in August 1944, very late in production.

The **Ascencio del Rio Trio**, a vocal group comprising Ofelia and Sara Ascencio and Emmy del Rio, had appeared previously in Paramount's *Tropic Holiday* (1938). In *La Piñata* they did not appear on-screen, but their voices were heard on the sound track singing the lovely melody of the Zandunga.

The **Padua Hills Players**, a troupe of actors and dancers in Los Angeles, regularly presented plays and musical performances at the Padua Hills Institute. They worked extensively with Graciela Amador, of Mexico City, a musicologist and specialist in traditional regional music and dances of Mexico. (Illustrating the complex, and sometimes problematic, web of relationships behind the Good Neighbor project, Amador was a friend of Eulalia Guzmán.) In *La Piñata* the Players danced the Jarabe Pateño, a traditional dance of Pátzcuaro that Amador had discovered and restored.

A publicity photo illustrating an inked and painted cel of the caballeros.

PANCHITO
WILL HAVE GUNS
AND HOLSTERS
IN SEQ.12.1
ONLY
THIS WILL BE CARRIED AS A HEAVY
PEN LINE IN PRODUCTION
HIGHLIGHT
CLEAN UP
MODEL OF
"PANCHITO"
PROD. 2725
#14-118
IN ALL OTHER
SEQUENCES HE WILL
HAVE JUST A BELT

In this Panchito model sheet, the final design of the character still has not quite been established.

Meanwhile, the studio was having second thoughts about the casting of Paco Miller as the voice of Panchito. Despite his eminent qualifications for the role, Miller was at a loss when recording the English-language sound track. "Paco didn't speak any English at all," unit manager Moray Foutz explained. "We had to write out the dialogue phonetically. He didn't know what he was saying; the words didn't mean anything to him. He couldn't get any feeling into it. We were on one thing two hours—that 'Bienvenidos,' the opening, you know." The studio quietly replaced him with **Joaquín Garay**, who was a native of Mexico but had spent most of his life in the U.S. and was fluent in both English and Spanish. Garay had dabbled in several areas of show business and had already made unbilled appearances in some Hollywood features, including Frank Capra's 1934 classic *It Happened One Night*. (In that film's celebrated scene of the bus passengers singing "The Man on the Flying Trapeze," Garay sings the third verse.) In the early 1940s he had established his own San Francisco nightclub, Joaquín Garay's Copacabana, and Larry Lansburgh contacted him there. By November 1943 Garay was at work at the Disney studio, recording Panchito's dialogue and songs.

By the end of 1943 *La Piñata* had far outgrown the slight concept Walt had described to the Mexican press a scant year earlier. Just as with *Baía*, a second and greatly expanded synopsis was submitted to the MPPDA in December 1943—two, in fact: one covering the main body of the film, submitted on 16 December, and a second describing the *torito* finale on the twenty-second. Taken together, these synopses come much closer than the July version to what we see in the finished film. The December version describes the opening, with Donald and Joe opening the large gift box; the raucous entrance of Panchito, Donald's encounter with the sound track, and the song number "The Three Caballeros"; the depiction of "Las Posadas"; all the business with the piñata; the magic sarape flying into the live-action scenes of Mexico in the folio; the combination scenes with human singers and dancers; Donald's delirious dream sequence; and of course the mock bullfight at the end. Carmen Molina and Dora Luz are not identified, and neither is some of the music, but it's clear that *La Piñata* is well on the way to its finished form.

There are still, however, some key differences. Most strikingly, this synopsis contains references to Xochimilco and Paricutín; the version of *La Piñata* that was current in December 1943 retained at least vestiges of these two sequences. By February 1944, both had been discarded to make room for yet another combination of live action and animation: the three caballeros' visit to the beach at Acapulco. This sequence would push the technological challenges of the combination scenes to a new level, as Donald Duck was seen frolicking with human, live-action bathing beauties on Acapulco Beach. Jack Kinney, director of the discarded "Xochimilco" and "Paricutín," was disappointed at the decision to cut them, and even in later years he expressed some resentment that they had been replaced with the Acapulco sequence. And yet the substitution may have been prompted by factors other than Walt's fascination with combination scenes. Traces of "Xochimilco" do survive in the finished version of *La Piñata*, during the folio sequence. As for Paricutín, in early 1944 the real Paricutín was still erupting, after nearly a year. In fact it would continue to erupt sporadically for the next *eight* years, in the process burying several villages in lava and driving four thousand people from their homes. Under the circumstances, it's not entirely surprising that Walt had second thoughts about playing such a destructive, catastrophic event for laughs.

In any case, the Acapulco sequence was added to the film early in 1944 and was carefully planned to showcase the most intricate interactions yet between human and cartoon characters. Apart from Dora Luz's song sequence, the bulk of the live action in *La Piñata* was filmed in January–February 1944. Harold Young, a veteran live-action director, was hired to work with Norm Ferguson in supervising both the Carmen Molina dance numbers and the Acapulco sequence.[131] The dance numbers were filmed on the Disney live-action stage, while the Disney parking lot, emptied of cars and covered with sand, became Acapulco Beach. Shooting on the "beach set" began Saturday, 29 January, and continued for the next week. Happily, amateur

[131] Young, a former film editor, had graduated to direction in the mid-1930s and, among his other credits, had directed the classic 1935 Alexander Korda production of *The Scarlet Pimpernel*, starring Leslie Howard. By the early 1940s, when he contracted with Disney, Young was directing routine program pictures, dividing his time between Universal and such poverty-row companies as Monogram and PRC. Some of his Universal credits were musicals such as *Swing It Soldier* and *Juke Box Jenny*, perhaps qualifying him to direct the musical sequences in *La Piñata*.

16 mm footage, shot behind the scenes, has survived to document the details of shooting this sequence: the wind machines that simulated the effect of the flying sarape zooming over the beach, knocking over beach umbrellas and kicking up sand; the large reflectors used for fill light; the high wooden platform and the crane from which overhead shots of the girls were filmed; the tracks and dolly that were used to shoot the rapid tracking shots, so that Donald would appear to be chasing girls along the beach. (At the end of one take the overenthusiastic crew pushes the dolly too far, and it falls off the end of the track.) The shots had been carefully planned in advance, storyboarded as if for an all-animated film. After they had been filmed, similar care was exercised in matching the animation to the live-action element, to create a convincing illusion that the Duck and the bathing girls were really inhabiting the same space.

Since most of the combination shots in *La Piñata* were to be effected with the optical printer, not the process screen, almost all the animation was drawn *after* the live-action elements had been completed. The "Las Posadas" sequence—which consisted of Mary Blair's still paintings of Mexican children, with only the addition of flickering candles or twinkling stars—was finished and shot in January 1944. All the other animated scenes, including the straightforward cartoon sequences with no live action, were executed several months later during the spring and summer. One of the landmark sequences in the film, and indeed in all of Disney animation history, is Ward Kimball's exuberant, wildly inventive animation of the "Three Caballeros" song number. In later years Kimball described this sequence to Michael Barrier as "the only animation I can look back on with pride." As Kimball remembered it, his rowdy, experimental animation was retained only over the objections of sequence director Gerry Geronimi. "When you see it now," Kimball commented to Barrier, "it's kind of old hat, you know, characters going out on the left and coming in from the right, with no hookups, sort of

On the "beach set," Harold Young and crew film a crane shot that will simulate the caballeros' aerial view.

magic animation. When Gerry Geronimi, who was the director on the sequence, saw this, he almost fainted. He said, 'I can't show this to Walt. There are no hookups. A guy goes out here and comes in at the top. What are you trying to do, get me fired?' I said, 'Aw, Gerry, for Christ's sake . . .' I even had a pistol pointed at the audience that talked with the end of the barrel. All this really blew his wig. I said, 'Well, I'm not going to fix it.' The big show was coming up with Walt, and I refused to change my animation, and Gerry had to run the sequence. He said he was embarrassed for my sake. When Walt saw the sequence he laughed his ass off and thought it was great." In fairness to Geronimi, it should be added that Kimball often told such stories in his later years, and that Geronimi, interviewed by Barrier a few years later, denied the truth of this one. In any case, the sequence is brilliant and a milestone in the art of animation.

Ward Kimball injects some of his own irrepressible personality into the character of Panchito.

As production proceeded, the studio continued to encounter various problems, including one that no one could have anticipated. Even after the role had been recast with Joaquín Garay, the voice of Panchito was still not entirely satisfactory. Garay had a fine singing voice and was technically a native of Mexico, but he had spent nearly all of his life in the United States, and to an experienced ear his accent and phrasing just did not sound convincingly Mexican. Jack Cutting, who was still the studio's resident "foreign expert," noted the problem as early as February 1944 when he heard the earliest recordings: "The Garay rendition of the song ['The Three Caballeros'] is excellent, but do not care for his handling of the narration back of 'Las Posadas.' It sounds as though he is striving too much for a Mexican accent. It seems artificial and the tone and tempo of the narration is out of keeping with the pictures and music of the sequence." The problem was underscored a few months later when "Alex" Buelna, head of the Mexican Department of Tourism, who had done so much to help the Disney artists during their various visits to Mexico, was himself a visitor at the Disney studio. As a courtesy he was shown the current work print of *La Piñata*, and he later wrote to Walt that he immensely enjoyed everything about the film—except the voice of Panchito. "Being perhaps somewhat high pitched," Buelna wrote, "it sounds a bit effeminate and, as you will appreciate we certainly want that rooster to be most manly in every respect. He represents to a certain extent our 'he-men' and believe me my worthwhile countrymen are just that."

This was putting a fine point on the studio's efforts at diplomacy. Walt turned to Cutting, who had been unaware of Buelna's comments but had been taking steps of his own. Cutting had engaged Felipe Turich, a veteran Mexican actor,[132] to work with Garay as a vocal coach,

[132] Turich had a long career of his own in both Mexico and the U.S. He had appeared in Spanish-language films in the U.S. as early as 1935, and his career would extend well into the late 1970s.

but Garay's readings had shown no appreciable improvement. "I suddenly realized," Cutting reported, "we were missing a bet in not trying to tie in Turich's speaking voice with Garay's singing. We have managed to do this quite successfully. I know Turich will be acceptable, first of all, because he has done a comic Charro type on the stage for years, and secondly, because he is really Mexican in his expression." The English dialogue tracks for *La Piñata* remained unchanged, but Turich's voice was substituted in the dialogue passages of the Spanish-language edition. The problem was solved.

Another unexpected problem came to light in the studio's ink and paint department. The Disney studio manufactured and mixed its own paints, and in creating a particular shade of green for the cacti in the "Jesusita" sequence, chemist Emilio Bianchi was unable to stabilize the chemical makeup of the paint. The cactus cels, once painted, stubbornly refused to dry normally and tended to stick together. "That was a stinker picture," said Ruthie Tompson, herself a veteran of the ink and paint department who had become a final checker by 1944. "We got these scenes—Camera had them, and they couldn't make them work, because they were sticking. So they sent them back to us, and we were patching them." Tompson recalled that inker Ruth Richards finally went to the camera department and touched up the cels as they were being filmed. "She went upstairs, because the paint was pulling the ink lines off, too. So she went up there, and she did everything to fix that. She practically re-animated half of that stuff."

ABOVE, AND ON PAGES 225 AND 227: Donald and Joe resort to increasingly extreme measures to silence Panchito's sustained high note.

By the fall of 1944, *La Piñata*—after expanding and evolving in a wildly unpredictable fashion for two years—had more or less settled into its finished form. Even with the excision of prime material, including the "Xochimilco" and "Paricutín" sequences, *La Piñata* was much lengthier than any of the other segments in the package feature, accounting by itself for nearly half the feature's running time. Like its Brazilian counterpart, this Mexican picture was divided into sequences—in this case eight of them. The first sequence begins with Donald and Joe, having just returned from Bahia, jumping back into Donald's giant gift box to retrieve whatever may still be inside. The premise that had once been suggested for *La Piñata*, a gift to Donald from his friends in Latin America, has by now been appropriated for the feature as a whole, and the filmmakers have established that this segment will follow *Baía* in the running order of the feature. Accordingly, *La Piñata* wastes no time on formalities; Donald and Joe simply leap inside the box and tear into its contents.

The contents consist of a large gift package labeled "México," and untying the ribbon unleashes a musical interlude built around the film's sound track. One of the innovative features in *Fantasia* had been a short sequence featuring the sound track: a white electronic line in the center of the screen, initially looking like a bona fide optical sound track, had gradually been elaborated with effects animation that provided a visual parallel to the instrumental sounds: an undulating movement of the line, surrounded by soothing ripples, when a harp was heard; pastel effects for woodwinds; sharp, abrasive colors for the brass. Characteristically, *La Piñata* begins where *Fantasia* left off, launching into its sound track animation without pausing for an explanation. The tune is a spirited rendition of "¡Ay, Jalisco, no te rajes!," and the on-screen sound track, animated by Josh Meador, offers hot Latin colors arranged in a pattern that features symmetrical guitar and trumpet motifs. The silhouetted Duck and Parrot dance in the foreground, Donald making vain attempts to grab one of the musical instruments until he's sucked into a trumpet—whereupon he's instantly trapped in the sound track himself, and symmetrical Duck patterns begin to appear in the ongoing display. (Viewers, swept up in this riot of color, sometimes fail to notice that Panchito is heard before he is seen, singing the original Spanish lyrics of "¡Ay, Jalisco!") The Duck pattern becomes a sarape that begins to bulge like a dangerously overinflated balloon. Joe touches the balloon with his cigar and explodes it, releasing both Donald and Panchito.

The explosion also serves to unleash Ward Kimball. In Kimball's contributions to some of the other Good Neighbor films he seems to be reining himself in (with effort), keeping his explosive energy in check as he follows the concepts established by other artists. Now *La Piñata* offers him an opportunity tailor-made for his talents. Panchito, a character as raucous and uninhibited as Kimball himself, bursts onto the screen, propelling himself across the floor with blasts from his six-shooters, punctuating his wild antics with loud charro yells, and generally frightening both Donald and Joe out of their wits. This is another decisive bonding of animator and character. If Fred Moore has already put his stamp on Joe Carioca, and Donald (then celebrating his tenth anniversary in show business) is community property, shared by a pool of animators, Kimball in this sequence unmistakably claims Panchito as his own.

But Panchito—and Kimball—are just getting started. After enthusiastically greeting his new friends and providing them with sombreros, Panchito launches into the legendary "Three Caballeros" number.[133] This wildly inventive sequence has earned its place in animation history, and whether we accept Kimball's or Geronimi's version of its creation (John Canemaker points out that most of the rapid-fire gags conform closely to the storyboard), it is Kimball's ebullient, reckless animation that brings it to life. The July 1943 synopsis had suggested that Panchito would be joined in song by his reflections in two full-length mirrors, but the finished sequence doesn't bother with such literal devices; instead it releases a volley of purely imaginary inventions, many of them triggered by the song lyrics. At the mention of "snappy sarapes," the caballeros suddenly sport bright fluorescent sarapes that promptly disappear again, their function discharged; "guitars here beside us" produces guitars for Panchito and Joe and a series of outlandish substitutes for Donald, who finally seizes a giant string bass and tries to strum it like a guitar. A pistol becomes a peso; "stormy weather" translates as a violent rainstorm that suddenly appears and as suddenly vanishes; Donald becomes a "book on the shelf" with a little "Vol. 1" label plastered on his belly—these and other sight gags pop up so rapidly that the eye can scarcely take in one before charging on to the next. The sequence climaxes

[133] There's no formal introduction as such, and in fact Panchito is never addressed by name at any time in the film. Like everything else in the Disney Good Neighbor films, this is probably not an accident. Recalling Buelna's concerns about the rooster's masculinity, we may note that U.S. ads for the film referred to the character by the diminutive "Panchito," whereas the Mexican ads identified him by the more macho appellation "Pancho Pistolas."

with a remarkable 56-foot scene,[134] Panchito holding the song's last note in a bravura performance far beyond the lung capacity of any human singer, while Donald and Joe, in a series of lightning gags, try vainly to silence him with water, blankets, insecticide, fire, axes, and artillery. (This final scene, with its artificially extended high note, *doesn't* conform to a storyboard precedent and was one of the ideas Kimball claimed to have improvised over Geronimi's objections.)[135]

[134] In other words, it lasts on-screen for nearly 38 seconds, which is longer than it sounds.

[135] For the record, Bob Carlson worked with Kimball on some of the scenes in this sequence, and three brief solo close-ups of Joe Carioca were animated by Fred Moore, who was not otherwise involved in the sequence. But the "Three Caballeros" number unquestionably belongs to Kimball.

By now the principle introduced in *Saludos Amigos*—allowing the North American character to bear the brunt of any slapstick gags—has become second nature. When the caballeros lean over backward to observe the stars in the sky, Donald is the one who falls flat on his back; when they flutter in the air like "birds of a feather," Donald is the one who can't stay airborne and gets unceremoniously trampled by the others a few seconds later. Yet he reacts with an uncharacteristically even temper, perhaps swept along by the momentum of the song. So the sequence maintains both its slapstick energy *and* its message of hemispheric unity.

The second sequence, "Las Posadas," is quietly reverent and gives the audience a much-needed respite from the hysteria of "The Three Caballeros." The *Baby Weems* idea, so celebrated at the time of the South American trip in 1941—a series of still drawings enlivened with minimal animation—is revived in "Las Posadas" to very different effect. This time the still images are Mary Blair's paintings of small Mexican children enacting the Christmas ritual of Las Posadas, which El Grupo had observed in Mexico City in December 1942. We've noted that Mary's art had been transferred directly to the screen in the "little train" sequence of *Baía*; here again her characteristic paintings of small children are presented in their original form, enhanced only by George Rowley's effects animation of twinkling stars and flickering candles. The Las Posadas ritual is recounted with simplicity and respect, culminating in an image of the children breaking the piñata—which leads to Donald's attempt to break the huge piñata that is his gift from Mexico. In these scenes, animated by Ollie Johnston, Donald is again the butt of the slapstick gags: Panchito and Joe contrive to keep the piñata out of reach of the blindfolded Duck, who repeatedly clobbers *himself* without ever coming near the piñata. Finally he does manage to smash the elusive object, releasing a flood of toys, masks, musical instruments, and other gifts (including the *torito* that will be seen again in the closing sequence).

One of the gifts is a huge folio labeled "Mexico," and in the third sequence the caballeros explore its pages. Panchito begins with an image of the Mexican flag, explaining the origins of its design in Mexican folklore, illustrated on the screen by the versatile Josh Meador. Remarkably, considering the manifestly respectful tone of this passage, it was nearly cut from the film for fear of giving offense. Santiago Reachi, president of Posa Films in Mexico, visited the studio during production and expressed some reservations about these scenes, suggesting that they might be taken as ridicule of the Mexican flag. Of course the studio's intention was to *honor* the flag, but an alarmed

Jack Cutting, galvanized by Reachi's comments, solicited the opinions of Manuel Aguilar, the Mexican consul, and several other Mexican nationals. Not surprisingly, they unanimously endorsed the sequence, confirming the viewer's impression to this day: the treatment is light but respectful.

The flag is followed by Carlos Ramírez's offscreen rendition of the song "Mexico," accompanied on the screen by another lovely succession of Mary Blair's paintings. This is a long way from the style of *Aquarela do Brasil* (or "Las Posadas," for that matter), but it is a watercolor of Mexico: sun-drenched markets and village squares, cool moonlit serenades under balconies, fishing boats on Pátzcuaro Lake with their picturesque nets, boatloads of flowers at Xochimilco. The music and images form an indelibly romantic combination, enhanced by the screen presentation of the paintings: at first they simply dissolve in and out; then the transitions become more elaborate, rippling and shimmering across the screen with the help of distortion glasses and matte effects. The song has the effect of a charming introduction, setting the stage for a more detailed exploration of Mexico. (Production papers indicate that the montage of paintings was originally meant to end with a scene suggesting that Panchito had been performing the song. That scene was eliminated from the final cut—happily, since Carlos Ramírez's rich baritone sounds nothing like Joaquín Garay's speaking voice as Panchito.)

Now, and only now, *La Piñata* unveils its live-action content. Walt's instincts as a showman are on display in both *Baía* and *La Piñata*: the live-action combination scenes, perceived as the show-stopping highlights of both segments, are given a careful buildup, teasing the audience before their full effect is revealed. In *La Piñata* the folio illustrations simply come to life and become living scenes of modern Mexico. The caballeros multiply the magic by entering those scenes themselves, taking off on a tour of Mexico by means of the magic sarape (the "flying carpet" of the *Arabian Nights* tales, given a south-of-the-border twist). These delightful scenes could not have been produced without the Iwerks printer: the caballeros glide alongside a car on the highway and appear to greet the occupants inside; they zoom over the surface of Lake Pátzcuaro while Donald leans over the edge of the sarape, trailing his finger in the water. These glimpses of Mexico serve as "establishing shots," leading us to the dance performances actually filmed at the studio.[136] The caballeros ostensibly visit Pátzcuaro, where the Padua Hills Players dance the Jarabe Pateño, then continue to Veracruz, where Carmen Molina and a company of dancers, also from the ranks of the Padua Hills Players, perform the Lilongo.

These episodes force the filmmakers to confront the major pitfall of combination scenes: they attempt to unite two worlds that operate by very different rules. Twice, consecutively, Donald Duck attempts to imitate the human dancers, and both times he fails and is corrected by Panchito. Animated cartoon characters are inherently free of limitations,

[136] These genuine views of Mexico, originally filmed by Wilfrid Cline, ASC, were acquired by the Disney studio from travelogue producer James FitzPatrick and his distributor, MGM. As we've seen, Walt, FitzPatrick, and MGM chief Louis B. Mayer had all been invited to Mexico City in August 1943 to be awarded the Aguila Azteca. The three honorees returned to Los Angeles on 28 August; less than a month later, on 23 September, the *La Piñata* production team screened eight of the recent FitzPatrick TravelTalks filmed in Mexico. Norm Ferguson sent the list of titles to Walt with a memo: "Attached is a list of the reels run on Thursday afternoon which you might want to review before contacting M.G.M. about them." Ultimately the Disney team used stock shots from three of the FitzPatrick shorts: *Picturesque Patzcuaro* (1942), *Motoring in Mexico* (1943), and *Glimpses of Mexico* (1943).

endlessly flexible, and capable of a full range of physically impossible movement, so it's a little jarring to see one straining unsuccessfully to imitate the movements of *human* performers. In these scenes, however, Donald is laboring in the service of both the Good Neighbor program and the studio's newest technological breakthrough, and he graciously forfeits some of his rights as a cartoon character—at first. When Panchito ridicules his efforts to dance with Carmen Molina, there's a flare-up of the characteristic Duck temper, and the agenda shifts again. Now, discarding the Lilongo, Donald begins to dance a wild North American jitterbug instead and regains his cartoon capacity for impossible movement, dancing on one hand and whirling in wild gyrations. Carmen displays a winning charm in these scenes: baffled at first by this strange dance, she makes an effort to adapt to it. The band and the other dancers, likewise, briefly tolerate this aberration, but then the Lilongo returns—for everyone but Donald. Surrounded by both human and cartoon characters performing the Lilongo, he's the oblivious Ugly American as he jitterbugs on.

The casting of animators for these scenes is worth noting. The Pátzcuaro scenes, and Donald's bashful introduction at Veracruz, are animated by Eric Larson, who does a creditable job with Donald's and Joe's laborious imitations of the Jarabe Pateño. When Donald loses his temper and breaks into the jitterbug, Ward Kimball takes over. We've seen little of Kimball's animation since the end of the riotous "Three Caballeros" number (although his handling of Panchito continues to set the standard for the rest of the crew), and it's surely no accident that Donald's wild, defiant dance sequence is assigned to him.

Dragging the squawking Duck away from Veracruz, the caballeros reboard the sarape and set off for Acapulco. More showmanship: the Acapulco scenes were originally meant to be seen *before* the visit to Pátzcuaro—which, given the location of both Acapulco and Pátzcuaro in western Mexico, would have made more geographic sense. But this would have placed the Jarabe Pateño at the end of the "Folio" sequence, creating a serious anticlimax. Accordingly, just as in *Saludos Amigos*, geographic continuity takes a backseat to dramatic effect, and the "Folio" sequence concludes with its strongest component: Acapulco. Following two aerial views of the real Acapulco Beach, the camera and the caballeros zoom down toward the scenes shot at the studio. The sarape imitates a fighter plane[137] as it executes three "attacks" on the beach, the live-action bathing girls playfully scattering in mock terror before the caballeros' assault. Donald's infatuation with Aurora Miranda in *Baía* and his bashful overtures to Carmen Molina in the Veracruz scenes were only the beginning; now he assumes a more aggressive sexuality, first in the macho symbolism of "machine-gunning" the bathing girls from the air, then by diving off the sarape and actively pursuing the girls on the beach. This is a natural progression from the earlier scenes, but it's unfamiliar territory for Donald Duck, and his sexual pursuits become more heated as *La Piñata* continues. Some critics at the time found this disturbing, and generations of later writers have busily occupied themselves analyzing Donald's exploits in this film.

[137] The story crew was specific: the sarape's maneuvers over the beach were meant to suggest a Lockheed P-38, coincidentally one of the subjects of the aircraft-identification series the Disney studio had produced for the army.

Of course the real point of the Acapulco section has nothing to do with sexual or imperialist aggression; it simply provides an opportunity for more combination scenes. As we've seen, the live-action elements here were the last ones filmed for *La Piñata*, and Walt characteristically raises the technological stakes to a new high. The Acapulco combination scenes represent the feature's most intricate interactions between human and cartoon characters. Walt took a justifiable pride in them in 1944, and today they retain their full power to amaze and delight, creating a convincing illusion that rewards repeated viewings. Donald, blindfolded for a game of blindman's buff, stands on a real beach chair that collapses under his weight; pulls a real cape from the shoulders of one of the fleeing girls and then, standing on the cape, is sent tumbling when she snatches it back again; is tossed in the air by several girls, repeatedly landing in their real beach blanket with convincing weight and mass and then bouncing high in the air. Needless to say, such illusions lean heavily on the capabilities of the Iwerks printer, but they also depend on meticulous attention to detail both before and after the shooting. The January–February 1944 "beach set" shoot was preceded by story conferences in which each detail was planned with precision. (The transcripts indicate that Walt, with his usual foresight, played a key role in this process, e.g.: "We should have the sand full of footprints so we don't have the problem of matching [shots].") The cartoon elements, animated months later by Milt Neil, Hal King, and Don Patterson, were linked to the live action with similar precision and were carefully color-controlled to maintain the convincing illusion. Donald's contact shadows[138] were animated separately, and some of them double-exposed to blend convincingly with the real shadows on the sand. If combination scenes are the distinguishing feature of *The Three Caballeros*, they reach their zenith on Acapulco Beach.

[138] Contact shadows are the shadows cast on the ground by an animated figure.

Once again the vehemently protesting Duck is dragged away from one display of pulchritude, only to fling himself even more violently into the next. This is the fourth sequence, in which Dora Luz sings Lara's "Solamente una vez," now fitted with English lyrics and retitled "You Belong to My Heart." This sequence marks a turning point for *La Piñata*, the point at which we shift into a kind of overdrive. In the earlier sequences the filmmakers have unleashed a wave of cinematic energy that has steadily gained momentum, and now there's no turning back. The technical crew, gaining increasing confidence, has become an unstoppable force, with a virtual obligation to keep topping the visual pyrotechnics of earlier sequences. Donald too is completely out of control. Continuing his libidinous trajectory from Veracruz and Acapulco, he has by now become downright delirious—and so has the film.

The "Solamente una vez" sequence is framed as yet another page in the folio, this time representing "the night life of Mexico City." Erwin Verity's 16 mm shots of city lights having been lost in transit, the studio fell back on its reliable strengths, and what appears in the film to be a live-action aerial shot of Mexico City by night is actually animated by effects animator George Rowley. This facilitates a series of transitional effects: the city lights dissolve into twinkling stars—and, in the midst of the heavens, Dora Luz makes her appearance.

Now the effects crew goes to work, flexing its technological muscle. No matter that Dora's scenes, filmed nine months earlier, are simple and straightforward and have none of the built-in tricks of the Acapulco Beach episode; they can still be transformed into combination scenes. And so they are: Dora's image appears, shimmering in the heavens, surrounded by animated stars, the whole framed as an image in an animated book; then she reappears as twin reflections in Donald's eyes; and Donald, observing her, noisily gets into the act. "You Belong to My Heart" *is* a lovely song, and Dora delivers a sensitive and affecting performance. But by this time Donald can scarcely contain himself, and intrudes on the song at every opportunity—singing along, hovering in the foreground, rump to camera, as he adores Dora's image, frantically knocking Joe and Panchito aside in his mad scramble to maintain eye contact with her, squirming in adolescent ecstasy as he utters frequent interjections ("Don't *do* that!").

This passage culminates in a flock of disembodied lips, and their kisses propel Donald (literally) even further into surrealism. On a technical level the fifth sequence, "Montage," is a special-effects workshop that is assembled almost entirely within the Iwerks optical printer. From the audience's point of view it's a riotous explosion of sound and color that takes on the explicit contours of a nightmare. Time and again the dreamy-eyed Duck is drawn to a vision of Dora, still gently crooning—only to have the vision explode in his face with the raucous intrusion of Joe and Panchito, firing random gunshots and madly reprising "The Three Caballeros" in sped voices. John Lounsbery, responsible for most of the Duck animation in both this and the previous sequence, is now joined by Josh Meador, who offers more wildly imaginative visuals: the Duck as a skyrocket zooming through a bizarre garden, the Duck as a neon hummingbird hovering among neon flowers. The effects crew continues to run amok with an orgy of pop-art juxtapositions: three animated caballeros with (female) human legs, Dora's face singing from the center of a flower, kaleidoscopic patterns that become quasi-Busby Berkeley overhead shots of the Acapulco bathing girls.[139] Images from earlier sequences crowd back in, now turned on their heads: the bathing girls take their turns riding the sarape and wearing blindfolds. Multiple Donalds race frantically toward the camera, pursued by rotoscoped silhouettes of the girls.

[139] This was fair enough; the previous year Berkeley had gotten into the Good Neighbor act himself, staging the spectacular "Lady in the Tutti-Frutti Hat" number for Carmen Miranda in Twentieth Century–Fox's *The Gang's All Here*.

This level of hysteria can't last indefinitely—and it doesn't. The insistent flower motif suddenly leads us into the relative calm of the sixth and seventh sequences, in which Carmen Molina dances the Zandunga and Jesusita. Wherever we've been for the last ten minutes, these sequences remind us why we came: Carmen performs these traditional regional dances with subtle grace and charm, clad in the regional costumes that were part of her standard wardrobe in Trío Mixteco.

These sequences also employ a level of craft that may not be fully appreciated on first viewing, especially by an audience whose senses have just been bombarded with the frenzy of the preceding sequences. Returning to the first principles of the *Baía* combination scenes, the Zandunga and Jesusita sequences make use of the process screen to provide Carmen with an animated backdrop—then add further physical set pieces and matte additional animation into the foreground, surrounding her with theme-oriented art. For the Zandunga, Carmen's Tehuantepec costume, with its floral headdress, is echoed in the animated setting, which surrounds her with a chorus of gently waving flowers. (Raw takes from the Zandunga sequence, with Carmen backed by the process plate and set piece but without the animated overlay, can be glimpsed in the *Three Caballeros* trailer.) For the Jesusita she returns in regional dress representing Chihuahua—jacket, skirt, sombrero, with smart high-topped boots and riding crop—against a process plate that begins with pure design elements suggesting the patterns of a sarape. As the number continues, this is replaced by a stylized late-afternoon sky. As the sky deepens into the rich gold of sunset it becomes even more stylized, finally resurrecting the sarape design. This is an important thematic touch; it extends the sarape motif that we saw in the opening sound track sequence and that has periodically resurfaced throughout *La Piñata*.

Of course the other major design element in the Jesusita sequence is a moving one: the long double line of animated cacti that join in the dance with Carmen. Inevitably, some writers have attempted to saddle these cacti with Freudian significance. In fact, of course, they're simply the most instantly recognizable feature of a desert landscape, given life by animation—a sort of desert equivalent of the mushrooms in *Fantasia*. They also serve as a collective foil for Donald Duck. (Panchito and Joe have mysteriously disappeared during "Solamente una vez"—except for their nightmare cameos during the montage—reinforcing the impression that this entire section of the film represents Donald's dream, or delirium.) Donald of course maintains his squawking presence throughout the Zandunga and Jesusita sequences; he seems to have spent some of his manic energy during the montage, but he's still very much taken with Carmen. Happily, his appearance has improved; he's animated by Les Clark throughout most of these sequences (with a major assist from Fred Moore at the beginning of the Jesusita). In the Zandunga there's another subtly impressive technical touch: Carmen joins hands with Donald and dances with him.[140] When she returns in the Jesusita he tries to dance with her again, and briefly realizes that goal. All too soon, however, he's intercepted by one dancing cactus, then another, and quickly finds himself absorbed into a botanical chorus line. Cactus to the left of him, cactus to the right, forced to stay in step with them, the grumbling Duck is constantly thwarted in his efforts to reunite with Carmen. As a crowning indignity, one cactus splits up into tiny duck-shaped cacti that surround Donald and trample over him. Carmen herself seems to materialize from a distant cactus at the beginning of the sequence; and as she retreats into the distance at the sequence's haunting conclusion, she transforms back into a cactus before Donald can reach her. . . .

And then, suddenly, we're back in the parallel universe with all three caballeros, preparing for a mock bullfight with the *torito* (that is, Donald) in the film's closing sequence. Of all the disjunctive transitions in this deliberately disjunctive film, this jump-cut is the most disorienting; we seem to be starting over again after the breaking of the piñata, and Donald, already playing his part inside the *torito*, seems to have been here all along. If this finale doesn't exactly bring closure to *La Piñata*, it does at least seem to return us to the setting where we started—wherever that is; we

[140] This direct contact is, like some of the Acapulco scenes, made possible by the Iwerks optical printer. The earlier *Baía* climaxes with a scene, accomplished with the process screen, in which Aurora Miranda hugs and kisses the rear-projected Donald—but she does so with her back to the camera, and only the Duck's arms and legs, flung wide in excitement, are seen from behind her. In the Zandunga sequence, thanks to the printer's new level of precise control, Carmen and the Duck are convincingly shown joining hands.

might assume we've been in Donald's home all along, but the surroundings have been kept purposely vague, and the fireworks at the end seem to soar unobstructed into the sky. Once again, principles of showmanship are on display in this sequence: *La Piñata* ends on a strong visual note by bringing back Fred Moore, one of the studio's top artists, to animate all three caballeros at the beginning of the sequence, as well as our last view of them, shoulder to shoulder, joining in one final harmonious note at film's end. In between, Moore is joined by two other animators. The *torito* has firecrackers attached to its tail, in the best tradition, and Joe Carioca casually lights them with his cigar. The explosions send the frantic Duck into a wild paroxysm of slapstick, animated by Don Patterson, culminating in a gag borrowed from *Alpine Climbers* (1936). In that short Donald, pursued by a large, angry mountain goat, finally turned the tables and charged his pursuer head-on. Being the harder-headed of the two, he left the *goat* dazed and reeling from the collision. In *Sea Scouts* (1939) he tried something similar with a shark, with similar results. Here, in 1944, he tries the same tactic with the *torito*, and the result is one final, gigantic explosion of fireworks. The fireworks are the work of effects animator George Rowley, who contributed the film's final image: a shower of tiny red, white, and blue stars spelling out the end title in all three Good Neighbor languages—FIN, FIM, and finally THE END. Rowley later told Michael Barrier that this effect was achieved by animating each color separately, using different layers of animation paper, but that the ink and paint department combined all the colors on a single cel level. He also recalled that, at the end of this monumentally laborious job, he saw the film several times in theatrical showings—and that the theater management invariably drew the curtains over the end title, obscuring his work!

A star-spangled moment from George Rowley's multicolored end title.

In the feature's opening sequence, Donald receives an assortment of birthday gifts from his Latin American friends.

INTERSTITIAL SCENES

At the time of *Saludos Amigos*, the decision to convert the four component shorts into a feature had been made at the last minute, after the shorts were already completed. As a result, *Saludos* looked like exactly what it was: four short cartoons strung together with connecting tissue. With the second Good Neighbor feature, things would be different. This time the filmmakers had *two and a half years'* notice that they were working on a feature, not individual short subjects, and they used the time to coordinate the sections into a cohesive whole. *The Cold-Blooded Penguin*, *The Flying Gauchito*, *Baía*, and *La Piñata* were each created as separate productions, but the latter two segments were planned from the beginning as parts of a feature, and another separate production number was issued for the interstitial scenes that would tie the segments together as seamlessly as possible.

The original story concept for *La Piñata*, as we've seen, had been framed as a Christmas celebration; the piñata of the title was a gift sent to Donald Duck by his friends in Mexico. Now the studio appropriated that device for the feature as a whole. The picture would begin with a large gift box sent to Donald by his friends in Latin America—not for Christmas, but for his birthday, Friday the thirteenth[141]—and new transitional scenes would be animated, showing Donald opening the various packages inside, leading to each of the four major segments. In *La Piñata*, the gift was a piñata with the wonders of Mexico hidden inside; in *Baía* it was a pop-up book in which a miniature Joe Carioca appeared, reducing Donald to his own size and

[141] The idea of placing Donald's birthday on Friday the thirteenth didn't originate here. Studio correspondence indicates that Bill Cottrell had suggested a promotional celebration of Donald's birthday on Friday the thirteenth as early as 1935. Subsequent links between Donald and the unlucky number had included *Donald's Lucky Day* (1939), in which the Duck survived harrowing danger on Friday the thirteenth, and *Donald Gets Drafted* (1942), in which his induction notice was "Order no. 13."

taking him for a visit to the Brazilian scenes inside the book. This led to another transitional sequence at the end of *Baía* in which Joe and Donald emerge from the book, still in miniature. Joe, using "black magic," simply blows on his finger to inflate himself back to normal size. Donald, still the inept North American foil, tries the same trick and inflates into wildly distorted shapes, like a toy balloon out of control, before Joe helps restore him to normal duckhood.

And what of *The Cold-Blooded Penguin* and *The Flying Gauchito*, already completed in 1942—how to integrate them into this gift box? This problem was solved with ingenious simplicity: the first package to be pulled from the box is a gift-wrapped projector and a supply of films. ("Oh boy, home movies!" Donald cries. "Just what I wanted!") The first film's title announces AVES RARAS, strange birds, a category that is improbably stretched to include both the penguin and the flying donkey.

Most of these interstitial scenes were produced under the direction of Jack Kinney, a fast and reliable worker who had directed *El Gaucho Goofy* in the first feature and the abandoned "Xochimilco" and "Paricutín" sequences in *La Piñata*. Kinney's adaptability was a real asset in producing these transitional sequences; as the four major segments of the feature were constantly modified and shifted, Kinney's sequences were revised in turn.

With the loss of "Xochimilco" and "Paricutín," Kinney's strongest showing in the finished film comes in "Birds," the sequence connecting *The Cold-Blooded Penguin* and *The Flying Gauchito*. Here the stories of these *aves raras* are bridged by fanciful scenes of other South American birds: the marrequito, the tijereta, the toucan. The "Birds" sequence was revised three times between January and March 1944. Among the material dropped from it was a 43-foot scene,[142] animated by Milt Kahl, which would have marked an encore appearance by the *avestruz*. The Argentine ostrich, who had appeared in *El Gaucho Goofy* and had been considered for his own starring short, was to be seen here disgustedly rolling eggs into a pile and sitting on them, while the narrator enthused about how he was looking forward to feeding them when they hatched. Most of the exotic birds remaining in the finished sequence—including the Aracuan, popping up in a surprise "preview" to pave the way for his appearance in *Baía*—were animated by Eric Larson.[143] (It's worth noting that Larson's work on these scenes took place during the spring of 1944, overlapping, but slightly preceding, Ward Kimball's work on the "Three Caballeros" song number. Today Larson is remembered for his gentle, charming animation of small birds and animals, but here his scenes of the uninhibited Aracuan display the same reckless disregard for continuity logic that marked Kimball's "Three Caballeros" sequence.)

As planned, these interstitial sequences help to ease the transitions from one segment to another. By introducing Pablo the penguin and the Aracuan before their stories actually get under way, and integrating Donald's reaction shots with the "home movies" he's watching, they make the feature seem less like an assortment of unrelated shorts and more

[142] This would have amounted to nearly half a minute of screen time.

[143] This sequence begins with a flock of birds fluttering and circling over a relief map of South America. The birds are rough animation from *Bambi*, cleaned up and inked and painted in a way that varies so greatly from their appearance in *Bambi* that the scene's origin is practically unrecognizable. The same animation, greatly simplified, turned up again after the war in *Fun and Fancy Free*.

like a unified whole. Much of the Duck animation in these scenes was assigned to Hal King, but other animators were available when their specialties were needed. Fred Moore, who had established the character of Joe Carioca in *Saludos Amigos*, animated Joe's first appearance in this picture, dancing on a miniature stage inside the pop-up book and playing his umbrella like a musical instrument. Donald and Joe, the two old friends last seen together dancing a vigorous samba in *Saludos*, enjoy a happy reunion in these scenes that lead directly into the opening of *Baía*—also animated by Moore.

As the individual segments of the feature took shape, the feature itself remained in a state of flux. Twice during 1943, once in May and again in December, *The Flying Gauchito* was dropped from the package and reclassified as a separate short subject, only to be reinstated in the feature within a couple of weeks. On the second of these occasions, when *The Flying Gauchito* was removed from the feature in December 1943, *The Near-Sighted Oven Bird* was announced as the short that would take its place. In January 1944 *The Flying Gauchito* returned to its place in the feature lineup, and the oven bird's story resumed its status as an independent short—and, as we've seen, was ultimately abandoned and not produced at all.

As for *The Flying Gauchito*, one of the first Argentine-themed shorts to be produced on El Grupo's return from South America in 1941, its Argentine identity was compromised by the time it reached the screen. In 1943 the CIAA received an ominous communication from an RKO affiliate in Uruguay who had seen advance reports on the second Disney Good Neighbor feature. "The movie-going public of that small country, now so closely allied to the United States, resented the fact that Uruguay was conspicuous by its absence in *Saludos*, not even mention being made of them, let alone a short pictorial sequence, and I feel certain that they will resent the fact that again in *Surprise Package* Uruguay is left out entirely. We have made an excellent deal for this picture in Uruguay, and I am only hoping that there will be no repercussions when the picture is released in the territory." *The Pelican and the Snipe*, which might have mollified the offended Uruguayans, was not yet completed at the time of this letter, and the studio decided to take no chances. At the beginning of *The Flying Gauchito* a new line of narration was hastily inserted: "It's a tale told by an old gaucho from Uruguay." In one quick stroke, *The Flying Gauchito* was converted from an Argentine story to an Uruguayan one. Jack Cutting, the studio's resident authority on foreign cultures, had not been informed of this change, and when he discovered it in February 1944 he was alarmed. Cutting routinely inspected the studio's Good Neighbor productions for verbal or cultural gaffes, and he quickly called attention to this one. "The statement 'An old gaucho from Uruguay' is not consistent with the contents of *The Flying Gauchito*," he wrote. "There are no high mountains for condor hunting in Uruguay. The sequence has characters styled in the well known Campos manner. The dialogue contains Argentine slang and statements like 'The pride of Mendoza'—Mendoza is in Argentina. If you did not want to mention Argentina, why not have the narrator say 'It's a tale told by an old gaucho?'" Needless to say, a separate version of the film was prepared for Argentina, omitting the reference to Uruguay *and* featuring the narration track recorded by F. Molina Campos in 1942.

This Mary Blair painting is similar to the title card that was used in the finished feature, introducing Aurora Miranda, Carmen Molina, and Dora Luz.

❖ ❖ ❖

Even the feature's title was uncertain. At first it was identified simply by the working title "South American Group Number 2," but because of the framing concept of the gift package from Latin America, the film was tentatively titled *Surprise Package*. This title appeared in CIAA correspondence as early as October 1942, and for several months afterward the trade press continued to refer to the feature as *Surprise Package*. Perhaps because this title had little Latin American connotation, in June 1943 the studio began to investigate the suitability of using the word *Latin* in a title.[144] Throughout the summer months the picture was alternately known as *Let's Go Latin* and *Latin for a Day*. But by October 1943 it was clear that the film's intended theme of hemispheric unity was succinctly summed up in the song "The Three Caballeros," and this was adopted as the feature's title as well. In Spanish-speaking countries it was of course known as *Los tres caballeros*, while in Brazil it bore the title *Você já foi à Bahia?* (Have You Ever Been to Bahia?), from the Dorival Caymmi song heard at the beginning of *Baía*.

As the film's completion approached, the studio began to gear up for promotion and exhibition. *Saludos Amigos* had had its world premiere in Rio de Janeiro, and as early as May 1943 (when production was just getting under way on *La Piñata*), Walt and Roy had tentatively determined to premiere the new feature in Mexico City. At this time the event was optimistically planned for September 1943, but in succeeding months it became clear that *The Three Caballeros* would be far from complete at that date. The studio bowed to reality and pushed the premiere date further and further back, but Mexico City remained the location of choice.

[144] Later, in 1944, Simon and Schuster published a Disney storybook titled *Surprise Package*. This was not a Good Neighbor publication but a "Giant Golden Book" featuring a variety of stories, adapted by Marion Palmer, all of them currently under consideration for future Disney films.

The Spanish-language edition of the film was of course assembled with special care. In several respects the Spanish edition differs markedly from the domestic version. The "Las Posadas" episode, for example, for which Jack Cutting had found Joaquín Garay's narration unsatisfactory, plays out in the Spanish edition with no narration at all—presumably because Spanish-speaking audiences would already be familiar with the Las Posadas tradition and would need no explanation. In this version the sequence unfolds visually, letting Mary Blair's paintings tell their own story, accompanied only by a chorus singing the traditional "Las Posadas" music—not the soft, wordless chorus of the English version, but an alternate recording with the Spanish lyrics. Similarly, the fiesta scenes in *The Flying Gauchito*, in which the English narrator enumerates the various dances and games, appear in the Spanish version against a strictly musical accompaniment. In other sequences, cultures sometimes collide in interesting ways: Mexican audiences must have found it an odd spectacle to hear Dora Luz singing the English lyrics of "You Belong to My Heart" while Donald, the gringo Duck, interrupted her in Spanish.

The Spanish version of the film's title song, "Los tres caballeros," presented a unique problem. Although Ernesto Cortázar's original lyrics from "¡Ay, Jalisco, no te rajes!" are briefly heard in both the English and Spanish versions of the film, we've already seen that the song was completely transformed as "The Three Caballeros." Gone was "Jalisco's" original theme; the new song was an encapsulation of the film's theme of hemispheric unity. What's more, Ward Kimball's animation was inseparably linked to the new lyrics; its lightning visual puns made sense only in their context. Clearly it would have been ludicrous to exhibit this sequence in Mexico with the original "¡Ay, Jalisco!" lyrics; new Spanish lyrics, appropriate to the cause, were called for. Early in 1944 Jack Cutting contacted Ralph Peer, the music publisher, explaining the situation. Peer assured Cutting that Cortázar, his client, would happily write the new "parody" lyrics for the film. Cortázar's efforts arrived at the studio in March 1944, and—while they qualified as a "parody" of the *original* lyrics—had no connection with "The Three Caballeros," its theme, or anything else in the film. Distant from the studio and never having seen the animation, Cortázar simply had no idea what was required. Felipe Turich, on the other hand, was already present at the studio, and Cutting called on him to write new Spanish lyrics for the film. Peer, informed of this arrangement, replied that it would be satisfactory—as long as Cortázar received all the credit and all the royalties. When Cutting protested this blatantly unfair stipulation, Peer doggedly held his ground, wielding vague threats of "complications" if any other lyricist's name should be credited. In the end, Turich was the real unsung hero of the film's Spanish edition; not only did he provide Panchito's speaking voice without credit, but he also supplied the Spanish lyrics for "Los tres caballeros" without compensation and without credit, even in the film's cue sheets. "This seems to be a nice bit of soft soap to Cortázar," Cutting observed acidly, "and it surprises me that a lyricist would want credit for lyrics he didn't write, or for that matter, that you [Peer] would be a party to such an arrangement. This is probably an ingenuous observation on my part," he added, "because after all, I should realize that the important thing is to arrange a payoff in one way or another." (Aloysio de Oliveira, also without credit, supplied the Portuguese lyrics for Brazil.) As if to compensate, Turich was also called upon to narrate *The Cold-Blooded Penguin* and, like Sterling Holloway in the English version, was prominently identified on the sound track.

In the meantime, the Disney and RKO publicity departments were joined by the CIAA in planning promotional schemes to help launch the new feature. The most elaborate of these was a series of radio programs, prerecorded in Hollywood in June 1944, featuring the music of *The Three Caballeros*. The songs were recorded in English, Spanish, and Portuguese on transcription discs and supplied, free of charge, to more than a thousand radio stations within the Western Hemisphere and beyond. The music was arranged and conducted by Al Sack, staff conductor of the Blue Network, and the recordings featured vocalists from the film—Aurora Miranda, Nestor Amaral, and the character voices of the three caballeros—along with nonfilm vocalists like Dona Lee and Rad Robinson. (Dora Luz was not available for these recordings because she was still in Mexico. Clarence de Lima, the studio's main contact in Mexico City, wrote to Norm Ferguson that he had encountered her unexpectedly while entertaining visiting Disney lawyer Gunther Lessing. "He said they visited a rather low class club in Mexico City and found that Dora Luz was singing there," Ferguson reported to Walt. "He did not mention the name but I am wondering if it might not be to the studio's advantage to see if some contact can't be made to get her a booking in a better class club before we start doing any exploitation work down there. . . . I definitely feel, considering her billing on *The Three Caballeros*, that her present work is hardly an asset to the picture.")

Another promotional activity was the introduction in North America of a new dance step, the samba-jongo, based on the dances performed on-screen in *Baía*. *Samba-jongo* is a musical term, used in Brazil to describe a samba accompanied solely by percussion

This Los Angeles store-window display promotes both the Decca *Three Caballeros* album and the upcoming opening of the film.

instruments. Now the term was applied by the Dancing Masters of America to a variant of the basic samba, and heavily promoted in connection with *The Three Caballeros*. The Disney studio also supplied a special *Three Caballeros* comic book to be distributed in multiple languages by the CIAA. Disney comics artist Floyd Gottfredson, who had begun drawing the "Mickey Mouse" comic strip in 1930 and had already achieved legendary status in the meantime, contacted Russell Pierce of the CIAA in the summer of 1944, sending him sample pages and suggestions for the project. Their correspondence is revealing: Gottfredson proposes the standard Disney comic-book page count and a minimal level of propaganda; Pierce counters by suggesting less than half the number of pages and *lots* of propaganda. "Could Jose Carioca be made to refer in some natural way to what Brazil has done for the United States, i.e., supplying quartz and many other critical war materials, making available the base at Natal, etc.? Could Panchito be given similar lines?" Happily, the studio's ideas prevailed; the finished product (penciled by another comics legend, Walt Kelly) was nearly the length of a standard Disney comic book and refreshingly free of overt propaganda. Meanwhile the "José Carioca" Sunday newspaper comic page, after a run of nearly two years, made its last appearance on 1 October 1944, and was replaced the following week by a new "Panchito" comic feature. Written by Bill Walsh, penciled by Paul Murry, and inked by Dick Moores, the "Panchito" page would run for another full year.

Walt and Lilly enjoy a dance at the *Three Caballeros* costume party in November 1944.

Some of the advance publicity was of questionable value. We've already seen that Alberto Soria, Hollywood correspondent for various Argentine periodicals, had been engaged as narrator of the Spanish-language edition of *Saludos Amigos*. This had seemed a judicious Good Neighbor gesture in 1942, but it backfired in 1943 when Soria used his inside connection to obtain an exclusive story on the studio's next feature. Appearing in the Buenos Aires newspaper *La Prensa* in September 1943, Soria's story referred to the feature by the already obsolete title *Latino por un día*, dissipated any possible publicity value by appearing more than a year before the film's opening, *and* created ill will toward Disney among competing Buenos Aires papers, in particular *La Nación*. "I know we can't stop these representatives from coming over, seeing stuff in work and talking with the boys," Roy grumbled, "but we definitely can refuse to give them artwork such as they had here."[145]

On 18 November 1944 the Disney staff celebrated the finish of production with a Latin American–themed costume party at the Oakmont Country Club. This celebration, under the direction of chairperson Mary Blair, mushroomed into a major social event in the Hollywood filmmaking community. Walt and Lillian Disney formally welcomed a guest list

[145] Actually the artwork illustrating Soria's story is fascinating to see today. Clearly slanted toward an Argentine audience, it suggests that the film features *four* characters of equal prominence—in the words of one caption: "el Gallo Mexicano, José Carioca, el Pato Donald y el Gauchito."

At the Mexico City premiere, Roy addresses the audience and presents bouquets to Carmen Molina and Dora Luz.

including such stars as Aurora and Carmen Miranda, Carlos Ramírez, Xavier Cugat, Lina Romay, and Desi Arnaz, along with Bob Hope, Jimmy Durante, Linda Darnell, Jack Haley, and others. Mary Blair, Retta Scott, and other Disney artists supplied elaborate decorations and a huge piñata. The festivities included a competition for the best costume—with a prize of $350 in war bonds—judged by no less than Edith Head, Howard Greer, and Walter Plunkett.

After numerous delays, the world premiere of *Los tres caballeros* finally took place in Mexico City on 21 December 1944, seven years to the day after the world premiere of *Snow White and the Seven Dwarfs* in Hollywood. The theater was the Alameda, one of the larger and more prestigious movie theaters in Mexico City, with a seating capacity of over three thousand. Accompanying the film was an elaborate stage program, featuring Dora Luz and Carmen Molina—this time performing with her brothers; Trío Mixteco, denied the opportunity to appear on-screen in the picture, did take part in the opening. The event, attended by a glittering multitude of dignitaries and celebrities from both sides of the border, was a smash success. Walt, having just returned to California from a trip to Washington, was unable to attend the Mexico City premiere, but Roy and his wife, Edna, were on hand to represent the studio.[146] The film was held over for an extended run at the Alameda, along with the stage show. ("Carmen tells me," Clarence de Lima wrote to Norm Ferguson, "that they play practically all the time to a full house.") The Alameda normally changed its program once a week; *Los tres caballeros* played there for more than two months.

[146] Walt did, however, host a showing of the Brazilian edition at the Disney studio on the previous day, 20 December. Among those present were Aurora and Carmen Miranda, Ary Barroso, and Brazilian consul general Raul Bopp.

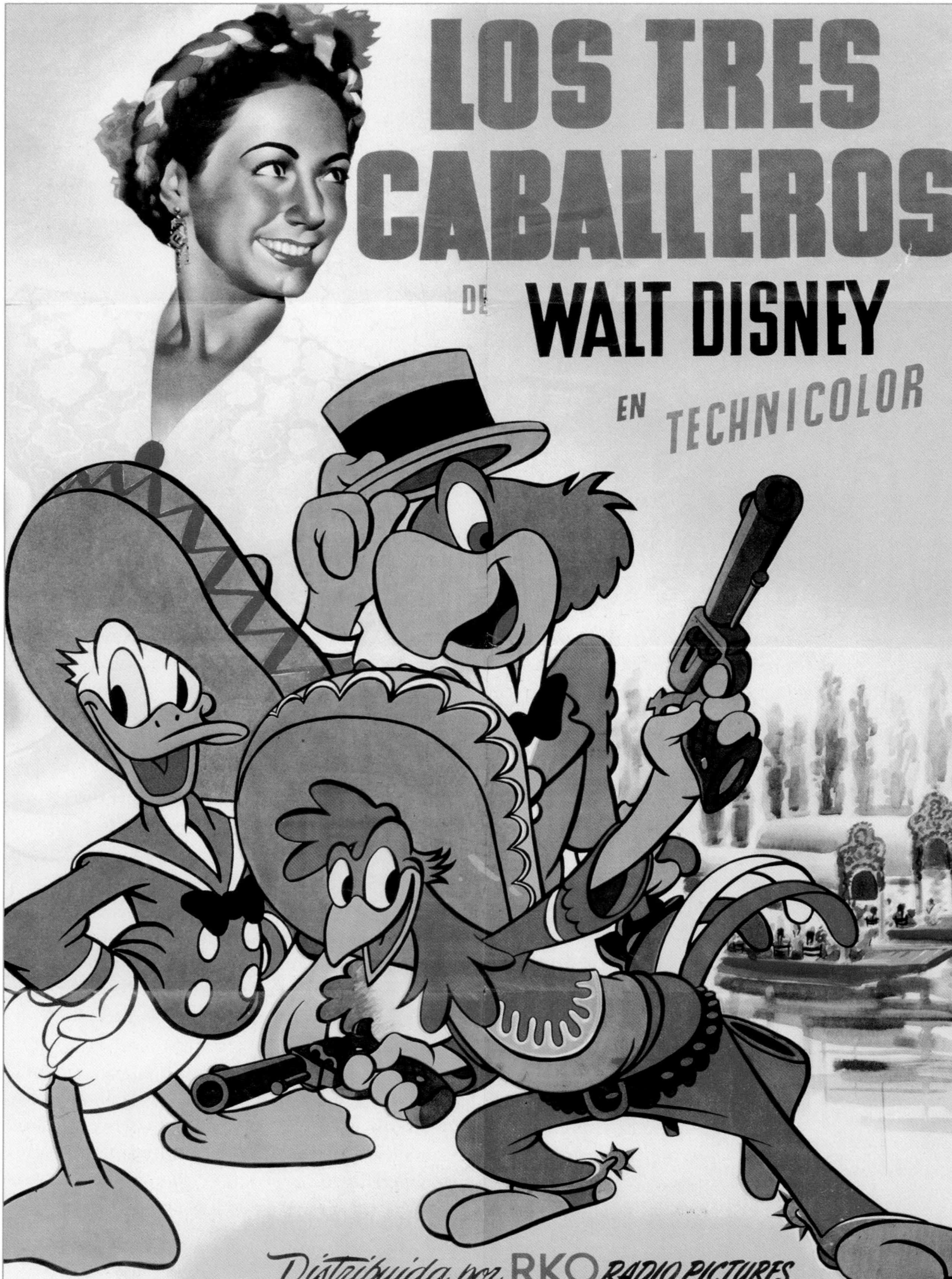
LOS TRES
CABALLEROS
DE WALT DISNEY
EN TECHNICOLOR
Distribuida por RKO RADIO PICTURES

The film's advertising served regional interests. Here, the Mexican poster art stresses Carmen Molina, Panchito (or Pancho Pistolas), and Xochimilco.

But there was still the North American opening to arrange. *The Three Caballeros*, into which Walt and his studio had poured such monumental effort, was starting to evoke a disturbingly ambivalent response. *Saludos Amigos* had been denied a Radio City Music Hall opening in 1943, and Walt had actively pursued that venue for *The Three Caballeros*, going so far as to solicit Nelson Rockefeller's help in obtaining a Music Hall booking. Rockefeller did submit the film to the Music Hall's manager, G. S. Eyssell, and received a sharply negative response. "Of all the Disney feature length pictures, this one I feel will have the most limited appeal. As for its entertainment value, it is nil. It seems to me that aside from its lack of story and continuity, it is a boisterous bore.... The charm and beauty of one of the sequences is marred by frenzied animation. Some of Disney's effects in color, animation and co-relation of animation and real life characters are breath-takingly beautiful, but others are nothing more than dull demonstrations of technical virtuosity." Rockefeller himself, on his first viewing of the film, had wired Walt immediately: "SIMPLY THRILLED WITH TREMENDOUS IMPACT OF NEW TECHNIQUE. FAR MORE BEAUTIFUL THAN I HAD IMAGINED POSSIBLE. HAS MANY OF THE QUALITIES AND BEAUTIES OF THE BALLET." Privately, however, he expressed a different sentiment to his staff: "Mr. Rockefeller liked it very much but suggested that the bird sequence might be eliminated and suggested that the beach scene in Acapulco be cut and the whole picture speeded up a bit."

These conflicting criticisms were symptoms of an increasingly apparent fact: the *Saludos Amigos* honeymoon was over. Walt, acting in good faith, had tried too hard to please too many people. By now three years had elapsed since El Grupo's triumphant return from South America, and that first flush of enthusiastic, wholehearted cooperation between Washington and Hollywood had begun to wane, overlaid by a new matrix of political opportunism and competing agendas. Walt himself was still solidly behind the Good Neighbor mission, but by the time *The Three Caballeros* was finished, his heart was really in the live-action–animation combination scenes. In interviews promoting the film, he could scarcely contain his enthusiasm for this amazing new effect. "I got the idea," he told one journalist, "because so many of my artists had been drafted, and so many of those that were left were busy on Government cartoons out at our Hollywood plant. I really thought that by putting real people in the film it would eliminate a lot of drawing. Of course, as it turned out, we got so fascinated doing tricks—like having Donald do a jitterbug with a girl—that in the end it took more drawing than if we'd done a straight full-length cartoon. But it mystifies people, I'll say that. They just sit there and look at the screen and try to figure out how we do it. But wait until you see Donald chasing dames all over the place. I guess it's the first time in history that a duck turned out to be a wolf." Press releases similarly stressed the film's technological wonders. *Popular Science* published a detailed account of the new techniques in its September 1944 issue—with one notable omission: the new optical printer, the Disney studio's secret weapon, was never mentioned at all.[147] The *Three Caballeros* trailer began by acknowledging the film's Pan-American flavor and the introduction of a new character (Panchito), but

[147] The article concentrates on the rear-projection process screen, and includes photos of the studio's multiplane crane with a projector mounted next to it, projecting live-action frames into a mirror that reflects them into the camera lens. This setup was used to align the images in order to generate matte elements, but the article implies that it was used for the final combination work, which in fact was performed on the optical printer.

saved its climactic excitement for "the newest thing to hit the movies since talking pictures came in"—the combination scenes.

Like its predecessor, *The Three Caballeros* had its New York opening not at Radio City but at the Globe, off Times Square. The opening took place 3 February 1945 and, despite "one of the worst snowstorms in the city's history,"[148] was a smash success. Overflowing with loud, dazzling, frenetic entertainment, the film overwhelmed its audiences and left critics struggling for a coherent response. As the prerelease reactions had suggested, that response was mixed: some reviewers (including many in the trade press) praised the film, but others were harshly critical. The *Variety* reviewer summed up the positive reactions by calling it "a new form of cinematic entertainment . . . a socko feature production . . . just right for popular consumption . . . bound to please generally," and vindicated the transitional sequences: "The off-screen narration is so skillfully blended with the dialog between Donald, Joe Carioca, et al., and it's all so smoothly cut and edited, one is only casually conscious of where one [segment] stops and the other begins." Of the naysayers, perhaps the most familiar to today's reader is Woolcott Gibbs, whose *New Yorker* review called the film "a mixture of atrocious taste, bogus mysticism, and authentic fantasy, guaranteed to baffle any critic not hopelessly enchanted with the word 'Disney.'" Other reviewers fell somewhere in between these poles, but a disconcerting majority weighed in with negative comments. Most of them (including Gibbs) were avowed admirers of earlier Disney films who felt *The Three Caballeros* represented a step in the wrong direction. More than a few decried the carefully wrought combination scenes, declaring that they preferred their Disney cartoons straight. Bosley Crowther, of the *New York Times*, even reversed himself in print. Under the spell of the opening night, he called *The Three Caballeros* "a brilliant hodgepodge of Mr. Disney's illustrative art—a literal spinwheel of image, color and music which tumbles at you with explosive surprise." But after a few days' reflection he published a second review with a very different tone, calling the film "little more than a brightly explosive demonstration of illustrative work" and referring to the combination of human actors and cartoons as "a cheap flea-circus."

[148] The opening at the Globe had been preceded by a special showing for children at Bellevue Hospital on 26 January.

A unique and refreshing perspective was that of music critic Walter H. Rubsamen, who praised Walt as the one Hollywood producer with the courage to bring a feature-length ballet to the screen. In Rubsamen's view, *The Three Caballeros* was "essentially a full-length dancing spectacle and pantomime . . . authentic Latin-Americana, a tour through the colorful regions of Brazil and Mexico that provides a rare opportunity to view and hear the folk-dances and songs of our southern neighbors, and be entertained as well by the three comical birds who symbolize the countries involved." Rubsamen compared the film favorably to *Fantasia*, which he felt had committed an egregious offense by reinterpreting the imagery of Beethoven's *Pastoral*. "Fortunately, similar lapses in taste are entirely absent from *The Three Caballeros*."

Unhappily, the ambivalence of the critics was reflected in the film's box-office performance. Not that it was a box-office disaster; at the Globe it was held over for more than two months, and *Hollywood Reporter* noted that "Walt Disney's *The Three*

In Brazil the film is retitled, and the poster art features Aurora Miranda.

WALT DISNEY
apresenta
VOCÊ JA' FOI A' BAHIA?
(THE THREE CABALLEROS)
em TECNICOLOR
com
PANCHITO
JOSE CARIOCA
PATO DONALD
AURORA MIRANDA
CARMEN MOLINA
DORA LUZ
DISTRIBUIDA PELA
RKO RADIO FILMES

Caballeros is being held over in every one of the nation's key cities where it has opened." But *The Three Caballeros* had been a *very* expensive film, and the public's response was not enough to compensate for the tremendous sums that had been expended on it. The studio's annual report described the film's receipts as merely "satisfactory." Meanwhile the songs "Baía" and "You Belong to My Heart" were recorded by popular singers and became international smash hits, far surpassing their earlier regional popularity. "Os quindins de Yayá," now supplied with English lyrics and retitled "Angel-May-Care," was not far behind, and the title song, "The Three Caballeros," was featured in a popular recording by no less than Bing Crosby and the Andrews Sisters. In May the film opened in London with a charity premiere at the New Gallery, the West End cinema where *Snow White* and *Pinocchio* had also been shown.

As Walt had predicted, audiences were much taken with the combination scenes. So were the other Hollywood studios, several of which—disregarding the tremendous difficulties experienced by the world's leading animation studio—attempted to create similar scenes of their own. Richard Irvine, who had been the art director on *Baía*, was working on *Billy Rose's Diamond Horseshoe* for Twentieth Century-Fox by the summer of 1944, and notified Norm Ferguson that combination scenes were being planned for that film. "I understand Hugh Harman is doing the cartoon process," Ferguson reported to Walt. "Thought this was interesting insofar as the news must be getting around. I believe Mary Blair was approached to work on it but she turned it down."[149] The finished version of *Billy Rose's Diamond Horseshoe* was produced without any animation, whereupon Harman sued Twentieth Century-Fox for breach of contract. Meanwhile, MGM put its cartoon department to work on a special sequence in *Anchors Aweigh*, in which Jerry the mouse danced a duet with Gene Kelly. And by 1948 Warner Bros. was prepared to combine Bugs Bunny and other characters with Doris Day and Jack Carson in a dream sequence for *My Dream Is Yours*. By that time the Disney studio, still maintaining its preeminence, had produced even more elaborate and sophisticated combination scenes for such films as *Song of the South* and *Melody Time*.

[149] Hugh Harman was an animation producer who had started his career by working at the Disney studio in the 1920s.

In fairness to the critics who savaged it in 1945, nothing in previous Disney films (or anywhere else) could have prepared them for *The Three Caballeros*. In producing *Snow White and the Seven Dwarfs*, *Pinocchio*, and the other classic early features, Walt had started with a vision and had followed it through to completion of the film—developing, ornamenting, embellishing, but always retaining his long-range focus on that original vision. *The Three Caballeros* was different. This time Walt had started with a mandate, imposed from without, and had been given autonomy to plot his course as he saw fit. *Saludos Amigos* had been his first response to that mandate, but it had been hastily reinvented as a feature-length picture at short notice. *The Three Caballeros* had evolved over a two-and-a-half-year period, sometimes in startling, unexpected ways, continually adding new layers of inspiration and innovation. At every turn Walt had insisted on "plussing" the film, striving to overlay the old ideas with new ones, to augment surprising effects with ever more dazzling and breathtaking ones. Audiences and critics had been privy to none of this evolutionary process, but were now confronted with the full cumulative force of the finished product. *The Three Caballeros* packed enough Latin American culture, evocative music, innovative animation, astounding visual effects, and sheer entertainment value for four or five ordinary features into one overwhelming, wildly colorful eight-reel package. Small wonder so many of the critics were confounded by it. In succeeding decades, like so many other Disney films that were underappreciated upon their initial release, it has reclaimed its place in the pantheon. In addition to the belated respect that often accrues to vintage films with the passage of time, *The Three Caballeros* has won the esteem of new generations of animation enthusiasts who gladly accept its unorthodox structure for the sake of its rich gallery of visual invention. Their appreciation has been enhanced in the video age, when individual sequences can be isolated and savored in detail, revealing the full range of cultural history and artistry concentrated within. Today, no less than during its own time, Walt's "Surprise Package" is still filled with surprises.

6 BLAME IT ON THE SAMBA

***Saludos Amigos*, *The Three Caballeros*, and . . .** Originally there was to be a third Good Neighbor feature. Or, more precisely, *originally* there were to be twelve Good Neighbor short subjects. As we've seen, the reinvention of *Saludos Amigos* as a feature in mid-1942 had caused a sensation and had led to general agreement that *each* group of four shorts should be reconstituted as a feature-length film. For a time it was assumed that all of these package features would be standardized along the lines of *Saludos Amigos*, and that the second one would be released late in 1943 and the third in the spring of 1944.

However, as we've also seen, no part of this plan remained stable for very long. Walt was capable of standardizing his films if need be, but he much preferred to strike out in fresh directions, to innovate, to break new ground. The second feature had evolved over an unexpected length of time, and along radically unexpected lines, before finally emerging late in 1944 as *The Three Caballeros*. In the meantime, supervising director Norm Ferguson had begun to assemble material for the third feature in this projected trilogy. By the spring of 1945 he had accumulated a variety of story material, music, and miscellaneous ideas for the new film. Considering the sweeping changes that had been made in *The Three Caballeros*, who could tell how the new film might evolve by the time of its completion?

In the end, after a long period of development, the third feature was abandoned. But parts of it did survive, sometimes in their original form, sometimes revised beyond recognition for later Disney productions. Thanks to this never realized and forgotten film, a surprising range of later Disney activities may be traced to roots in the Good Neighbor program.

CUBA

One thing about the third Good Neighbor feature was agreed from the start: it must include a major segment on Cuba. This was regarded as such a certainty that the studio publicly announced its plans for a Cuban film as early as May 1943. This may seem surprising today, in the wake of the Castro era and the political upheavals of the late twentieth century. In the 1930s and '40s, however, most U.S. citizens shared an entirely different perception of Cuba. Distant enough to represent an escape from domestic mores, yet near enough to be reached conveniently by boat, Cuba was regarded by many as a vacation getaway for the idle rich. Its image in popular American culture was glamorous, exotic, perhaps a little dangerous. The contemporary vogue for Latin American music, into which the Good Neighbor program had tapped so serendipitously, had originated largely in Cuba, and Cuban musicians such as Xavier Cugat and Ernesto Lecuona maintained a strong presence on the U.S. popular-music charts. This was the era of "The Peanut Vendor," "She Went to Havana," and "Siboney," of *Havana Widows* and *Weekend in Havana*.

Walt and his artists had established a pattern with their successful survey trips to South America in 1941 and to Mexico in 1942, and now the U.S. ambassador to Cuba

Scenes from the 1944 Cuban research trip. **TOP:** The Pepin Feurer orchestra performs outside the *bohio* as Fred Moore sketches. **BOTTOM:** Rosita, a popular performer, flanked by Moore and Norm Ferguson.

suggested a similar Disney visit to that country. The CIAA responded enthusiastically. In March 1943 Nelson Rockefeller received a memo from the Coordination Committee for Cuba, suggesting interesting sights, such as the harvesting and processing of sugarcane, that Walt and his visiting artists might like to see.[150]

[150] The letter also recommended that Walt contact Ernesto Lecuona, then on tour in the U.S., to discuss Cuban music.

By the time this memo reached Rockefeller's desk, Walt had already dispatched to Cuba a survey group of one: Mary Blair. The Disney Good Neighbor project was in full swing in the spring of 1943: *Saludos Amigos* was in general release in the U.S., the studio's technical crew was experimenting with process shots for *Baía*, a party (including Walt) was in Mexico auditioning musical talent for *La Piñata*, Bill Cottrell and Jack Cutting were touring Central America researching the nontheatrical health and educational films, and plans were being laid for the international seminar that would be held at the studio a couple of months later. In the midst of all this activity, Mary Blair departed to conduct her own personal five-week survey of the sights, music, customs, and general atmosphere of Cuba, accompanied by Jack Halpern of the CIAA. By this time Mary had become an indispensable part of the studio's Good Neighbor activities, and Walt had decided that her visual and cultural impressions of Cuba would provide a preliminary guide for future work.

While in Havana, Mary and Halpern were joined for two weeks by Cutting and Cottrell, who detoured from their Central American travels to provide any help they could. Together the four made their customary formal contacts in diplomatic and artistic circles. Ernesto Roca, local representative of Southern Music, was also on hand and eager to help. Because of wartime restrictions, there had been no Carnival in Cuba in 1943, but the party visited nightclubs and radio stations, scouting for musical talent—much as other Disney parties were concurrently doing in Mexico City for *La Piñata*. They also explored some of the more rural, traditional areas of Cuba. In Santiago they found a colorful array of survey material, including the Tumba Francesa, a Haitian society dedicated to preserving traditional rites and ceremonies. Mary continued such exploration after Cutting and Cottrell departed, and returned to California in late April with a portfolio full of paintings and sketches. She told one journalist that she had found Cuba filled with charm, despite strict rationing and other wartime hardships. "Love of music by the natives was outstanding, Mrs. Blair said. At the sound of 'claves,' orchestra sticks, the people will drop anything and work up an orchestra on boxes, tin pans or anything at hand. . . . She especially enjoyed her trips to the cigar factories, sugar centrals and the native dance halls."

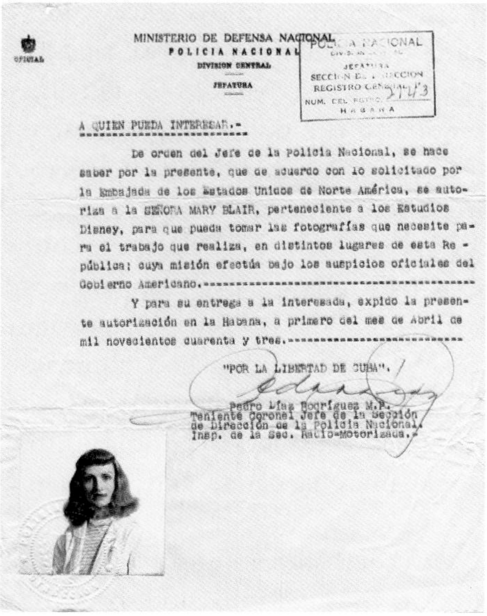

OFICIAL

MINISTERIO DE DEFENSA NACIONAL
POLICIA NACIONAL
DIVISION CENTRAL
JEFATURA

POLICIA NACIONAL
JEFATURA
REGISTRO
NUM. DEL
HABANA

A QUIEN PUEDA INTERESAR.-

De orden del Jefe de la Policia Nacional, se hace saber por la presente, que de acuerdo con lo solicitado por la Embajada de los Estados Unidos de Norte América, se autoriza a la SEÑORA MARY BLAIR, perteneciente a los Estudios Disney, para que pueda tomar las fotografías que necesite para el trabajo que realiza, en distintos lugares de esta República; cuya misión efectúa bajo los auspicios oficiales del Gobierno Americano.-

Y para su entrega a la interesada, expido la presente autorización en la Habana, a primero del mes de Abril de mil novecientos cuarenta y tres.-

"POR LA LIBERTAD DE CUBA".

Pedro Díaz Rodríguez M.P.
Teniente Coronel Jefe de la Sección de Dirección de la Policia Nacional.
Insp. de la Sec. Radio-Motorizada.-

Before Mary Blair's departure for Cuba, she was issued a permit allowing her to explore, sketch, and photograph.

After this preliminary taste, the studio's Cuban activities were temporarily sidelined by the crush of production on other films,

In this evocative story sketch, fireflies spell out a title card.

principally *The Three Caballeros*. It was not until a full year later, in the spring of 1944, as *The Three Caballeros* began to approach completion, that the Cuban project was revived. Now Walt began seriously to consider the prospect of a full-fledged survey trip to Cuba, comparable to the earlier South American and Mexican expeditions. Norm Ferguson laid tentative plans for an extended tour in November 1944, by a group that might or might not include Walt himself. He also suggested to Walt a preliminary visit by a smaller advance group in August–September; this "would eliminate all unnecessary and uninteresting material, saving time and effort on the part of yourself and group when and if visit is made in November." In the end a compromise was reached: this reconnaissance trip was moved back to September–October, slightly enlarged in scope, and made *instead* of the large-scale November tour.

A new and smaller El Grupo was formed for this trip. This time Mary Blair, Jack Cutting, and Bill Cottrell were all absent from the lineup. Instead the group consisted of three other long-standing veterans of Good Neighbor expeditions—Norm Ferguson, Chuck Wolcott, and Larry Lansburgh, all of whom had participated in the 1941 South American tour—along with two relative newcomers. Writer Homer Brightman had become an integral part of the studio's Latin American team after making major contributions to *Saludos Amigos*, and had participated in some of the survey trips to Mexico for *La Piñata*. Fred Moore, one of the studio's leading animators since the early 1930s, had lent his inimitable touch to the Good Neighbor features, especially with his animation of Joe Carioca. Like the earlier Latin American tours, this one involved months of preparation. Research material, from the previous year's visit and from other sources, was gathered and absorbed; the studio's Cuban contacts were notified of the impending visit and paved the way for the group's arrival; the party's camera equipment was scrupulously documented and registered to prevent any security concerns. All the studio's previous experience with survey trips was brought to bear to ensure a successful venture. By the time El Grupo left Burbank on 8 September, Ferguson had thoroughly prepared for every possible circumstance—or so he thought.

Arriving in Mexico City, the party prepared for the next leg of their flight, which would take them to Havana on the eleventh. Here they were met with an unpleasant surprise: the air priorities for their flights—a requisite formality for air travel in wartime—had not been provided. El Grupo was grounded. The studio, having been expressly invited by the Cuban government and having followed all the usual advance procedures, had assumed that all the paperwork was in order. Now even Alejandro Buelna of the Mexican Department of Tourism, who had been able to smooth over all difficulties during earlier survey trips, was unable to help. A worried Ferguson wired the Disney studio in Burbank, where Jack Cutting in turn wired the Cuban ambassador in Washington. What a difference three years had made! The 1941 trip to South America had seemingly been charmed; the U.S. and South American governments had been so eager to cooperate with the Disney studio that any problems had been instantly and efficiently swept away to avoid inconveniencing Walt and his artists. Now *this* entire survey trip was jeopardized by the absence of this most fundamental and necessary formality, and the CIAA not only seemed powerless to help but might have been partly responsible. For a time, there lingered a dark suspicion that the "oversight" had been intentional, triggered by petty internal politics within the CIAA staff. Whatever the cause of the problem, the Disney studio was momentarily nonplussed but quickly rallied its resources. Larry Lansburgh enlisted the help of his old friend, Mexico City newspaperman José Soto, and between Soto's efforts and those of the Cuban ambassadors to the U.S. and Mexico and the Cuban government itself, the problem was resolved. Belatedly, the priorities were issued.

Arriving in Havana on 20 September, nine days later than planned, El Grupo set to work. For the remaining two weeks allotted for the trip, their activities were a scaled-down version of earlier survey trips: sketching, photographing, note-taking, reviewing musical talent, social and formal contacts with important names in government and the arts. Wolcott conferred on Cuban music with Southern Music representatives Ernesto Roca and Russel Goudey and with the prominent bandleader Miguel Matamoros. Ferguson met the caricaturist Conrado Masaguer, found his work comparable to that of Disney artist T. Hee, and considered engaging him to work on the Cuban subject. Dr. Roberto Machado, one of Jack Cutting's contacts from the previous year, screened his 16 mm films of various Cuban regions for the group. After the first five days in the cosmopolitan atmosphere of Havana, Ferguson, Lansburgh, and Moore left to photograph and sketch the picturesque historical settings of Cienfuegos, Camaguey, and Santiago. Walt, who had tentatively planned to join the group partway through their visit, canceled his plan when their travel schedule was disrupted.

Larry Lansburgh was the group's designated 16 mm cameraman. Mindful of the studio's experience with *Saludos Amigos*, he filmed his footage so that it would be useful as reference material, but also with an eye toward possible use in the finished film. His notes on the trip indicate that the group's problems were not confined to their travel arrangements: he was unable to shoot for the first four days because the sky remained stubbornly overcast, and his effort to film a sunrise over Morro Castle was thwarted by an unreliable motor launch that left him floating aimlessly in Havana Bay. Ultimately he was able to shoot two thousand feet of Kodachrome,[151] documenting specific locations such as San Juan Hill and the Upman cigar factory as well as general scenery and atmosphere. The group discovered the importance of the *bohio*, a thatched hut, as a feature of Cuban culture, and made arrangements to shoot film of a representative example near Caney. On Saturday, 30 September, a special shooting session took place with this *bohio* as a setting. The subjects included dancers and an orchestra hired for the occasion, as well as a domino game and a cockfight.

[151] This would have given the studio nearly an hour of reference footage.

Early in October the party returned to the Disney studio and began to organize the material they had collected. What kind of Cuban film did they have in mind? It had long since been agreed that the studio should develop a new character who would symbolize Cuba. Bill Cottrell and Jack Cutting, arriving in Havana in March 1943 to join forces with Mary Blair, had found such a sentiment already widespread in Cuba. "We find the government people as well as certain other people that we have met . . . have all seen *Saludos* and are hoping that we can find a Cuban Joe Carioca, although no one can suggest an animal or bird that is typical of the country," Cottrell wrote to Walt. "The only lead we have along this line so far is the fighting cock. As you know, the fighting cock is as important [to Cuba] as the bull-fight is to Mexico. I understand the ruffles on the fancy costumes of the rhumba bands here are significant of the rooster."

In the spring of 1943, of course, the studio was already developing a Latin American rooster character: Panchito, the charro rooster who would represent Mexico in *The Three Caballeros*. Despite the similarity, the idea of a Disney *guajiro*, or fighting cock, persisted at the studio. Norm Ferguson, on his return from Cuba in October 1944, wrote to Walt: "After checking for a representative character, the Cubans agreed a rooster or fighting cock would be it. But in discussing possible angles, most Cubans kept talking about a 'Kikirigui,' which we found out was their name for a bantam rooster. Their fighting cock is a big, skinny rooster that is brave, tough etc., but the 'kikirigui' is small and, as they say, 'No good, for nothing.' He thinks he's tough. They apply the name to humans, short people who think they are tough. In an argument they call them 'kikirigui' or say, 'just like a kikirigui,' derisively." This seems an unpromising start for a character who was meant to cement good relations between the U.S. and Cuba, but Fred Moore had made some tentative sketches of the character, and Ferguson was counting on the inherent appeal of Moore's drawings. He added, "The cuteness of the little guy together with animation possibilities would tend to offset the disdain for the actual bird in Cuba, although it isn't a feeling of dislike as much as a feeling of appreciation of the comic aspects of the little person being tough. His size is in good contrast to the Duck, Joe Carioca, and Panchito. The costuming is authentic and with a fast Spanish patter, as they speak in Cuba, he offers great possibilities. He could be

Fred Moore made numerous story sketches of Donald's and Joe's encounter with the new *guajiro* character.

tough but also a happy little guy, full of rhythm and clever." For the character's name, Ferguson (again with input from the studio's Cuban contacts) suggested "Miguelito Maracas" or something similar.

A profusion of surviving story sketches offers further clues to the artists' ideas at this time. Numerous ideas were suggested, but all of them were based on the idea of a visit to Cuba by Donald Duck and Joe Carioca. (Joe was a Brazilian parrot but was, after all, invariably seen smoking a cigar.) The two were to journey through Cuba—perhaps on a little train similar to the one in *Baía*—through landscapes featuring palm trees and sugarcane. There they would meet the *guajiro* character as they had met Panchito in Mexico. A wide variety of ideas were sketched for the subsequent adventures of the three, some with a musical theme, some featuring such oddities as an animated, dancing cigar, and one, incongruously, depicting their observation of a cockfight (though the *guajiro* was himself supposed to be based on the fighting cocks). Larry Lansburgh, writing to Ferguson in November 1944, suggested alternate ideas: "The point on which I feel most strongly is that we should do something on Cuba from the sea angle. Cuba as seen from a ship, with a little of the buccaneer feeling, landing in the ports that are full of pirate history and memories of Spanish gold." Lansburgh also favored a story that might be weighted toward live-action content. "This story should take the opposite approach [to the one] we took on *The Three Caballeros*," he wrote. "In *The Three Caballeros* we introduced our cartoon characters to real people. In this picture let's introduce our real people to cartoon characters. And incidentally, how about bringing the Duck in toward the end of the picture rather than having him throughout the picture[?]"

The filmmakers did pursue the idea of extensive live action, possibly filmed on location in Cuba with Technicolor's new Monopack system, which had already been tested on the short subject *Defense Against Invasion*. Lansburgh contacted the distinguished Mexican cinematographer Gabriel Figueroa, with whom the studio had maintained contact since his participation in the 1943 visual-education seminar, about the possibility of his taking a camera crew to Cuba to shoot live action for the picture. Following the precedent set by *The Three Caballeros*, Ferguson conducted an intensive search for Cuban musical talent for the new film. El Grupo had returned from Cuba in October 1944 with a large assortment of records showcasing prominent singers and orchestras, and shipments of additional records continued to arrive at the studio for weeks afterward. One obvious candidate for the picture was Xavier Cugat, who had a previous connection with the Disney studio and who had become extraordinarily popular in Hollywood by the mid-1940s.[152] At the same time, Ferguson was also impressed with another bandleader, Miguel Matamoros, who had conferred with Chuck Wolcott during the group's Cuban visit. "Matamoros has, according to Cubans, the best orchestra representative of Cuban music, popular and typical," Ferguson wrote to Walt. He also strongly endorsed the popular singer Miguelito Valdes, a fiery tenor who had just crashed Hollywood by way of an appearance in RKO's *Pan-Americana*. For a time Valdes was considered as a possible voice for the *guajiro* character.

The problem with searching for Cuban musical talent, Ferguson quickly discovered, was that most of the top names had been snatched up by other countries. At the time of the Disney talent hunt, most of the top Cuban musicians were performing in New York or Mexico City. One New York discovery who received the studio's attention in early 1945 was a young singer named Elsa Miranda. Elsa was no relation to Carmen or Aurora and was, in fact, a native of Puerto Rico. At the time the CIAA's Jack Halpern brought her to the studio's attention, Elsa was working as a secretary in New York by day and, after hours, appearing on a semiweekly shortwave radio program, *Canciones*, which was broadcast to South America. Halpern arranged for a photographer to shoot stills of

[152] The little-known early connection between Cugat and the Disneys dates to 1929, when Cugat, on the threshold of his starring career, was featured in an all-talking Spanish-language musical revue titled *Revista musical Cugat*. The sound track for this independent production was recorded by the Disney Film Recording Company. The film was not a success, but Cugat's career continued to gather momentum throughout the 1930s, and shifted into high gear with his appearance in Columbia's *You Were Never Lovelier* (1942).

Elsa Miranda, a singer considered for an appearance in the Cuban film.

her, and sent them to the Disney studio in February 1945 along with transcriptions of her radio performances. On the strength of this evidence, Ferguson seriously considered signing Elsa for the Cuban film. But the wheels of progress turned too slowly to suit Elsa. In April 1945, Disney's New York office received a note from her: "Have been too busy to drop in. Got ried [*sic*] of waiting for Mr. Disney, and signed contract with C.B.S. This coming Thursday (and every other week thereafter) will be on Viva America, 11:30 to 12 midnite."

CARNIVAL

For a time, the proposed Cuban film—intended as one component of a package feature—was known by the working title *Cuban Carnival*. During the spring and summer of 1945 that theme was adopted for the feature itself, which was identified simply as *Carnival*. Like its two predecessors, the *Carnival* feature was to be made up of four sections, each identified with a separate Latin American country. The Cuban segment was in progress, and Norm Ferguson proposed new segments on Brazil and Mexico, the countries that had been most prominently featured in *The Three Caballeros*. For the fourth segment, some consideration was given to Colombia, a country that had not yet been featured in

Joe Carioca, resplendent in evening wear, enjoys the night life in a *Carnival* story sketch (*see* page 117).

the studio's Good Neighbor program. In assembling material for these films, Ferguson concentrated on music. Much of his Latin American activity in early 1945 consisted of gathering songs from these various countries for Walt's review, auditioning musicians who might perform the songs, and trying to coordinate tentative shooting schedules.

There was, to be sure, a wealth of music to choose from. As before, the studio relied on its relationship with Southern Music for guidance in selecting suitable material, and Southern obligingly provided a steady supply of top Latin American tunes—all from its own catalogue, of course. "[Ernesto] Roca was very helpful but naturally kept plugging Southern Music," Ferguson wrote to Walt after the 1944 Cuban trip. Roca had been especially enthusiastic about a number by Osvaldo Farres titled "Tres palabras." "It is a very good melody," Ferguson conceded, "and we agree it has possibilities but did not commit ourselves as there is a lot of music in Cuba." Another popular song, "Amor de mi bohio," offered a natural connection with the *bohio* theme that the studio was developing for the Cuban short, and Ferguson even considered a swing arrangement of the old standard "The Peanut Vendor" ("El manisero"), the song that had started a craze for Cuban music in the U.S. more than a decade earlier.

Similarly, a variety of music was available to represent the other countries; the studio had hardly exhausted the musical riches of Brazil or Mexico. For the Brazilian section, Ferguson considered yet another Ary Barroso song, "Terra seca." Another possibility was suggested by Aloysio "Luis" Oliveira, who returned from a visit to Brazil with a short film depicting a dance, the Frevo. "The history of the dance," Ferguson reported to Walt, "is that it comes from the north of Brazil and is done by the natives up there. You will notice the use of umbrellas; these are used for two purposes—one, against the heat of the sun, and the other, in the manner of a tightrope walker, to maintain equilibrium while dancing. According to Luis the dance is done in Rio as a sort of competitive dance between groups. . . . The dance is very colorful in costuming and umbrellas . . . We might make use of it by having Joe Carioca, with his umbrella, do a bit of it with some other cartoon character." Oliveira had also brought a recording of a new Dorival Caymmi song, "Dora," which described its title character as the "Queen of the Frevo." He suggested it for possible use in such a picture.

The Mexican section likewise offered an array of musical possibilities, including the traditional "Las chiapanecas." "This is the number with the hand-clapping," Ferguson noted, "and has audience participation appeal." The studio had been pleased with Carlos Ramírez's performance of "Mexico" in *The Three Caballeros* and made tentative plans for his return appearance in their new Mexican production. Ferguson considered several songs as possible material for Ramírez, and at one point suggested that he might sing Augustín Lara's "Granada"—apparently overlooking Ramírez's previous performance of the same number in MGM's *Two Girls and a Sailor*. Ramírez himself, a native of Colombia, suggested a song he might sing for the possible Colombian segment: "Romanza de amor." "From a commercial standpoint I think it is questionable," Ferguson noted, "but from the Goodwill side it is a number which is 'typical' in Colombia. It gives Ramírez a chance to show his voice and with our own arrangement (possibly adding more rhythm) would give us something to work against a Colombian background."

All these ideas and many more circulated in the Disney studio through mid-1945. And then suddenly they were dropped. The office of the Coordinator of Inter-American Affairs, the Washington agency that had launched the entire Good Neighbor program in 1940 and under whose authority all the Disney Latin American films had been made, was itself on the brink of demise by early 1945. The CIAA's brief tenure had been marked by an uneasy coexistence, and sometimes outright conflict, with the State Department. Nelson Rockefeller had been a newcomer to government circles in 1940, but had brilliantly maneuvered his way through countless political labyrinths for several years, keeping the CIAA on a solid footing and laying the groundwork for its continued activities in a postwar world. His winning streak came to an end in the spring of 1944, with the formation of a new interdepartmental committee on hemispheric development that effectively usurped most of the functions of the CIAA. From that point on Rockefeller's agency was steadily drained of its power, and Rockefeller himself was gradually reduced to a mere figurehead (a source of personal frustration that was relieved by Rockefeller's own appointment to the State Department late in 1944). The CIAA would not be officially terminated until May 1946, but by that time the writing on the wall had been visible for two years. With the end of the war in the summer of 1945, it became unmistakably clear that the Good Neighbor program had served its purpose and was no longer needed—and neither was Hollywood's contribution. The Disney studio, for its part, was not strongly motivated to continue with another Latin feature for its own sake, considering the tepid box-office response to *The Three Caballeros*. In the summer of 1945 the *Carnival* picture was quietly abandoned.

But some of the ideas developed for *Carnival* did survive in later Disney productions, adapted in surprising ways.

WITHOUT YOU

Ernesto Roca's enthusiasm for the song "Tres palabras," expressed during El Grupo's visit to Cuba in 1944, was not a passing fancy. After Ferguson's return to the Disney studio, Roca continued to mail him alternative recordings of the song and to query him periodically as to Walt's reaction. Southern Music intended to promote "Tres palabras" heavily in the U.S., and was clearly hoping that exposure in a Disney film would transform the song into an international hit, as had already happened with previous Barroso and Lara compositions. Apparently Walt's reaction to the song was favorable, and some of Ferguson's memos during the spring of 1945 indicate that he considered it as a vehicle for Elsa Miranda, then for Carlos Ramírez. By late May, English lyrics were being written by studio lyricist Ray Gilbert, and an English title had tentatively been chosen: "Without You."

A moody "background" painting from *Without You*. In the film the empty space is filled with effects animation of trickling raindrops on the window.

By the time the *Carnival* feature was abandoned, *Without You* had gathered enough momentum that its production continued independently. A story number was issued in September 1945; the story crew was one person—the studio's first emissary to Cuba, Mary Blair. A scant month later, production started under the direction of Bob Cormack. The vocal was performed not by Carlos Ramírez but by a singer of Mexican extraction: Andy Russell, whose real name was Andrés Robago.

In the end *Without You* was absorbed into the Disney studio's first postwar package feature, *Make Mine Music*, released in 1946. Seen today, *Without You* strikes the viewer as a somber little mood piece, dominated by Mary Blair's melancholy images of separation and loneliness: an empty room, an unread letter, drooping or stark, bare trees. There is no character animation at all; as in "Las Posadas," the still paintings are given movement mostly by George Rowley's effects animation of trickling raindrops, twinkling stars, ghostly shadows. It's a subtle and affecting piece of filmmaking—but, surrounded by more colorful and dynamic sequences in *Make Mine Music*, it's often overlooked, and probably doesn't represent the kind of hit-making showcase for which Southern Music had hoped.

TWO SILHOUETTES

Make Mine Music includes another minor sequence, *Two Silhouettes*, which today endures the nearly universal scorn of animation enthusiasts. It features a vocal rendition of the romantic title song by Dinah Shore while, on the screen, the silhouettes of two human dancers perform a quasi-classical dance against a painted background of gardens, woods, and abstract views of the heavens, accompanied by the silhouettes of two animated cupids. The dancers who modeled for the film were major stars: Tatiana Riabouchinska and David Lichine.[153] In *Two Silhouettes* these dancers, or their silhouettes, are matted by the Iwerks printer into a kaleidoscope of romantic abstract imagery, trailed by the two silhouetted cupids who are animated by Les Clark. The result is only a step away from rotoscoping and today is widely decried as a descent into kitsch and the nadir of Walt's art—although, to be fair, it does represent a continuing attempt to create new and different effects in animation.

In any case, the finished film doesn't seem particularly Latin American, and in fact its production was largely complete by the end of 1944, when Ferguson's ideas for *Carnival* were still in a formative state. But *Two Silhouettes* has bloodlines that suggest the Good Neighbor project: the song is an original composition by Chuck Wolcott and Ray Gilbert, and the visual design is the work of Mary Blair. (And the layout artist is John Hench, who also worked on *Without You*

[153] Riabouchinska, who was first made famous in the 1930s by choreographer George Balanchine as one of his "baby ballerinas" with Colonel Wassily de Basil's Ballets Russes de Monte Carlo (one of the successor companies to Serge Diaghilev's Ballets Russes), was at the time a principal dancer with de Basil's so-called Original Ballet Russe—De Basil renamed his company many times—and a frequent guest artist with Ballet Theater in New York. Lichine, a choreographer as well as a dancer, was also associated with both these companies, and worked in Hollywood occasionally throughout the 1940s. Lichine and Riabouchinska may have had a previous connection with the Disney studio: in later years it was claimed, sometimes by Riabouchinska herself, that she had performed as one of the models for the hippos in the *Dance of the Hours* segment of *Fantasia*. It is known for certain that the main animation model for Hyacinth Hippo, the prima hipporina, was dancer Marge Champion (who had already modeled for earlier Disney features and who would later star in film musicals choreographed by her husband and dance partner, Gower); Hyacinth's *body*, however, was modeled by actress-singer Hattie Noel. Special thanks to both Christopher Caines and Mindy Aloff for all this information.

and *Destino.*) The most decisive link comes from Walt himself, who made reference to this film while discussing his prized live-action-animation combination scenes in *The Three Caballeros.* "We won't use this system in every picture we make, but in those that lend themselves especially," he told one journalist. Then he expanded on the subject: "In the next Latin-American film, which we are tentatively calling 'Cuban Carnival'—although that will not be the final title—there will be the blending. Lichine and Riabouchinska will dance among the stars and planets, and meet with many imaginary and visionary phenomena." This is a fair partial description of *Two Silhouettes,* but ultimately—whatever one's opinion of this film—it ended up a long way from Latin America.

The supporting characters in *Two Silhouettes* were a "boy" and "girl" cupid who trailed the star dancers.

DESTINO

Of all the films generated by the Disney Good Neighbor project, none followed a more unlikely and convoluted evolutionary trail than *Destino.* This subject has acquired a certain notoriety as the aborted collaboration of Walt Disney and Salvador Dalí, but it was first conceived in 1945 as a musical number for the Mexican segment of *Carnival.* Dora Luz had scored a success with her performance of "You Belong to My Heart" in *The Three Caballeros,* and in addition had endeared herself to the Disney staff. As Walt and his crew considered ideas for the studio's next Mexican production, a favorite candidate was an encore appearance by Dora Luz. Ferguson selected Armando Domínguez's song "Destino" as a musical vehicle for her, and Dora recorded the song on a return visit to the Disney studio in February 1945. Once again Ray Gilbert contributed English lyrics, and the recording featured an instrumental arrangement by Al Sack and a choral backing arranged by Ken Darby.

This 1945 session was made possible by Dora's return to California for the Los Angeles opening of *The Three Caballeros.* Her visit was sandwiched in between two engagements in Mexico City—she arrived in California in February direct from her stage appearance at the Cine Alameda, and was due to return to Mexico City in late March for a radio commitment—and the sound recording of "Destino" took place before a visual treatment had been established. At the same time, however, Ferguson was at work on the visual element. He assigned story artist Dick Kelsey to create a storyboard, and worked with the live-action crew, preparing to film Dora's performance to a playback of the recording. Following the precedent established two years earlier with "You

Belong to My Heart," Ferguson was evidently hoping to film a simple performance of the song while Dora was available, then fill in the animation and effects later on. But the weeks flew by, and by the time Dora's departure date arrived a Technicolor camera was still not available. She returned to Mexico City with the live action still unfinished. At the time, Ferguson speculated that she might be brought back to the studio in June to complete the filming.

In the summer of 1945, then, when the *Carnival* feature was abandoned, *Destino* existed at the Disney studio only as a series of story sketches and two optical-track recordings of the song by Dora Luz. The production remained dormant until Salvador Dalí, having met Walt Disney at a Hollywood party, agreed to work on an animated film at the Disney studio. The exact nature of the planned Disney–Dalí collaboration was not decided for some time; at one point late in 1945, dancer Maria Gambarelli was tentatively engaged for the project. Early in 1946, the studio decided to base the film on the unused "Destino" recording. Dick Kelsey's story sketches, created the previous year, were quickly discarded in the excitement over the famous surrealist's arrival at the studio. Clearly, neither Dalí nor John Hench, who worked with him on the project, had any interest in the original concept of the production or in the Latin American films in general; apparently Dalí was attracted to the song simply because its title appealed to his interest in the concept of destiny. John Hench confirmed as much in an interview with Dave Smith, of the Walt Disney Archives, many years afterward. Hench dismissed the song itself as "banal" and seemed to have no idea how the studio had acquired it in the first place.

Itself abandoned after eight months of work, the Disney-Dalí-Hench *Destino* became the stuff of legend—until half a century afterward, when a later generation of Disney animators undertook to finish the project. Unveiled in 2003, the completed short attracted international attention and was nominated for an Academy Award. By that time its roots in the Good Neighbor project had been completely forgotten—and, indeed, the surviving connection is so thin as to be almost coincidental.

BLAME IT ON THE SAMBA

Of all the ideas Ferguson proposed for the *Carnival* feature, only one reached the screen—eventually—in something approximating its original form.

During the early 1940s, as the U.S. entertainment industry busily pitched in to cooperate with the Good Neighbor program, numerous entertainers on both sides of the border found themselves pressed into service as goodwill ambassadors. One member of this group was U.S.-born Ethel Smith, a native of Pittsburgh who performed on the Hammond organ. If this seems an unlikely background for an exponent of Latin American music, Ethel came by her distinction honestly; long before the CIAA proposed an official program of cultural diplomacy, Ethel was fascinated with Latin music. Already an accomplished musician, she discovered the electric organ in the mid-1930s when it was still a relatively new instrument and took to it partly because it responded so sensitively to the exotic rhythms she loved. By the end of the decade she had performed extensively in South America, and in

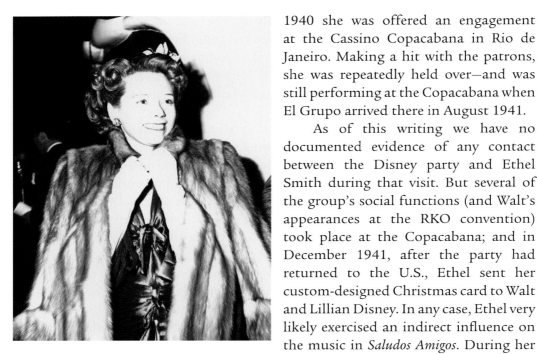

Ethel Smith arrives at the Los Angeles opening of *The Three Caballeros* in March 1945.

1940 she was offered an engagement at the Cassino Copacabana in Rio de Janeiro. Making a hit with the patrons, she was repeatedly held over—and was still performing at the Copacabana when El Grupo arrived there in August 1941.

As of this writing we have no documented evidence of any contact between the Disney party and Ethel Smith during that visit. But several of the group's social functions (and Walt's appearances at the RKO convention) took place at the Copacabana; and in December 1941, after the party had returned to the U.S., Ethel sent her custom-designed Christmas card to Walt and Lillian Disney. In any case, Ethel very likely exercised an indirect influence on the music in *Saludos Amigos*. During her residence in Rio she had voraciously pursued all manner of local and regional music, and had discovered a catchy and very popular melody that was eventually identified as Zequinha de Abreu's 1917 composition "Tico-tico no farelo," later retitled "Tico-tico no fubá." Ethel adopted the tune and created her own organ arrangement, and it became one of her specialty numbers. It's possible that El Grupo became aware of the song through Ethel's performances. We've already seen that they were immediately interested in "Tico-tico" and negotiated for the film rights (although, unlike the Barroso songs, it proved to have a nebulous copyright status), and that they later introduced it to U.S. movie audiences in *Saludos Amigos*.

Meanwhile, after Pearl Harbor was attacked and the U.S. entered the war, Ethel took the advice of her colleagues and returned to the States. She had performed extensively in the U.S. before her Brazilian sojourn, but now, with her vast new South American repertoire and the increased domestic interest in Latin music, Ethel Smith was in the right place at the right time. She quickly established herself as a major musical personality of the 1940s, notably on the radio, where she became a regular featured performer on *Your Hit Parade* and its offshoot, the *All-Time Hit Parade*, for more than a year. When MGM beckoned her to Hollywood, she happily responded. In the summer of 1944 she reasserted her claim on "Tico-tico," performing her high-energy rendition of the song both in MGM's Esther Williams musical *Bathing Beauty* and on a hit record for Decca.

By late 1944, then, when Norm Ferguson began assembling material and musicians for the projected *Carnival* feature, one obvious candidate for the film was practically on his doorstep. The studio contracted with Ethel in early 1945, and Mary Blair began working on preliminary costume sketches for her, each representing a different nationality. Ferguson's memos make it clear that he was considering Ethel as a performer in each one of the *Carnival* segments, perhaps as one of the connecting threads that would tie the feature together. A rented Hammond organ was installed on the sound-effects recording stage, and there, in February 1945—around the same time Dora Luz was recording "Destino" on another stage—Ethel recorded the Cuban number "Cachita paran pan pin." The studio also secured the rights to a Mexican song, "La parranda," as a vehicle for Ethel. "All these numbers," Ferguson noted, "have possibilities for combination of cartoon characters and Ethel Smith."

To represent Brazil, Ferguson endorsed an up-tempo *chôro* (a form of instrumental music born in Rio in the nineteenth century) known as "Apanhei-te, cavaquinho." This instrumental number was apparently suggested by Ethel herself; Ferguson enthused to Walt that "it has the possibilities of 'Tico Tico.'" Like "Tico-tico," however, "Cavaquinho" was an older composition, written by the late Ernesto Nazareth, and its copyright status was a mystery. Ferguson wired José da Rocha Vaz, one of the studio's Brazilian contacts since the 1941 trip, and asked him to investigate the possibilities for rights clearance. In the meantime, several alternate Brazilian songs, some of which

The Aracuan's costuming and design changed with each of his three appearances. This model sheet was created for *Blame It on the Samba*.

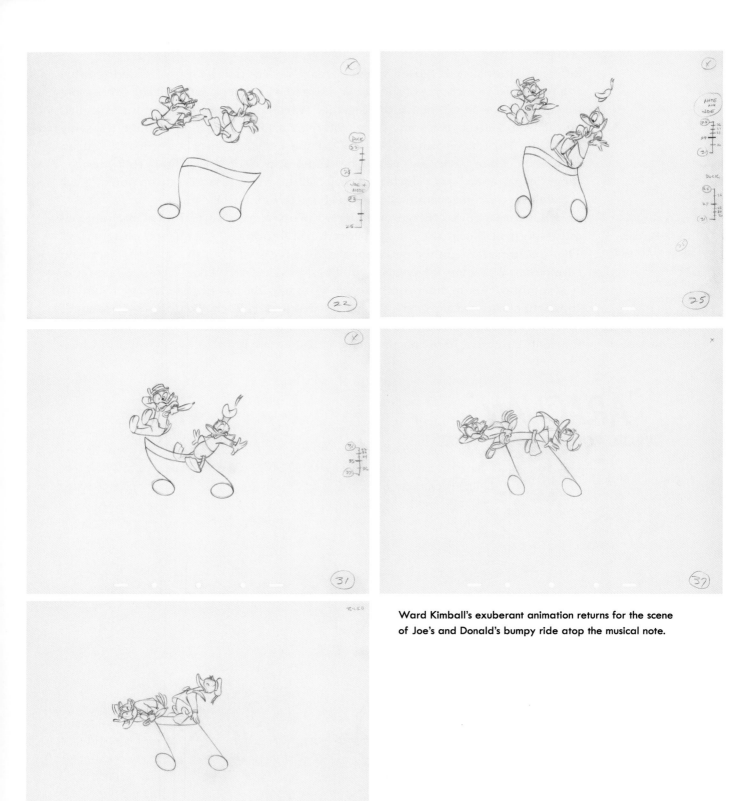

Ward Kimball's exuberant animation returns for the scene of Joe's and Donald's bumpy ride atop the musical note.

Ethel had already recorded commercially, were considered as substitutes, but Ferguson continued to pin his hopes on "Cavaquinho." Finally, in May 1945, the studio obtained clearance, and Ethel recorded the song for the studio. Disney lyricist Ray Gilbert, who had provided English lyrics for so many Latin songs, performed the same service for "Cavaquinho." The song now became known as "Blame It on the Samba."

Like the other planned segments for the *Carnival* feature, the unfinished *Blame It on the Samba* was shelved when the feature was abandoned in the summer of 1945. *Unlike* the other segments, it was later revived and completed, more or less intact.[154]

[154] In the meantime "Apanhei-te, cavaquinho" was heard in another Hollywood film: Paramount's *Road to Rio* (1947), one of the Bob Hope–Bing Crosby "Road" series. However, this was an instrumental performance and was played in the background of a dialogue scene, not as a featured number.

At the close of World War II, the Disney studio found itself in a precarious position—its strong momentum of the late 1930s and early '40s broken by the war, its wartime government contracts abruptly vanished, facing a suddenly urgent need to produce new theatrical films quickly in order to generate income at the box office. One way of meeting this need was to produce "package features" made up of shorter sections, each of which could be produced relatively economically and then combined with others to make a feature-length film.[155] The first of these "package features" was *Make Mine Music*, which appeared in the spring of 1946 and included the finished *Without You* and *Two Silhouettes* segments, along with other, better-remembered entries such as *Peter and the Wolf*, *All the Cats Join In*, and *The Whale Who Wanted to Sing at the Met*. *Make Mine Music* was sufficiently successful that another, similar feature seemed in order, and by the end of 1946 the studio was at work on more short films that would eventually be combined into the new feature, *Melody Time*. By now the studio's official involvement in the Good Neighbor program was, like the program itself, a thing of the past, but *Blame It on the Samba* offered a tempting prospect for the new feature. Its musical and visual possibilities were as strong as ever, and some of the production work was already completed. In the meantime Ethel Smith had become a more prominent screen personality through her continued guest appearances in other studios' live-action features, and the Disney studio had extended its option on her services through the spring of 1947. This was too much to waste. Late in 1946, production of *Blame It on the Samba* was revived.

[155] By this definition it could be argued that *Saludos Amigos* and *The Three Caballeros* were also "package features," and in fact they were produced along very similar lines. The difference was that *Saludos* and *Caballeros* were driven by their strong Latin American themes and their mandated diplomatic mission, while the later "package features" were far more generic, their segments more or less interchangeable and linked only by their common accent on music.

There exists a fascinating set of storyboard drawings for a proposed version of the picture, which would have featured both Ethel Smith and Carmen Miranda. In this version, Donald Duck and Joe Carioca visit a theater where Carmen and Ethel are appearing. Crashing the backstage area while Ethel is performing, the two make their way to Carmen's dressing room. After a brief introduction to Donald, Carmen goes onstage and performs "Blame It on the Samba" to Ethel's accompaniment. Meanwhile Donald and Joe are still in her dressing room, and Donald, intoxicated by a kiss from

Carmen and by the heady aroma of her perfume, listens to Joe's romantic tales of Rio and succumbs to further delirious fantasy images like those in *The Three Caballeros*. From here on the sketches suggest one final, spectacular Brazilian extravaganza, incorporating both the Frevo idea and the still-unused *Caxangá* story line. As in earlier treatments, caxangá leads Donald into a surreal nightmare involving giant matchboxes, and this in turn leads to a "Bonfire Ballet" celebrating the incendiary revels of the Festa de São João. This elaborate scenario would have closed the Disney studio's Latin American chapter on a wildly extravagant note. It would have made use of Ethel Smith's already-recorded organ track, but Ethel herself would have appeared as little more than a supporting character.

As of this writing it's not clear whether this version of the story was proposed in the spring of 1945, before the project was abandoned, or late in 1946 when it was revived. In any case, this ambitious plan had been dropped and replaced by a more scaled-down concept, with Ethel back at the forefront, by the time serious production began in December 1946. As with the animation–live-action combinations in *La Piñata*, the live action came first. The production team devised a scenario for Ethel's scenes and, coordinating their production schedule with her radio commitments in New York, arranged for Ethel to appear at the Disney studio for two weeks in February 1947. Once again the Disney connection with RKO came in handy; in 1945 Ethel had made an appearance in RKO's *George White's Scandals*, and now the Disney studio prevailed on RKO wardrobe mistress Adele Balkins to design Ethel's costume. Because of the shots that would show her feet working the pedals, her shoes were a key consideration; they must coordinate with the rest of the costume and look good in Technicolor, but also allow Ethel maximum flexibility for performance. The Disney studio also sought RKO's advice on the prop organ console to be used in Ethel's scenes.

After some initial tests shot on Tuesday, 4 February 1947, the live-action components of *Blame It on the Samba* were filmed during the week of 10 February under the direction of Ken Anderson. A two-manual Hammond console, dismantled for shipping to Hammond for repairs, was supplied by the Penny-Owsley Music Company in Los Angeles. This, along with the pedal unit, was mounted on a rotating platform on the Disney live-action stage. As the organ console slowly rotated before the camera, Ethel re-created her performance to a playback of the recording she had made nearly two years earlier. The distinguished Technicolor cameraman Winton Hoch, who had supervised the first live-action tests for *The Three Caballeros* fully *four* years earlier, was the director of photography.

Meanwhile, the animated portion of the picture was also taking shape. Ken Anderson, a veteran of the earlier Good Neighbor features, served as both story director of the cartoon scenes and director of the live-action scenes. He and his crew devised a story that neatly avoided the costly excesses of the proposed Carmen Miranda–Ethel Smith scenario, but packed its own share of visual pyrotechnics and high energy. Norm Ferguson's earliest plans for the picture had proposed that "the Three Caballeros" might be featured on-screen along with Ethel, but now one of the caballeros, Panchito, was excluded because the number had nothing to do with Mexico. Instead the "three boisterous birds of a feather" featured in *Blame It on the Samba* were Donald Duck, Joe Carioca, and the Aracuan—who *was* appropriately Brazilian and who was now making his third screen appearance for Disney (having previously appeared in *The Three Caballeros* and in the short *Clown of the Jungle*). Taking its cue from Ray Gilbert's lyric, which cited the various Brazilian percussion instruments as ingredients in a "musical cocktail," this version of the story mixed all three birds with Ethel in a large cocktail glass, a special-effects challenge that would have been unthinkable without the new possibilities opened up by the Iwerks optical printer.

The animation crew assembled for this picture was a cast of familiar names: Les Clark, John Lounsbery, Harvey Toombs, Hal King, and Ward Kimball, with effects animation by Josh Meador and George Rowley. Conspicuous by his absence was Fred Moore, who had temporarily left the Disney studio. Moore's inimitable animation had established the character of Joe Carioca five years earlier, and his sure touch with the character was missed in this film. Ray Gilbert's lyrics were sung on the sound track by a young vocal trio, the Dinning Sisters, who had earlier been heard in *Fun and Fancy Free*.[156]

As completed in late 1947, *Blame It on the Samba* opens with a dejected Donald and Joe, literally blue in color, dragging themselves wearily along a Rio sidewalk. They are intercepted by the Aracuan, the proprietor of a sidewalk "Café do Samba," who brightens their spirits and restores their natural colors by producing the necessary ingredients for "the fascinating rhythm of the samba." Rejuvenated by its pulsing beat, Donald and Joe are soon happily samba-ing. The Aracuan then dumps them, and himself, into a large cocktail glass, and soon Ethel is heard and seen rendering a lively performance of the song inside the glass, surrounded by swirling animated bubbles, flowing colors, and the Duck, Parrot, and Aracuan themselves. Donald and Joe, rendered as tiny creatures, continue to samba on top of the console.[157] Donald's lecherous interest in live-action women, introduced in *The Three Caballeros*, had led him into vaguely disturbing territory before that film's end, and the aborted Carmen Miranda version of *Blame It on the Samba* might have followed the same trend. Instead, the filmmakers neatly sidestep any such issues by depicting Donald and Joe on such a Lilliputian scale that each could easily be held in the palm of Ethel's hand. The accent is on special-effects wizardry: Donald falls off the console and stands next to the organ pedals; the Aracuan appears and strikes Ethel's knee with a cartoon stick; her reflex response kicks Donald out of the frame.

Having displayed a solicitous concern for Donald and Joe in their dejected state, the mischievous Aracuan reverts to type after their spirits revive. He periodically disrupts the number, each time catapulting it to a new level of frenzy and bizarre imagery. Halting Ethel's performance by covering her eyes, he triggers

[156] The Dinnings had backed Dinah Shore singing "Lazy Countryside" in the *Bongo* segment of *Fun and Fancy Free*. They also cultivated a Disney connection in their commercial recording career; their first Capitol session in 1943 had produced one of the many English covers of "Brazil" ("Aquarela do Brasil") in the wake of *Saludos Amigos*, and they went on to record other Disney songs: "Fun and Fancy Free," and "Very Good Advice" from *Alice in Wonderland*.

[157] Their steps, animated by Les Clark, are correct, thanks to 16 mm samba reference footage featuring Nico Charisse and his partner, Claudia de Borga Lewis, photographed at the studio by Larry Lansburgh in April 1947.

a new, strongly rhythmic section in which Donald and Joe run through a painted jungle, menaced by giant drums and percussion instruments. In a clearing in this "jungle" Ethel displays some of her talents away from the keyboard, playing the drums and (multiplied into five identical Ethels) dancing. Now, on the sound track, the Dinning Sisters reprise the song's chorus in a rapid-fire succession of double-talk lyrics. In a bewildering profusion of images the bubbles become lips (representing the Dinnings' voices), the lips become butterflies, the butterflies become marionettes manipulated by the Aracuan, and he dangles Joe and Donald on strings as, riding an eighth-note unicycle, he careens madly along the top of a musical staff. The two caballeros are unceremoniously dumped onto a runaway musical-note vehicle of their own, and from there back onto the organ console, where Ethel is still pumping away. But the Aracuan is not finished yet; he lights a match and inserts it into one of Ethel's carefully designed shoes, giving her a hotfoot that kicks the tempo into a higher gear—then tops that with a stick of dynamite, which blows the Hammond to bits. Can this minor annoyance slow the momentum of the samba? Not a chance. Ethel continues to play energetically as pieces of the console float back down through the liquid in the cocktail glass, reassembling themselves while Donald and Joe tumble back into the scene and the song finishes with a triumphant flourish.

In hindsight, it's tempting to see this—the last major film to emerge from the Disney Good Neighbor project—as a summation of all the others, at least the Brazilian ones. Familiar sights and themes, recalling the whole story of the studio's Latin American venture, are on display in *Blame It on the Samba*. The picture begins with echoes of the 1941 South American trip: the mosaic sidewalks and lush vegetation of Rio, which had so charmed El Grupo and had been seen in their earliest Brazilian films, reappear here as if by second nature in the opening scene; and Ethel Smith herself provides a link with the Copacabana in August 1941. The first major Good Neighbor production, *Saludos Amigos*, is suggested partly by the presence of our old friend Joe Carioca, but also by what had been that film's great breakthrough in the world of propaganda filmmaking: the introduction of bona fide elements of South American culture (in this case the Brazilian percussion instruments: the cabaça, cuíca, and pandeiro)[158] not as dry "educational" material but in a thoroughly entertaining way. Echoes of *The Three Caballeros* are felt here too, thanks to the dazzling combinations of animation and live action that had defined that film, as well as by the maddening antics of the Aracuan. (Even the Aracuan's action of "magically" donning his bathing suit before diving into the cocktail glass recalls Donald's similar action before diving from the sarape in *The Three Caballeros*.)[159]

[158] The cabaça is a gourd shaker; the cuíca is a side drum. The pandeiro is a hand drum that we've already heard during the "Flauta e pandeiro" section of *The Three Caballeros*.

[159] For that matter, we can find echoes of non-Latin Disney films here too. As Ethel Smith pounds the conga drums in the "jungle" clearing, they illuminate at her touch like the live-action orchestra instruments in *Fantasia*. And her nonstop performance at the climax, continuing to pound out the melody even as chaos swirls around her, recalls the similar sequence in the classic 1935 Mickey Mouse short *The Band Concert*.

But *Blame It on the Samba* is more than an exercise in nostalgia. It marshals all these souvenirs of the studio's Latin American activities during the previous six years but, following Walt's natural inclination, goes on to build something new and exciting on that foundation of the past. This is no sentimental farewell but a picture that pulses with infectious energy, its visual effects surpassing even those in *The Three Caballeros*. The music, too, authentic as always, maintains a high level of excitement, starting at a moderate tempo but steadily building to an explosive climax. If the Disney Good Neighbor project had continued past 1945, the film seems to say, this is one direction it might have taken.

The package feature *Melody Time* opened in U.S. theaters in mid-1948, with *Blame It on the Samba* featured prominently among its segments, second only to Roy Rogers and *Pecos Bill*. Audiences and reviewers responded well; *Variety* called the segment "an infectious combination of sound track and drawing that pays off." Along with *The Flying Gauchito* and the four individual segments from *Saludos Amigos*, *Blame It on the Samba* was reissued separately as a short in 1955.

And with this disarming, happily energetic short, the Disney Latin American venture officially came to an end. The studio had traveled a long road since that day in October 1940 when Jock Whitney and Francis Alstock had first asked Roy Disney about the possibility of inserting "some South American atmosphere" in a few of the short subjects. The CIAA's Good Neighbor program itself had, perhaps inevitably, produced mixed results, accomplishing some good but simultaneously leaving pockets of resentment in its wake at war's end. For their part, however, Walt and his studio had far surpassed at every turn the efforts requested of them by the CIAA. What in other hands might have been a dreary exercise in propaganda became, instead, a series of strikingly original and enduring contributions to film history. The very existence of *Blame It on the Samba* in 1948, not to mention the viability of this and the other shorts in the reissue market in later years, is evidence that the Disney Latin American films were brilliantly capable of standing on their own, independent of any outside diplomatic agenda.

By 1948, of course, the series had ended and would not be revived. In these postwar years, Walt's straitened circumstances would have ruled out further independent survey trips along the lines of the sponsored tours that had produced *Saludos Amigos* and *The Three Caballeros*. Even apart from this consideration, it was not in Walt Disney's nature to repeat himself. By 1948 he had moved on to fresh challenges and, characteristically, never looked back.

But by now the experience of his Latin American years had been absorbed into the fabric of his studio. The Disney artists had responded to the challenges of the Good Neighbor project with fresh new ideas and techniques, and now the studio continued to build on those innovative animation concepts, and such startling technical feats as the combination scenes, in *Song of the South*, *Melody Time*, and other films. Too, the invaluable experience of producing educational films for the CIAA paved the way for an extensive postwar program of Disney educational films that crossed the theatrical/nontheatrical boundary. On one hand the studio expanded

its production of 16 mm educational reels for classrooms; on the other hand, the making of *The Amazon Awakens* provided a template for theatrical films like the groundbreaking True-Life Adventure nature series (which invariably opened with the animated paintbrush from *Aquarela do Brasil*).

Joe Carioca makes a television appearance in 1960 in the "Two Happy Amigos" episode of *Walt Disney Presents.*

With the arrival of television in the 1950s, the Disney Good Neighbor themes and characters found a new outlet. As early as 1954, the Christmas offering of the *Disneyland* series was a truncated version of *The Three Caballeros*, shown under the title "A Present for Donald." *Saludos Amigos* followed a few years later, and various Good Neighbor shorts were incorporated into other programs. Along with the original films, the Disney television series also presented new encore appearances by Joe Carioca in such episodes as "Two Happy Amigos" (1960) and "Carnival Time" (1962), as well as a 1955 performance by his alter ego, José Oliveira, on *The Mickey Mouse Club*. The advent of home video brought yet another showcase for the Latin American films: *The Three Caballeros*, with its dazzling assortment of animation effects, was eagerly snatched up by the new medium, and *Saludos Amigos* and the shorter films were not far behind. And so they live on today, remarkable souvenirs of a unique chapter in Disney history—colorful, exhilarating films that once strove to unite a hemisphere.

APPENDIX A: FILMOGRAPHY

The following is a filmography of the films described in this book. Every effort has been made to provide the fullest and most accurate documentation possible, based not only on screen credits but on production papers preserved by the Disney studio. The index is divided into three parts: features, theatrical shorts, and nontheatrical shorts. Each entry is preceded by the film's production number. The film's title, as known in the U.S., is given first, followed by variant Spanish and Portuguese titles, where known.

Animation credits for these films are compiled mainly from two kinds of production papers: *drafts* and *exposure sheets*. Drafts are assignment sheets on which the director breaks the picture down into scenes and assigns each scene to an animator. Exposure sheets chart the changes in each scene as it moves through production, in order to provide a reliable guide for the camera department. To the historian, a combined view of both documents offers a useful "before-and-after" view of production of each scene. Wherever possible I have worked from both sets of papers, but in some cases only one or the other has been preserved.

Although I have tried to make this filmography as complete as possible, some details have been omitted for lack of space. In particular, "salvage" animation reused from earlier films—accounting for a significant percentage of such shorts as *The Grain That Built a Hemisphere*—is not detailed here. (No animation credits at all are listed for the four literacy films because all were assembled from animation in the corresponding health films; *see* chapter 4.) All the theatrical films in this index were originally distributed by RKO Radio Pictures.

Please note these standard abbreviations: LS (long shot); CU (close-up); efx (effects); o/s (off-screen).

I. FEATURES

Because *Saludos Amigos* and *The Three Caballeros* both involve complicated sets of credits—each of them being composed of four discrete sections, each of *them* having its own production number and credits—this section of the filmography is divided into three parts: one each for *Saludos Amigos*, *The Three Caballeros*, and *Blame It on the Samba* (which of course was absorbed into the 1948 feature *Melody Time*).

IA. SALUDOS AMIGOS

2015
SALUDOS AMIGOS
SALUDOS
ALÔ, AMIGOS
World premiere: 24 August 1942, Rio de Janeiro, Brazil (Plaza, Astoria, Olinda, Ritz, Parisiense)
Argentine opening: 6 October 1942, Buenos Aires (Ambassador)
North American opening: 6 February 1943, Boston (Majestic)
New York opening: 12 February 1943 (Globe)
U.S. copyright: © Walt Disney Productions, 9 July 1942 (LP12268)
Library of Congress: FGB 9255–FGB 9256
Length: 4 reels (3,776 ft)
Supervising director: Norm Ferguson
Story research: Ted Sears, Bill Cottrell, Webb Smith
Story: Homer Brightman, Ralph Wright, Roy Williams, Harry Reeves, Dick Huemer, Joe Grant
Live-action camera (16 mm): Walt Disney, Lee Blair, Larry Lansburgh
Art supervision: Mary Blair, Lee Blair, Herb Ryman, Jim Bodrero, Jack Miller
Backgrounds: Hugh Hennesy, Al Zinnen, Ken Anderson, McLaren Stewart, Al Dempster, Art Riley, Claude Coats, Dick Anthony, Yale Gracey, Merle Cox

Musical director: Charles Wolcott
Song: "Saludos Amigos," lyrics by Ned Washington, music by Charles Wolcott
Additional music: Ed Plumb, Paul J. Smith
Foreign supervision: Jack Cutting
Associates: Gilberto Souto, Alberto Soria, Edmundo Santos
Narration: Fred Shields (English), Alberto Soria (Spanish)

Feature composed of the following four segments:

2712
LAKE TITICACA
EL LAGO TITICACA
LAGO TITICACA
Director: Bill Roberts
Layout: Hugh Hennesy
Animation: Milt Neil (Duck's introduction to Lake Titicaca, siroche and balsa boat scenes and bakery, native walks downhill, Duck tries to place planks ahead of walking llama on suspension bridge, Duck with single plank)
Milt Kahl (native orchestra, natives walking with and against wind, Duck with baby, young boy and llama, Duck's flute-playing sequence, most of suspension bridge sequence)
Bill Justice (natives walking with and against wind, Duck poses in costume, Duck hangs from rope and is yanked back up to bridge, Duck piles planks under llama, Duck with llama on back and trying to tie rope, falling into pottery market, rolling into lake, and paddling away)
Josh Meador (LS silhouette of Duck and llama, CU of unraveling rope)
Art Palmer (Duck and llama's first scene on suspension bridge, planks fall into gorge)
[Kahl and Justice worked together on scene of natives walking with and against the wind, with Duck following behind.]
Efx animation: Ed Aardal, John McManus
Voice: Clarence Nash (Donald Duck)
Assistant director: Mike Holoboff
Working titles: *The Bolivian Story, Donald in Bolivia*
Reissued as a short 18 February 1955

2714
PEDRO
Director: Ham Luske
Story director: Bill Cottrell
Layout: Ken Anderson
Animation: Bill Tytla (papa plane, second part of Pedro's return flight through the storm, papa and mama at end)
Ham Luske (mama plane, first signal tower scene, Pedro flies through the pass, Pedro runs from lightning bolt)
Fred Moore (Pedro introductory scenes and takeoff, first half of his flight through retrieval of the mail, Pedro returns at the end)
Josh Meador (oil pressure gauge, Christ of the Andes, upshot of Aconcagua with rain and lightning, lightning bolt, windshield scene with rain, altimeter dial, general rain efx, airfield lights and signal tower at end)
Ward Kimball (Pedro saunters out for takeoff, Pedro scurries behind cloud and comes out cockily, first part of Pedro's return flight with condor chase and encounter with Aconcagua)
Assistant director: Larry Lansburgh
Reissued as a short 13 May 1955

2711

EL GAUCHO GOOFY
BUCEFALO GAUCHO
PATETA, O GAUCHO

Director: Jack Kinney
Layout: Al Zinnen
Animation: Hugh Fraser (Goof in Texas and whisked away, Goof and horse pose for picture, Goof saddles horse, avestruz solo scenes)
Woolie Reitherman (most of Goof and horse in Argentina, including avestruz chase)
Harvey Toombs (panuela and poncho on Goof, Goof on fire and whisked out of scene, Goof in water trough at end)
Andy Engman (barbecue smoke and nighttime efx, Goof's return flight and landing)
Dan MacManus (fire efx at end)
Voice: Pinto Colvig
Backgrounds: inspired by F. Molina Campos
Assistant director: Lou Debney
Working titles: *Goofy Gaucho, El Goofo Gaucho*
Reissued as a short 10 June 1955

2717

AQUARELA DO BRASIL
ACUARELA DE BRASIL

Director: Wilfred Jackson
Layout: McLaren Stewart
Animation: Josh Meador (opening paint and paintbrush scenes until introduction of Joe, closing Rio scene)
Paul Allen (introduction of Duck)
Bill Tytla (introduction of Joe and his meeting with Duck)
Les Clark (Duck reads Joe's card and produces his own, crowd samba scene)
Milt Neil (Duck consults dictionaries)
Fred Moore (Duck and Joe in "Tico Tico" number, Joe walks with Duck and teaches him the samba, Duck and Joe at sidewalk café, girl dancing samba alone and with Duck)
Dan MacManus (paintbrush action beginning with painting Joe, cachaça fire, brush paints scenery as Duck and Joe walk and paints musical instruments)
Voices: Aloysio Oliveira (singer, "Aquarela do Brasil"), Clarence Nash (Donald Duck), José Oliveira (Joe Carioca)
Assistant director: Jacques Roberts
Reissued as a short 24 June 1955

Linking sequences
Director: Norm Ferguson
Animation: John McManus (planes fly over landscape)
Assistant director: Gail Papineau

1B. THE THREE CABALLEROS

2016

THE THREE CABALLEROS
LOS TRES CABALLEROS
VOCÊ JÁ FOI À BAHIA?

World premiere: 21 December 1944, Mexico City (Alameda)
New York opening: 3 February 1945 (Globe)
U.S. copyright: © Walt Disney Productions, 28 October 1944 (LP13147)
Library of Congress: FGB 9219–FGB 9222
Length: 8 reels (6,482 ft)
Supervising director: Norm Ferguson
Story: Homer Brightman, Ernie Terrazas, Ted Sears, Bill Peet, Ralph Wright, Elmer Plummer, Roy Williams, Bill Cottrell, Del Connell, Jim Bodrero, Joe Grant, Dick Huemer, Webb Smith
Process efx: Ub Iwerks
  Process technician: Dick Jones
  Operator: Bob Broughton
Color supervision: Phil Dike
Art supervision: Mary Blair, Ken Anderson, Bob Cormack
Film editor: Don Halliday
Backgrounds: Al Dempster, Art Riley, Ray Huffine, Don Douglass, Claude Coats
Musical director: Charles Wolcott
  Additional music: Paul J. Smith, Ed Plumb
Sound: C. O. Slyfield
Foreign supervision: Jack Cutting
  Associates: Gilberto Souto, Aloysio Oliveira, Sidney Field, Edmundo Santos

Feature composed of the following four segments:

2718

THE COLD-BLOODED PENGUIN

Director: Bill Roberts
Story director: Bill Cottrell
Layout: Hugh Hennesy
Animation: Harvey Toombs (other penguins, farewell committee, and Pablo melting through the ice, Pablo encased in ice, Pablo finishes sawing his boat, Pablo looks through telescope, Pablo reads chart, Pablo's meeting with Neptune)
  Josh Meador (smoke efx, snowball crashes igloo, boat sails in LS, fog efx, storm cloud, telescope views of island, stove silhouette, chart, Viña del Mar and Quito, sun and melting igloo, stopper squirts and tub sinks)
  Milt Kahl (Pablo warms himself at stove, Pablo's attempted departures, Pablo starts to saw ice boat, Pablo in "rainstorm," Pablo enjoys the sun, Pablo with his sinking tub and making for the island, Pablo on the island at end)
  Bill Justice (Pablo in fog, Pablo with melting igloo)
  Ed Aardal (Pablo overtaken by storm cloud)
  Dan MacManus (miscellaneous water efx)
    [Ed Aardal also worked with Kahl on the "rainstorm" and with Justice on Pablo with the melting igloo.]
Voices: Sterling Holloway (narrator, English edition), Felipe Turich (narrator, Spanish edition)
Assistant directors: Mike Holoboff, Larry Lansburgh
Working title: *Pablo Penguin*

2713

THE FLYING GAUCHITO

Directors: Norm Ferguson, Eric Larson

Story director: Jim Bodrero

Layout: Herb Ryman, McLaren Stewart, Ken Anderson

Animation: Eric Larson (introduction of hornero and donkey, gauchito and donkey by campfire, LS town, gambling gauchos, first starter scene, townspeople shadows, gauchito and donkey trail other riders, last part of race and ending)

Frank Thomas (introduction of gauchito, gauchito goes hunting, pursues and captures donkey, dancers, second starter scene, gauchito struggles with the rope, then cuts it and takes off)

Ollie Johnston (gauchito climbs along path, gauchito and donkey before race, preparations for race, most of race until gauchito and donkey are knocked down)

John Sibley (dancers' feet, musical instrument montage)

[LS of the town, assigned to Larson, may actually have been animated by Ken O'Brien.]

Efx animation: Dan MacManus

Voice: F. Molina Campos (narrator, Spanish edition)

Assistant director: Larry Lansburgh

Working titles: *The Remarkable Donkey, The Flying Gaucho*

Reissued as a short 22 July 1955

2721

BAÍA

Sequence 1. Have you ever been to Bahia?

Layout: Yale Gracey

Animation: Fred Moore (Joe and Duck at beginning, Joe interrupted by Aracuan)

Eric Larson (Aracuan runs around the frame line)

Les Clark (Joe scolds the Aracuan and begins his song)

John McManus (Brazil map)

[Extended CU of Joe was assigned to Clark but apparently animated jointly by Clark and Moore.]

Sequence 2. Baía

Song: "Na baixa do sapateiro" by Ary Barroso, English lyrics by Ray Gilbert

Layout: Bob Cormack, John Hench

Animation: Josh Meador (light and dewdrop efx, boats on river, two doves in cathedral tower)

John McManus (dove flies through scene, doves' reflections in pool)

George Rowley (doves fly into garden)

Sequence 3. Baixa do Saparteiro ([*sic*] the Barroso song titled "Na baixa do sapateiro" is actually the basis of the previous sequence here titled "Baía.")

Song: "Você já foi à Bahia?" by Dorival Caymmi, English lyrics by Norm Ferguson

Layout: Ken Anderson, Yale Gracey

Animation: John Lounsbery (Joe finishes "Baía," Duck and Joe alight from train and look at next pages of book)

Fred Moore (all of number: "Have You Ever Been to Bahia?")

Eric Larson (book reveals train station, Duck and Joe run in, train cars separate)

Les Clark (most of train's trip, including Aracuan action)

Marvin Woodward (train through forest, last car hops curve)

[Scene of the cars separating was jointly assigned to Clark and Josh Meador, but animated by Larson.]

Efx animation: Jerry Hathcock

Sequence 4. Os quindins de Yayá

Song: "Os quindins de Yayá" by Ary Barroso

ANIMATION

Layout: Ken Anderson

Animation: John Lounsbery (Duck and Joe investigate book and hear singing, Duck and Joe hear o/s guitarist, Duck and Joe with pencil player, Joe's "fast worker" line, Duck misses the first kiss, Duck and Joe watch fight)

Josh Meador (Yayá's shadow on wall)

Fred Moore (Duck and Joe meet Yayá, walk along wall behind her, Duck and Joe regard guitarist, Joe dances with Yayá, Duck edges him out, Joe and Duck as guitarist returns with girls)

Ward Kimball (Duck pursues Yayá, Joe holds him back, Duck on wall as Yayá sings to him)

Eric Larson (Duck and Joe compete for Yayá's attention, jealous Duck, Joe gives him the mallet, Duck and Joe dance down street with Yayá)

Les Clark (Joe and Duck join dancing, group dancing scene, Duck misses orange peddler with mallet and is hit himself, Duck's musical hallucination and cockfight, dancing buildings, book slams shut)

Ollie Johnston (Duck gets second kiss from Yayá and is love-struck, Joe leads dancers at end)

John Sibley (dancing lamppost, Duck with dancing chair and fountain elephant)

[Kimball also worked with Lounsbery on pencil-player scene. George Rowley worked with Clark on the cockfight and with Lounsbery on the scene of Duck and Joe watching the fight. Clark worked with Sibley on one scene of dancing buildings, and with Meador on the closing scene of the book slamming shut.]

Efx animation: Jerry Hathcock (cartoon scenes), Ed Aardal (live-action dancing scene)

LIVE ACTION

Director: Norm Ferguson

Art director: Richard Irvine (set dresser: Bill Kiernan)

Camera: Ray Rennahan, ASC

Second camera: Lee Davis

Camera technician: Harry Wolf

Assistant cameraman: David Kesson

Wardrobe design: Walter Plunkett

Dance director: Billy Daniels

Makeup: Walter Herman

Hairdresser: Alice Ribal

Cast: Aurora Miranda (Yayá)

Luis (Aloysio de) Oliveira (Guitar)

Ivan Lopes* (Trumpet)

José Oliveira* (Pencil Tambourine)

Affonso Ozório* (Cabaça)

Stênio Ozório* (Cuíca)

Oswaldo Gogliano* (Tom-Tom)

Nestor Amaral* (Orange Peddler)

Billy Daniels (Rival)

(*Members of Bando da Lua)

[Lopes, Gogliano, and the Ozórios also served as doubles. Modern spellings, as a result of orthographic reform: Afonso Osório and Stênio Osório.]

Dancers

Men:	Women:
Mike Fernandez	Naomi Becker
Enrique Valadez	Louise Burnett
Alexander Nohera	Frances Grant
Fernando Ramos	Elizabeth Dow
Carlos Barbe	Helene Garon
Vincent Gironda	Patsy Bedell
Paul Lopez	Melba Snowden
Carlos Albert	Carmen Moreno
Ivan Jordan	Carmen Lopez
Wally Kreuter	Lolita Lindsay
	Italia de Nubila

Casting: Walt Pfeiffer
Treadmill operator: T. W. La Mar
Assistant directors: Barton Adams, Martin Santell, Herb Hirst

2725
LA PIÑATA
Sequence 1. Intro to Charro
Director: Gerry Geronimi
Layout: Hugh Hennesy, Herb Ryman
Animation: Les Clark (Duck and Joe leap into box and pull ribbons on package)
Josh Meador (sound track)
Milt Neil (Duck and Joe dance and interact with sound track)
Ward Kimball (Duck grabs Joe, introduction of Panchito and his opening song, most of "Three Caballeros" number)
Fred Moore (CUs of Joe in "Three Caballeros" number)
Ollie Johnston (Duck puzzled by piñata, Panchito begins explanation of Christmas)
[As indicated above, all the Duck-Joe silhouette dancing scenes were assigned to Neil, but two of them may actually have been animated by Clark. Bob Carlson worked with Kimball on some scenes in the "Three Caballeros" number.]
Miscellaneous efx animation: Jerry Hathcock
Assistant director: Rusty Jones
Sequence 2. Las Posadas & Breaking Piñata
Director: Gerry Geronimi
Layout: Herb Ryman, Hugh Hennesy
"Las Posadas" paintings: Mary Blair
Animation: George Rowley (animated efx on "Las Posadas" paintings, club misses, then hits piñata, flood of gifts, miscellaneous efx)
Ollie Johnston (Duck prepares and tries to break piñata, Panchito and Joe pull rope, piñata toys march to music, caballeros catch them, Duck with pig and bull, Duck runs and has sarape draped over head)
Ward Kimball (Panchito in piñata sequence?)
[Inconclusive evidence suggests that Kimball and Johnston may have worked together on Panchito in this sequence.]
Assistant director: Rusty Jones

Sequence 3. Folio

ANIMATION

Director: Gerry Geronimi

Layout: Hugh Hennesy, Charles Philippi

"Mexico" paintings: Mary Blair

Animation: Ollie Johnston (Panchito shows book to Duck and Joe, introduction of magic sarape, caballeros ride sarape through first live-action shots and arrive at Pátzcuaro)

Josh Meador (Mexican flag and historical tableaux)

Eric Larson (caballeros dance Jarabe Pateño, then leave on sarape, Duck tries to join dancing and Joe and Panchito urge him to dance with Carmen)

Don Patterson (caballeros fly from Pátzcuaro to Veracruz, Panchito and Joe fly away with protesting Duck, aerial "attacks" on Acapulco, Duck lands in water and continues chasing girls, Panchito and Joe sweep him up on sarape)

Ward Kimball (caballeros watch Lilongo, Duck dances with Carmen, Joe and Panchito pull him away)

Fred Moore (Joe and Panchito dance during Lilongo sequence)

Milt Neil (caballeros fly over Acapulco beach, Duck lands on beach as Panchito and Joe watch him, Duck tossed in blanket by girls, caballeros on sarape after leaving Acapulco)

Hal King (caballeros on sarape pursue last girl, Duck's quick-change and dive from sarape, Duck chases girls on beach)

Efx animation: Jerry Hathcock

Assistant director: Rusty Jones

LIVE ACTION

Director: Harold Young

Art director: Richard Irvine

Camera: Ray Rennahan, ASC

Second camera: Tom Brannigan

Camera technician: Paul Weddell

Assistant cameramen: Chuck Adler, Monty Steadman, W. Eagan

Camera, Mexico Stock Footage: Wilfrid Cline, ASC

Hairdresser: Alice Ribal

Cast: Carmen Molina (Lilongo dancer)

Pátzcuaro and Veracruz dancers (Padua Hills Players):

Anita de la Rosa
Dolores Vigil*
Mina Morales*
Casilda Amador
Ernesto de Soto*
Inez Torres
Porfidia Lopez*
Hilda Ramírez de Jara
Jacinta Vigil
Lupe Mireles*
Ignacia Jara
Rafael Artíz*
Jesus Concha*
Abigael Chavez*
Alfonso Gallardo*
Maximino García*
Manuel Mireles
Arturo Soto*
Juan Cuellar*

(*Pátzcuaro sequence only)

Assistant directors: Barton Adams, Don Bush

Sequence 4. Solamente una vez

Song: "Solamente una vez" by Agustín Lara; English lyrics ("You Belong to My Heart") by Ray Gilbert

ANIMATION

Director: Norm Ferguson

Layout: Ken Anderson, Bob Cormack

Animation: John Lounsbery (caballeros leave Acapulco, Panchito introduces Mexico City scene, Duck listens to Dora and fantasizes)

George Rowley (aerial scene of Mexico City, star efx)

Les Clark (Duck fantasy during instrumental section)

Assistant director: Larry Lansburgh

LIVE ACTION

Cast: Dora Luz

Art director: Richard Irvine

Camera: Ray Rennahan, ASC

Second camera: Billy Tuers

Camera technician: Paul Weddell

Assistant cameramen: George Gall and Monty Steadman

Makeup: Harry Ross

Hairdresser: Era Lynn

[Note: These are the technical credits recorded for 28 September 1943, when Technicolor makeup tests were shot for both Dora Luz and Carmen Molina. By this time the Dora Luz vocal track for "You Belong to My Heart" had already been recorded, and her test was filmed to playback. Documentation from the actual production of the number has not been preserved, but it took place within ten days after this session and likely involved the same technical personnel.]

Sequence 5. Montage

Director: Norm Ferguson

Layout: Ken Anderson

Animation: Les Clark (Duck kissed by lips, Duck as hummingbird)

Josh Meador (Duck as skyrocket and neon hummingbird with neon flowers, Duck with flying patterns of girls and ducks)

John Lounsbery (Duck floats toward Dora fantasy images, Panchito and Joe disrupt images, caballeros with girls' legs)

John McManus (Duck and girls against red background, Duck and final fantasy images of Dora)

[Production materials suggest that Clark and Meador worked together on the scene of Donald as a neon hummingbird.]

Assistant director: Larry Lansburgh

Sequence 6. Zandunga

ANIMATION

Director: Norm Ferguson

Layout: Ken Anderson

Animation: Les Clark (Duck watches Carmen and dances with her, swaying flowers)

[Jim Moore may have worked with Clark on some of the process plates.]

Efx animation: Jerry Hathcock

Assistant director: Larry Lansburgh

LIVE ACTION

Director: Harold Young
Cast: Carmen Molina
Dance director: Carmelita Maracci
Assistant: Marie Groscup
Art director: Richard Irvine
Camera: Ray Rennahan, ASC
Second camera: Tom Brannigan
Camera technicians: Paul Weddell, Henry Imus
Assistant cameramen: Chuck Adler, Monty Steadman, W. Eagan
Makeup: Jack Casey
Hairdresser: Alice Ribal
Assistant directors: Barton Adams, Don Bush

Sequence 7. Jesusita (The Cactus March)

ANIMATION

Director: Norm Ferguson
Layout: Ken Anderson
Animation: Fred Moore (first part of dance: Duck and cacti, Duck watches Carmen and tries to dance with her)
Les Clark (second part of dance: Duck surrounded by cacti and with cactus ducks)
[As in the previous sequence, Jim Moore may have animated some of the process plates.]

LIVE ACTION

Director: Harold Young
Cast: Carmen Molina
Stand-in: Lynn Sarli
Dance director: Carmelita Maracci
Assistant: Marie Groscup
Art director: Richard Irvine
Camera: Ray Rennahan, ASC
Second camera: Tom Brannigan
Camera technicians: Henry Imus, Paul Weddell
Assistant cameramen: Chuck Adler, W. Eagan
Makeup: Jack Casey
Hairdresser: Alice Ribal
Assistant directors: Barton Adams, Don Bush

Sequence 8. Finale

Director: Gerry Geronimi
Layout: Hugh Hennesy, Charles Philippi
Animation: Fred Moore (Panchito and Joe ride straw horses out of horn, first part of bullfight through Joe lighting firecrackers with cigar, final scene of caballeros looking up at fireworks)
George Rowley (firecracker efx, explosion and "End" title)
Don Patterson (second half of bullfight: Duck out of bull, bull chases Duck, Duck and bull charge each other)
Miscellaneous efx animation: Jerry Hathcock
Assistant director: Rusty Jones

INTERSTITIAL SEQUENCES

Director: Jack Kinney

1. Opening—into Penguin Picture

Animation: Hal King (Duck opens packages, looks at film, sets up and runs projector)
Jack Boyd ("Aves Raras" title)

Assistant director: Bee Selck

2. Birds—Insert from Penguin to Gauchito

Layout: Don Da Gradi

Animation: Hal King (most of Duck animation, Marrequito builds nest and Aracuan destroys it)
Eric Larson (exotic birds, introduction of Aracuan, Duck attempts to imitate flamingos)

Assistant director: Ted Sebern

3. Lead into Baía

Layout: Ken Anderson

Animation: Hal King (opening scene of Duck with unreeled film)
Josh Meador (large box with smoke)
John Lounsbery (Duck runs to box, pulls out and drops package)
Les Clark (Duck unwraps package and opens book)
Fred Moore (all of Joe Carioca, Duck reacts to Joe)
[John Reed may have worked with Clark on Duck unwrapping package.]

Efx animation: Jerry Hathcock

4. Duck-Parrot Blowing Up

Animation: John Lounsbery (Duck and Joe emerge from book, Duck in trance, Joe reminds him of gifts, Duck runs up side of box and falls)
Eric Larson (Joe reassures Duck and inflates self, Duck begins his attempt)
John Sibley (Duck's unsuccessful attempts, distorted body, Duck listens to Joe)
Fred Moore (Joe's laughter, Duck successfully inflates self and happy reaction)

Efx animation: Jerry Hathcock

1C. BLAME IT ON THE SAMBA

2060

BLAME IT ON THE SAMBA

Released as part of the package feature *Melody Time*

***Melody Time* New York opening:** 27 May 1948

***Melody Time* Los Angeles opening:** 29 July 1948

***Melody Time* general release:** August 1948

Copyright: © Walt Disney Productions, 7 April 1948 (LP1721)

Library of Congress: FGB 9228–FGB 9232

Length: 10 reels (6,776 ft)

Song: "Apanhei-te, cavaquinho" by Ernesto Nazareth, English lyrics ("Blame It on the Samba") by Ray Gilbert

Vocal: Dinning Sisters

ANIMATION

Director: Gerry Geronimi

Story: Ken Anderson

Layout: Bob Cormack, Hugh Hennesy, Lance Nolley

Animation: Hal King (blue Duck and Joe, Aracuan seats them at table, Aracuan snaps staff, slices up instruments, and mixes musical cocktail, Duck and Joe fall off console, CU of Aracuan riding note, Duck and Joe dance wildly after Ethel's hot foot, Aracuan at end)

John Lounsbery (Duck and Joe look at menus, Aracuan starts to take orders, then tears up menus, introduction of number, Duck and Joe watch Ethel play drums, characters blown into air by explosion)

Les Clark (Duck and Joe land in cocktail glass, watch Ethel play and samba on organ console, Duck knocked off, underneath, and pulled back up to top of console)

Harvey Toombs (Aracuan draws hole and follows Duck and Joe into it, Aracuan lights dynamite and buildup to explosion)

Ward Kimball (most of riding-notes sequence, from Aracuan painting lips through Duck and Joe's bumpy ride, Aracuan gives Ethel hot foot)

Efx animation: Josh Meador

Backgrounds: Jimi Trout, Dick Anthony, Ralph Hulett

Special processes: Ub Iwerks

Assistant director: Ted Sebern

LIVE ACTION

Director: Ken Anderson

Cast: Ethel Smith

Camera: Winton Hoch, ASC

Operator: Harvey Gould

Props: Ken Walters

Makeup: Joe Bonner

Hairdresser: Vera Peterson

Wardrobe: Violet Smith

Assistant director: Joe Lefert

Reissued as a short 1 April 1955

II. THEATRICAL SHORTS

All the films listed in this section are one-reel shorts.

2715

PLUTO AND THE ARMADILLO

Copyright: © Walt Disney Productions, 27 August 1942 (LP11871)
Released: 19 February 1943
Director: Gerry Geronimi
Layout: Charles Philippi
Animation: Les Clark (armadillo in opening scenes, armadillo's friendly overtures)
Marvin Woodward (Mickey and Pluto exit plane, all of Mickey scenes)
Nick Nichols (Pluto stretches, Pluto and armadillo make friends, end of chase and Pluto destroying ball, Pluto imitates ball action, Pluto and armadillo on the plane)
John Lounsbery (Pluto confuses ball with armadillo, confronts armadillo, remorse scenes ending with happy surprise)
George Nicholas (bouncing-ball sequence through armadillo winking)
Norman Tate (underground chase)
Efx animation: George Rowley (airport bell, propeller)
Music: Paul J. Smith
Song: "The Armadillo Samba" (English lyrics Bob Musel; Spanish lyrics Palo Sacás)
Voices: Walt Disney (Mickey Mouse), Fred Shields (narrator)
Assistant director: Ralph Chadwick

2716

THE PELICAN AND THE SNIPE

Copyright: © Walt Disney Productions, 29 November 1943 (LP12603)
Released: 7 January 1944
Director: Ham Luske
Story director: Bill Cottrell
Layout: Ken Anderson
Animation: Ham Luske (most of opening sequence through first rescue, plane buzzes pelican, second rescue, planes drop bombs)
Ollie Johnston (opening scene, snipe nails blanket down, pelican admires plane, pelican pulls snipe up in air, snipe's dream sequence, lighthouse tower, pelican's awakening and bomb sequence, snipe rescue through end sequence, miscellaneous snipe animation)
Ward Kimball (pelican's exercise sequence, pelican into water, angry pelican orders snipe out, miscellaneous pelican animation)
Music: Ollie Wallace
Voice: Sterling Holloway (narrator)
Assistant directors: Riley Thomson, Larry Lansburgh
Working titles: *Percy Pelican, Down Uruguay Way*

2302

CONTRARY CONDOR

Copyright: © Walt Disney Productions, 13 March 1944 (LP12631)
Released: 21 April 1944
Director: Jack King
Story: Harry Reeves
Layout: Ernie Nordli
Animation: John McManus (footsteps in opening, Duck tosses dummy and mama dives after it, then cries)

Judge Whitaker (Duck yodels and climbs mountain, Duck's first encounter with mama through cloudburst, Duck applauds Jr.'s flight, Jr. glides into scene and lands, Duck's clumsy landing, Duck thinks up a new plan)
Nick Nichols (Duck discovers nest and hides in egg, hatching sequence through Duck jabbing mama, jealous Jr., Jr. scuffles with Duck and snaps him off limb, Duck "flies" and lands, mama applauds, mama misses dummy and it falls in water, closing sequence from Jr. running with the egg)
Paul Allen (mama pushes Jr. off limb, mama encourages Duck to fly and Duck's reaction, Duck tries to escape with egg and Jr. intercepts it)
George Nicholas (Jr. falls and tries to fly)
Don Towsley (Jr. lowers legs like landing gear, mama's card trick with Duck)
Hal King (mama's attempts to push Duck off limb, Duck fakes bad wing)
Marvin Woodward (mama tricks Duck with berry)

Efx animation: Jerry Hathcock
Voices: Clarence Nash (Donald Duck), Florence Gill (mama condor)
Backgrounds: Merle Cox, assisted by Leonard Kester
Music: Paul J. Smith
Sound effects: Earl Hatch
Assistant director: Joel Greenhalgh
Working titles: *Contrary Condors, Egg Collector, The Colombian Condor*

2344
CLOWN OF THE JUNGLE
Copyright: © Walt Disney Productions, 31 December 1946 (LP1131)
Released: 20 June 1947
Director: Jack Hannah
Story: Ray Patin, Payne Thebaut
Layout: Yale Gracey
Animation: Bill Justice (hummingbirds, Aracuan in scenes with hummingbirds, Duck and Aracuan after machine gun scenes)
Volus Jones (Duck attempts to photograph parrot and flamingo, Duck behind camera reacts to Aracuan, Duck tries to photograph hummingbirds and tangles with Aracuan, imaginary motorcycle chase and house-building sequence, Duck in closing scene)
Judge Whitaker (Duck frames and poses stork, Aracuan cries and tries to hang himself [first time], Duck forgives him, Aracuan mimics Duck and Duck reacts)
Hal King (Aracuan dances through scene and snips film, boxing glove and elevator gags, machine gun and second suicide sequence)
Al Coe (Duck attempts to photograph mechanical birds, cigar and skyrocket sequence)
[Jones animated the Duck-Aracuan fireman scene jointly with Whitaker, and the machine gun firing scene jointly with King.]

Efx animation: Josh Meador (opening scenes), Andy Engman (machine gun efx)
Backgrounds: Thelma Witmer
Music: Ollie Wallace
Voice: Clarence Nash (Donald Duck)
Assistant director: Bee Selck
Working title: *Feathered Frenzy*

III. NONTHEATRICAL SHORTS

This section details the short films that were distributed in 16 mm through nontheatrical channels in Latin America. The first and last films listed in this section, *South of the Border with Disney* and *The Amazon Awakens*, each have a length of four reels; all other titles listed here are one-reel shorts.

2614

SOUTH OF THE BORDER WITH DISNEY
POR TIERRAS DE AMERICA CON WALT DISNEY
POR TERRAS DA AMÉRICA COM WALT DISNEY

Copyright: © Walt Disney Productions, 6 November 1942 (MP16208)
Library of Congress: FCA 1702
Director: Norm Ferguson
Camera (16 mm): Walt Disney, Lee Blair, Larry Lansburgh
Additional live action supplied by: National Geographic Society, Moore-McCormack Steamship Lines
Pencil animation: Les Clark (armadillo)
Fred Moore (Joe Carioca, Pedro)
Woolie Reitherman (Goofy)
Frank Thomas (Flying Gauchito with burro)
Music: Charles Wolcott
Voice: Art Baker (narrator)
Assistant director: Gail Papineau
Working titles: *Walt Disney Sees South America, Walt Disney Sees Latin America*

2732

THE WINGED SCOURGE
PESTE ALADA

Copyright: © Walt Disney Productions, 11 January 1943 (MP13619)
Library of Congress: FAA 326, FAB 8466
Director: Bill Roberts
Layout: Hugh Hennesy
Animation: John McManus (mosquitoes and larva, fish eat larva, wigglers in dipper and sardine can)
Milt Kahl (introduction of dwarfs, Doc and Sneezy in boat, Happy sprays oil, Dopey with dipper and oil can, Bashful and birds apply Paris green, Sleepy and mole dig ditches, Grumpy chops stump, dwarfs with deer and cart, Doc with cans in wheelbarrow, Grumpy and woodpecker)
Frank Thomas (Dopey and mosquitoes sequence, with Grumpy)
Harvey Toombs (Happy covers rain barrel, dwarfs and birds hang screens, Sleepy and birds with netting, dwarfs in bed snoring)
Efx animation: Josh Meador (parasites taken out of bloodstream, sprayed oil)
Andy Engman (parasites injected into bloodstream)
Ed Aardal (Paris green, dirt shoveled into water)
George Rowley (dust shoots from chimney)
Assistant director: Mike Holoboff
Working title: *The Mosquito and Malaria*

2736

THE GRAIN THAT BUILT A HEMISPHERE
LA SEMILLA DE ORO

Copyright: © Walt Disney Productions, 28 January 1943 (MP13739)
Library of Congress: FAA 111, FAB 8506
Director: Bill Roberts
Layout: Hugh Hennesy, Leo Thiele
Animation: Bill Tytla (all of Indian animation)
Josh Meador (ear of corn, corn god temple, corn picker and husker)
Ed Aardal (corn-breeding process, hand affixing stamp and pouring syrup, stream of syrup, car)
John Reed (corn "wedding" and offspring)
George Rowley (salad, donuts, ice cream and pudding, clothes dummy, bill poster's brush, surgeon's shadow, streams of sugar)
Frank Thomas (steer with cuts of meat outlined on side, boy eyes pie)
Milt Kahl (woman feeds baby, distorted image of chemist)
Backgrounds: Warren Williams
Music: Paul Smith, Ed Plumb
Assistant director: Mike Holoboff
Working title: *Corn and Corn Products*

2731

WATER—FRIEND OR ENEMY

Copyright: © Walt Disney Productions, 6 April 1943 (MP13620)
Director: Norm Wright
Layout: Ernie Nordli, Leo Thiele
Animation: Ed Aardal (opening scenes of river, hands washing clothes and first hands dipping water, skull in contaminated water, water fills glass, smaller family at table, cross-sections of spring and construction of well, hands dipping bucket into well, pollution traveling underground, water boiling over charcoal fire, hand operates water jar, closing scene of river)
Bill Tytla (small boy washed in river, reflection of woman walking, first scene of family at table)
Josh Meador (second hands dipping water, water in strata at bottom of driven well, construction of driven well, boiling water in lab, CU of glass filled from water jar)
Voice: Fred Shields (narrator)
Working title: *Water Supply*

2733

DEFENSE AGAINST INVASION
DEFENSA CONTRA LA INVASION

Copyright: © Walt Disney Productions, 5 August 1943 (MP13826)
Library of Congress: FBA 1748
Director: Jack King
Story directors: Carl Barks, Jack Hannah
Layout: Bill Herwig
Animation: Josh Meador (buildings, germs seen through lens, LS traffic and people in city, corpuscles run in and out of buildings, germs effuse from windows and roofs and cover corpuscles, candle, whistle blowing, factory lights and smoke, corpuscles close in on green germs, tanks approach and fire, red and black armies approach each other and meet, corpuscles overflow ground)

Marvin Woodward (introduction of corpuscles and germs, bread enters tunnel, germ multiplies, germs pour over roofs and through windows, corpuscles take guns from rack, germs form pincers and snap closed, needle with green germs, corpuscle blows whistle, doors open and planes and tanks exit building, germ army approaches, corpuscle paints bomb, germ swallows it and explodes, corpuscles spray liquid, corpuscle plays "Chicago piano")

Judge Whitaker (germ enters with slice of pie, germ leaps toward corpuscle and swallows him, corpuscle sounds alarm and others run out of buildings, corpuscles hand out guns, corpuscle beats up green germ, shells, planes attack building and separate into germs, trumpets, corpuscles run out of building, plane sequence with bombs, parachutes, and tommy guns, germ runs up ladder pursued by corpuscles)

Hal King (germs overflowing tanks, wave of germs engulfs corpuscles and falls over building, workers and riveters in factory, corpuscle kicks green germ through crack, germs around corner and down steps, lookout in tower, germs leap over wall and are shot as they leap, corpuscle fires machine gun in jump-rope pattern and germs jump)

Paul Allen (introduction of heart "building" and green germ, cauldron rounds corner and goes toward BG, corpuscle in factory pulls shell, jeep and corpuscles on cannon, tanks approach head-on, tanks cut inroads, corpuscles fire machine gun and hit germ)

Milt Neil (germ leaps toward camera, corpuscle pulls lever and germ enters)
[Neil may have worked with Whitaker on the scene of the black germ swallowing the corpuscle.]

Assistant director: Jack Atwood

Live action unit manager: Dan Keefe

Live action assistant director: Lowell Farrel

2754

TUBERCULOSIS

LA TUBERCULOSIS

Copyright: © Walt Disney Productions, 13 August 1945 (MP2724)

Director: Jim Algar

Story: Jim Algar, Glen Scott, Retta Scott, Don Griffith

Layout: Don Griffith, John Niendorff

Animation: Josh Meador (diagram man, leaves, cloud casts shadows, Mr. and Mrs. Brown at home, doctor examines Mrs. Brown, two men on chart, TB germs blowing in wind)

Jack Boyd (pages turning in book, sick man spits)

Ed Aardal (TB eats away lungs, germs passed from man's lungs to woman's lungs, X-ray scenes, germs enter the friend's lungs, boiling water, woman washing hands, special drinking cup)

John Reed (candle, Mrs. Brown coughs, walks out of scene and goes home, Mr. and Mrs. Brown go to doctor, Mr. Brown in garden)

Sandy Strother (Mr. and Mrs. Brown watch doctor at blackboard, family in beds with woman coughing, hands washing dishes, dishes set apart, milk in kettle for boiling, cross-section of boiling pot)

Backgrounds: Retta Scott

Voices: Art Baker (narrator), Jim Macdonald, Violet Bayerl (coughs)

Music: Paul Smith

Titles: Warren Williams

Working titles: *Sunshine—The Plague Killer*, *The Disease that Lives in Darkness*, *The White Plague*

2760

CLEANLINESS BRINGS HEALTH
LA LIMPIEZA TRAE BUENA SALUD

Copyright: © Walt Disney Productions, 4 June 1945 (MP16119)
Library of Congress: FAA 3431, FAA 3432
Director: Jim Algar
Layout: Don Griffith
Animation: Ed Aardal (opening scene of hand painting on two easels, CU hand sifts dirt, kid scrubbed, clothes washed)
Murray McClellan (Juan's wife cooks on brick stove, Juan and son work in field, Pedro and son sick, Juan's son, Pedro sits down to rest, dusts hands, goes home and eats, sick again, Juan's son in latrine and thatch applied to framework)
Sandy Strother (stove with fire and steam cycles)
Josh Meador (pig enters house and hand pulls it out, hands kneading dough, father and son washing, sweeping house and burying refuse)
John McManus (CU hand picks up corn, construction of latrine)
Ollie Johnston (closing scene: Juan's family dancing)
Backgrounds: Al Dempster, Retta Scott
Voice: Art Baker (narrator)
Assistant director: Toby Tobelman
Working title: *Personal Cleanliness*

2761

INFANT CARE
EL CUIDADO DEL NIÑO

Copyright: © Walt Disney Productions, 10 March 1945 (MP16188)
Library of Congress: FAA 4029, FAA 4030
Director: Jim Algar
Story: Norm Wright, Jesse Marsh
Layout: Don Griffith
Animation: John McManus (introduction of family, foods, milking goat, mother eating [including scene with cross-section], mother nursing, brush draws foods, brush draws bed and netting around sleeping baby)
Sandy Strother (boiling milk, fruits, flies on net, boiling water, cereals, rice and corn, drinking glass)
Murray McClellan (husband hoeing, baby drinking, mother giving baby drink, baby being spoon-fed, baby crawling)
Jack Boyd (vaccination, baby lying in blanket, mashed foods, and soft-boiled eggs)
Backgrounds: Retta Scott
Working title: *Infant Care and Feeding*

5000

THE HUMAN BODY
EL CUERPO HUMANO
O CORPO HUMANO

Copyright: © Walt Disney Productions, 13 August 1945 (MP2727)
Director: Bill Roberts
Story: Ed Penner, Herb Ryman
Layout: Al Zinnen, Herb Ryman
Animation: Bill Justice (introduction of José and possessions [house and animals], José and muscles, José eats, slaps self after breathing fresh air, CU of José, closing scene)
Ed Aardal (José's possessions lost or stolen)
Jerry Hathcock (LS of ruins and José)
Josh Meador (José standing and breathing, hand paints window on house)
Harvey Toombs (CU of things in José's head)
[Murray McClellan may also have animated some scenes. Justice and Meador worked together on scene 43: José's shirt painted back on, takes hat off.]
Backgrounds: Bill Layne
Voice: Larry Keating (narrator)
Assistant director: Harry Love

5001

LA HISTÓRIA DE JOSÉ

5009

A HISTORIA DE JOSÉ

Copyright: © Walt Disney Productions (as *A historia de José*), 29 December 1944 (MP15713)
Library of Congress: FAA 119, FAA 120
Directors: Dan MacManus, Graham Heid
Story: Dan MacManus
Layout: Tom Hayward
Backgrounds: Dusty Farnam, Bill Layne

5002

JOSÉ COME BIEN

5010

JOSÉ COME BEM

Copyright: © Walt Disney Productions (as *José come bem*), 29 December 1944 (MP15714)
Library of Congress: FAA 143, FAA 144
Director: Graham Heid
Story: Dan MacManus
Layout: Tom Hayward
Backgrounds: Bill Layne
Voice: Dan MacManus (narrator)

5003

WHAT IS DISEASE?
¿QUÉ ES ENFERMEDAD?
O QUE E A DOENÇA?
THE UNSEEN ENEMY
EL ENEMIGO INVISIBLE
O ENEMIGO INVISÍVEL

Copyright: © Walt Disney Productions (as *El enemigo invisible*), 13 August 1945 (MP2725)
Director: Bill Roberts
Story: Ed Penner
Layout: Al Zinnen, Herb Ryman
Animation: Harvey Toombs (Ramón hoeing in field, Ramón eating in house gets nervous and runs outside)
Murray McClellan (hand catches Ramón, Ramón drinks from stream, scratches head)
Ed Aardal (cloud and rain in opening sequence, doctor, removing doctor's glasses, beetles eating tree)
John McManus (progressive views of fly, microscope, germs multiplying, amoeba, mosquito)
John Reed (hand with dipper)
Josh Meador (flies on food, fly's leg)
Backgrounds: Bill Layne
Voice: Larry Keating (narrator)
Assistant director: Harry Love

5004

LA HISTÓRIA DE RAMÓN

Not copyrighted
Directors: Graham Heid, Dan MacManus
Story: Dan MacManus
Layout: Bill McKee, Tom Hayward

5005

RAMÓN ESTÁ ENFERMO

Not copyrighted
Director: Graham Heid
Story: Dan MacManus
Voice: Felipe Turich (narrator)

5006

HOW DISEASE TRAVELS
LA ENFERMEDAD SE PROPAGA

Copyright: © Walt Disney Productions, 11 June 1945 (MP16189)
Library of Congress: FAA 3980, FAA 3981
Director: Bill Roberts
Story: Ed Penner, Norm Wright
Layout: Herb Ryman, Al Zinnen
Animation: Josh Meador (paintbrush, Joe's house, village, rain and filth, group on riverbank, flies in cornfield and on filth, swarming and visiting houses, pencil draws latrine, villagers cough)
Harvey Toombs (family and "you," Joe, house and cornfield, "you" drinking water and eating food, finding place for latrine, boy visits Johnny, mother takes glass, family works)
John McManus (germs)

John Reed (water, fly on food)
Sandy Strother (flies on pan and on food)
Backgrounds: Claude Coats, Bob Ferguson
Voice: Larry Keating (narrator)
Assistant director: Harry Love
Working title: *Transmission of Disease*

5008
HOOKWORM
UNCINARIASIS
Copyright: © Walt Disney Productions, 4 May 1945 (MP16118)
Library of Congress: FAA 3970, FAA 3971
Director: Jim Algar
Story: Dan MacManus, Ernie Terrazas
Layout: Don Griffith
Animation: John McManus (brush paints house, sun, and cloud, hookworms in intestine and laying eggs, rain cloud and rain, eggs hatch, sick family and shabby house, worms die, latrine cover, cross-section of latrine)
Ollie Johnston (introduction of healthy and sick Charlie, Charlie puzzled, Charlie feels stronger)
Josh Meador (worms through magnifying glass)
Murray McClellan (scared Charlie in tree, Charlie comes out of tree and falls, hand catches him)
Ken O'Brien (Charlie in and out of cornfield, family walks on bad ground, Charlie reacts to bare feet, Charlie proud of himself, then does take, Charlie runs, trips on rock and accidentally "builds" latrine housing, Charlie and son hoeing, Charlie tips hat good-bye)
Hal Ambro (Charlie at the clinic and wearing shoes, Charlie digs latrine and builds cover)
Backgrounds: Retta Scott, Bob Ferguson
Voice: Art Baker (narrator)

5012
INSECTS AS CARRIERS OF DISEASE
INSECTOS QUE TRANSMITEN ENFERMEDADES
Copyright: © Walt Disney Productions, 13 June 1945 (MP16117)
Library of Congress: FAA 4091
Director: Bill Roberts
Story: Ed Penner, Ernie Terrazas
Layout: Al Zinnen
Animation: Ward Kimball (Charlie eats food, shoos fly, and catches louse)
Harvey Toombs (Charlie shoos fly and catches louse, Charlie with stomachache, Charlie shivers with malaria, Charlie scratches head, Charlie drains pool, Charlie takes a bath)
Al Coe (Charlie shrinks and introduction of large insects, fly walks on filth and flies away, Charlie starts to confront insects and is stopped by pencil, mosquito stands on head, pencil stops Charlie again, CU louse, second sick neighbor, Charlie and neighbor, Charlie starts after insects with fork, then runs from them, Charlie grows, angry Charlie)
John Reed (fly goes in window, mosquito flies to neighbor's house and back to Charlie's house, louse on arm and goes under sleeve, Charlie boiling clothes)
Josh Meador (fly lands on food)
George Rowley (first sick neighbor, mosquito on Charlie's arm)
[The scene of Charlie with fly and louse was roughly animated by Kimball; Toombs followed through and completed the scene.]
Efx animation: Ed Aardal

Backgrounds: Claude Coats, Bob Ferguson, Art Riley
Music: Paul Smith
Voice: Larry Keating (narrator)

5011
PLANNING FOR GOOD EATING
ES FACIL COMER BIEN
Copyright: © Walt Disney Productions, 3 April 1946 (MP2726)
Director: Gerry Geronimi
Layout: Lance Nolley
Animation: Harvey Toombs (brush paints ox, lion and worm, three types of food, Charlie's house and farm, "Careful" family at table, Charlie bows and hand pulls in kitchen, hog and chicken eating, cow and goat, Charlie chopping wood and his bone structure, skeleton of man, family working on farm)
Andy Engman ("Careless" family at table, beans on plate, pie-cuts of farm, children growing, animal products)
Vern Papineau (raw beans and corn)
Voice: Art Baker (narrator)
Assistant director: Rusty Jones
Working title: *Nutrition*

5013
ENVIRONMENTAL SANITATION
SANEAMIENTO DEL AMBIENTE
Copyright: © Walt Disney Productions, 3 April 1946 (MP2728)
Directors: Graham Heid, Earl Bench, Ben Sharpsteen
Layout: Tom Hayward, Philip Barber
Animation: Fred Jones (growing village, many people at well, coffins, water running in washtub, water running in sink, pan from city to outhouses, pools of stagnant water)
John Reed (hands dip water from well, people washing and bathing in river, tiny stream, clean street, garbage cans, storm drains, market exterior)
Hal King (crowded, dirty street, laundry)
Music: Paul J. Smith
Voice: Art Baker (narrator)

2735
THE AMAZON AWAKENS
Copyright: © Walt Disney Productions, 11 April 1944 (MP15379)
Library of Congress: FCA 1708, FCA 1709
Director: Bill Roberts
Camera (16 mm): Herbert E. Knapp
Story: Winston Hibler
Layout: Al Zinnen, Glen Scott
Animation: Ed Aardal (Acuna stoops over, picks up and sifts dirt)
Al Zinnen (Manaus airways)
Josh Meador (bud grafting diagram, world shipping lanes)
Backgrounds: Claude Coats, Warren Williams
Voice: Art Baker (narrator)
Assistant director: Harry Love

Franklin Thomas

APPENDIX B: ARY BARROSO DISCOGRAPHY

COMPILED BY DANIELLA THOMPSON

This discography lists contemporary recordings of the three Ary Barroso songs used in the Disney Good Neighbor films: "Aquarela do Brasil" (used in *Saludos Amigos*), "Os quindins de Yayá" and "Na baixa do sapateiro" (both used in *The Three Caballeros*). The index is adapted from materials compiled by Daniella Thompson for her Web site, daniellathompson.com. Grateful acknowledgment is hereby made to Ms. Thompson for permission to reproduce this material (and she, in turn, acknowledges the input of Paulo Cesar de Andrade and the Funarte database).

This is a highly selective discography, including only the records made in Brazil and in the United States (along with some radio broadcasts) in the years before and immediately after release of the films. It does not include more recent recordings, film sound tracks, or the numerous recordings of "Aquarela do Brasil" and "Na baixa do sapateiro" made in England in the 1940s. All this material and much more, encompassing a comprehensive survey of Barroso's career and those of other Brazilian musicians, can be found at Ms. Thompson's Web site, which is highly recommended. The present index deals only with recordings directly contemporary with the Disney Good Neighbor project and films.

"AQUARELA DO BRASIL"

* Indicates U.S. recordings, issued under the title "Brazil" and using the English lyrics by S. K. Russell (not heard in the film).

Francisco Alves with Radamés Gnattali and his Orchestra [premiere recording]
18 August 1939 (released October 1939)
Odeon 11768-A and B (mx. 6179–6180)

George Brass (accordion) and his Rhythm Players [as part of medley: "Cocktail Copacabana"]
14 July 1941 (released September 1941)
Odeon 12.033-A (mx. 6713)

Lee Broyde (organ) and Lazla Muller (piano)
25 July 1941 (released October 1941)
Victor 34816-A (mx. S-052274)

*Eddy Duchin and his Orchestra (vocal by Tony Leonard)
4 September 1941
Columbia 36537 (mx. CO31221)

*Xavier Cugat and his Waldorf-Astoria Orchestra, with La Chata and Chorus
December 1941 (released 1942)
Columbia 36651 (mx. CO32077)

*Fred Waring and his Pennsylvanians
6 May 1942 (released 1942)
Decca 18412 (mx. 70719)

Silvio Caldas with Orquestra RCA Victor
29 May 1942 (released August 1942)
Victor 34949-A (mx. S-052542)

*André Kostelanetz and Orchestra (vocal by Allan Jones)
31 May 1942
The Coca-Cola Hour (CBS radio broadcast)
Library of Congress LWO 5585 r20B1

George Brass with Rogério Guimarães and his Conjunto
27 August 1942 (released October 1942)
Odeon 12.212-B (mx. 7041)

*Jimmy Dorsey and his Orchestra
with Bob Eberly and Helen O'Connell
(released 1943)
Decca 18460/18808/25122 (mx. 71055)

*Kay Kyser and his Orchestra
with Harry Babbit, Julie Conway, Diane Pendleton, Jack Martin, and Max Williams
(released 1943)

Zaccarias and his Orchestra
18 October 1943 (released June 1944)
Victor 80.0177-A (mx. S-052863)

*The Dinning Sisters
with Jack Fascinato's Orchestra
10 December 1943
Capitol BD-7 (album: *Songs of the Dinning Sisters*) (mx. 136)
(Single disc: Capitol 938)

*Charles Wolcott and his Orchestra
Decca 23330-A (Decca album 360: *Saludos Amigos*) (mx. L3296A)

Ethel Smith with Bando Carioca
(formerly Bando da Lua)
(13 June 1944) Decca

*Andre Kostelanetz and his Orchestra
8 October 1944
The Coca-Cola Hour
(CBS radio broadcast)
Library of Congress tape no. RXA 9751 A2

Anjos do Inferno with Regional Pixinguinha-Benedito Lacerda
30 January 1946 (released November 1947)
RCA Victor 80.0539-A (mx. S-078710)

*Carmen Cavallaro (piano) and his Orchestra
19 November 1946
Decca 23847-B (mx. L4332)

*Desi Arnaz and his Orchestra
January 1947
RCA Victor

Quatro Ases e um Coringa
30 January 1947 (released March 1947)
Odeon 12.763-A (mx. 8179)

"OS QUINDINS DE YAYÁ"

Ciro Monteiro with Orchestra
4 December 1940 (released January 1941)
Victor 34703-B (mx. 52070)
reissued as Victor 80.0273-A (April 1945)

Simon Bountman and his Orchestra do Cassino Copacabana (vocal by Nuno Roland)
25 July 1941 (released October 1941)
Victor 34811-A (mx. S-052281)

Fernando Alvarez with Regional
20 September 1941 (released March 1942)
Victor 34885-A (mx. S-052363)
Decca 18134 [same recording reissued later in the U.S.?]

Charles Wolcott and his Orchestra
Decca 23342-B (Decca album 373: *The Three Caballeros*) (mx. L3298A)

"NA BAIXA DO SAPATEIRO"

* U.S. recordings, issued under the title "Baía" and using the English lyrics by Ray Gilbert.

Carmen Miranda with Orchestra Odeon
(conducted by Simon Bountman)
17 October 1938 (released November 1938)
Odeon 11667-B (mx. 5937)

Ary Barroso (piano), Laurindo de Almeida and Garoto (guitars)
26 June 1939 (released August 1939)
Odeon 11746-A (mx. 6126)

Silvio Caldas with Orquestra RCA Victor
29 May 1942 (released August 1942)
Victor 34949-B (mx. S-052543)

*Charles Wolcott and his Orchestra
Decca 23342-A (Decca album 373: *The Three Caballeros*) (mx. L3297A)

*Bing Crosby with Xavier Cugat and his Waldorf-Astoria Orchestra
11 February 1945
Decca L3736-A /Brunswick 0.3587-A (mx. L 3736A/L 3736-ATI)

*Andre Kostelanetz and his Orchestra
1 November 1945
Music Millions Love (CBS radio broadcast)
"From musical film *The Three Caballeros*"
Library of Congress tape no. RGA 4125, track 7

Anjos do Inferno with Regional Pixinguinha-Benedito Lacerda
30 January 1946 (released November 1947)
RCA Victor 80.0539-B (mx. S-078711)

Quatro Ases e um Coringa
31 May 1946 (released August 1946)
Odeon 12.714-B (mx. 8053)

APPENDIX C: COMICS

As indicated in the main text of the book, the Disney Good Neighbor films produced numerous promotional spinoffs, including comics. To be more specific, there were two Sunday newspaper comic pages, running consecutively from 1942 through 1945, and a *Three Caballeros* comic book, produced by agreement with the CIAA but issued by Dell (Western Publishing Company) under Disney's standard comic-book arrangement. This appendix offers details on each.

JOSÉ CARIOCA

(The title panel in each page actually reads "José (Joe) Carioca.")
11 October 1942–1 October 1944
Written by Hubie Karp
Penciled by Bob Grant and Paul Murry
Inked by Karl Karpe and Dick Moores
Most of the comic strips based on classic Disney characters modified the character's screen persona in some way to produce a somewhat different character, and the "José Carioca" Sunday page was no exception. The character who appears on the screen is smooth, debonair, unflappable; the comic character is not only a smooth talker but an outright con man. He has a taste for the good life and lives by his wits, finding ways to enjoy good meals, clothes, and so forth, while getting others to pay his way. He constantly makes up stories about his wealth and accomplishments, then finds himself in embarrassing predicaments and has to bluff his way out. None of the story material has any connection with *Saludos Amigos* or *The Three Caballeros*. During the two-year run of the page, Joe's adventures include an ocean cruise with a beautiful girl aboard her father's yacht, which he tries to represent as his own; a stint as manager of a performer he thinks is a U.S. opera star but who turns out actually to be a burlesque dancer; a duel with a rival who is a master swordsman; and, when he misrepresents himself as a big-game hunter, a trip up the Amazon in search of the "Slingshot Indians" who are rumored to have discovered a special strain of rubber that needs no refining. (The rubber turns out to be a crate of inner tubes dropped from a North American plane.) One of the characters in the strip (the owner of the yacht) is given the name Rocha Vaz, the name of one of the studio's real-life contacts in Brazil. In April 1944, months before the real-life opening of *The Three Caballeros*, a guest star appears in the strip: Panchito, who has been hired by a rich family because of his expertise with horses. Of course Joe pretends to be an expert horseman too, launching a rivalry marked by frequent, very un-Good Neighborly outbursts of temper. Panchito exits the strip in late August. The last installment has Joe, in a happy mood on a beautiful day, embracing all his friends, only to wind up in the hospital with all of them because the first one had measles.

PANCHITO

8 October 1944–7 October 1945
Written by Bill Walsh
Penciled by Paul Murry
Inked by Dick Moores
Following his preview appearance in the "José Carioca" strip, Panchito debuted in his own series the week after Joe's adventures ended. In this strip Panchito rides through Mexico on his horse, "Señor Martinez," who is drawn like the horse in *How to Ride a Horse*. Unlike the "Joe Carioca" stories, these are separate weekly gags, again unrelated to any of the story material in the Disney films. Without the con-man character devised for Joe Carioca or any such characteristics, Panchito comes across as more or less a straight man, and frequently the last panel finds the joke on him. One installment, for example, is an ironic twist on "The Pied Piper": the mayor of a town asks Panchito to stay *in* the town and sing, and his voice drives the rats away. Neither Donald Duck nor Joe Carioca appears in any of the "Panchito"

pages, and apart from Panchito and his horse, the only continuing character (who actually reappears only a few times) is Chuy, a short duck with a long bill. Some of the pages do include oblique references to Disney films: in the very first page (8 October 1944) Panchito is seen singing "Ay! Jalisco!," and in August 1945 he sings "I am the three caballeros" (a takeoff on Frank Crumit's "I am a gay caballero"). Another page has him dreaming about the days of knighthood (!), in which he saves a princess from a dragon; the dragon looks like the Reluctant Dragon from the Disney film of the same title, and Panchito wakes from his dream in disgrace because he kills the dragon and then discovers that the baby dragons are mourning their papa. This setting is a departure, however; most of the stories are built around a popular conception of Mexico—deserts, mountains, adobe villages (no cities), and bullfights.

THE THREE CABALLEROS

One-shot comic book

Dell Four Color #71, 1945

Penciled by Walt Kelly

48 pages

Unlike the Sunday comic pages, which bore no relation to the Disney films except for the characters of Joe and Panchito, this promotional comic book (see chapter 5) draws heavily on story material from the film *The Three Caballeros*. The story is a very free adaptation of *most* of the material in the film, with some significant omissions and some completely original material. In this version, Donald is awakened at the unearthly hour of 9:30 in the morning by a postman delivering a large package for his birthday. Donald is disappointed to find it's only a "rug" until Joe Carioca appears and explains to him that it's the flying sarape. Joe and Donald fly the sarape to Mexico and meet Panchito; then all fly to South America. Donald and Joe fall off, land near an island, and meet Pablo the penguin, who tells them his story. In a surprise reference to *Saludos Amigos* Joe identifies the local ostriches as rheas, demonstrates the bolas, and, like Goofy in the film, catches himself. They board the little train after an argument with the engineer/conductor, a turtle, but the train doesn't make it to Bahia. Instead Donald and Joe commandeer the engine, derail the train, fall out, and find Panchito waiting for them. The *Flying Gauchito* story is told to all three caballeros by the adult gaucho himself. After hearing his story they fly away and immediately see, not the burrito, but a *lobo volante*, a harpy. Escaping into the jungle, they land in the water and encounter the surinam toad (with cups on its back to carry its young), a crocodile, and a jaguar. Donald has had enough and, escaping from the jungle, they depart for Mexico. Donald is welcomed to Mexico and there's an explanation of Las Posadas and the piñata. Donald breaks his piñata—accidentally, with his head—and Panchito says he's a real caballero now, so Donald wants a horse. The horse bucks him high in the air, and the sarape catches him and carries him back home, ending the story. Missing is all the material about Aurora Miranda, Carmen Molina, and Dora Luz, along with anything else about Donald pursuing human women. The artwork by Walt Kelly, later legendary as creator of the "Pogo" comic strip, gives this comic book an added measure of historical interest. It occasionally veers into a completely different style, as in the drawings of the adult gaucho who tells the Flying Gauchito story, or the Las Posadas passage, which dispenses with panels and employs a free-form, full-page format to explain the tradition (and approximates the Mary Blair drawings very well).

NOTES

References to sources included in the bibliography are given below in short form; for complete references, please see the bibliography.

INTRODUCTION

11 *In the field of world policy* Franklin D. Roosevelt, first inaugural address, 4 March 1933.

11–12 *The essential qualities* Roosevelt, address to the Governing Board of the Pan-American Union, Montevideo, 12 April 1933.

13 *Walt Disney is not considered* Bob Carr, memo to Walt Disney, 5 June 1941 (part of a studio booklet labeled "South American Research," now in the collection of the Walt Disney Archives). Paulo Einhorn, a Rio de Janeiro representative for Pan American Airways, was cited as the source of this and other information on Brazil.

CHAPTER 1: AMBASSADORS OF GOODWILL

17 *been appointed by/Whitney also wanted* Memo, Roy Disney to Walt Disney, 31 October 1940 (Walt Disney Archives, hereinafter identified as "WDA").

18 *revealing their complete ignorance* This and other diplomatic gaffes were later enumerated by the Chilean writer Manuel Seoane in his article "If I Were Nelson Rockefeller," published in English in *Harper's Magazine*, February 1943, pp. 312–18.

19 *audiences were so infuriated* See "Killing Kindness," *Time*, 12 May 1941, p. 34.

19 *Those charged with their entertainment* "Latin America Tired of Parties" (UP), *San Diego Union*, 6 July 1941 (WDA).

19 *The next good-will mission* Oswaldo Aranha quoted in *Time*, 9 June 1941, p. 34.

19 *If I were Disney* Letter, Julien Bryan to Bob Carr, 6 June 1941 (WDA). Bryan's letter to Carr, written before he knew the full scope of the Disney program, was a response to Carr's request for advice.

19 STOP SUCH PICTURES/*Miami may be happy* J. R. Josephs, Report on Use of Walt Disney Films in South American Good Will Program, 6 August 1941 (National Archives and Records Administration, hereinafter identified as "NARA").

19 *The Walt Disney project has been approved* Weekly report, CIAA Motion Picture Section, Whitney to Don Francisco, 1 July 1941 (NARA).

19 *Whitney personally offered* State Department Memorandum of Conversation, 26 June 1941 (NARA).

19–20 LABOR IS OF COURSE Telegram, Kenneth Thomson to Whitney, 17 July 1941 (NARA).

20 COMMITTEE DESIROUS Telegram, John Rose to Mary Goodrich, 31 July 1941 (WDA).

20 *Believe me* Letter, George Strehlke to Rose, 15 November 1941 (WDA).

22 *rough sketches of a new character* Letter, Rose to H. W. Peterson, Pan American Airways, 18 July 1941 (WDA).

22 Note: *In the early 1930s* See Reich, *The Life of Nelson A. Rockefeller*, pp. 99, 136; and Okrent, *Great Fortune*, p. 251.

22 *Mr. Disney plans to ask* CIAA Project Authorization, "Walt Disney Field Survey and Short Subjects on the Other American Republics," 16 June 1941 (Rockefeller Archives Center, hereinafter identified as "RAC").

22 *After all, General Motors* Memo, Jack Cutting to Walt, 9 June 1941 (WDA).

22 *he was already denying* "El famoso dibujante Walt Disney llego ayer a Montevideo," *El Día*, 13 September 1941. Courtesy Bonnie Ferguson Brown.

23 *Ignorant and arrogant Hollywood* Memo, Bob Carr to Walt, 5 June 1941 (WDA).

24 *Despite local rivalries* Ibid.

24 *an article by Carleton Sprague Smith* Carleton Sprague Smith, "The Song Makers," *Survey Graphic*, March 1941, pp. 179–186.

24 *one of the funniest comics* Memo, Rose to Walt, 9 July 1941, subject: "Ni Sangre Ni Arena" (WDA). (*Ni sangre ni arena* was a parody of Twentieth Century–Fox's recent remake of *Blood and Sand*.)

24 Note: *internal CIAA document* Report of the CIAA Motion Picture Section, 6 August 1941, p. 25 (NARA).

25 *Campos had told him* Anonymous, undated report in a pretrip research notebook preserved at the Walt Disney Archives. This notebook, with specialized information on South American artists and other subjects, was apparently prepared especially for Walt; unlike the "South American Research" notebook, which was reproduced and distributed to the staff, this one appears to be unique and is labeled simply "Mr. Disney."

25 *one staff member compared* Anonymous, undated report, "Brazilian Composers—Villa Lobos," "Mr. Disney" booklet (WDA).

25 *had captured international attention* See "Music From Mountains," *Time*, 1 April 1940, p. 54. One of Villa-Lobos's "musical profiles" (composed after this article was published) was *Rudepôema*, introduced by, and intended as a musical portrait of, Villa-Lobos's friend Artur Rubinstein.

25 *His weird method* Memo, Carr to Walt, 5 June 1941, subject: Heitor Villa-Lobos. From the "Mr. Disney" booklet (WDA).

25 *a musical group/a comedy group* Undated page at the beginning of Bill Cottrell's research notebook (WDA). This document probably predates plans for the trip; it begins with an explanation of "a series of Short Subjects for South American release" but makes no mention of the trip.

26 *Walt met with the writers* Memo, Rose to Norm Ferguson, 16 July 1941, subject: South American Production Program (WDA). This memo served as the minutes of Walt's meeting with the story department on 11 July.

26 *An undated document* "Suggestions re South American Films from Ted Sears and Bill Cottrell," undated (WDA).

26 *would not be a boy* Ted Sears, "First Notes on The Little Gaucho Character," 11 June 1941 (WDA).

26 *submitted another outline* Ted Sears, "Gaucho Story," 18 June 1941 (WDA).

26 *featuring the beautiful birds* This description actually comes from the undated "Suggestions re South American Films from Ted Sears and Bill Cottrell" list (WDA).

26 *special Samba pop tune* Memo, Rose to Ferguson, 16 July 1941, subject: South American Production Program (WDA).

26 Note: *suggested on two other occasions* The page at the beginning of his research notebook, and the "Suggestions re South American Films" document.

26 *Thanks for sending in* Memo, Walt to Lee Blair, 25 July 1941. Courtesy John Canemaker. The story idea that elicited this response seems not to have been preserved.

27 *Roy tried repeatedly* Roy broached the subject to Whitney in a letter on 11 July and in a telegram on 1 August (both WDA). Easby's name appears in tentative plans for the trip as late as 5 August.

27 *Similar efforts to recruit* Letters to that end were written to H. W. Peterson of Pan Am by John Rose (18 July 1941) and Roy (22 July 1941, both WDA).

28 *Walt came around* Thomas to author, 26 April 1997.

29 *I went out to the parking lot* Lansburgh to author, 7 May 2000.

31 *Walt vetoed this idea* Memo, Janet Martin to Rose, 29 July 1941 (WDA).

31 *A new Eastman camera* Purchase of the Eastman camera is confirmed in a memo, Lansburgh to Walt, 8 August 1941, subject: Camera Equipment—S.A. (WDA). Walt's Bell & Howell camera is preserved today in the Walt Disney Archives.

31 *call for 16 mm film* "Government SOS For 16 mm. Films," *Hollywood Reporter*, 12 August 1941, p. 1 (Margaret Herrick Library, Academy of Motion Picture Arts and Sciences, hereinafter identified as "AMPAS").

31 *WOULD LIKE VERY MUCH* Telegram, Kenneth Macgowan to Walt, 5 August 1941 (WDA).

31 *MOST MEN CONTEMPLATING TRIP* Telegram, Roy to Alstock, 15 July 1941 (WDA).

31 *SUGGEST YOU TELEPHONE* Telegram, Gunther Lessing to Roy (who was in New York at the time), 25 June 1941 (WDA).

32 *This sounds like pure imagination* J. R. Josephs, Report on Use of Walt Disney Films in South American Good Will Program, 6 August 1941 (NARA).

32 *NO SIGNED CONTRACT* Telegram, Roy to Alstock (WDA). The copy of this telegram preserved in the Walt Disney Archives has no date, but is placed in the Disney legal file between items of 1 and 4 August 1941.

32 *HAVE JUST SEEN* Telegram, Rose to Roy, 8 August 1941 (WDA).

32 *The initial newsbreaks* Memo, Janet Martin to Walt, 9 August 1941 (WDA). The press release had been issued the previous day.

33 *Silveira recalled in later years* Silveira's recollections were reported by Mário de Moraes in *Recordações de Ary Barroso*, p. 83.

33 *They were met by a crowd* Jack Cutting, in a letter to Roy on 20 August 1941 (WDA), described the crowd as "in the neighborhood of 1,000 people." John Rose, in his formal posttrip report to the CIAA (WDA), put the figure at "approximately 2,000."

33 *Rio was an exciting* Cottrell to author, 24 September 1989.

33 *There just seemed to be* Thomas to author, 26 April 1997.

33 *I saw all the street vendors* Ibid.

33 *Brazilian* Fantasia*-type short* John Rose, "Report on the Walt Disney South American Field Survey," p. 6 (WDA). This 39-page report, submitted to Francis Alstock on 21 December 1941, was compiled after the fact as a master record of the group's activities.

34 *We are extremely pleased* Letter, Rose to Alstock, 1 September 1941 (WDA).

34 Note: *Jack Cutting had called it to Walt's attention* Memo, Cutting to Walt, 12 June 1941 (WDA).

34 *sings, dances, and talks Portuguese* Norm Ferguson's note in margin of an unidentified newspaper clipping sent to his family. Courtesy Bonnie Ferguson Brown.

34 *We have publicly announced* Letter, Rose to Alstock, 1 September 1941 (WDA).

36 *[The Glória] was a nice old hotel* Thomas to author, 26 April 1997.

36–37 *Walt Disney is far more successful* Report of John Hay Whitney, 29 August 1941 (forwarded by Alstock to Nelson Rockefeller 8 September 1941; RAC).

37 *We were supposed to have* Letter, Jack Cutting to Roy, 20 August 1941 (WDA).

38 *The only thing* Ibid.

39 *Fortunately* Fantasia *was an enormous success* Whitney report, 29 August 1941 (RAC).

40 *which we are told* Letter, Rose to Leo Samuels, 1 September 1941 (WDA).

40 *I think they were like studio musicians* Thomas to author, 26 April 1997.

40 *Spent about five hours* Letter, Chuck Wolcott to Harriett Wolcott, 6 September 1941. Courtesy Sheila Wolcott Banani.

41 *These efforts were appreciated* "Talent and Technical Facilities" research notebook, ca. 25 November 1941, p. 1 (WDA). This and other research notebooks, compiled after the trip, were unsigned but were probably written by Rose.

42 *to concentrate on Argentine material* Telegram, Rose to Mary Goodrich (Disney studio), 31 July 1941 (WDA).

42 *a stinging five-column assault* This was reported by Vincent de Pascal, the Buenos Aires stringer for *Hollywood Reporter*. "Latin Nazis Lie in Wait for Walt Disney Plans," *Hollywood Reporter*, 26 August 1941, p. 13 (AMPAS).

43 *the largest crowd* This assessment was conveyed to John Rose by Sylvester "Spec" Roll, the general manager of Pan Air's office in Buenos Aires. Rose, daily activity reports (Argentina), p. 2 (WDA).

43 *Welcome, then, greatest pictorial genius* Undated transcript, Ramón Columba welcoming speech (WDA).

43 *swarmed onto the airfield* This story was related to John Canemaker by Marc Davis (who was, of course, not present at the time). See Canemaker, *Before the Animation Begins*, p. 72.

43 *the first good food* Janet Martin, journal, 8 September 1941 (WDA).

43 *suggested the Continental Hotel* Letter, Smith to Rose, 3 September 1941 (WDA).

44 *The frequency of Don Ramón's visits* Doug Clark, "Summary of Local Reactions to Walt Disney's Visit to Argentina" (WDA). Clark's undated notes were placed in the studio's legal file between items of 28 and 29 August 1941, but were clearly written about a month after that date, around the time of El Grupo's departure from Buenos Aires.

44 *You never saw such a mob* Janet Martin, journal, 9 September 1941 (WDA).

45 *When we arrived* Janet Martin, journal, 13 September 1941 (WDA).

46 *The whole gang's there* Letter, Ted Sears to Violet Sears, 16 September 1941. Courtesy Cindy Garcia.

46 *And it's obvious* Janet Martin, journal, 15 September 1941 (WDA).

46 *When this big thing arrived* Thomas to author, 26 April 1997.

47 *The Brazilian theme* Ryman, "Recollections of a Friendship" (1968). Courtesy Paul Anderson.

48 *The yards are immense* Lansburgh, journal, 10 September 1941 (WDA).

48 *He had the dark eyebrows* Ryman to Katherine and Richard Greene, spring 1988. Courtesy Katherine and Richard Greene.

49 *I remember one time* Lansburgh to author, 7 May 2000.

49 *The newspapers devoted columns* Vincent de Pascal, "Walt Disney Proves Real U.S. Good-Will Ambassador," *Hollywood Reporter*, 25 September 1941, p. 5 (AMPAS).

49 *urged a boycott* "The Artists and Workers of Walt Disney Ask the Argentines Not to Patronize His Films" (English translation), *La Hora*, 9 September 1941 (WDA). The source of this translation is unknown; Janet Martin provided it to Walt in late October after returning to California.

49 *Curiously enough* Vincent de Pascal, "Disney Steals Latin Heart with Good-Will Gestures," *Hollywood Reporter*, 6 October 1941, p. 12 (AMPAS).

50 *Walt was introduced* This diplomatic feat took place on Monday, 15 September. See "Walt Disney's Busy Day," *Buenos Aires Herald*, 16 September 1941. Courtesy Bonnie Ferguson Brown.

51 *So we finally decided* Thomas to Peri, 24 November 2002. Courtesy Don Peri.

51 *Walt took it very well* Letter, Ferguson to Roy, 16 September 1941 (WDA).

51 Note: *I was very sorry* Letter, Sears to Roy, 19 September 1941 (WDA).

51 *She'd always been following* Thomas to author, 18 September 1996. See John Canemaker, *The Art and Flair of Mary Blair*, pp. 12–19.

52 *the artists tentatively suggested* Rose, undated schedule for 17–21 September 1941 (WDA). (Numerous schedules like this, reflecting the evolving plan for upcoming activities, were written and discarded during the tour as plans continued to change by the day, sometimes by the hour.)

53 *As you know* Memo, Lansburgh to Walt, 8 May 1941 (WDA).

54 *exchanged tales over cocktails* Mary Blair, journal, 3 October 1941. Courtesy John Canemaker.

58 *a tourist's delight* This and subsequent quotes, Frank Thomas to author, 18 September 1996.

60 *The manner in which* Letter, Walt to Sara Short and Diana Bohm, 24 September 1941 (WDA).

60 *the two largest* Rose, "Report on the Walt Disney South American Field Survey," p. 25 (WDA).

60 Note: *He walked on his hands* Roig to Thomas, 10 April 2006. Translation by Gustavo Kletzl. Courtesy Ted Thomas.

61 *And you Americans* Leonard Lyons, "The Lyons Den," *New York Post* (undated clipping in WDA).

61 *On that flight/This plane that we saw* Cottrell to author, 24 September 1989. See "Snowy Death in Chilean Andes," *Life*, 8 December 1941, pp. 46–48.

62–63 *The reason I'm in on it* Letter, Ted Sears to Violet Sears, 30 September 1941. Courtesy Cindy Garcia.

63 *offering his services* Letter, Robert Chalumeau to Walt, 3 October 1941 (WDA).

64 *the trials and tribulations* Rose, "Report on the Walt Disney South American Field Survey," p. 29 (WDA).

64 *They are just giving* Invitation, Carlos Trupp and Jaime Escudero to Walt, undated but circa 1 October 1941 (WDA).

64 *Walt Disney has aroused* CIAA Latin American newsletter, 10 October 1941 (Bulletin/Reports section), p. 3 (RAC).

65 *ELEVEN TIRED DISNEYITES* Telegram, Rose to Walt Disney Productions (New York), 5 October 1941 (WDA).

65 *We're on the homeward lap* This excerpt from Walt's "memorandum book" was quoted in "Disney Picture No Sedentary Job These Days," *New York Herald-Tribune*, 14 February 1943, section 6, p. 3 (as part of the domestic publicity for *Saludos Amigos*).

66 *You should enjoy your stopover* Letter, Janet to Rose, 6 October 1941 (WDA).

67 *So we all went on this cruise* Cottrell to author, 24 September 1989.

67 *Captain Parker was talking* Ibid.

68 *THIS PERMISSION NEVER GRANTED* Telegram, Gulbransen to Rose, 14 October 1941 (WDA).

68 *And they said to us* Cottrell to author, 24 September 1989.

68 *the cleanest subways* "Disney Ends His Tour of South America," *New York Times*, 21 October 1941, 28:3.

68 *I'd been warned* Eileen Creelman, "Walt Disney, Just Back From South America, Talks of His New 'Dumbo,'" *New York Sun*, 21 October 1941.

69 *After all, friendship* Thomas M. Pryor, "Film News and Comment," *New York Times*, 26 October 1941, IX:4:1.

69 *While Walt had enhanced* Doug Clark, "Summary of Local Reactions to Walt Disney's Visit to Argentina," undated (WDA).

69 *Hollywood owes Disney the finest bunch of orchids* Vincent de Pascal, "Disney Steals Latin Heart with Good-Will Gestures," *Hollywood Reporter*, 6 October 1941, p. 12 (AMPAS).

CHAPTER 2: SALUDOS AMIGOS

73 *The frank truth of the matter* Memo, Rose to Leo Samuels, 25 November 1941, subject: South American Survey (WDA).

73 *The music to be especially composed* This document, part of an immediate posttrip list of story ideas, is undated and unsigned but appears to have been written by Bill Cottrell (WDA).

74 *Mary Blair and Jack Miller were working* Memo, Ferguson to Walt, 31 October 1941, subject: Report on Unit (WDA).

75 *In parts of Bolivia* Walt, "Getting Hep On Latins," *Variety*, 7 January 1942, p. 7 (AMPAS).

75–76 *Mary Blair . . . had that nice watercolor painting* Brightman to Gray, 14 February 1977. Courtesy Michael Barrier.

76 *I didn't have the pipes* Wolcott to David Tietyen, 26 September 1978 (WDA).

76 *What we need* Walt in story meeting, "Walt Disney Sees South America," 19 February 1942 (WDA).

78 *It just fit* Grant to author, 18 September 1989.

80 *at Walt's specific request* "Also, Walt again mentioned utilizing Tytla on P.T.O.2.L. as soon as possible." Memo, Hal Adelquist to Norm Ferguson, 2 December 1941 (WDA).

81 *I have liked your other characters* Letter, Harriet Van Tobel, Cranston, Rhode Island, to Walt, 4 April 1943 (WDA).

81 *There has been some criticism* "Ray," *Saludos Amigos* review, *Variety*, 9 December 1942, p. 8 (AMPAS).

81 *She was born and raised* Letter to Walt, 1 April 1943 (WDA). The letter was officially a report from Jack Cutting and Bill Cottrell, but was actually written by Cottrell.

83 *I have also found out* Memo, Ferguson to Walt, 31 October 1941, subject: Report on Unit (WDA).

83 *somewhat similar/He also acknowledged* Sears, gaucho story notes, 18 June 1941 (WDA).

84 *He was a cocky little guy* Kinney to author, 14 September 1989.

85 *The horse sat down* Thomas to author, 21 September 1997.

85 *Our relationship grew* Ryman, "Recollections of a Friendship" (1968). Courtesy Paul Anderson.

85 *So we used his backgrounds* Kinney to Barrier, 28 November 1973. Courtesy Michael Barrier.

89 *Pan-American Symphony* Sears and Cottrell, "Suggestions re South American Films," undated but preceding the South American trip (WDA).

89–90 *making it a complete* Memo, Ferguson to Walt, 31 October 1941, subject: Report on Unit (WDA).

90 *Papagaio is quite a comic* Sears, undated story notes (WDA).

90 *It's [Walt's] idea* "Virginia Wright, Drama Editor," *Los Angeles News*, 17 December 1941, p. 25.

91 *requesting permission/JOE CARIOCA ONLY TENTATIVE NAME* Memo, Samuels to Rose, 26 December 1941; telegram, Rose to Samuels, 30 December 1941 (both WDA).

92 *He's from New York* Marc Davis, "Staging Humor and Comedy" panel discussion, Chouinard School of Art animation class, 27 May 1960. Courtesy Michael Barrier.

92 *He worked me over* Jackson to Barrier, 5 November 1976. Courtesy Michael Barrier.

93 *They [Brazilians] can get rhythm* Walt in *Aquarela do Brasil* story meeting, 15 January 1942 (WDA).

94 *Before he had done the work* Memo, Cutting to O. B. Johnston, 10 June 1942 (WDA).

96 *The notion was to do a feature* Memo, Selznick to Whitney, 3 February 1942, subject: Walt Disney—Pan-American Follies (NARA).

96 *Couldn't the shorts* Memo, Selznick to Whitney, 17 February 1942, subject: Pan-American Follies (NARA).

97 *They found out* Thomas to author, 26 April 1997.

97 Note: *HOPKINS ARRANGING* Telegram, Walt to Ferguson, 24 May 1942 (WDA).

99 *In Shields you haven't got* Walt in *Saludos* sweatbox session, 17 June 1942 (WDA).

99 *Hollywood correspondent* "Ray," *Saludos* review, *Variety*, 9 December 1942, p. 8 (AMPAS).

99 *This is a much better order* Walt in *Saludos* sweatbox session, 20 May 1942 (WDA).

99 Note: *asked to retake the last scene* Memo, Tommy Alcorn to Production Camera, 5 June 1942 (Walt Disney Animation Research Library, hereinafter identified as "ARL").

100 Hollywood Reporter *announced* "Well! Carmen Miranda Is Tech Advisor To Disney," *Hollywood Reporter*, 15 July 1942, p. 2 (AMPAS).

100 *Thank you ever so much* Letter, Rockefeller to Walt, 30 July 1942 (RAC).

100 *including a private showing* "Latin Consuls See New Disney Reels," *Hollywood Reporter*, 14 December 1942, p. 7 (AMPAS).

100 *rewrote their original contract* Rockefeller's first amendment to contract NDCar-110 was dated 19 April 1943, but the contract was further revised on several occasions.

100 *I think up to now* Walt on *The Coca-Cola Hour*, WABC-CBS, 27 December 1942.

100 *I tried to find a way* Letter, Molina Campos to Reed, 9 July 1942, quoted in letter from Reed to Cordell Hull, U.S. secretary of state, 27 July 1942 (NARA).

100 Note: *playing a guitar/real he-men* Letter, Klock to Hull, 28 July 1942 (NARA).

101 *After witnessing yesterday* Letter, Molina Campos to Walt, 24 July 1942 (WDA). Translation by Dan MacManus.

101 *That was stopped by audiences* Kyle Crichton, "Riot from Rio," *Collier's*, 19 December 1942, p. 91.

101 *SALUDOS OPENED RIO* Telegram, Reisman to Alstock, 26 August 1942 (NARA).

102–103 *Audiences here [in Argentina]* "Ray," *Saludos* review, *Variety*, 9 December 1942, p. 8 (AMPAS).

103 *Walt Disney's* Saludos *looks* Ibid.

103 *The sequences, particularly those dealing with Argentina* Memo, Josephs to Coordination Committee, 8 October 1942, subject: Argentine opening of Walt Disney's *Saludos* (NARA).

103 *Goofy is not a gaucho* *Estampa*, translated and quoted in Worth Cheney, "Disney's Ambassador Duck," *The Pan American*, January 1943, p. 17.

103 *I have seen Walter Disney's last picture* Excerpt from anonymous confidential report to CIAA, 8 June 1943 (NARA).

103 *Apparently we do not exist* Ibid.

104 *Nelson Rockefeller had prevailed* Telegram, Rockefeller to Gus Eyssell, manager of Radio City Music Hall, 27 August 1942 (NARA).

104 *I deplore the booking* Letter, Brooks to Walt, 6 January 1943 (WDA).

104 *at once a potent piece* Barnes, *Saludos Amigos* review, *New York Sun*, 13 February 1943, p. 8. Courtesy Bonnie Ferguson Brown.

104 *A delightful surprise* Hartung, *Saludos Amigos* review, *The Commonweal*, 19 February 1943, p. 445.

104 *it will do more* *Saludos Amigos* review, *Hollywood Reporter*, 15 December 1942, p. 3 (AMPAS).

104 *Now you'll like propaganda* Corby, *Saludos Amigos* review, *Brooklyn Eagle*, 13 February 1943, p. 14. Courtesy Bonnie Ferguson Brown.

105 *One page* "José Carioca," *Good Housekeeping*, January 1943, p. 121.

105 *irresistible entertainment* *Cinema* (London), 5 November 1943.

105 *The sum total* *Daily Film Renter* (London), 8 November 1943.

105 Note: *the Russian actor Leonid Kinskey* See "Disney Doing Three Pictures In Russian," *Hollywood Reporter*, 1 December 1943, p. 1 (AMPAS).

CHAPTER 3: SELECTED SHORT SUBJECTS

108 *We're going to have to go* Walt in "The Laughing Gaucho" story meeting, 16 January 1942 (WDA).

108 *A guy madder than hell* Ibid.

108 *He would not be a boy* Sears, "First Notes on The Little Gaucho Character," 11 June 1941 (WDA).

109 *Catch and Go* "Survey By-Products" notebook, ca. 16 December 1941 (WDA).

109 *tie in with the Diamond Match Company* Memo, Ferguson to Walt, 14 November 1941, subject: South American Subjects (WDA).

109 Note: *was paid a flat sum* Memo, Cutting to Jack Lavin, 4 August 1944, subject: Brazilian Music (WDA).

111 *We need history* Letter, Ferguson to Rocha Vaz, 26 July 1944 (WDA).

111 *The only thing we remember* Letter, Rocha Vaz to Ferguson, 12 October 1944 (WDA).

112 The Near-Sighted Oven Bird *would take the place* Memo, Dick Pfahler to Runar Ohls, 27 December 1943 (WDA).

112 The Flying Gauchito *was reinstated* Memo, Pfahler and Red Meyer to Ohls, 10 January 1944 (WDA).

114 *based on Street Peddler's song* Memo, Norm Ferguson to Walt, 10 April 1942, subject: South American Prod. (WDA).

114 *might have just the opposite/if we could announce* Letter, Bottome to Rockefeller, 24 August 1942 (Motion Picture Society for the Americas [hereinafter identified as "MPSA"] collection, AMPAS).

114 *The story told of the efforts* Synopsis, "The Blue Orchid," by Lucila Palacios, music by María Luisa Escobar (MPSA collection, AMPAS). Along with the synopsis, Bottome enclosed two libretti and recordings of some of the music.

114 *I have read the synopsis* Letter, Walt to Richard Rogan, CIAA, 15 September 1942 (MPSA collection, AMPAS).

118 *burlesque on society/we do not intend* Sears, undated story notes. Courtesy John Canemaker.

120 *proposed a setting* Memo, Norm Ferguson to Walt, 23 December 1941 (WDA).

121 *Exciting, isn't it?* "Pablo Pelicano" script, p.18 (WDA). Although undated and unsigned, this script was probably prepared by Bill Cottrell; it appears to have been typed on his typewriter.

121 *It is not absolutely necessary* Memo, Production Management (H.T.) to "Those Listed" (list of seven names), 17 March 1943 (WDA).

121 *it had been discarded* Memo, Ferguson to Walt, 16 February 1943, subject: Condition of Latin American Material (WDA).

122 Note: *Two Production Management memos* 9 November 1942 and 5 February 1943 (both WDA).

122 Note: *Barks's own records of his story work* Published by Barrier in *Funnyworld* 21 (Fall 1979), pp. 12–13, and in *Carl Barks and the Art of the Comic Book* [New York: Mark Lilien, 1981], p. 216.

CHAPTER 4: FILMS FOR THE AMERICAS

125 *taken by stars/All footage* "Government SOS for 16mm. Films," *Hollywood Reporter*, 12 August 1941, p. 1 (AMPAS).

125 *John Rose had received a telegram* Telegram, Leo Samuels (of Disney's New York office) to Rose, 8 October 1941 (WDA).

125 *What we have in mind* Letter, Rose to Macgowan, 15 November 1941 (NARA).

125–126 *I had never shot* Lansburgh to author, 7 May 2000.

126 *Such scenes as Walt* Letter, Rose to Raymond A. Disney, 10 December 1941 (WDA). Ray Disney, Walt and Roy's brother, was an insurance agent and had handled the insurance for the South American tour.

126 *Have the studio in Rio* Walt in "Walt Sees South America" story meeting, 19 February 1942 (WDA).

128 *Maybe one of the guys* Ibid.

128 *tried to explain to an Argentine innkeeper* *Saludos Amigos* review, *Time*, 25 January 1943, p. 86.

128 *The trouble is we selected stuff* Walt in "Walt Disney Sees South America" sweatbox session, 16 July 1942 (WDA).

130 Note: *Golden expressed his ambitions* Letters, Golden to Leighter, 3 November and 10 November 1942 (MPSA collection, AMPAS).

130 Note: *without first securing written permission* Letter, Cutting to Carroll Dunning, 27 November 1942 (WDA).

130 *Walt Disney has volunteered* "Disney Makes Special Material For Inter-American Committee," *Hollywood Reporter*, 12 January 1942, pp. 1–2 (AMPAS).

132 *The only reason/If you make it look* Walt in "Malaria & Mosquito" story meeting, 14 May 1942. A partial transcript of this conference was reprinted in "Walt Disney: Great Teacher," *Fortune*, August 1942. These quotes appeared on pp. 91–92.

133 *much more subtlety* Johnston to Andreas Deja, 15 September 1987, quoted by John Canemaker in *Walt Disney's Nine Old Men and the Art of Animation*, p. 143.

134 *Our records show/This might indicate* Letter, Pierce to Cutting, 15 May 1944 (NARA).

134 *Malaria, it seems* Letter, Walt to Guy Cox, 24 June 1943 (NARA).

135 *This footage is nearly* Letter, Roy to Jock Whitney, 1 May 1942 (WDA).

135 *animation's Michelangelo* Canemaker's essay "Vlad Tytla: Animation's Michelangelo" first appeared in *Cinefantastique* (Fall 1976), was abridged and anthologized in Gerald and Danny Peary, eds., *The American Animated Cartoon* (New York: Dutton, 1980), then was expanded and updated (under a different title) in *Animation Journal*, vol. 3, no. 1 (Fall 1994).

136 *it is a sound exposition* Charles Wilson in conference with Bill Cottrell and Jack Cutting, 12 July 1943 (WDA).

138 *In Salvador we went* Letter to Walt, 23 March 1943 (WDA). This letter was nominally from both Cottrell and Cutting but was written by Cutting.

139 *written authority to lead the seminar* Letter, Rockefeller to Walt, 19 May 1943 (RAC).

139 *attracted international attention* See "Literatizer," *Time*, 28 June 1943, pp. 79–80.

140 Note: *the Hyperion animation building . . . had been built in an L shape* See David R. Smith, "Disney Before Burbank," *Funnyworld* 20 (Summer 1979), pp. 32–38.

141 *He said that in Latin America* Dr. Murgeytio, quoted in Proceedings of the Inter-American Seminar on Visual Education, p. 255 (WDA).

141 *For the Latin mind* Dr. Martínez Mont, ibid., p. 22.

141 *In the same picture* Karl Van Leuven quoted in Proceedings of the Hollywood Writers' Mobilization/University of California Writers' Congress, October 1943, p. 121. Courtesy Michael Barrier.

141 *The argument was clinched* Proceedings of the Inter-American Seminar on Visual Education, p. 260 (WDA).

141–142 *The group was especially interested* Ibid., p. 264.

142 *You want to teach them* This comment was made by Doris LeRoy at a preseminar conference with Cottrell, Cutting, and Enrique de Lozada, 4 May 1943 (WDA).

142 *numerous books, including* Charles Morrow Wilson, *Ambassadors in White: The Story of American Tropical Medicine* (New York: Holt, 1942).

143 *A simple analogy* Robert Spencer Carr, "Ideas for More Walt Disney Films for South American Release" (February 1942), p. 23 (WDA).

143 *Advised at every step* "Walt Disney: Great Teacher," *Fortune*, August 1942, p. 154.

143 *was to compare the body* Ibid., p. 152.

145 *would go way over the heads* Wilson in conference with Bill Cottrell and Jack Cutting, 12 July 1943 (WDA).

145 *has not been approved* Letter, Pierce to Cutting, 15 May 1944 (NARA).

145 *Tuberculosis is the Number One* Wilson in conference with Cottrell and Cutting, 12 July 1943 (WDA).

145 *changing the word* tubercular Letter, Wilson to Walt Disney Productions, 25 August 1943 (WDA).

146 *like a comic strip* Walt in "Infant Care and Feeding" story meeting, 9 May 1944 (WDA).

146 *Walt stressed his feeling* Notes from *Tuberculosis* story meeting, 11 January 1944 (WDA).

147 *a rather theoretical point* Letter, Wilson to Walt Disney Productions, 25 August 1943 (WDA).

148 *films on the construction of toilets* Dr. Sutter, 27 May 1943, quoted in Proceedings of the Inter-American Seminar on Visual Education, p. 23 (WDA).

149 *I have never seen* Major Christopherson in "Infant Care and Feeding" story meeting, 5 April 1944 (WDA).

149 *I don't see any reason* Walt in "Infant Care and Feeding" story meeting, 9 May 1944 (WDA).

149 *One turning page/The idea of these things* Algar and Walt in "Infant Care and Feeding" story meeting, 9 May 1944 (WDA).

150 Note: *The waiver was granted* Memo, Jim Algar to Erwin Verity (unit manager), 25 October 1944, subject: Music—#2761 (WDA).

150 *albino baby* The transcript of the meeting in which Walt made this comment has apparently not been preserved, but references appear in several later documents, e.g.: "You will recall that upon viewing the 35 mm composite copy print on this subject, Walt criticized the 'albino baby.' Accordingly, the last scenes in the picture were re-shot to make this correction." (Memo, Erwin Verity to Fred Maguire, 13 July 1945, subject: Production #2761 "Infant Care," WDA.)

150 *It may be a tough job* Robert Spencer Carr, "Ideas for More Walt Disney Films for South American Release," February 1942, p. 24 (WDA).

150 *Take the hookworm* Walt quoted in "Walt Disney: Great Teacher," *Fortune*, August 1942, p. 156.

151 *It would be worth developing* Madison in Literacy Project story meeting, 18 November 1943 (WDA).

152 *This should be much easier* Carr, "Ideas for More Walt Disney Films for South American Release," February 1942, p. 24 (WDA).

152 Note: *Captain Madison . . . objected* Comments attached to memo, Madison to Fran Alstock, 2 August 1943, subject: Walt Disney Story Boards on THE FLY and EVER-NORMAL GRANARY (NARA).

152 *such changes would* Letter, Madison to George C. Dunham, attn. Dr. Clark Yeager, Dr. Janet Mackie, and Phillip Riley, 16 August 1944 (WDA).

152 *I have looked at the story boards* Letter, Dr. Janet Mackie, Medical Section, to Madison, 22 August 1944 (WDA). By this time Madison had returned to Mexico, and this letter was addressed to him in care of the American embassy in Mexico City.

153 Note: *Jack Cutting and Bill Cottrell . . . had suggested a film* Memo, Cutting and Cottrell to Walt, 15 February 1943, subject: Visual Education Program (WDA).

154 *a lot of cels have been painted* Memo, Geronimi to Sharpsteen, 27 September 1945, subject: NUTRITION—Prod. 5011—Seq. 1 (WDA).

154 *Sharpsteen . . . wrote back to the CIAA* Letter, Sharpsteen to Charles Zippermann, 6 December 1945 (WDA).

154 *responded with a list* Letter, Zippermann to Sharpsteen, 20 December 1945 (WDA).

155 *We had in mind* Letter, Dr. Mackie to Madison, 14 October 1944 (WDA).

155 *I took environmental sanitation* MacManus to Gray, 22 March 1977. Courtesy Michael Barrier.

155 *The pump handle* Excerpts from "'Environmental Sanitation' Changes," submitted to Sharpsteen by Madison, 22 March 1945 (WDA).

157 *produced in black and white* Letter, Cutting to Alstock, 16 June 1943 (WDA).

157 *For example the duck* Cutting in discussion on educational films with Bill Cottrell and Bob Carr, 10 May 1943 (WDA).

157 *was very enthusiastic* Letter, Cutting to de Lozada, 30 June 1943 (WDA).

157–158 *Furthermore, we believed* Memo, Cutting to Walt, 3 August 1943, subject: Educational Program (WDA).

158 *Eliminating color and personality animation* Memo, de Lozada, 2 August 1943 (WDA). This long memo, detailing de Lozada's criticisms, was intended for Nelson Rockefeller but was never sent to him. Cutting did read it, however, and forwarded it to Walt.

158 *I don't believe the solution* Ibid.

158 *We plan to study* Memo, de Lozada, Tavares de Sa, LeRoy, Cutting and Cottrell, 15 August 1943, (WDA). This long memo took the place of de Lozada's earlier missive and was addressed simultaneously to Walt, Roy, and Francis Alstock.

158–159 *The recent discussions* Memo, Cutting to Walt, 19 August 1943 (WDA).

159 *this system is not practical* Jack Cutting diary, 20 September 1943 (NARA).

160 *Unfortunately, Wiese displayed* Ibid.

161 *Mr. Alstock was sore as hell* Letter, Verity to Jacques Roberts (at the Disney studio), 27 September 1943 (WDA).

161 *We have learned* Letter, Verity to Roberts, 5 October 1943 (WDA).

162 *He is of Indian extraction* Cutting, memo on personnel, ca. 25 September 1943 (NARA).

162 *Keep stressing the intellect* Walt in Literacy Project story meeting, 18 November 1943 (WDA).

163 *Let us not be forever Yankees* Memo, Cutting to Walt, ca. 1 October 1943 (NARA).

163 *It looks as if these people* Verity, "Miscellaneous comments" in weekly report (*La história de José*), 18 February 1944 (WDA).

166 *What a germ is* Carr, "Ideas for More Walt Disney Films for South American Release," February 1942, p. 23 (WDA).

168 *These people know man and nature* Walt in Literacy Project story meeting, 18 November 1943 (WDA).

169 Note: *a letter written to Wallace Harrison* Letter, Rothschild to Harrison, 23 July 1945 (NARA).

170 *a later editorial by a Mexican journalist* "Even Mr. Disney, with respect to the taste of the Mexicans, was opposed to this idea. . . ." María Elena Sodi de Pallares, "Walt Disney's Good Will Abused," *El Universal*, date unknown (RAC, CIAA translation).

171 *I am very happy* Memo, Madison to George C. Dunham (assistant Coordinator), 16 September 1944 (NARA).

172 *She began to anticipate/You know, I just love* Subjective Report on Health and Literacy Film Testing Trip, 16 December 1944, p. 6 (RAC).

172 *Let's make it clear* Carlos Denegri, "Diary of a Newspaper Reporter," *Ultimas noticias*, 13 September 1944 (NARA; translation by Salvador Mendoza, who forwarded the clipping to Roy Disney).

172 *The lessons were prepared* Eulalia Guzmán, "La voz del agora," *Ultimas noticias*, 15 September 1944 (RAC; CIAA translation).

172 *José is a healthy young man* Guzmán, *Excelsior*, 6 October 1944 (RAC; CIAA translation). She had expressed similar sentiments to Walt in a letter, 10 August 1944 (WDA).

172 *came to regret her smear campaign* "Since then she has privately said that she regretted sincerely the whole incident, that she knows now she should not have . . . responded publicly to the charges made." Letter, Clarence de Lima (Departamento de Turismo) to Jack Cutting, 29 September 1944 (WDA).

172–173 *It is true that we cannot produce* María Elena Sodi de Pallares, "Walt Disney's Good Will Abused," *El Universal*, date unknown (RAC; CIAA translation).

173 *They do not question* Letter, Cerwin to Rockefeller, 16 October 1944 (RAC).

173 *It is therefore recommended* Airgram, Burley, U.S. embassy in Mexico City, to secretary of state, 2 November 1944 (RAC).

173–174 *far below the Disney standard* In fairness, ERPI's earliest educational films had been linked to the company's major role in the talking-picture revolution of the 1920s. For a profile of these activities, *see* Robert Finehout, "Pioneering the Talkies," *American Cinematographer*, vol. 69 no. 1 (January 1988), pp. 36–40.

174 more *effective than the teachers* MacManus to Milt Gray, 22 March 1977. Courtesy Michael Barrier.

174 *It is obvious* Memo, Holland to board of directors, Inter-American Educational Foundation, 18 December 1945, subject: Motion Picture and Visual Education Materials, B-EF-62 Change Order No. 2 (NARA).

174 *an ever-normal granary film simply wasn't needed* Memo, Ryland Madison to Francis Alstock, 2 August 1943, subject: Walt Disney Story Boards on THE FLY and EVER-NORMAL GRANARY (NARA).

175 *We're going to call this one* Walt quoted in "Walt Disney: Great Teacher," *Fortune*, August 1942, p. 156.

175 *shelved and never revived* Memo, Roy to Walt, 10 September 1943, subject: Coordinator General (WDA). This memo included a list of subjects that were to be shelved, according to Roy's telephone conversation with Francis Alstock the same day.

175 *Don't overlook the Amazon* Walt in *Aquarela do Brasil* story meeting, 13 November 1941 (WDA).

175 The Amazon Awakens *started production* The title change had been made official on 18 March 1942, but some interoffice correspondence continued to refer to the film as "Amazon Basin" as late as November.

176 *spent afternoon and evening* Letter, Knapp to Sharpsteen, 18 May 1943 (WDA).

177 *would now be produced in* four *reels* Letter, Walt to Gerald Smith (CIAA), 19 November 1943 (WDA).

178 *His point is well taken* Verity, "Miscellaneous Comments" in the weekly report, 24 March 1944 (WDA).

178 *the best documentary film I've ever seen* Alstock quoted by Verity in "Miscellaneous Comments," weekly report, 18 April 1944 (WDA).

178–179 *All who reviewed the picture* Letter, Pierce to Sharpsteen, 9 May 1944 (WDA).

179 *As a matter of fact* Letter, Pierce to C.F. Woit, 31 October 1944 (WDA).

179 *singled out for praise* "Engel, Toland, Disney Win CIAA Praise for Latin Pix," *Daily Variety*, 13 February 1945, p. 3 (AMPAS).

180 *the studio had received 10,000 feet* Letter, Roy to Col. Harold B. Gotaas, director, Institute of Inter-American Affairs, 5 November 1945 (NARA).

180 *recommending . . . that the proposed list . . . be reduced* Memo, Madison to Gotaas, 19 November 1945 (NARA).

180 *farming out production* Letter, Iverson to Madison, 20 December 1945 (NARA).

CHAPTER 5: THE THREE CABALLEROS

183 *completed research of the music* "Disney Plans Film In Color On Mexico," *Hollywood Reporter*, 5 August 1942, p. 5 (AMPAS).

184 *We impressed Hastings with the fact* Memo, Ferguson to Walt, 15 October 1942, subject: Mexican Trip (WDA).

185 *Disney has a new creation* *Población*, February 1943 (NARA; CIAA translation).

185 *Six months from now* Curtis Vinson, "Senor Gallito By Disney Due In Six Months," *Dallas Morning News*, 27 December 1942, Art and Music section, p. 1.

185 *Mexicans in every walk of life* "Disney Finds U.S.–Mexico Bond Strong," *Los Angeles Examiner*, 24 December 1942 (NARA).

186 *Brazil or any other S.A. country* Memo, John Rose to Norm Ferguson, 16 July 1941, subject: South American Production Program (WDA).

186 *We would like to feature* Ted Sears, "The Penguin Story (Paul Penguin)," undated outline (but written immediately after the South American trip; WDA).

186 *happens to be 100 miles inland* Ibid.

190 *Horse racing is a top sport* Memo, Lansburgh to Walt, 8 May 1941 (WDA). Lansburgh was pitching an unrelated story idea, which was not used.

190 *built around a race* Sears, "Suggestions for 'Little Gaucho' Series," 27 June 1941, p. 6 (WDA).

190 *The little Gaucho* Sears, "Gaucho Series," undated story notes (WDA).

191 *would not be a boy* Sears, "First Notes on The Little Gaucho Character," 11 June 1941 (WDA).

191 *In order to steer away* Sears, gaucho story notes, 18 June 1941 (WDA).

192 Note: *might occasionally contradict or argue* Sears, "Suggestions for Little Gaucho series," 27 June 1941 (WDA).

193 *It is a mistake to talk* Memo, Roy to Joe Reddy and Vern Caldwell, 25 March 1943, subject: South American Pictures (WDA).

194 *We come to Rio* Walt in *Aquarela do Brasil* story meeting, 13 November 1941 (WDA).

194 *Before the streamlining of the Brazilian language* Memo, Cutting to Norm Ferguson, 7 April 1944, subject: Baía-Bahía (WDA).

196 *engaged her as a "technical adviser"* "Well! Carmen Miranda Is Tech Advisor To Disney," *Hollywood Reporter*, 15 July 1942, p. 2 (AMPAS).

197 Note: *The Disney contribution to* Servants' Entrance For my own account of this and another 1934 Disney combination sequence, created for MGM's *Hollywood Party*, see J. B. Kaufman, "Before Snow White," *Film History*, vol. 5 no. 2 (June 1993), pp. 158–175.

198 *This all had to be figured out* Ken Anderson to Milt Gray, 14 December 1976. Courtesy Michael Barrier.

201 *"flesh troupes"* "Five Flesh Troupes Working For Disney," *Hollywood Reporter*, 15 April 1943, p. 5 (AMPAS).

201 *Air of mystery* Edwin Schallert, "Disney Dance Sequence Called Revolutionary," *Los Angeles Times*, 20 May 1943.

201 *Only on the little train* Letter, Mary Blair to Ross Care, 18 February 1977, quoted in Canemaker, *Before the Animation Begins*, p. 124.

202 *SHOWING SHIPS, FORTS, ETC.* This text is actually taken from a memo from Dunham to secretary Betty Kay, 10 August 1943 (WDA), asking her to send the night letter to Knapp. The wire was presumably sent the same or the next day.

209 *the film was simply to depict* This description is based on the account published in "Creator of Immortal Characters," *Caminos del Aire*, a periodical published in Mexico City by Pan American Airways, in February 1943 (NARA; CIAA translation).

209 *reworking "La Piñata"* Memo, Ferguson to Walt, 15 February 1943, subject: Report on Latin American Pictures (WDA).

209 *an official synopsis was registered* *La Piñata*, original MPPDA synopsis, 9 July 1943 (AMPAS).

209 *best marimba band in the world* "List of Artists Tried Out for Mr. Disney, Ferguson, Wolcott & Santos—Who Offered Best Possibilities," undated (WDA).

210 Note: *Two other Hollywood filmmakers* See "Mayer, Disney Party Home With Honors," *Hollywood Reporter*, 30 August 1943, p. 12 (AMPAS).

212 *One of the first things Walt asked* Letter, de Lima to Keefe, 11 October 1943 (WDA).

213 *the quintessential Mexican singing charro* Carl J. Mora, *Mexican Cinema*, p. 56. As a further source, Mora cites Francisco Pineda Alcalá, *La verídica histórica del cine mexicano* (Mexico City, no date), pp. 49–51.

215 *Xochimilco, as you probably know* Kinney to author, 14 September 1989.

215 *The idea for the short* Letter to Walt, 1 April 1943, nominally from both Cutting and Cottrell but actually written by Cottrell (WDA). Much of the Disney studio staff was on the move in spring 1943: by the time this letter was written, Cottrell and Cutting had moved on to Havana, and they wrote to Walt in care of the Hotel Reforma in Mexico City.

216 *He was able at that time* Letter, de Lima to Norm Ferguson, 20 May 1943 (WDA).

216 *Now 'Paricutín' had a little story* Kinney to author, 14 September 1989.

216 *If now we could secure* Letter, Keefe to de Lima, 27 July 1943 (WDA).

217 *singing the praises of Walt* Letter, de Lima to Keefe, 11 October 1943 (WDA).

217 *It was exciting because* Broughton to author, 15 November 2004.

218 *Shortly after Walt's arrival* Letter, Verity to Jacques Roberts, 20 October 1943 (WDA).

218 *voice the part of one of the caballeros* "Ramírez to Disney," *Hollywood Reporter*, 23 August 1944, p. 8 (AMPAS).

219 *Paco didn't speak any English* Foutz in interview with Joaquín Garay, 3 November 1943 (WDA).

221 *the only animation/When you see it now* Kimball to Barrier, 6 June 1969. Courtesy Michael Barrier.

222 *The Garay rendition of the song* Memo, Cutting "To whom it may concern," 16 February 1944, subject: The Three Caballeros (WDA).

222 *Being perhaps somewhat high pitched* Letter, Buelna to Walt, 5 June 1944 (WDA).

223 *I suddenly realized* Memo, Cutting to Walt, 30 June 1944 (WDA).

223 *That was a stinker picture* Ruthie Tompson to author, 13 November 2004.

226 Note: *Attached is a list* Memo, Ferguson to Walt, 27 September 1943, subject: Latin American Unit (WDA).

228 *We should have the sand* Walt in "Beach Sequence" story meeting, 22 January 1944 (WDA).

231 *this effect was achieved/drew the curtains over the end title* Rowley to Barrier, 15 October 1988. Courtesy Michael Barrier.

234 *The movie-going public of that small country* Excerpt from anonymous confidential report to CIAA, 25 May 1943 (NARA).

234 *The statement 'An old gaucho from Uruguay'* Memo, Cutting "To Whom It May Concern," 16 February 1944, subject: *The Three Caballeros* (WDA).

236 *This seems to be a nice bit of soft soap* Letter, Cutting to Peer, 2 August 1944 (WDA).

237 *He said they visited a rather low class club* Memo, Ferguson to Walt, 25 April 1944, subject: Dora Luz (WDA).

238 *Could Jose Carioca be made* Letter, Pierce to Gottfredson, 19 July 1944 (NARA).

238 *I know we can't stop* Memo, Roy to Vern Caldwell, 11 October 1943, subject: *The Three Caballeros* Publicity (WDA).

238 Note: *the artwork illustrating Soria's story* "Nueva película de Walt Disney sobre motivos sudamericanos: 'Latino por un día'," *La Prensa*, 26 September 1943 (WDA).

239 *Carmen tells me* Letter, de Lima to Ferguson, 4 January 1945 (WDA).

241 *Of all the Disney feature length pictures* Letter, Eyssell to Rockefeller, 29 November 1944 (RAC).

241 *SIMPLY THRILLED WITH TREMENDOUS IMPACT* Telegram, Rockefeller to Walt, 14 November 1944 (RAC).

241 *Mr. Rockefeller liked it very much* OEM memo, Fran Alstock to William Phillipson, 22 November 1944 (NARA).

241 *I got the idea* Walt quoted by Dorothy Kilgallen in *New York Journal-American*, 25 October 1944 (WDA).

241 Popular Science *published a detailed account* "How Disney Combines Living Actors with His Cartoon Characters," *Popular Science*, September 1944, pp. 106–111.

242 *one of the worst snowstorms* "'Caballeros' Preem Is Tops Despite Storm," *Hollywood Reporter*, 6 February 1945, p. 3 (AMPAS).

242 *a new form of cinematic entertainment/The off-screen narration* "Abel," *The Three Caballeros* review, *Variety*, 13 December 1944, p. 8 (AMPAS). (This review was based on a New York trade showing preceding the opening.)

242 *a mixture of atrocious taste* Gibbs, "What Hath Walt Wrought?" (*The Three Caballeros* review), *The New Yorker*, 10 February 1945, p. 36.

242 *a brilliant hodgepodge* Crowther, *The Three Caballeros* review, *New York Times*, 5 February 1945, 20:1.

242 *little more than a brightly explosive demonstration/a cheap flea-circus* Crowther, second *The Three Caballeros* review, *New York Times*, 11 February 1945, II:1:7.

242 *essentially a full-length dancing spectacle/Fortunately, similar lapses in taste* Rubsamen, *The Three Caballeros* review, *Arts and Architecture*, January 1945, pp. 24, 48.

242–244 The Three Caballeros *is being held over* "'*Caballeros*' Holding Over In All Openings," *Hollywood Reporter*, 6 March 1945, p. 7 (AMPAS).

244 *satisfactory* Walt Disney Productions annual report, 1945, p. 4 (WDA).

244 *I understand Hugh Harman* Memo, Ferguson to Walt, 20 July 1944 (WDA).

247 *the studio publicly announced its plans* "Third South American Film to Salute Cuba," *Brooklyn Eagle*, 17 May 1943; "Disney Plans to Include Cuba in Next Musical," *Motion Picture Herald*, 22 May 1943, p. 46 (AMPAS).

248 *Rockefeller received a memo* Letter, Coordination Committee for Cuba to Rockefeller, 17 March 1943 (NARA).

248 *Love of music by the natives* Helen Ewing, "Wartime Living in Cuba Described by Disney's Aide on Return From Trip," dateline 27 April 1943, unidentified clipping in Blair family collection. Courtesy John Canemaker.

249 *would eliminate all unnecessary* Memo, Ferguson to Walt, 15 July 1944, subject: Cuba—Research Trip (WDA).

251 *We find the government people* Letter to Walt, 1 April 1943 (WDA). The letter was nominally from both Cottrell and Cutting but was actually written by Cottrell.

251 *After checking for a representative character/The cuteness of the little guy* Letter, Ferguson to Walt, 14 October 1944 (WDA).

252–253 *The point on which I feel/This story should take the opposite approach* Memo, Lansburgh to Ferguson, 17 November 1944, subject: Cuba (WDA).

253 *contacted the distinguished Mexican cinematographer* Night letter, Lansburgh to Figueroa, 13 November 1944 (WDA).

253 *Matamoros has, according to Cubans* Letter, Ferguson to Walt, 14 October 1944 (WDA).

254 *Have been too busy* Quoted in memo, Jack Lavin to Ferguson, 13 April 1945, subject: Elsa Miranda (WDA).

255 *Roca was very helpful/It is a very good melody* Letter, Ferguson to Walt, 14 October 1944 (WDA).

255 *The history of the dance* Memo, Ferguson to Walt, 26 July 1945, subject: "Frevo" reel (WDA).

255 *This is the number with the hand-clapping* Memo, Ferguson to Walt, 16 January 1945, subject: Latin American production (WDA).

255 *suggested that he might sing . . . "Granada"* Memo, Ferguson to Walt, 25 May 1945, subject: Talent (WDA).

255 *From a commercial standpoint* Memo, Ferguson to Walt, 7 April 1945, subject: Carnival (WDA).

257 Note: *Special thanks to . . . Mindy Aloff* See Mindy Aloff, *Hippo in a Tutu: Dancing in Disney Animation* (New York: Disney Editions, 2009).

258 *We won't use this system/In the next Latin American film* Walt quoted in *The Three Caballeros* review in *Los Angeles Times*, 18 February 1945, part III, p. 3.

259 *Ferguson speculated that she might be brought back* This is one of several tentative plans put forth in a memo from Ferguson to Walt, 19 March 1945, subject: Report on "Carnival" (WDA). (A handwritten note at the top of the memo reads: "Not sent.")

259 *Hench dismissed the song itself* Hench to Dave Smith, 1 May 2002 (WDA).

261 *All these numbers have possibilities* Memo, Ferguson to Walt, 19 March 1945, subject: Report on "Carnival" (WDA). (Handwritten note: "Not sent.")

261 *it has the possibilities of "Tico-Tico"* Memo, Ferguson to Walt, 16 January 1945, subject: Latin American Production (WDA).

264 *"the Three Caballeros" might be featured on-screen* Memo, Ferguson to Walt, 17 February 1945, subject: Report on Cuban Production (WDA).

367 *an infectious combination* "Brog," *Melody Time* review, *Variety*, 19 May 1948, p. 13 (AMPAS).

BIBLIOGRAPHY

Albaroa Martíez, Gabriel. *El flaco de oro*. Mexico City: Grupo Editorial Planeta, 1993.

Canemaker, John. *Before the Animation Begins*. New York: Hyperion, 1996.

___________. *The Art and Flair of Mary Blair*. New York: Disney Editions, 2003.

___________. *Walt Disney's Nine Old Men and the Art of Animation*. New York: Disney Editions, 2001.

de Moraes, Mário. *Recordações de Ary Barroso*. Rio de Janeiro: Edição Funarte, 1979.

Mora, Carl J. *Mexican Cinema: Reflections of a Society 1896–1980*. Berkeley, Los Angeles, London: University of California Press, 1982.

Okrent, Daniel. *Great Fortune: The Epic of Rockefeller Center*. New York: Penguin, 2003.

Reich, Cary. *The Life of Nelson A. Rockefeller: Worlds to Conquer, 1908–1958*. New York: Doubleday, 1996.

Ryman, Herb. "Recollections of a Friendship." J. E. Reynolds (Bookseller) Catalog 102, Winter 1968.

Taibo, Paco I. I. *La musica de Agustín Lara en el cine*. Mexico City: Filmoteca de la UNAM, Universidad Nacional Autonoma de México, n.d.

P-212

INDEX

Page numbers in *italics* refer to picture captions.
Page numbers followed by *n* refer to notes.

ASOCIACION DE DIBUJANTES
ARGENTINOS
1941
WITH SINCERE APPRECIATION FOR THEIR COOPERATION AND THE MANY KINDNESSES RECEIVED AT THEIR HANDS_
Herb Ryman
John P. Miller
Lee Blair
Jim Bodrero
Walt Disney
John Rose
Mary Blair
Franklin K. Thomas
Larry Lansburgh
WEBB SMITH
Hazel B. Cottrell.
NORM FERGUSON
TED SEARS

ACKNOWLEDGMENTS

The road that led to this book began in 1988, when I was contacted by Bonnie Ferguson Brown, daughter of the great Disney animator and director Norm Ferguson. Bonnie offered me a chance to review a box of material left by her late father. As it turned out, most of the material was related to his trip to South America in 1941 with the Walt Disney survey group. Poring over those priceless photographs and other memorabilia reawakened my long-dormant interest in the Disney Latin American films. In succeeding years, Bonnie and her husband, Stan, became friends of mine, and I hereby gratefully acknowledge all their kindnesses.

Beginning with that incident I had several opportunities to write and lecture on the Good Neighbor films, but nothing on the scale of this book was remotely possible until Diane Disney Miller and the Walt Disney Family Foundation offered their practical and moral support for the project. Thanks to them I have enjoyed a long period of intensive research, marked by extraordinary autonomy and an absolute lack of pressure—as well as the blessing of their warm and enduring friendship. I cannot possibly ever thank them enough for either one.

An indispensable part of the research for this book has come from personal interviews with several of the artists and filmmakers who actually produced the films, and other eyewitnesses who shed additional light on the story. Some of them are no longer with us at this writing, but my sincere thanks go out to them all: Bob Broughton, Bill Cottrell, Joe Grant, Don Iwerks, Jack Kinney, Larry Lansburgh, Frank Thomas, and Ruthie Tompson.

Needless to say, most of the work on this book would have been impossible without the kind cooperation of the Walt Disney Company, in particular several very special people. Howard Green, who has facilitated so many projects for so many writers, did the same for me with his usual unflappable grace. All the films described in this book owe their present-day existence to the tireless work of Scott MacQueen, during his years as the studio's manager of library restoration, and I personally benefited from his vast storehouse of technical knowledge. Didier Ghez, who worked for both the Brazilian and Argentine offices of the company during the time of my research, supplied much rare material, not least access to the *Cine jornal Brasileiro* newsreel through the kind offices of the Cinemateca Brasileira. Much of my preliminary research into these films derives from work on the 1995 Disney Home Video laser disc set of *Saludos Amigos/The Three Caballeros*, and the tireless research of producer Harry Arends and his staff added greatly to the quality of my own.

My research for this book has relied upon two vital divisions of the Disney company. The Walt Disney Archives, headed by Dave Smith and featuring, during my research, the sterling team of Robert Tieman, Rebecca Cline, Collette Espino, and Edward Ovalle, became a very comfortable second home during much of this book's preparation. The archivists went far beyond the call of professional courtesy, not only fielding the most obscure requests I could throw them, but volunteering rare studio files I wouldn't otherwise have known about. Similarly, Lella Smith and her staff at the Animation Research Library—in particular Ann Hansen, Vivian Procopio, Fox Carney, Doug Engalla, Jackie Vasquez, and Mary Walsh—went far out of their way to make my research trips vastly productive, as well as pleasant, experiences. Thanks to their kindness, I had access not only to invaluable production papers but also to much of the precious original animation artwork that can be seen in this book's illustrations.

Other archives too have produced a rich fund of information on the Disney Good Neighbor films. Many important documents were found at the Rockefeller Archives Center in Sleepy Hollow, New York, and I'm especially thankful for the help of Rockefeller archivists Carol Radovich and Michele Hiltzik. The staff of the National Archives and Records Administration in College Park, Maryland, unearthed many rare treasures that had previously been overlooked. Special thanks are also due to the staffs of the Motion Picture, Broadcasting, and Recorded Sound division of the Library of Congress (in particular Madeline Matz and Mike Mashon), of the Margaret Herrick Library of the Academy of Motion Picture Arts and Sciences (in particular Barbara Hall, Jennie Romero, and Howard Prouty), of the USC Film and

Television Library (especially the indispensable Ned Comstock), of the UCLA Film Archives (especially Mark Quigley and Dino Everett); to Dennis Millay, Director of Programming, Turner Classic Movies; and to Lee Tsiantis, Corporate Legal Manager, Turner Broadcasting.

I'm blessed to have contact with a community of distinguished Disney historians, many of whom are also good friends and have provided materials essential to this research. In particular, my thanks go out to Robin Allan, Mindy Aloff, Paul F. Anderson, Michael Barrier, Christopher Caines, John Canemaker, Bill Cotter, Rod Learned, Katherine and Richard Greene, and Don Peri. All of them have contributed materially to the information collected in this book. Less Disney-centric, but equally valuable, have been the contributions of other historians and specialists: Joaquín Alvarado, Jim Bedoian, Karen Latham Everson, Maureen Furniss, Judith Johnson, Laura Lee McKay, Russell Merritt, James Parten, Rick Prelinger, and Catherine A. Surowiec. My brother Kenn Kaufman has lent his invaluable expertise on bird life of the hemisphere; Daniella Thompson has freely given of her inexhaustible knowledge of Brazilian music and culture. Many of the above have also read all or portions of the manuscript and offered extremely valuable suggestions and comments.

One of the great blessings of this project has been an association with the documentary film *Walt & El Grupo*, produced by the highly talented husband-and-wife team of Ted Thomas and Kuniko Okubo. Not only have Ted (son of the great Disney animator Frank Thomas) and Kuniko become very dear friends of mine during the course of this work, but they've also generously shared the fruits of their own research, which has immeasurably enriched mine and, in turn, this book. In addition, Ted generously allowed me access to his father's letters from South America; similar use of Charles Wolcott's correspondence was very kindly granted by his daughter, Sheila Wolcott Banani, and that of Ted Sears by *his* daughter, Cindy Garcia. My connection with Ted and Kuniko also led to a meeting with Angelic Christine Márquez Núñez, who made a tremendous contribution of her own, tracking down elusive information, correcting my Spanish, and warding off cultural infelicities.

It's a great thrill to be able to present, along with the *facts* of the Disney Good Neighbor story, the illustrations in this book, some of them representing extremely rare and precious images. These illustrations have come from several sources. In addition to the Walt Disney Animation Research Library, already mentioned, the company's Photo Library, an extraordinarily rich storehouse of Disney-related images, has contributed some of the best and rarest to these pages. Ed Squair, manager of the library, and his dedicated staff, particularly Andrea Carbone, Rick Lorentz, and LaToya Morgan, accorded me every courtesy in making these treasures available, along with the benefit of their expertise. And many rare and previously unknown photos and art treasures have been provided by the Walt Disney Family Museum. Michael Labrie, Mark Gibson, Martín Salazar, Anel Muller, Rachael Zink, and Bob Moseley have given me their kind assistance in locating and reproducing these visuals, not to mention the pleasure of their company.

For translations of various Spanish and Portuguese documents, I'm indebted to Didier Ghez, Gustavo Kletzl, Santiago Moratto, Charles Oelfke, and Judith Procter. And for miscellaneous help of other kinds along the way, many thanks to Tracey, Jim, Molly and Sam Doyle, to Paul and Holly Anderson, and to the late Sally Dumaux. Many of my projects have owed a tremendous debt to the help of Howard Prouty; this one is no exception.

The process of turning this manuscript into a book, which could have been an agonizing ordeal, has been made painless and even quite pleasant by the smooth professionalism of Wendy Lefkon and Jessica Ward of Disney Editions. Along with other kindnesses, they have afforded me the opportunity to work with two additional extraordinary individuals: Christopher Caines, an editor of rare sensitivity, taste, and ingenuity (as well as patience!), and Jon Glick, a brilliant designer who has worked his magic on the overall appearance of the finished book. Whatever virtues this book has, many of them can be traced directly to Christopher and Jon.

Special thanks are due to Margaret and Chris Kaufman, who patiently endured my years of concentration on this project and also contributed material assistance of their own. Little Ali was no help at all, but meant well. Last but not least, I want to thank my sixth-grade teacher, Mrs. Ebell, in whose classroom—without her knowledge, and quite apart from whatever she was trying to teach me—I first discovered *The Three Caballeros*.

J. B. Kaufman
January 2009

mines
ARAGUAY
BRAZI
PACIFIC OCEAN
Valparaiso
Santiago
URUGUAY
ARGENTINA
Lake country
N
W
E

copper mines
PARAGUAY
BRAZIL
PACIFIC OCEAN
ANDES MOUNTAINS
Valparaiso
Santiago
ARGENTINA
URUGUAY
CHILE
Lake country
N
W
E